Y0-BSW-103

AN ANALYSIS OF MOTION PICTURES ABOUT WAR RELEASED BY THE AMERICAN FILM INDUSTRY 1930-1970

Russell Earl Shain

ARNO PRESS

A New York Times Company

New York · 1976

This volume was selected for the
Dissertations on Film Series
of the ARNO PRESS CINEMA PROGRAM
by Garth S. Jowett, Carleton University

Editorial Supervision: Sheila Mehlman

First publication in book form, Arno Press, 1976

Copyright © 1973 by Russell Earl Shain

THE ARNO PRESS CINEMA PROGRAM
For complete listing of cinema titles see last pages

Manufactured in the United States of America

Library of Congress Cataloging in Publication Data

Shain, Russell Earl.
An analysis of motion pictures about war released by the American film industry, 1930-1970.

(Dissertations on film)
Originally presented as the author's thesis, University of Illinois at Urbana-Champaign, 1971.
1. War films--History and criticism. 2. Moving-pictures--United States--History. I. Title.
II. Series: Dissertations on film series.
PN1995.9.W3S5 1976 791.43'0909'3 75-21435
ISBN 0-405-07536-7

AN ANALYSIS OF MOTION PICTURES ABOUT WAR RELEASED
BY THE AMERICAN FILM INDUSTRY, 1939-1970

BY

RUSSELL EARL SHAIN
A.B.J., University of Kentucky, 1966
M.S., University of Illinois, 1967

THESIS

Submitted in partial fulfillment of the requirements
for the degree of Doctor of Philosophy in Communications
in the Graduate College of the
University of Illinois at Urbana-Champaign, 1971

Urbana, Illinois

ACKNOWLEDGMENT

Thanks are extended to many people, including the staff at the Library of Congress for assistance in screening some older motion pictures and Colin Young of U.C.L.A. for advice in the initial stages of the project. Primary appreciation, however, goes to Thomas H. Guback, whose advice was invaluable during the research and writing of the thesis.

TABLE OF CONTENTS

INTRODUCTION

INTRODUCTION

The past thirty-two years in the United States have been marked by a chronic state of war or war-readiness. Since 1939, the country has sustained an efficiency of war alertness--economically, militarily, and emotionally. Constitutionally, only one war has been fought, but constitutionality has little relevancy for a nation's mental or physical involvement. Besides, Korea and Vietnam have had the attributes if not the official title of war, and the Cold War has had all the preliminaries to battle without the conclusion.

For twenty years, the threat of atomic annihilation, so compellingly illustrated by Hiroshima, has fluctuated from crucial to the brink of disaster. At the same time the military rose in the 1950's to a peak of influence within the American power structure. The legitimacy of the military's role in policy decisions has been challenged recently, but despite current controversy the military establishment is a factor to be considered in any analysis of recent American history.

Politicians have risen and fallen with the contemporary international conflicts. For nearly twenty-five years the major criterion of political success was the capacity to deal with international conflict or with internal threats supposedly instigated by external enemies.

However, the contemporary conflicts are not the exclusive bailiwick of soldiers or politicians. Modern warfare threatens everyone and thereby involves everyone. While war's ultimate threat is physical, the individual's involvement generally is emotional. The continental United States was never actually attacked during World War II, but fear of such an attack pervaded the West Coast. Fear turned to hysteria for some one night in Los Angeles when air raid sirens sounded and anti-aircraft guns opened up on something, or nothing.[1] The incident is an extreme example of the consequences of emotional involvement but illustrates that the civilian does not have to be physically in the fighting to feel a part of the war.

Once the United States entered World War II, the nation's opinion front solidified. National opinion appeared almost monolithic during the most frigid of the Cold War years, an image only recently altered. In the 1960's and 1970's one component of American society has rejected the black-and-white view of international relations and concomitantly turned its primary attention to internal devils. The new crusade and the response to it by the old guard, still preoccupied with external threats, have evolved into an internal conflict of some magnitude.

However, this introduction does not propose to recount the events of the past thirty years. The introductory remarks are intended to emphasize the dominant place of war in American life during the past three decades. From this beginning the discussion will move to the problem of the thesis: an analysis of fictional, feature-length motion pictures about war produced by the American film industry from 1939 through 1970.

---

[1]The California coast was shelled in one isolated incident, and the Japanese released booby-trapped balloons into the atmosphere killing some persons in Oregon. Generally, though, the home-front fear of physical harm from the Japanese or Germans was just fear. For a more detailed account see A. A. Hoehling, Home Front U.S.A. (New York: Thomas Y. Cromwell Company, 1966), pp. 28-46.

Review of the Literature

America's contemporary wars have been frequently and prominently portrayed in the mass media—fictionally as well as factually. Naturally, the importance of the wars dictated prime attention in the news media. Fictional accounts, though somewhat less conspicuous, have nevertheless been extensive. From 1941 to 1945 popular songs about World War II abounded, praising heroics, ridiculing the enemy, arousing patriotism, and consoling loved ones. War songs almost disappeared after 1945 but the 1960's saw a resurgence. This time, the songs frequently condemned rather than promoted war.

The radio networks were dominated by war news during 1941-1945 and a good portion of fictional presentations were war related. About 7 per cent of regular radio series during 1941-1945 featured the war.[2] The percentage includes entertainment programs expressly focusing on the war but not drama series which may have included war stories among their offerings. As in the case of songs, the number of war programs declined drastically following the war, although a few survived and a trickle of such programs later transferred to television.

War stories also have been frequent subjects in popular magazines, comic strips, novels (Publishers' Weekly counted 270 about World War II between 1939 and 1948),[3] and motion pictures (815 meeting

[2]Percentage derived from information in Harrison B. Summers, Radio Programs Carried on National Networks, 1926-1956 (Columbus, Ohio: Ohio State University, 1958).

[3]"The Novels of the Second World War," Publishers' Weekly, CLIV (October 23, 1948), p. 1806.

the criteria of this study).[4] However, scholarly examination, or any kind of examination, of war fiction has been sparse, generally subjecting the exceptional to assessment rather than the ordinary to analysis.

According to William J. Smith, novels about war are of two types: war as history and social dialect as represented by War and Peace and war as psychological catalyst and personal experience as represented by Red Badge of Courage. The American novelist, Smith said, "has tended to see war in purely personal terms and admit history to his pages only as remotest implication . . ."[5]

Smith and Joseph Waldemeir agreed that novels of World War I were generally pessimistic while those of World War II were generally optimistic.

> No one . . . has been quite willing to admit that World War II was quite the futile and meaningless cruel holocaust that World War I seemed to be. The attitudes of the war novel have changed accordingly, if not to the glorification of war at least to the glorification of the brave men who fought it.[6]

Waldemeir traced the optimism of World War II to commitment of the novels' characters to an idealistic struggle.

> But, through traumatic experiences with war and fascism in enemy, comrade, and ally . . . each man gradually comes to realize that indifference and timidity have made him guilty of and responsible for the fact of the war. Each man commits himself to the

---

[4]The list of 815 films was compiled from a search of Variety, Motion Picture Herald, Motion Picture Review Digest, Film Daily, The Green Sheet, and Film Facts.

[5]William J. Smith, "The War Novel," Commonweal, May 11, 1956, p. 146.

[6]Ibid., p. 148.

struggle; a struggle no longer simply with German or Japanese, but with a hated ideology under whatever guise.[7]

The novels of Vietnam have been somewhat less idealistic, according to Clinton R. Sanders displaying "patterns of affirmation" and "patterns of despair." "The former are either overt or covert apologetics for the war in which the style is commonly romanticized naturalism and there is usually little questioning of the basic moral aspects of the war and business of killing by the main character."[8] The novels of despair "are particularly concerned with this frustrating, senseless, strange war in which no final victory seems possible."[9]

While the major characters of World War II arrived at the conclusion that they were partly responsible for the war because of indifference, the major character of the Vietnam novels of affirmation reject any responsibility for the war itself. They may fight because of ideology--but nationalistic ideology. The other motivation is survival. Another interesting contrast is that while the character of the World War II novel frequently concludes that his safety and security is bound with that of others, "the G.I. in the novels dealing with the war in Vietnam is portrayed essentially as an atom floating free of social bonds other than the formal ties of army organization . . . the soldier defines the chances of his own survival being bettered by his

---

[7] Joseph Waldemeir, "Novelists of Two Wars," Nation, Nov. 1, 1958, p. 306.

[8] Clinton R. Sanders, "The Portrayal of War and the Fighting Man in Novels of the Vietnam War," Journal of Popular Culture, III (Winter, 1969), p. 554.

[9] Ibid., p. 558.

avoidance of social ties."[10]

Propaganda rather than characterization was found by Vernon
McKenzie in an analysis of pre-Pearl Harbor magazine fiction of World
War II.[11] Making extensive use of stereotypes, the fiction made a
black-and-white distinction between British hero and Nazi villain.
Germans frequently were depicted as gallant, courageous, and efficient
but driven to war by their Nazi leaders. One of the major themes in
the fiction emphasized that Americans could not be disinterested in
the world.

Comic strips are also a source of propaganda. Daniel J. Leab
assessed Cold War comics as "on the whole . . . defending and promoting
an American point of view that is jingoistic, often highly belligerent,
and meant to be taken seriously."[12] Leab said Cold War comics either
had a central character as a Cold War warrior, an adventurer of the
1930's and 1940's given new life by attachment to the Cold War or are
not primarily about the Cold War. In the latter kind of comic "a
political point of view is eased into the surroundings that the illus-
trators have created. The insidiousness of this material is that a
hard-line view of the Cold War becomes a part of everyday life in the
comics."[13]

A few authors have approached the subject of war films. However no single study has examined the entire lot of war films of the

[10]Ibid., p. 563.

[11]Vernon McKenzie, "Treatment of War Themes in Magazine Fiction,"
Public Opinion Quarterly, V (June, 1941), pp. 227-232.

[12]Daniel J. Leab, "Cold War Comics," Columbia Journalism Review,
III (Winter, 1965), p. 42.

[13]Ibid.

past thirty years. Included among the writings about war films are
two catalogings of World War I pictures; an analysis sponsored by
the Office of War Information during World War II; an assessment of
battle films of 1952-1962; a commentary on the war hero of the years
of World War II; an evaluation of the status of war movies in 1967;
and comments by several historians.

Jack Spears' analysis of World War I themes traced a change
in sentiment in the films that corresponded almost exactly to changes
in public opinion, shifting from pacifism to neutrality, militancy,
vengeance, and disillusion.[14] Aviation movies of the same era capitalized on action rather than politics. Such films, according to
Rudy Behlmer, "comprise a colorful, but limited, genre, for their
plots, characters, situations, and dialogue quickly became repetitive
and stereotyped. And the same aerial footage was used over and over
again."[15] Repetition was necessitated by the time, effort, and
expense required to film the new aviation technology. However, expenses were defrayed by the War Department, which recognized the
promotional value of such films. For example, when What Price Glory
was produced in 1925, the War Department agreed to furnish manpower
and equipment and provide shooting sites, logistics, and engineering
as long as those were handled according to Army specifications and
regulations.[16]

---

[14]Jack Spears, "World War I on the Screen," Films in Review,
XVII (May and June-July, 1966), pp. 274-292 and 347-365.

[15]Rudy Behlmer, "World War I Aviation Films," Films in Review,
XVIII (August-September, 1967), p. 413.

[16]Ibid., p. 414.

A systematic examination of war films was made by Dorothy Jones while she was director of the Film Reviewing and Analysis Section of the Hollywood branch of the Office of War Information from 1942 to 1944. Her primary objective was "to evaluate how far Hollywood has aided interpreting the war at home and giving a better understanding of America's role in the conflict."[17] Jones said that 376 of 1,313 films produced by Hollywood during 1942-1944 related to the war. Only about 45 or 50 aided in understanding the war. More aids to understanding were not produced, according to Jones, because Hollywood was unprepared for the war and lacked experience in making films dealing with social problems. Thus, producers lapsed into formulas in which the material was secondary to the development of a stereotyped plot. A major problem was timing. Themes could not be tied too closely to current events because by the time the film was released, it might be dated, hindering its economic potential.[18]

Arthur Knight's The Liveliest Art devotes about six pages to World War II films of the 1940's. He praised the realism of the films.

> Rarely did these films seek to glorify war, or attempt to make it seem a great advantage. On the contrary, most of them stressed the average American's distaste for killing and for regimentation-- as well as his ability to rise to deeds of heroism when his country needed him.[19]

In Hollywood in the Forties Charles Higham and Joel Greenberg

---

[17] Dorothy B. Jones, "Hollywood Goes to War," Nation, Jan. 27, 1945, p. 93.

[18] Ibid., p. 19. Jones' list of war films is published in Dorothy B. Jones, "Hollywood's War Films, 1942-1944, Hollywood Quarterly, I (October,1945), pp. 1-12.

[19] Arthur Knight, The Liveliest Art (New York: The New American Library, 1957), p. 245.

present a rather critical recounting of the war films. They concluded
that the story of the war was told in stereotypes--in particular depicting the Nazis as cultured swine. "They knew what vintage to order,
relished Goethe and Wagner, but didn't hesitate to shoot hostages or
torture prisoners whenever it suited their purposes."[20] In the
Pacific the Japanese "were portrayed as repulsive, sadistic, libidinous
little monkeys, grinning bespectacled, and sporting king-size choppers."[21]

Although generally critical of the 1940 war films, Higham and
Greenberg concede one significant point: ". . . despite themselves
they (the films) captured something of the mood of the time, something
of the fervour and exhilaration of an experience central to the lives
of all who lived through it."[22]

In a chapter of a book in progress, Lewis Jacobs said that the
war films of the 1940's changed with the progression of the war. Before
the entry of the United States into the war, a frequent picture was one
glorifying war's modern instruments--planes, tanks, dive bombers, carriers. After Pearl Harbor and a request from the President to explain
war aims to the public, the industry responded by tying old plots to
new themes. Later, again responding to the government, Hollywood
probed deeper into character, tackling the political aspects of fascism
and avoiding a romantic view of combat.[23]

---

[20]Charles Higham and Joel Greenberg, Hollywood in the Forties
(New York: A. S. Barnes and Co., 1968), p. 90.

[21]Ibid., p. 98.

[22]Ibid., p. 86.

[23]Lewis Jacobs, "World War II and the American Film," Film
Culture, Fall, 1969, pp. 28-42.

Views of a more analytical nature are provided by three authors: Barbara Deming, Colin Young, and Peter A. Soderbergh. Deming's analysis of films of the 1940's is restricted but incisive. She focused on the hero of the war films, finding him as a disillusioned cynic, criminal, gambler, profit-seeking adventurer caught in a crisis of faith. He claims non-involvement but ultimately marches to battle to confirm his faith.[24]

Young provides an interesting assessment of combat films in Robert Hughes' Film: Book II.[25] In addition to Young's article Hughes' book contains evaluations and opinions of film makers and critics concerning the production of anti-war films. As it appears, Young's essay is one-third its original length. The unpublished parts "contain formidable ammunition in their analysis of Hollywood war-film production over the past ten years (1952-1962), trends and costs, plus a jaunty (and depressing) list of synopses."[26]

Young criticized war films of the early 1960's as being too simplistic for their era of production.

> It is no longer possible to maintain the simple contrast between good and evil which was applied in 1939 in Europe and after Pearl Harbor in the United States. But if this is true the basis of the traditional patriotic argument is undermined, and we are only beginning to fumble for something to replace it. Current World War II pictures involve a grotesquely anachronistic return to the simple days of 'hurrah for our side' when such simplicity no longer applies, and defense is now inseparable from self destruction . . . What is needed is a thorough appraisal of all

---

[24]Barbara Deming, Running Away from Myself: A Dream Portrait of America Drawn from the Films of the Forties (New York: Grossman, 1969), pp. 9-38.

[25]Colin Young, "Nobody Dies" in Film: Book II, ed. by Robert Hughes (New York: Grove Press, Inc., 1962), pp. 87-110.

[26]Robert Hughes, ibid., p. 65. In a letter Young said he no longer could put his hands on the rest of the essay.

our military values, at the intellectual as well as the emotional
level. The Hollywood film has failed to reflect an intellectual
and emotional process that has been at the heart of political
discussion for the past ten years.[27]

A more optimistic assessment of the status of anti-war films
was given by Soderbergh in 1967.[28] He said that structural changes
in the film industry had provided a greater independence which would
allow Hollywood's war films to make a more realistic comment on contemporary situations.

It is evident, then, that some attention has been devoted to
war films. Generally, though, the attention has been limited in scope
and depth. Treatment usually has been isolated to a particular time
period. Young's study covered ten years but has never been published
in its entirety. The article by Soderbergh hints that he has examined
the evolution of war films of the past thirty years but his treatment
of content is superficial. Deming delves beneath the superficial but
her analysis is limited to the 1940's. The problem, as Young acknow-
ledges in a slightly different context, is:

> . . . a tendency in critical journals to concentrate on the well
> made or the pretentious films and to forget that the routine
> picture is also produced, distributed and seen--that it reaches
> its audience, has its effect (or fails to), and returns its cost
> to the producers who go on, presumably, to make another. This
> selective practice on the parts of critics and through them on
> the part of the so-called informed public, allows a more optimis-
> tic impression of Hollywood's influence on the status quo than the
> record merits. I do not know of any other way to support this
> negative report than to examine the product.[29]

---

[27] Young, "Nobody Dies," p. 91.

[28] Peter A. Soderbergh, "On War and the Movies: A Reappraisal,"
Centennial Review, XI (Summer, 1967), pp. 405-418.

[29] Young, "Nobody Dies," pp. 104-105.

This thesis, then, is an examination of the product--i.e., an examination of the content and environment of war films produced in the United States over the past thirty years.

Content Study: A Rationale

A primary assumption in any examination of mass media content and its role in society is given by the statement with which Kenneth Boulding launched The Image: "The first proposition of this work is that behavior depends upon image."[30] His observation is not unique (and does not preclude the possibility that behavior determines image), but, if accepted, it provides a foundation for a discussion of the social role of mass media content.

Ernst Cassirer observed that a clue to man's nature is the symbol, and it is the capacity to produce and use symbols that distinguishes man from other animals.[31] All animals possess receptor and effector systems by means of which they perceive and react to the physical world, but man's symbolic capacity acts as intermediary between the receptor and effector systems. "No longer can man confront reality immediately; he cannot see it, as it were, face to face. Physical reality seems to recede in proportion as man's symbolic activity advances."[32] Man lives no only in a physical world but to a great

---

[30]Kenneth Boulding, The Image (Ann Arbor: The University of Michigan Press, 1966), p. 6.

[31]Ernst Cassirer, An Essay on Man (New Haven, Conn.: Yale University Press, 1966), pp. 23-26.

[32]Ibid., p. 25.

extent also in a world of symbols, created by him and shaping him.

Cassirer argued that an understanding of man can be gained from inspecting his symbol systems, and, then, he examined a group of the symbol systems (language, art, myth, religion, history, and science). Walter Lippmann advanced similar arguments. "The only feeling that anyone can have about an event he does not experience is the feeling aroused by his mental image of that event. That is why until we know what others think they know, we cannot truly understand their acts."[33]

It would be foolish to claim that a study of American motion pictures would reveal the full range of Americans' opinions about war. However, war films as a cultural product can serve as a pulse of American feelings about the subject.[34] To approach the subject of man's image of war, one should ask: what are the raw materials from which that image is built? In contemporary times a partial answer is provided in motion pictures.

Support for this view can be borrowed from symbolic interactionism and George Herbert Mead's discussion of the role of communication

---

[33]Walter Lippmann, Public Opinion (New York: The Free Press, 1965), p. 9.

[34]George Gerbner has argued in several articles for the study of mass mediated messages as cultural indicators of man's symbolic environment. For an elaboration of his argument see: George Gerbner, "The Film Hero: A Cross-Cultural Study," Journalism Monographs, no. 13 (Minneapolis: University of Minnesota, 1969), pp. 1-7; George Gerbner, "Toward 'Cultural Indicators': The Analysis of Mass-Mediated Public Message Systems," in The Analysis of Communication Content, ed. by George Gerbner et al. (New York: Wiley & Sons, 1969), pp. 123-132; and George Gerbner, "Cultural Indicators: The Case of Violence in Television Drama," The Annals of the American Academy of Political and Social Science, CCCLXXXVIII (March, 1970), pp. 69-81.

in society. In an analysis of the social act from the perspective
of symbolic interactionism, J. Edward Hulett said that behavior is
motivated partly by anticipated consequences of the act. This antici-
pation is formulated in part from information derived from an individual's cognitive map, which includes knowledge of self concepts, of
roles of the participants, and of the generalized other, i.e., the
general values, norms, and structure governing the situation.[35] The
contents of the cognitive map are built through role taking and communication. The self develops when the individual is able to act
toward himself as toward others, to view himself as others view him.
It is through language that he acquires meanings and definitions of
those around him, providing knowledge for use in role taking and
ultimately viewing himself as others view him. Similarly, the mind
is social in origin, i.e., the individual acquires the perspectives
of others and internalizes their definitions, which are transmitted
through linguistic symbols.[36]

Mass communication is part of the process of sociation. "The
vast importance of media of communication such as those involved in
journalism is seen at once, since they report situations through

[35]J. Edward Hulett, Jr., "A Symbolic Interactionist Model of
Human Communication. Part I," AV Communication Review, XIV (Spring,
1966), pp. 24-29.

[36]A number of books summarize Mead's position or include parts
of his work. See Charles W. Morris, ed., Mind, Self and Society
(Chicago: University of Chicago Press, 1934); Andrew J. Reck, ed.,
Selected Writings: George Herbert Mead (New York: The Bobbs-Merrill
Company, Inc., 1964); and Anselm Strauss, ed., George Herbert Mead on
Social Psychology (Chicago: University of Chicago Press, 1964). Also
useful is Jerome G. Manis and Bernard N. Meltzer, eds., Symbolic Inter-
action: A Reader in Social Psychology (Boston: Allyn and Bacon, 1967).

which one can enter into the attitude and experience of other persons."[37]
However, mass communication is not identical to interpersonal communication because it is more likely to convey societal values and norms
than those belonging to any particular individual. Another distinction
is that mass communication is more likely than interpersonal communication to bring distant situations to the individual. Mead referred
to this distinction when, discussing the similarity of function of
drama, novel, and journalism, he said the importance of the novel is
that it "presents a situation which lies outside of the immediate pur-
view of the reader in such form that he enters into the attitude of
the group in the situation."[38]

Motion pictures about war enable the individual to partake in
the experience of events which may not immediately impinge upon his
daily life and to ascertain (perhaps intentionally but probably incidentally) the view of his society toward war. Any particular individual's view would not necessarily correspond to those of films nor to
that of society. Nevertheless, the individual builds his views from
various informational sources and motion pictures are one of the
sources.

The image of war conveyed by a film does not necessarily match
those of Americans in general, but motion pictures' broader themes over
time will more or less correspond to those of society. As Hortense

---

[37] Morris, ed., Mind, Self and Society, p. 257.

[38] Ibid.

Powdermaker indicated, Hollywood can be classified as a "dream factory."[39] That fact, however, should not detract from the value of an analysis of film content. Siegfried Kracauer argued that beneath surface meanings of films is a clue to a nation's mentality.[40] An examination of film content, then, should yield a fairly accurate characterization of a nation. Such an examination is one way of attaining what Raymond Williams called, "the most difficult thing to get hold of, in studying any past period . . . this felt sense of the quality of life at a particular place and time; a sense of the ways in which the particular activities combined into a way of thinking and living."[41]

A full understanding of films' meanings is not gained from content study alone. Films are produced and viewed within a particular historical context, and their meaning is gained from that context. Thus, an understanding of the context is necessary for comprehension of the content.

The context of films is institutional and societal. As an adjunct to the economic order in American society, the film industry is subject to economic pressures.[42] An inquiry into the economic relationships of the film industry should provide some insight into why certain kinds of films are produced. Other institutional relationships--

---

[39]Hortense Powdermaker, Hollywood, the Dream Factory (Boston: Little, Brown and Co., 1950).

[40]Siegfried Kracauer, From Caligari to Hitler: A Psychological History of the German Film (Princeton, N.J.: Princeton University Press, 1947).

[41]Raymond Williams, The Long Revolution (New York: Harper & Row, 1966), p. 47.

[42]Theodore Peterson, Jay W. Jensen, and William L. Rivers, The Mass Media and Modern Society (New York: Holt, Rinehart and Winston, Inc., 1966), pp. 19-20, 25-26.

particularly with the political order—should also be investigated. A war film is by nature political comment, and, under emergency conditions, the film industry has had a history of moving into close relationships with the political order.

At the societal level the context of war films includes two major elements. First is the progression of international relations of the past thirty-two years, the events which provide war films with a base of reality. An account of international relations should include not only instances in which the United States is directly involved with another nation but also internal consequences of those relations such as the rise of the influence of the military. Society's second contextual element is the prevailing mentality of the nation— the values, beliefs, and emotions of its people—concerning the relevant war, problems, and solutions.

In summary, this study approaches war films from the viewpoint that they have provided Americans with a portion of the material from which their images of war have been built. Because of the institutional nature of the film industry, one would expect that an analysis of war film content would yield an image quite representative of the society of which it is a part. War films provide the individual with clues by which to determine society's view of war. However, the relationship between individual and film should not be interpreted as one which the individual enters with the purpose of forming opinions. Indeed, he may be watching the film purely for relaxation and opinion forming is far from his purpose. Nevertheless he is partaking of a cultural product, an examination of which can be expected to yield some sense of the temperament of the times.

Procedure

Two lines of inquiry characterized the gathering of information for this study. An historical analysis was necessary to provide a context for the war films. Trade publications, primarily Variety, and the New York Times proved valuable for this purpose as did a number of general and cinema histories, investigations of American social conditions, and commentaries on motion pictures.

The other line of inquiry combined a formal content analysis with a more subjective analysis in an attempt to reach some generalizations about war film content. It was recognized that a formal content analysis has weaknesses--especially if the statistical data represent the ends rather than the means. However, the number of films to be studied (815) dictated the use of some systematic procedure in which similar questions would be asked about all films and which would allow the answers to be easily compared for groups of films. The decision to use the formal analysis in no way dictated the analyst suspend his critical powers. Rather, it was felt that the formal analysis would discourage selective attention to the more critically acclaimed films at the expense of the mediocre and encourage a uniform analysis of each film.

A list of war films was compiled from a search of motion picture trade literature. Variety was the primary source supplemented by Motion Picture Herald, Film Daily, The Green Sheet, Film Facts, and Motion Picture Review Digest. A list compiled from such sources may be incomplete. However, there is really no better source than trade journals since the industry itself does not publish synopses for general consumption.

To be included on the list, a film had to meet the following requirements:

1. The film had to fit the definition of a war film. A war film is one dealing with the roles of civilians, espionage agents, and soldiers in any of the aspects of war (i.e. preparation, cause, prevention, conduct, daily life, and consequences or aftermath). Under this definition war films did not have to be situated in combat zones. The broad definition seemed useful because comment about war is not restricted to combat and because contemporary wars do not belong exclusively to the military.

Many comedies about military life do not comment on war _per se_. However, such films do make indirect statements about war--i.e. about an organization charged with making war. Service comedies thus were included. On the other hand, not all films with military characters are on the list. For example, if the major character was a soldier on leave and the plot focused on a love affair in which his military membership had no bearing, e.g. Seven Days Ashore (1944), the film was not included.

2. The film had to be a feature-length, fictional drama. This requirement excluded documentaries and short-subjects but included dramatizations of real events, such as The Longest Day (1962) and Mission to Moscow (1943).

3. The film had to be produced and released by the commercial motion picture of the United States between January 1, 1939, and December 31, 1970. It had to be distributed in commercial theaters.

During the past ten years the distinction between American-produced and foreign-produced films has been blurred. It has become increasingly difficult to determine a film's nationality.[43] For example,

films like Is Paris Burning? (1966) and The Dirty Dozen (1967) were in

one sense foreign produced but had American cast or production staff

or were financed by American companies. Such films as this pair, pro-

duced by American companies in conjunction with foreign producers and

those financed by American companies, were included, when it was pos-

sible to ascertain such conditions. Foreign films, though not included,

were screened whenever possible.

4. The film had to portray a war in which the United States had

been involved during the past thirty-two years. Thus, the plot had

to relate in some way to World War II, the Cold War, Korea, or Vietnam.

Science fiction was excluded, e.g. War of the Worlds (1953) and The

Day the Earth Stood Still (1951) if the opposition was non-human. Also

excluded were some of the recent spy films, such as those featuring

Matt Helm, Flint, and James Bond, when the adversary did not represent

a nation involved in one of the specified wars.

Viewing a film is the best way to gain some sense of its meaning.

It would have been preferable to screen all 815 films, or, failing that,

to screen a representative sample of them. Neither alternative was

feasible. The entire lot of films is not available for screening.

Some of the pictures of the 1940's no longer exist, or they are danger-

ous to handle because they have not been transferred from the combustible

base on which they were first made.

Jack Schwartz encountered similar problems in studying the

---

[43]Thomas H. Guback, The International Film Industry (Bloomington:
Indiana University Press, 1969).

portrayal of education in films.[44] His solution was to rely on film
reviews for his data collection and to screen a number of films to
check the reliability of reviews as a source of information. A similar procedure was followed in this study except that there was more
of an attempt to integrate information from reviews with that from
screenings. The procedure followed was to consult as many reviews as
possible on each of 815 films and to screen as many of those films as
possible. The number of reviews per film ranged from one to more than
thirty. At least one review was read for each film. The average reviews per film was 5.8. A total of 226 movies were screened, 27.7 percent of the 815.

The primary source of reviews was various trade journals in
libraries at the universities of Illinois and Colorado. Such journals
as Variety, Film Daily, Motion Picture Herald, The Green Sheet, and
Film Facts review practically every Hollywood production. Unfortunately,
with the exception of Variety and Film Facts the combined holdings of
these two libraries are incomplete. However, additional reviews for
the majority of films can be found in the New York Times, Time, Newsweek, and Commonweal. The trade journals were searched issue by issue
as were others, such as Films in Review and Hollywood Quarterly. For
many other publications reviews are indexed in Reader's Guide to Periodi-
cal Literature, Educational Index, International Index to Periodicals,
and the New York Times Index.

Possible sources for screening films include theaters, television,

---

[44]Jack Schwartz, "The Portrayal of Education in American Motion
Pictures, 1931-1961" (unpublished Ph.D. dissertation, University of
Illinois, 1964).

rental companies, motion picture studios, and film archives. Four of the five sources proved useful. Motion picture studios provided none of the films screened as letters to two motion picture organizations failed to bring any help from the industry. Television was the source of 186 screenings, rentals 12, theaters 16, and the Library of Congress 12.

Television is not a perfect source, however. Time and commercial requirements cut and sometimes distort films on television, a possibility that must be considered when using such movies for analysis. If adequate financing is available, film archives and rentals are better sources. One directory of films available for rental in the United States listed 337 war films.[45] Few films rent for less than $10 and it would require liberal financing to rent all 337.

Archives providing facilities for scholarly research are the Museum of Modern Art in New York, the George Eastman House in Rochester, New York, and the Library of Congress. The Museum of Modern Art has a large collection but its emphasis is on "art" films. Its facilities are neither large nor inexpensive. The Eastman House does not charge for use of its facilities but its collection generally predates 1939.

For scholars seeking a cross-section of recent movies, the Library of Congress is the most liekly source. Its collection was begun in 1942 and includes a selection of average as well as highly regarded films. The Library did not begin a systematic accumulation of motion pictures until the 1950's. Its holdings of American films include relatively few of the 1940's, 40 to 60 percent of the 1950's,

---

[45]James L. Limbacher, ed., A Directory of 8 mm and 16 mm Feature Films Available for Rental, Sale and Lease in the United States (New York: Educational Film Library Association, Inc., 1968).

and practically all of those produced in the 1960's. However, the
Library's research facilities are limited and ordinarily a scholar
is given one week use of them. Additional time may be granted if
demand for facilities allows. The expense of an extended stay in
Washington, however, would be a prime consideration if unlimited
access were provided.

The content analysis coding form was modeled after one used
by George Gerbner in an investigation of the portrayal of education
in the mass media.[46] The form (Appendix I) went through five revisions
before finalized. The revisions were the consequence of testing the
form on films and reviews and discussing it with a number of colleagues.

The form is divided into two parts. One focuses on the impression of the film as a whole, the other on the major character. Each
part asks questions intended to categorize surface characteristics of
the film as well as trying to obtain broader, more latent qualities,
such as norms, values, and symbols of legitimation advocated by the
picture. Questions thirty through thirty-four and forty-three of Form
A were designed to serve the latter function as were questions twenty-
four through thirty-one of Form B.

Problems of reliability are always encountered when using a
content analysis. In this study the problem had two facets. First,
as in any content analysis, was the question of coder reliability.
The second part of the problem was whether information from reviews is

---

[46]George Gerbner, Mass Communications and Popular Conceptions
of Education: A Cross-Cultural Study, Cooperative Research Project
No. 876 (Urbana: Institute of Communication Research, University of
Illinois, 1964). See also Gerbner, "The Film Hero: A Cross-Cultural
Study."

an accurate reflector of film content.

Coder reliability was checked in a normal manner. Coding responses of the researcher were compared with those of seven different colleagues while the form was being shaped and after it was finalized.[47] Comparing results alerted the researcher to personal interpretations that might differ from those of others. As great, if not more, benefit, though, was gained from discourse during the formative period which sharpened ideas and broadened perceptions.

As might be expected, the questions of greatest disagreement called for greater interpretation on the part of the coder. Answers to questions about demography or actions of the characters are rather obvious. Questions calling for judgments about motivations or intentions are apt to vary more with individual interpretation and thus be less consistent across coders. For example, question forty-three of Form A called for a ranking of themes in a film according to primary, secondary, and three others. The seven coders listed the five themes fairly consistently but their rank-orders were rarely uniform. Likewise questions thirty through thirty-four of Form A and twenty-five through thirty of Form B elicited less agreement. Form A questions asked for judgments about political messages, causes of war, symbols of justification, responsibility for war, and reasons for victory. Form B questions asked for primary and secondary goals, obstacles, and means of the major character.

One solution for less consistent answers is to throw them out.

---

[47]Helping test the coding form were Larry Bellman, John Erickson, Thomas H. Guback, Donald W. Jugenheimer, Peter R. Knights, Albert Kreiling, and Joseph M. Webb.

That was not the procedure here because in most cases the inconsistency was not intolerable since an interpretive question should elicit a greater variety of response than a question of a factual nature. Thus, the preceding discussion of variability of answers was intended to pinpoint answers of a subjective nature and to work within whatever restrictions that situation may entail. In other words, some answers may vary according to the coder and the reader should recognize that possibility.

Schwartz found that information from reviews was generally an accurate reflector of motion pictures. He reached his conclusion after comparing coding results based on reviews with coding results based on motion pictures. A similar procedure was followed in this study. Answers based on the 226 films that were screened were compared to those based on reviews of the same 226 films and categorized according to the following two-by-two classification.

Does Response Appear in Film?

		Yes	No
Does Response Appear in Review?	Yes	a	b
	No	c	d

Desirable classifications were "a" and "d" since in those cases the response in reviews matched the response in the films. Undesirable were "b" (which would indicate the reviews were misleading in information) and "c" (which would indicate the reviews were deficient in information). Once the frequencies for each category were established, a chi square test was used to statistically determine the probability that the differences appearing in the two-by-two table could have occurred by chance. A high number of responses in "a" and "d" in combination with a low probability was taken as indicating the reviews accurately reflected the films. A high grouping in "b" and "c" in combination with a low probability called for the opposite conclusion.

The chi square test pointed to eight questions in which the differences in screening and review data were great enough to warrant caution in using the analysis results. Having probabilities above .20 were questions 29AB (second most frequent ally spy activity), 29EC (third most frequent enemy spy activity), 41A and 41B (consequence of events in film for war effort), and 43B (second dominant theme) of Form A and questions 26 (second major goal), 30 (second major means), and 38 (priority of concern) of Form B (see Appendix IV).

Several other questions had so few frequencies in some of the squares that it was impossible to calculate a chi square. A peculiarity of the chi square test is that it is not always reliable if some of the table's cells have too few frequencies. In such cases it was necessary to develop another way to judge the reliability of the analyses. Thus, consideration was also given to the percentage of "correct" answers ("a" and "d") compared to the percentage of "incorrect" answers ("b" and "c"). If the "correct" answers were overwhelmingly in the majority, it was concluded that the lack of reliability was due to the peculiarity of the chi square rather than misinformation in reviews.

Judged by this added criterion, questions 41A, 41B, and 43B of Form A and 26 and 30 of Form B still should be viewed with caution. All of them have more "correct" than "incorrect" answers but not much more. None of the discussions in later chapters was based on these questions, but the results are carried in Appendix III.

Overall, then, the results of the coding based on reviews was found to reflect fairly accurately the coding according to screenings. However, a word of caution should be inserted against a broad application of this comparison of reviews and screenings. First, the films used in the comparison were not selected in any scientifically random fashion, and, thus, there was no way to scientifically determine if they were representative of the entire group of films. Second, because the same person coded both the films and the reviews, a possibility exists that one coding influenced the other. This interaction, rather than accuracy of reviews, could provide an alternative explanation for high agreement between film responses and review responses. This may have occurred despite the fact that coding from reviews and coding from a screening for a particular motion picture were separated in time.

Structure of the Discussion

The body of this study is divided into four parts, which together are intended to give a balanced view of war films and their place in society. The influence of the environment on production of war pictures is examined in Part One. Particular attention is given to relationships between the government and the motion picture industry, changing economic conditions within the industry, and changing social and cultural conditions within the United States as they relate to war films. Parts Two, Three, and Four focus in detail on war films content, examining changing concepts of the American war hero, of allies and enemies, and of justifications, methods, and consequences of warfare.

PART ONE

WAR FILMS AND THEIR HISTORICAL CONTEXT

INTRODUCTION

With the exception of a few years, Hollywood has produced war films at a fairly steady rate since 1939 (See Table 1). The major exceptions were the four years of World War II and the years immediately following the war. The war years accounted for 41.9 per cent of the thirty-two year total of war films while the exhaustion-induced lull following the war bottomed at two films in 1947. The two years preceding World War II also recorded a low rate of production but generally war pictures have accounted for approximately 6 to 16 per cent of Hollywood's annual releases.

Fluctuations in rate of production can be attributed to some degree to changes in the national situation. Given the fervor of concern and purpose during 1942-1945, the production heights are understandable as is the drop in numbers of films after the war. It is logical that the production rate should vary with changing political conditions, given the intrinsic political nature of war pictures, the institutional and culture character of films, and the commercial potential of contemporary war stories.

Of course, film and environment may also be related in that the content of specific films may be derived from particular events. Such derivations will be mentioned but only in passing. The primary purpose of this section is to trace the broad influences of the environment upon the film industry as they relate to war films and in turn the industry's responses to those influences.

Broadly, the past thirty-two years in the United States can be divided into three epochs, roughly falling into 1939-1947, 1948-1962,

TABLE 1

AMERICAN-PRODUCED FILMS BY YEAR AND WAR

Year	WWII	Cold	Korea	Vietnam	Total War	Total Films	War Pct.
1939	6	–	–	–	6	483	1.2
1940	12	–	–	–	12	477	2.5
1941	32	–	–	–	32	492	6.5
1942	121	–	–	–	121	488	24.8
1943	115	–	–	–	115	397	29.0
1944	76	–	–	–	76	401	19.0
1945	28	–	–	–	28	350	8.0
1946	13	–	–	–	13	378	3.4
1947	2	–	–	–	2	369	0.5
1948	11	1	–	–	12	366	3.3
1949	8	6	–	–	14	356	3.9
1950	6	7	–	–	13	383	3.4
1951	17	12	6	–	35	391	9.0
1952	8	17	5	–	30	324	9.3
1953	12	12	8	–	32	344	9.3
1954	3	6	6	–	15	253	5.9
1955	6	7	7	–	20	254	7.9
1956	11	4	2	–	17	272	6.3
1957	9	11	4	–	24	300	8.0
1958	23	7	4	–	34	241	14.1
1959	13	4	3	–	20	187	10.7
1960	9	1	2	–	12	154	7.8
1961	14	5	2	–	21	131	16.0
1962	10	4	3	–	17	147	11.6
1963	8	4	2	–	14	121	11.6
1964	11	4	1	1	17	141	12.0
1965	11	2	–	–	13	153	7.8
1966	6	4	–	–	10	160	6.3
1967	7	2	–	–	9	165	5.5
1968	10	4	1	1	16	180	8.9
1969	3	2	–	–	5	182	2.7
1970	8	1	1	–	10	*	*

[a]War film totals arrived at by searching various trade journals. American film totals are estimates found in Film Daily Yearbook of Motion Pictures.

and 1963-1970. The dividing lines of the three periods were selected after considering political developments of the past thirty-two years and in particular the relationships of the film industry and the government during that time. The general logic behind the choice of dividing points is this:

1. The years 1939-1947 roughly contain the antecedents, conduct, and immediate consequences of World War II. During the four years of the war the United States was united in effort and sentiment as seldom before or since. Hollywood's response to the situation matched that of other industries. It played a role in the war effort and was not averse to advertising its contribution. Patriotism partly motivated Hollywood but there were other inducements. The war created a more or less captive audience and a timely film subject, and the government through the Office of War Information and the War Production Board possessed powerful, if indirect, control over the industry.

The initial year of the period was selected because it marked the beginning of the war in Europe and of Hollywood's major propaganda enslaughts against the Axis. The end of the period stretched into 1947 because the phobia over communism did not begin to peak until 1948.

2. The first few years of 1948-1962 were paramount to Hollywood and the entire nation. The Berlin blockade, the witch hunts by Congress, and the Korean War cast the Soviet Union and communism as the new enemy. The ideas formed during the early portion of this era were to govern United States policy into the mid-1960's and to a lesser extent even today.[1]

---

[1]This premise is not unique to any one person. One place it is developed is Charles O. Lerche, Jr., The Cold War . . . and After (Englewood Cliffs, N.J.: Prentice Hall, 1965).

The film industry served as a scapegoat for the right wing during these formative years. Two investigations of Hollywood by the House UnAmerican Activities Committee led to an industry blacklist banning some of its top left-wing artists and to a succession of films with a Cold War message. Again, part of Hollywood's behavior during this period may be traced to patriotism--but probably to a lesser extent than during World War II. Right-wing coercion and economic uncertainty probably were greater influences in Hollywood's political acquiescence during this period.

War film underwent a slight evolution during 1948-1962. By the end of the period the films had deviated from some of the old stereotypes--particularly those dealing with World War II and later those featuring Korea. Cold War films generally retained the flavor of the formative years.

3. A valid argument might be made for placing the dividing line between the second and third periods a few years earlier or later. However, 1963 follows the Berlin and Cuba crises, which dramatically illustrated the potential holocaust of either the United States or the Soviet Union pursuing complete victory. That particular "truth" had been subscribed to for years but had paled until the reality seemed close to fulfillment. Following the Cuba crisis, the so-called thaw in the Cold War began.

An American introspection accompanied the thaw, a self analysis leading a large plurality of the citizenry to dethrone communism as the primary villain and replace it with social problems. Some, though, retained the older images and an open conflict, provoked and epitomized by Vietnam, ensued.

In the meantime, Hollywood had been trying to resolve its financial difficulties. It had internationalized, becoming dependent upon foreign, predominantly European, audiences for a profit. This dependency, the shift toward a younger audience in this country, and the general divisiveness of the country have discouraged war films about Vietnam. In fact, only two such battle pictures have been made. Lacking in this era was political pressure for the production of such movies—pressure that was much in evidence in the two previous periods. At the same time fewer "Americanized" films about past wars appeared, being partially replaced by denationalized slicks or by critical examinations of war.

CHAPTER I

A PARTIAL CRUSADE

Prewar Thrusts

Prior to World War II, Hollywood had little reputation as a social critic. The movies of the 1930's generally ignored problems of the depression. Some comedies alluded to the depression but their subjects ordinarily were the upper classes, those who escaped the crash. Raymond Durgnat has argued that these comedies were a form of reverse comment on the depression, but, if so, it was certainly not intended by Hollywood.[1] Standard procedure for the industry during the 1930's was to follow Samuel Goldwyn's famous remark:

"If you have a message, send it Western Union."[2]

Hollywood's artists also followed the advice during the early years of the decade. During the 1934 California gubernatorial campaign, however, the artists underwent a transformation from "elf-like creatures fondly believed (and expected) to behave like the fairy-tale princess who only knew she was blessed and thought of nothing but love"[3] to forthright activists. The reformulation began in Upton Sinclair's 1934 campaign for governor and manifested itself later in leftist politics.

---

[1] Raymond Durgnat, The Crazy Mirror: Hollywood Comedy and the American Image (London: Faber and Faber Limited, 1969), Passim, chaps. xix-xxii.

[2] Activism--Hollywood Style," Newsweek, Aug. 28, 1967, p. 74.

[3] Leo G. Rosten, Hollywood: The Movie Colony and the Movie Makers (New York: Harcourt, Brace, and Co., 1941), pp. 139-140.

Representing the Democrats, Sinclair shook the movie barons with radical plans. His EPIC party took its title from its campaign slogan: "End Poverty in California." Finances for the project were to come from the rich, including the state's corporations and especially Hollywood. Sinclair's intentions were made clear by a rhetorical question he posed to a New York reporter: "Why should not the State of California rent one of the idle studios and let the unemployed actors make a few pictures of their own?"[4]

Film studios, other businesses, the Hearst papers, and radio stations formed an alliance to stop Sinclair. The alliance warned that Sinclair's election meant shifting movie production to Florida, and studio employees were told not to campaign for Sinclair. Employees making $100 a week were asked to donate one day's wage to the opposing candidate, Frank E. Merriam, bolstering Republican campaign funds by $1 million.

More significantly, theaters throughout the state carried political messages. "Every cinema in the state showed anti-Sinclair movies . . . (one feature film had) young hooligans getting off a train which purported to be a crowd of bums lured to California by the prospect of enjoying the beneficence of Sinclair's welfare state . . ."[5]

The studios' profit-motivated excursion into politics was successful as Sinclair lost, but Hollywood's artists had been liberated. They organized mass meetings against fascism, Nazism, communism, and

---

[4] Upton Sinclair, "The Movies and Political Propaganda," in The Movies on Trial, ed. by William J. Perlman (New York: The Macmillan Company, 1936), p. 191.

[5] Ibid.

"all other dangerous isms."[6] A Motion Picture Artists Committee sprang to action to aid China and loyalist Spain, and the Hollywood Hussars, "a band of knights prepared to gallop on their steeds to any emergency,"[7] came into being.

The public's reaction was disbelief and consternation "not (arising) from what the demigods of the screen said, but from the fact that they talked at all . . . They were betraying public faith by stepping out of the romantic function they were supposed to serve."[8] Studio heads were not particularly enthusiastic about the activity either. However, they could not eliminate it, and the screen continued its settled pattern of escapism and ignoring social problems. That aloofness was soon to change--if only slightly.

Hitler's rise to power, his confrontation with the Allies at Munich, and Germany's subsequent march into Austria were events toward which the United States was officially neutral. They were events, however, that physically and emotionally involved American citizens. Some Americans were trapped in the Nazi advance while back home sides were being chosen. More important for American business was the loss of a vital market in Hitler's assimilation of the European continent. This fact was especially true for the movie industry.

After the depression, Hollywood's move toward recovery in the late 1930's was clouded by potential antitrust action. When Germany invaded Poland in 1939, about 33 per cent of American film revenue

---

[6] Rosten, Hollywood: Movie Colony and Movie Makers, p. 139.

[7] Ibid., p. 140.

[8] Ibid., pp. 133-134.

came from the foreign market.[9] More than half of that 33 per cent was earned in belligerent countries. The Axis countries were already being written off when Roosevelt's containment of the belligerents speech aroused fears that income from the Allies would also be eliminated.

All major producers except Paramount, MGM, and Twentieth Century Fox departed Europe in front of German expansion. All belligerents were not closed to Hollywood, though. The Allies remained open, an economic fact often cited as evidence that later anti-Nazi films were produced for strictly economic reasons.[10] Such an assertion is an over-simplification. Certainly, the economic situation influenced production policies. One does not produce a pro-German movie for an anti-German audience. However, other explanations are also feasible.

Animosity between the industry and the Axis could have contributed to anti-Nazi films. Mussolini had sent his son to Hollywood to learn film production techniques and he had been snubbed. Subsequently, Mussolini waged war on American films, finally banning most of them before 1939. A short while later Berlin noted, "the American film industry stands under predominating Jewish influence,"[11] and removed all American pictures from first-run Berlin theaters. In addition a Warner Brothers representative was killed by the Nazis in Berlin before the war's beginning. Thus, a foundation of mistrust and dislike existed between the Axis and Hollywood before 1939.

---

[9]*Variety*, Oct. 4, 1939, p. 1.

[10]John McDonald, "Films," *Public Opinion Quarterly*, V (March, 1941), p. 128.

[11]"Film War," *Current History*, L (March, 1939), pp. 46-47.

Profit and animosity were not enough alone to elicit anti-Nazi films. There is some evidence that some studio heads believed their propaganda films were serving humanitarian causes.[12] However, the political climate in the United States had to be favorable to such pictures as well. As Lewis Jacobs noted, "It wasn't until after Hitler haa seized Czechoslovakia; Japan had taken over the Spratly Islands in the Pacific; Mussolini had snatched up Alabania; Franco had captured Madrid; and Roosevelt had reacted by arousing the government to re-examine its neutrality legislation that the American screen broke its complacency about political events."[13]

Complacency was broken by Confessions of a Nazi Spy, a 1939 Warner Brothers production that deviated from previous espionage films of the era. Spy films of the late 1930's frequently used an international context without specifying nationality. For example, Lone Wolf Spy Hunt (1939) placed the hero detective in the role of protecting the secrets of an antiaircraft gun against villains who were obviously German but were labeled as representatives of a foreign government. Confessions . . . broke that pattern by calling Hitler Hitler, Goebbels Goebbels, and Germans Germans. Based on an actual incident in which the FBI captured and brought to trial German agents operating within the German-American Bund, the film was described by New Republic's Otto Ferguson as

---

[12] Jack Warner, My First Hundred Years in Hollywood (New York: Random House, 1965), p. 262.

[13] Jacobs, "World War II and American Film," p. 28.

a hate breeder if there ever was one . . . The picture is specific
about the thousands of good non-Nazi German Americans, but the old
human tendency to mass identification is bound to make trouble
there. Also it overstresses the theme of a Nazi America and the
importance of swiping secrets for that or any other end.[14]

No little controversy accompanied the production and release of
the picture. Threats on the lives of Jack and Harry Warner and stars
Edward G. Robinson, Paul Lukas, and Frances Lederer were reported.
Fritz Kuhn, head of the American Bund, threatened a $5 million libel
suit against Warner Brothers. The German Consulate filed an official
complaint and some neutral nations banned the picture. Other producers
tried to dissuade Warner Brothers from the picture, according to Jack
Warner.

> 'Look Jack,' one studio owner told me, 'a lot of us are still
> booking pictures in Germany, and taking money out of there. We're
> not at war with Germany, and you're going to hurt some of our own
> people there.'
> 'Hurt what?' I said angrily, 'Their pocketbooks? Listen, these
> murdering bastards killed our own man in Germany because he wouldn't
> heil Hitler. The Silver Shirts and the Bundists and all the rest
> of these hoods are marching in Los Angeles right now. There are
> high school kids with swastikas on their sleeves a few blocks from
> our studios. Is that what you want in exchange for some crummy
> film royalties out of Germany? I'm going to finish this picture,
> and Hitler and Goebbels can scream all they want. And so can guys
> like you.'[15]

One must wonder if all the ballyhoo surrounding the film was
real or manufactured—for example extra Horace Brown's reported quitting
the picture when forced to give the Nazi salute. Brown explained, "I'll
be darned if I'll salute that so and so even if it is just a movie."[16]
The premiere at Manhattan's Strand was protected by a police guard of

---

[14] Otis Ferguson, "They're Down! They're Up!" The New Republic, May 10, 1939, p. 20.

[15] Warner, My First Hundred Years in Hollywood, p. 262.

[16] Hollywood Spectator, April 15, 1939, p. 16.

104, and, according to _Time_, the picture "drew hisses, cheers, and
last week's biggest Broadway gross ($45,000)."[17]

Undoubtedly, some public relations was involved, but producers
and players believed the film was serving a nobler cause. Jack Warner
said, "I hope to do for the persecuted victims of Germany--Jews and
Catholics--what we did for law and order with _Public Enemy_. The
immediate result of that picture was to arouse the public to the horrors
of gangsterdom and put Al Capone behind bars."[18] Lederer, an activist
in the World Peace Federation, dissolved in 1938, concurred:

> Our appeals for world peace were drowned out by blood-thirsty cries
> for war. We decided then that the dictators had made our ideals
> and methods of operation obsolete and that the time had come to
> fight fire with fire. I was delighted to have opportunity to de-
> pict Schneider, as unsympathetic and low a character as he is, and
> to play my part in awakening the United States to the menace of
> foreign propaganda and espionage.[19]

Despite outcries from pacifists and isolationists (E. Raymond
Wilson, secretary of the American Friends Service Committee, warned
that Hollywood was leading the country to war)[20] apparently no
Washington administrative effort was made to discourage _Confessions_. . . .
The FBI gave technical assistance to the picture in the person of
Leon G. Turrou, who actually participated in the events, as an adviser.
Jack Warner counted Roosevelt as a close friend, and it would seem a
word from the President would have been enough to stop, or alter, the

---

[17]"Totem and Taboo," _Time_, May 15, 1939, pp. 58-59.

[18]_Hollywood Spectator_, April 15, 1939, p. 17.

[19]_Ibid._

[20]_Variety_, Jan. 25, 1939, p. 1.

picture.[21]

Subsequent individual films raised less controversy but carried similar messages. In Espionage Agent, produced later in 1939, Warner Brothers again spotlighted Nazi espionage, this time using a peace organization as a front. That film implied, "We are lenient fools about the peeping Fritz. But the implication is that it would be a lovely world if it weren't for the German people, a shilly-shally Congress and perhaps a little too much freedom."[22]

Some 1940 films refused to label the villains but most stamped them emphatically. Escape, The Man I Married, The Mortal Storm, and So Ends Our Night analyzed the problems of Nazi victims. Arise My Love, Foreign Correspondent, and Women in War placed individual Americans or British in direct confrontation with the Nazis. The first pair explicitly warned the United States that it should arm itself against totalitarianism.

The most controversial film in 1940 was Charlie Chaplin's The Great Dictator. Chaplin played two roles: Adenoid Hynkel, the dictator of Tomania, and a timid barber caught in the horrors and persecutions that befell the Jews in Germany. Critics lamented that Chaplin was simply warmongering, that Hitler was not a humorous subject, or that Chaplin betrayed his artistry at the end of the picture when the barber, mistaken for the dictator, mounted a platform to proclaim:

---

[21]Warner, My First Hundred Years in Hollywood.

[22]Otis Ferguson, "Three for the Show," The New Republic, Oct. 18, 1939, p. 301.

And the good earth is rich and can provide for everyone. The
way of life can be free and beautiful, but we have lost the way.
Greed has poisoned men's souls--has barricaded the world with
hate--has goose-stepped us into misery and bloodshed. We have
developed speed, but we have shut ourselves in. Machinery that
gives us abundance has left us in want . . . Knowledge has made
us cynical. Our cleverness, hard and unkind. We think too much
and feel too little. More than machinery we need humanity. More
than cleverness we need kindness and gentleness; without these
qualities, life will be violent and all will be lost.[23]

The comic could not be forgiven for becoming solemn social critic.

By mid-1940 the film industry was given a legal excuse for mak-

ing pictures favorable to a military buildup in the form of the

National Defense Act. In August, 1940, Variety reported:

Heads of both branches of the nation's armed service have tipped
all picture companies that they're ready to go the limit in assistance on any cinematic effort that will help to increase the air
mindedness of the American people and coax more recruits into
uniforms. This is a far cry from the cagey policy toward Hollywood
assumed by the admirals and generals a few months back, when their
attitude toward extending a helping hand was seemingly one of
thumbs down.[24]

For the promotion effort a number of officers were detached from regu-

lar duty to line up special pictures.

The promotion films made little direct comment about Europe but

the reason for a military buildup should have been evident to every

cinema patron. Asides sometimes made the reason clearer. In I Wanted

Wings (1940) the Army's flying service became a gallant melting pot

with lower class mechanic and wealthy playboy united for the country.

The supreme compliment came from a woman photographer describing the

mechanic: "You'll never catch this guy goose-stepping in a yellow

[23]Quoted in Theatre Patrons, April 4, 1941, p. 83.

[24]Variety, Aug. 21, 1940, p. 22.

shirt with his arm outstretched."

The official sanction for service pictures did not extend to anti-Nazi films but the output continued in 1941 just the same. Confirm or Deny attacked the principle of neutrality as journalist Don Ameche concluded in the middle of a London bombing attack that he could not remain merely an observer. Such films as A Yank in the R.A.F. and International Squadron praised Americans already fighting the Nazis.

In relation to total movie production during 1939-1941, the war films were few (3.4 per cent) but received more than their share of attention, especially from isolationist and anti-Roosevelt forces. As early as 1938 the forerunner of the House UnAmerican Activities Committee, chaired by Martin Dies of Texas, investigated the film industry. The Dies committee was formed to attack un-Americanism on the right and the left. In truth more than three-fourths of its 1939 investigations were directed toward the left.[25]

Dies' primary inquiry into Hollywood took place in late 1940. Little of consequence resulted--despite testimony by John A. Leech, former Communist organizer, that several top actors, writers, and directors were members of the party. Typical of Dies' conclusions was that Shirley Temple and Humphrey Bogart were not Communists.[26]

The America First Committee and Senator Burton K. Wheeler, Republican from Montana, followed Dies as Hollywood's critics. Wheeler, chairman of the Interstate Commerce Committee, complained in

---

[25] August Raymond Ogden, The Dies Committee (Washington: The Catholic University of American Press, 1945), p. 133.

[26] Ibid.

February, 1941, that motion pictures were a hotbed of war-mongering propaganda.[27] Newsreels irritated him most. He claimed newsreels did not give equal footage to both sides of the war question, an assertion confirmed by a study conducted by College Men for Defense First. The group found that of 1,175 newsreel subjects between January 28 and April 17, 1941, 553 dealt with issues of defense. Only seven presented isolationist views.[28]

Wheeler proposed a bill to force newsreels to give equal footage to both sides of any controversy. The bill was never passed but his Interstate Commerce Committee launched an investigation into Hollywood's activities in September, 1941.

Eugene Lyons, former New York Times correspondent in Moscow and at that time New American Mercury editor, charged that Communists had milked $2 million from Hollywood. Naming Donald Ogden Stewart, Dudley Nichols, Dalton Trumbo, and Lillian Hellman as having Red ties, Lyons said Communist front organizations included: Theater Committee for the Defense of the Spanish Republic (whose leaders included George Abbott, Heywood Broun, and Franchot Tone); Hollywood Citizens Committee for the Federal Theatre; and Films for Democracy (headed by Walter Wanger).[29]

Hollywood paid $100,000 to Wendell Wilkie to defend the industry. The primary defense was the First Amendment. Wilkie argued that movies had freedom of speech and that restricting content violated that right.

---

[27]McDonald, "Films," p. 128.

[28]Variety, May 14, 1941, p. 3.

[29]Variety, Sept. 3, 1941, p. 3.

The defense also stressed that anti-Nazi films appeared only after the value of the foreign market faded, and that the trend of American public opinion was in favor of the British. "Who would put up $200,000 to make an anti-aid-to-Britain feature film--just one--as against all pro-British films?"[30]

Finally, the industry argued its movies were consistent with the government's Lend Lease policy. Besides, noted Walter Wanger, president of the Academy of Motion Pictures Arts and Sciences, the feature films objected to by Wheeler were made with the full cooperation of the War Department. He added that the films were not subversive because they were intended to educate North and South Americans in the principles of democracy and the dangers of totalitarianism.[31]

The hearings were conducted in a tense and authoritarian atmosphere without allowable objections or cross-examinations. The industry countered claims of subversive propaganda with charges of anti-Semitism against the committee and particularly against Gerald F. Nye, a Republican from North Dakota. Nye responded, "If anti-Semitism exists in America, the Jews have themselves to blame."[32] Pearl Harbor left the hearings unresolved.

This immediate prelude to World War II is interesting since it is one of the few times Hollywood has been vocally antagonistic toward a powerful plurality of its audience. Normally in an ambivalent situation Hollywood has chosen non-action.

---

[30]McDonald, "Films," p. 128.

[31]Variety, March 5, 1941, p. 3.

[32]Variety, Sept. 10, 1941, p. 1.

War and Cooperative Propaganda

World War II was to be a different kind of war. In his State of the Union address in 1942 President Roosevelt said that winning the war would require the full participation of the entire population, not just the fighting men. Full participation included the motion picture industry to which he assigned the responsibility of fully informing the public concerning the following: the issues and the American way of life; the enemy; the united nations and neutral countries; the American production front; the American home or civilian front; and the American fighting forces.[33]

That the movie industry should have a role in the war fit logically with the contemporary concern with the power of the mass media, propaganda, and morale. Lessons of Hitler's rise to power were not lost on American leaders. The use of propaganda was an integral part of the Nazi strategy and seemed at least partly responsible for Hitler's success. Hollywood was supposed to play a vital part in psychological defense against German strategy, which was "to attack the enemy in its weak spots . . . to undermine and break down its resistance, and to convince it that it is being deceived, misled, and brought to destruction by its own government."[34]

The reaction of Hollywood to the President's message was not

---

[33]Cited in Jones, "Hollywood Goes to War," p. 93.

[34]Statement by German military writer Banse quoted in America Organizes to Win the War (New York: Harcourt, Brace and Co., 1942), p. 243.

complete and immediate compliance. Its leaders were ambivalent. John Howard Lawson said, "They wanted films which stimulated patriotism and strengthened civilian and military morale. But they did not want to probe too deeply into the causes of the war or the meaning of fascism."[35] They were not sure such films would sell. In addition the industry was not convinced the public would buy very many war films. The prewar scale of propaganda films was practically nil compared to the effort envisaged by the government.

Other American businesses had similar experiences. They were willing to sacrifice normal practices and convert to war production but not necessarily at the expense of profit. Nevertheless, conversion took place, and American businesses were more than willing to admit to their wartime roles. If you believe some of the advertisements of the early war years, the war was being won because of the contributions of typewriters, screwdrivers, and chewing gum.

While Roosevelt asked Hollywood to play an informational role, the industry saw this function as only one of three and not the primary one. Will H. Hays, president of the Motion Picture Producers and Distributors of America, divided cinema's role into recreation, education, and inspiration. The need for recreation was illustrated by Britain's experience, according to Hays.

> Shortly after the war began, the English government thought it advisable to close down the motion picture theaters, both as an economy and as a measure of protection for civilian population subject to air raids. But they soon discovered that neither economy nor protection counterbalanced the deprivation of amusement. It was easier to ration food and clothing as a war measure

---

[35]John Howard Lawson, Film: The Creative Process (New York: Hill & Wang, 1964), pp. 139-140.

than to withdraw from the people what some had thought to be only a luxury, not a necessity. The theaters remained open even during the period of the heaviest air raids. Furthermore, the wisdom of this decision is attested by the fact that last year the motion picture attendance in England was reported as 33 per cent higher than the average pre-war year.[36]

In effect, Hays was saying that movies should continue in wartime as in peacetime. No major shift in film topics was needed. What Hollywood was already doing was providing recreation and entertainment, which now would alleviate the strain of war.

Movies should also inspire, Hays said. Energy recuperated by relaxation must be charged by emotional stimulation. "Here is work which the motion pictures have shown they can do . . . by taking their fictional materials from past or current history, by making the heroism of their characters reflect the highest values which Americans respect, by focusing the climaxes of their plots upon actions or events which command our admiration."[37]

According to Hays, the fictional, feature-length picture was best suited for providing recreation and inspiration, but the short subject was the ideal vehicle for conveying information. From an economic standpoint this division of labor proved of some benefit to the industry. Instead of underwriting and using its own raw film stock to produce short subjects, Hollywood through its War Activities

---

[36] Annual Report to the Motion Picture Producers and Distributors of America, March 30, 1942, p. 9. A similar argument is presented in Walter Wanger, "The Role of Movies in Morale," American Journal of Sociology, XLVII (November, 1941), pp. 378-383.

[37] Annual Report, p. 13.

Committee cooperated with the Office of War Information in making informational shorts. The government's share of the cooperation included
financing and providing raw film. Thus, more commercial raw film, in
short supply, could be devoted to the more profitable feature-length
pictures.

Whether it wished or not, it is doubtful whether Hollywood
could have abstained from the war effort. The film industry was not
nationalized, but public sentiment was such that any impression of a
stall by Hollywood could have been costly at the box office. In addition the government included persons of some influence within the
industry and possessed sanctions which could have forced cooperation.

Cooperation of the industry operated under the auspices of the
OWI, born by executive order 9182 on June 13, 1942.[38] The order combined a number of governmental services in the OWI, which was to be
headed by newsman Elmer Davis. The Motion Picture Bureau, directed
by Lowell Mellett, a former Scripps-Howard editor, served as liaison
between Hollywood and the government.

> (The bureau) interpreted the government's needs and policies to
> the motion-picture makers, supplied them with the special infor-
> mation required for the production of certain war films, and at
> the request of the studios . . . analyzed short subjects and
> feature scripts for their potential effect on the war effort. The

---

[38]For a discussion of the OWI see Robert L. Bishop and LaMar
S. Mackay, "Mysterious Silence, Lyrical Scream: Government Information
in World War II," _Journalism Monographs_, no. 19 (Lexington, Ky.:
University of Kentucky, 1971). Accounts are also found in Robert Lee
Bishop, "The Overseas Branch of the Office of War Information," (un-
published Ph.D. dissertation, University of Wisconsin, 1965) and
LaMar S. Mackay, "Domestic Operations of the Office of War Information
in World War II," (unpublished Ph.D. dissertation, University of
Wisconsin, 1965).

functions of the office . . . (were) purely advisory. In accord-
ance with the wishes of both the industry and the administration,
final responsibility for the films made in Hollywood during the
war . . . rested with the motion-picture industry.[39]

The bureau was also responsible for creation and production of govern-

ment war films, coordinating the motion picture activities of other

governmental agencies, and obtaining the greatest possible distribu-

tion of government films in commercial theaters.[40]

Mellett worked closely with Hollywood in preparation of films

for defense. Since he had no real control over the industry, Mellett

resorted to public admonishment from time to time in trying to dissuade

Hollywood from certain kinds of films. In reserve, Mellett had the

possibility of asking the War Production Board (WPB) to invoke sanctions

against the industry.

The WPB was established in January, 1942, to set priorities on

raw materials in order to maintain high production and keep the armed

services supplied. Its director was Donald M. Nelson, former president

of Sears, Roebuck and Company, who was invested with almost complete

control over the nation's industrial and economic resources. Nelson

recognized that industry was "reluctant to stop peacetime production

and convert their factories to war use."[41] Reluctance could not be

tolerated. "Just ahead of us are the hardest years we have been through

[39]Jones, "Hollywood Goes to War," p. 93.

[40]Cedric Larson, "The Domestic Motion Picture Work of the Office
of War Information," Hollywood Quarterly, III (Fall, 1947), p. 436.

[41]A. A. Hoehling, Home Front U.S.A. (New York: Thomas Y. Crowell
Co., 1966), p. 49.

since Valley Forge . . . We're going to build so many planes and tanks

that when this is all over those of us who had anything to do with it

are going to be criticized because we built too much."[42]

To produce so much required depriving non-essential industries

of raw materials. Motion pictures were not an essential industry.

Ruling L-41 of the WPB limited spending for new materials to $5,000

for set construction on any one picture. Previously, costs were running

approximately $50,000 for "A" productions and $17,500 for "B" pictures.

This restriction along with scarcity of material found Hollywood in a

totally unfamiliar situation; it could not spend money.

> Statistics can be dull. Hollywood finds these deadly: in a normal pre-war year it used almost 21,000,000 board feet of lumber and more than 5,500,000 feet of composition board. Lumber is now on the priority lists, cannot be bought directly from the mills; composition board cannot be bought at all. Former average use of iron and steel was 850 tons; none may be had at the present.
> The annual hardware bill was $274,205; today studios must shop around for a few dollars' worth. They used to pound in 12,462 kegs of nails a year; with a War Board okay a studio now may actually buy a few kegs a month. Normal yearly consumption of paints, shellacs, alcohol, lacquer and thinners ran 158,740 gallons; they used 254,620 pounds of dry paints, colors, aluminum and bronze powders and pastes. Same story: frozen or doled out by the quart or ounce.
> Rubber, of course, is just a memory. Camel's-hair brushes for applying make-up are just off the market; the aircraft industry wants them for dusting precious instruments. Wigs were made of human hair from China; studio hairdressers thought they could get along with silk wigs; then silk was frozen. They started experimenting with lace; lace comes under M-73 and L-75. To keep their precious plywood and wallboard unmarred, efficiency experts hit on the idea of covering them with cheesecloth before pasting on wallpaper; to remove the paper, they would just grab one end of the cheesecloth, rip it--and the paper off. Cheesecloth cannot be bought today; wallpaper is hard to get.[43]

---

[42]Ibid.

[43]Frank S. Nugent, "Hollywood Counts the Pennies," New York Times Magazine, Aug. 30, 1942, p. 28.

Hollywood encountered other inconveniences. An anti-inflation limit on salaries restricted annual income to $25,000 after taxes, affecting stars and studio executives the most. In the beginning the Selective Service declared films an essential industry and exempted its employees from the draft. Adverse reaction led to revocation so that ultimately only film workers assigned to Army and Navy contract projects were deferred.[44] Gas rationing drew complaints from industry representatives who argued that they would need a larger ration if they were going to sell the war.

The deficiencies and restrictions were inconveniences Hollywood could live with. The WPB had the power of life and death over Hollywood, however, in its control of the raw film supply. The film industry received less than a normal supply because the government had entered movie making on a mass scale, and fear was almost constantly expressed during 1942 that further reductions were imminent.[45]

Hoping that voluntary reduction in film consumption would placate the government, Hollywood tried a conservation program. A suggestion that all credits, except those of stars and featured players, be omitted from all prints outside Los Angeles would have saved an estimated 10 million feet of film a year. That idea never got off the ground. Instead, trailers were limited to 200 feet for super stars, 150 feet for "A" productions, and 100 feet for all others. It was also decided to distribute 30 per cent fewer prints. A radical suggestion by Samuel Goldwyn that double features be eliminated elicited

---

[44]Variety, Nov. 18, 1942, p. 5.

[45]See various issues of Variety during Summer, 1942.

a collective glare from the industry and got no backing even with governmental support.[46] The voluntary concessions did not stop further reductions in the film supply. In September, 1942, the film supply for the rest of the year was reduced by 10 to 24 per cent for various companies and was cut by 25 per cent in 1943. This left about a billion feet for Hollywood's use.[47]

The WPB's priority list for raw film placed money-making films at the bottom. Newsreels received first priority, followed by Army and Navy pictures, feature-length war pictures, and finally all other features.[48] A partial consequence of the reduction in raw film was a cut in movie production—a decline of 18.7 per cent in number of productions in 1943 and another 12.5 per cent in 1945.

As mentioned earlier, the government making its own short subjects was a financial break for Hollywood. When the raw film reduction was first announced, Variety reported that one major studio was losing $10,000 weekly on shorts. After government production hit its peak, as much as 50 per cent of screen time available for shorts went to the government.[49] Hollywood concentrated on the more profitable feature productions—until later in the war when the government stopped making films.

Despite requirements of a war role and deficiency of materials

---

[46] Nugent, "Hollywood Counts Pennies," p. 28.

[47] Variety, Dec. 2, 1942, p. 5.

[48] Nugent, "Hollywood Counts Pennies," p. 28.

[49] Variety, Dec. 9, 1942, p. 1.

the movie industry prospered during the war years. A previously fluc-
tuating and declining attendance stabilized at a weekly average of 85
million. The figure had been 80 million in 1940 and reached 90 million
in 1946.[50]

The Motion Picture Research Bureau conducted a study in New York
in 1942 to determine the influence of the war on attendance. Reasons
cited for less attendance were: working at night and overtime; participating in war activities; husbands and boy friends not there to
take wives and girl friends; increased night school attendance by
youth working in industry; and higher admission prices. Factors leading to increased attendance included: better jobs and more money;
nightshift workers having afternoons off; women passing away free time
because boy friends or husbands worked late or were in the armed forces;
and a special interest in war pictures.[51] The special audience for
war pictures amounted to 11.2 per cent of the 1942 sample. This total
made war pictures the third favorite behind musical comedies (12.4 per
cent) and love stories (11.6 per cent).[52]

Many of the factors leading to increased attendance merely
offset those leading to decreased attendance. What kept attendance
fairly high and stable was the fact that most persons had increased
disposable income and motion pictures had the leisure market practically
cornered. No luxury or recreational items were being manufactured and
gas rationing restricted mobility.

---

[50]Film Daily Yearbook of Motion Pictures (New York: Film Daily,
1941-1947).

[51]Leo A. Handel, Hollywood Looks at Its Audience (Urbana:
University of Illinois Press, 1950), p. 116.

[52]Ibid.

Popular Sentiment

The lack of recreational outlets during 1942-1945 was quite symbolic of the country's mood during that time. A grim, determined attention to the task at hand gripped the nation during those four years. Optimism flared briefly in 1944 but fatigue brought a simple desire to get it over.[53] Immediately after the war, Allan Nevins cited four reasons for the home front's solemnity:

1. Unlike previous wars the American people knew "it was a war they might lose--that it would cost, in treasure, effort, and possibly lives, far more than any previous struggle. They were too anxious, busy, and determined to waste time cheering."[54]

2. The blood letting and aftermath of World War I was fresh in American minds. War was no longer noble; it killed, maimed, and destroyed.

3. "In 1917 there had been many pro-Germans; in 1941 nobody was blind enough to be pro-Japanese."[55] On the European front the years of warnings about the Nazis came to have real meaning. The enemy was evil--completely and unequivocally.

4. A deeper element entered American thinking.

Many millions of reflecting people were troubled by a feeling for which no counterpart had existed in the first World War; a feeling that the nation was partly to blame for the catastrophe. The origins of the first war were not our affair . . . We were dragged into it--or so we believed. But not so with this far greater

---

[53]Jack Goodman, ed., While You Were Gone (New York: Simon & Schuster, 1946), pp. 9-12.

[54]Ibid., p. 9.

[55]Ibid., p. 11.

collision. It was our affair, because we had been given a chance
in 1918-1920 to help stop all future conflicts, and had turned
our back on the opportunity. When we might have furnished mankind continued leadership, we had failed it. We were paying the
penalty. Beyond question this sense of a partial responsibility,
this troubled conscience, imparted to tens of millions of Americans
a feeling of moral obligation. Never had we been more acutely conscious of both past failure and future opportunity. We had been
given a second chance, in which we could rectify our errors, atone
for our failure, and write a better page.[56]

The Depression magnified the feeling of responsibility as did
the recognition that modern means of communication and transportation
removed the privilege of isolation from all nations.

Few educated and thinking Americans did not know by 1941 that
for better or worse they must henceforth share the general future
of mankind. They could play a cheap, mean, shrinking part to
their own injury, or a firm, generous, well-planned part to their
own benefit. But the world . . . (had) shrunk too far and too
fast to make it impossible to play no part at all.[57]

The character of that part was disputed by leaders at various
spots on the political continuum. They agreed that the postwar would
not see the United States slip back into isolationism. The right
visualized an American-dominated peace and prosperity through technology and capitalism. The left saw a world in which nations worked
together for the common welfare. The middle doubted the idealists of
the left and mistrusted the nationalism of the right.

Disagreement over postwar aims was academic at the time and
relatively minor compared to other home front difficulties. Despite
unity of war purpose, internal conflicts continued. Political par-
tisanship remained, and New Deal vestiges were especially fair game.
Congress challenged Roosevelt's enlarged authority. Labor broke

---

[56]Ibid., pp. 10-11.

[57]Ibid., p. 12.

no-strike promises while big business drew huge profit margins. Family

problems, particularly juvenile delinquency, multiplied as a consequence

of greater mobility required for the war effort. Conscientious objectors

enraged middle America. And racial clashes surfaced in Detroit.

Prompted by the social problems, the WPB asked Thomas North

Whitehead to tour the country and report American reaction to the war.[58]

> My own observation is that most people are behaving like patri-
> otic, loyal citizens and that, almost without exception, they all
> wish to do so . . .
> But the capacity of most people to rise above their local cir-
> cumstances and public opinion is always limited; and when I have
> personally witnessed indifferent or poor behavior it has usually
> seemed to me that the people involved were placed in circumstances
> which, in their thinking, did not make sense or at least did not
> correspond with the demands being made of them.[59]

Included among those patriotic, loyal citizens were many of

Hollywood's top personalities. They joined the war effort gladly,

many enlisting, others touring to boost morale. Gene Autry relinquished

his lucrative western role to enlist. Douglas Fairbanks Jr. arranged

a transfer from naval public relations to combat off the coast of

Corsica. Raymond Massey was invalided out of the Canadian Army after

eight months as a major. Burgess Meredith and Gene Raymond served as

captains and Jimmy Stewart as a major in the Air Force while Jackie

Coogan as a glider pilot landed one of the first load of troops behind

enemy lines in Burma.[60] Touring entertainers included Bing Crosby,

Rita Hayworth, Frank Sinatra, Fred Astaire, Ginger Rogers, Humphrey

Bogart, Jimmy Cagney, Joan Crawford, Linda Darnell, Marlene Dietrich,

---

[58]Cited in Hoehling, Home Front U.S.A., pp. 122-124.

[59]Quoted in ibid., p. 123.

[60]Ibid., p. 132.

Jinx Falkenberg, Al Jolson, Errol Flynn, Spencer Tracy, and Boris Karloff.

The tours were arranged through the United Service Organization (USO), founded by the YMCA, YWCA, National Catholic Community Service, National Jewish Welfare Board, and the Salvation Army at the suggestion of Roosevelt. The USO included 3,000 clubs in the United States and nearly 100 in thirty-five foreign countries. The stars volunteered their talents and the armed services paid the expenses.

Responsibility for tour recruiting was given to the Hollywood Victory Committee, which in four years arranged for stars to travel 5 million miles to entertain soldiers. The committee's final report took credit for providing 56,037 free appearances by 4,147 persons in 7,700 events, including 13,555 playing days by 176 persons on 122 overseas tours.[61]

Charged with integrating the movies' war effort was the War Activities Committee--Motion Picture Industry (June 5, 1940 to January 7, 1946), self-proclaimed as "the vehicle through which all branches of the industry, between Dunkerque and Pearl Harbor, cooperated with the United States Government to make America the arsenal of democracy and thereafter worked to speed total victory over Germany and Japan."[62] The committee acted as liaison with the OWI, provided technical assistance for production of government short subjects, and arranged screen time for these shorts. In addition the committee

---

[61] Annual Report to the Motion Picture Producers and Distributors of America, March 25, 1946, p. 50.

[62] Ibid., p. 51.

promoted seven bond drives which netted $36,874,436.37 from audiences admitted during 29,913 bond premiers.[63]

The Screen's Response to War

Roosevelt's proclamation that the war was total, that it would be won or lost on the home front set the pattern of the government's conception of the kinds of movies that should be made. Hollywood was to inform and inspire the home front by making pictures about the home front. Industrial changeover and production had to be accelerated, and the government believed Hollywood could significantly aid the effort.

This role should not have disturbed the industry too much. At that moment home-front film had more commercial possibilities than battle pictures. An audience will accept a stretch in credibility but not a complete perversion of reality. Reality was catastrophe at Pearl Harbor and the Japanese spreading rapidly through the South Pacific—events hardly appropriate for Hollywood's happy endings and the triumph of good over evil. Thus, while there were some early battle films involving American soldiers, they were the exception rather than the rule.

Also discouraging battle pictures was expense. Such films normally require much more than the $5,000 in materials allowed by the WPB. Past movies had been defrayed by technical assistance from the War Department. During most of 1942-1945 the War Department

---

[63]Ibid.

usually was not in a position to lend assistance.

The home-front film, then, was a natural component of the 1942-1945 propaganda releases. As Table 2 shows, slightly more home-front than war-front pictures were released in both 1942 and 1943. It was not until 1944 that war-front films were more plentiful than home-front pictures.

TABLE 2

PERCENTAGE OF FILMS BY CHARACTER-LOCALE
AND YEAR, 1939-1947

Classification	1939-1941	1942	1943	1944	1945	1946-1947	Total
Espionage-War	12.0%	24.0%	7.8%	6.6%	7.1%	26.7%	13.6%
Soldier-War	6.0	12.4	18.3	22.4	35.7	13.3	17.0
Civilian-War	28.0	12.4	23.5	28.9	25.0	13.3	21.5
Espionage-Home	24.0	35.5	13.9	9.2	10.7	13.3	20.7
Soldier-Home	26.0	5.8	7.8	9.2	-	-	8.9
Civilian-Home	2.0	9.9	28.7	23.7	17.9	33.3	18.3
Total	100.0	100.0	100.0	100.0	100.0	100.0	100.0
Number	50	121	115	76	28	15	405

Hollywood's interpretation of the home front differed from that of the OWI, which wanted stories about industry, workers, rationing, civil defense, etc. It got some, but the overwhelming majority of the early films featured espionage agents. It was relatively inexpensive for the film industry to relabel gangsters as Nazis, Fascists, or Japanese just as it was relatively simple for an audience to make a transfer of identification. Espionage films were not limited to the home front. A total of 59.5 per cent of 1942 war films were about espionage activities. The figure dropped in the following years with a corresponding increase in films about soldiers and civilians on the war front.

The OWI was dissatisfied with Hollywood's performance. In late 1942 Mellett embarked on a campaign to "nix the spy under every bed" approach.[64] It would be easy to conclude he had weighty persuasive powers since in 1943 only 21.7 per cent of the films were about espionage. However, by then some combat material was available for filming, and the hint of final success was beginning to form. Military pictures became easier to sell. Earlier combat films had evolved from defeats--Wake Island, Corregidor, Bataan--and they were fairly successful. However, defeats can be rationalized only so often.

It is interesting that the total of military films did not exceed civilian pictures at any time during 1942-1945. This is indicative, again, of the promotion of the conflict as a total war to be won as much on the home front as on the war front. Other factors encouraged civilian films also.

Roosevelt asked for movies that examined the character and ideology of the enemy. A battle setting is not the most efficient vehicle for this purpose, but a civilian war-front film does quite well. Such a picture repeatedly dissected the Nazi and promoted the courage of the partisans of Europe in the war years. Such films were used to place democracy and totalitarianism in direct confrontation and to demonstrate that democratic forces would survive regardless of the weight of modern instruments of warfare against them.

Then, in 1945 the country neared emotional exhaustion. It was obvious the war would be over soon, and all that was desired was a quick ending and return to normalcy. Battle pictures were not

---

[64]Variety, Sept. 28, 1942, p. 82.

commercially exploitable in such a situation. In addition governmental pressure to produce propaganda films lessened as the end neared.

As servicemen returned to civilian life, readjustment problems emerged. At the same time, artists, who had become accustomed to a more realistic form of film making in the services, rejoined commercial pictures. Directors in particular were not anxious to resume the dream world and sought ways to insert more reality into commercial productions. The adjustment problems of returning servicemen was a convenient subject for this purpose.

A listing of film types and numbers hardly is sufficient for understanding the screen mood. Specifying mood is one of the purposes of this thesis. An in-depth analysis occupies the latter chapters, but it would be useful at this time to mention in passing some of the films of 1942-1945, examining them by year of release.

1942

As mentioned previously, the predominant kind of film in 1942--in numbers anyway--was espionage tales, which frequently merely placed new labels on old characters. Some of the time-proven hero-detectives fought crucial battles during the war--including Sherlock Holmes, Michael Shayne, Ellery Queen, and the Falcon. Even the Invisible Man's formula was resurrected and used literally to boot the Nazis in the seat of the pants (Invisible Agent). Humphrey Bogart's supporting cast in Maltese Falcon returned to help him flush a quarry of Japanese agents in Panama (Across the Pacific).

Home-front sabotage was a favorite topic. Alfred Hitchcock's Saboteur traced a defense worker's escape route as he tried to prove himself innocent of destroying an aircraft plant. In so doing, Bob Cummings puts the finger on a fifth columnist, outwardly a clean, forthright patriot--and isolationist. Other films had a bomb being placed aboard a bus and timed to explode along the West Coast in order to light a target for Japanese submarines (Busses Roar); Nazi Bela Lugosi performing plastic surgery on a Japanese to make him appear American and then escaping a prison cell to avenge a double cross (Black Dragons); and a private detective discovering a double murder is linked to a Nazi spy ring (Crime by Night). In Foreign Agent Hollywood glamorized its studio technicians, one of whom supposedly invents a searchlight filter sought by the Nazis. The enemy agents are aided by a subversive peace organization financed by the Axis.

Espionage was sometimes funny as well as dangerous. Bob Hope and Percy the Penguin aid a beautiful British agent in My Favorite Blonde; Red Skelton and Bart Lahr thwart enemy spies in Ship Ahoy; expert kegler Joe E. Brown literally bowls over the Nazis in The Daring Young Man; and Judy Canova brings a barrage of assassination attempts to an end by shooting a carrier pigeon in Joan of Ozark.

On the less dangerous side of the home front, the isolationist argument took a beating. The War Against Mrs. Hadley featured the widow of a Washington newspaper publisher (who supposedly resembled Cissie Patterson of the Washington Times-Herald)[65] staunchly resisting the war provoked by the radical Roosevelt. After breaking with her children and a son's heroism in battle, she makes a remarkable about

---

[65]"The New Pictures," Time, Sept. 28, 1942, p. 82.

face, affirming an overwhelming patriotism and showing a sudden understanding of the middle and lower classes.

Industrial and consumer problems received a measure of attention.
Pittsburg (coal), Powder Town (explosives), Wings for the Eagle (Lock-
heed aircraft), and Priorities on Parade (women workers) glamorized
essential industries. At the same time Rubber Racketeers and The
Boss of Big Town attacked economic opportunism.

Even Blondie did her part. In Blondie for Defense she organizes
neighbors into Housewives for America. They wear uniforms and do the
usual civil defense stints, even guarding the local dam.

Westerns were updated. In Riders of the Northland Charles
Starret and two other Texas Rangers try to resign and join the Army.
Before that can happen they are sent to Alaska to track down spies
fueling subs and building a hidden airport. Along the way one of the
Rangers sings "We'll Carry a Torch for Miss Liberty."

The films just mentioned were not particularly good, but they
were typical of the productions ground out by Hollywood in a dutiful
manner. Not all war films were mediocre, as indicated by Table 3,
which lists a number of films cited as "outstanding" in 1942-1945.

The outstanding picture of 1942, war or otherwise, was Mrs.
Minniver, the story of the home life of a normal, middle-class British
family during the war and concomitant heartaches and fears. Two other
films about the British received acclaim. This Above All focused on
the dilemma of a lower class Englishman who doubts he should fight for
a country whose rulers discriminate against the poor. Journey for
Margaret drew sympathy for orphans of the war.

One movie about American combat received praise. Wake Island
eulogized the resistance of a handful of Marines during the first days
of the war. They were all killed and the Japanese captured the island,

TABLE 3

OUTSTANDING WAR FILMS, 1942-1945[a]

Year	Films
1942	Mrs. Minniver, Wake Island, The Pied Piper, This Above All, Journey for Margaret, Across the Pacific, Joe Smith, American, Flying Tigers, Saboteur, To Be Or Not To Be, Captains of the Clouds, Eagle Squadron
1943	Casablanca, Watch on the Rhine, So Proudly We Hail, Stage Door Canteen, The More the Merrier, Air Force, The Moon Is Down, Bataan, Keeper of the Flame, Journey for Margaret, Mr. Lucky, Action in the North Atlantic, Five Graves to Cairo, This Land Is Mine, Corvette K-225, Sahara, Commandos Strike at Dawn, Edge of Darkness, Hangmen Also Die, Hitler's Children, Crash Dive, The Fallen Sparrow
1944	Dragon Seed, Since You Went Away, A Guy Named Joe, Story of Dr. Wassell, Lifeboat, Destination Tokyo, See Here, Pvt. Hargrove, The Sullivans, Up in Arms, Hail the Conquering Hero, Guadalcanal Diary, Thousands Cheer, Purple Heart, Eve of St. Mark, North Star, Tender Comrade, Wing and a Prayer, Passage to Marseilles, Address Unknown, The Hitler Gang, Thirty Seconds over Tokyo, Janie
1945	Story of G.I. Joe, House on 92nd Street, Objective Burma, God is My Copilot, Hollywood Canteen, Pride of the Marines, They Were Expendable

[a]Compiled from films listed as outstanding in Annual Report to Motion Picture Producers and Distributors of America, 1943-1946, which gathered it from awards of various trade publications and other periodicals.

but the ending elicited determination and vengefulness rather than despair.

1943

The plight of the conquered nations of Europe was a favorite film topic in 1943. As in most American war films the accounts were not history but tales of individuals and small groups defying great odds and adversity.

An exception was Mission to Moscow, a semi-documentary of the diplomatic mission of Joseph E. Davies in 1937-1938. Costing more than $2 million, the movie reportedly was made by Warner Brothers at the suggestion of Roosevelt. Jack Warner was especially enthusiastic about the picture: "By gosh, we'll put Russia on the map."[66] If nothing else, the film renewed animosity between left and right in the United States. Mission . . . advocated the righteousness and courageousness of Stalin and absolved him of sin in the 1937 Purge. (According to the film the victims of the purge were Nazi agents.)

As propaganda Mission . . . was superb. It made its point in a politically and artistically effective manner, that premise being that the Soviet Union recognized Hitler's intentions early and the only reason Stalin signed a pact with Germany was to delay an attack in order to build his forces. The Soviets came out of the picture as one of the United States' strongest and most loyal allies—a view undoubtedly regretted by the Warners during later HUAC investigations.

Another pro-Soviet film was North Star, which depicts invading Nazis ravaging a village in rural Russia. The film preached postwar brotherhood and peace. In the late 1950's an attempt was made to turn the picture into anti-Communist propaganda. A narrator was added to

---

[66]"The New Pictures," Time, May 10, 1943, pp. 23-24.

attempt to cast Soviet leaders as traitors to peace-loving Russians because of the Hungarian intervention.

Hostages, Hitler's Madman (or Hangman; there seems to be confusion over the second word of the title), and Hangmen Also Die exploited a 1941 Czechoslavkian incident in which the Germans executed a number of hostages while they were seeking the murderer or Reinhard Heydrich, their premier henchman in the country. Most notable of the trio was Hangmen . . ., starring Brian Donlevy. The set resembled an American main street, and the suspense and technique were those of the traditional crime thriller. Through it all, though, the undying spirit of freedom loving Czechs reigned supreme.

An analysis of Nazi Germany, Hitler's Children, proved the bargain of the year. RKO produced the film for $170,000 and grossed well over $1 million. Featuring a Frauenklinik where women were sterilized, the picture was soon followed by Behind the Rising Sun with a slightly larger budget and slightly less return. In this film an American-educated Japanese abandons his civilized (i.e. American) culture upon return to his home land and ultimately is completely corrupted by the militaristic system.

Casablanca with Bogart and Watch on the Rhine with Bette Davis were the class of the year. Casablanca, which has become a favorite of film buffs, followed Bogart's conversior from individualistic cynicism to social responsibility. Watch . . . features a German partisan and his American wife in her wealthy mother's home near Washington. The family is completely disheveled but ignores exhaustion because fascism must be defeated.

On the home front the number of espionage pictures declined,

although Bob Hope submitted another entry, They Got Me Covered. Nothing was particularly striking about most of the home-front films as
they depicted farms (Hoosier Holiday), aircraft factories (Top Man and
Swing Shift Maisie), housing shortage (So This Is Washington), and
conserving scarce materials (He Hired the Boss).

Hollywood celebrated its contribution to morale with Stage
Door Canteen, based on an actual club for servicemen in New York.
Numerous stars and songs were thrown around a thin plot to promote one
of the Hollywood Victory Committee's pet projects.

Laurel and Hardy, who previously had been praised for their
USO efforts, evoked great wrath for Air Raid Wardens. Their usual
antics tie up a community after they are infected by patriotism and
volunteer for Civil Defense. Although the Civilian Defense Organization did not care for such a satirical portrayal, some reports indicated that the ineptness in the film was not too far from reality.

Battle films began to multiply. Robert Taylor, George Murphy,
and eleven others delayed the Japanese empire in Bataan, and America's
first offensive step in the Pacific (Mackin Island) was celebrated in
Gung Ho, taken from a Chinese phrase meaning work together. Sahara
put Bogart in North Africa with a tank crew and he came through in
usual fashion. Typical military pictures, however, (Aerial Gunner,
Bombardier, and Crash Dive) devoted 80 per cent of their time to training and concluded upon entry into battle with the hero proving himself.

1944

Some thought of postwar problems began to creep into 1944 releases. Lifeboat and None Shall Escape expressed interest in what to

do with the Nazis and whether prewar mistakes would be repeated.
None . . . advocated severe punishment in retribution while Lifeboat,
a Hitchcock allegory set in a row boat in the middle of the Atlantic
Ocean, noted the Nazis would be defeated but would resurface in the
face of weakness on the part of the rest of the world.

The Sullivans, Tender Comrade, and Since You Went Away approached
home-front difficulties from a deeper and more serious perspective than
had predecessors. The Sullivans was based on the story of an actual
Iowa family which lost five sons when a destroyer went down in the
Pacific. The film traced the lives of the five boys from birth to
death and glorified their American peculiarities.

In Since . . . a typical, middle-class American family (Claudette
Colbert, Jennifer Jones, and Shirley Temple) encounters and overcomes
problems related to father's hitch in the armed services. With
Joseph Cotten and Monty Wooley adding flavor, the picture was dedicated
in the introduction to "the unconquerable fortress, the American home."

Tender Comrade sympathized with difficulties of war widows and
orphans. The picture concludes with Ginger Rogers receiving a telegram
with the message of the death of her husband. She addresses her baby,
Chris, and tries to explain that the death was worthwhile.

The more light-hearted home-front pictures continued. Women
in industry found Dixie Dugan in a film of the same name giving up
driving a taxi to work for the Office of Mobilization of Women Power
and Rosie Warren as Rosie the Riveter becoming a welder to insure
production of more planes. Rationing was a late entry promoting the
necessity for such a policy.

Something of an inspiration itself, the Doolittle raid brought forth <u>Destination Tokyo</u>, <u>Thirty Seconds over Tokyo</u>, and <u>The Purple Heart</u>. <u>Destination . . .</u> portrayed a submarine entering the Sea of Japan to obtain weather readings for the raid; <u>Thirty . . .</u> depicted the raid itself and the experiences of the flyers trying to escape out of China; and <u>The Purple . . .</u> essayed the inhumanity of the Japanese as they executed several flyers as criminals.

On April 28, 1942, Roosevelt lauded an Arkansas doctor for sticking with ten basket cases (injured who could not move under their own power) during the evacuation of Java. He disobeyed orders to insure their safety. The report is that Cecil B. DeMille heard Roosevelt's fireside chat and immediately latched onto the topic. <u>Dr. Wassell</u> resulted with naval and Paramount collaboration and Wassell's personal assistance.[67]

1945

In some ways the exhaustion beginning to grip the country was reflected in Hollywood's 1945 productions--not just in film content but also in the scarcity of war pictures. Scarcity was also due to readjustment of governmental priorities. The urgency for counter-propaganda seemed to have died.

The notable battle film of the year was <u>The Story of G.I. Joe</u>, based on the writings of Ernie Pyle. Burgess Meredith as Pyle wandered through the battlefields of North Africa and Italy as a one-man Greek chorus. The picture's American fighting man was something of a deviation from past portrayal. He was as dedicated as ever but somewhat

---

[67]"Winning His Navy Cross," <u>Newsweek</u>, June 12, 1944, p. 72.

less heroic and bothered more by physical and material inconveniences.

From events surrounding the atomic bomb evolved The House on
92nd Street, an image builder for the FBI. It features Lloyd Nolan
ferreting out Nazi agents and protecting a secret formula, process 97.
Although not explicitly labeled, the formula supposedly represented
the atomic bomb.

Physical and emotional problems of returning servicemen were
solved in Identity Unknown and Pride of the Marines. In Identity . . .
Richard Arlen travels the country seeking his amnesia-forgotten identity.
All the while he explains to whomever he encounters that their loved ones
did not die in vain. Blinded during heroic action in the Pacific, Al
Schmid returns to civilian life in Pride . . . without any will to
live. Thanks to friends, family, and fiancee, he regains his sensi-
bilities and discards his bitterness.

Two pictures took rather critical views of the establishment.
A Medal for Benny condemned commercialism associated with war heroes.
Benny, a local bad boy, is exiled from his Southern California community
but later wins the Congressional Medal of Honor by killing 100 Japanese
single-handedly. The community is elated until they find out the boy's
name is pronounced Marteen rather than Martin. The boy's father, however, reminds the community that regardless of background all are
Americans.

The military received some measure of criticism in A Bell for
Adano, a story of the administration of a small Italian village. The
criticism is directed toward insensitivity of military bureaucracy
toward the human condition and did not censure the military and war.
However, the film along with A Medal . . . is indicative of the nearing

end of the war. Such pictures, critical of some middle-class values and of one aspect of military leadership, probably could not have been made in 1942 and 1943, when urgency demanded unity from all and criticism only of those who did not agree with the war purpose. Governmental control over the movie industry was much tighter during those two years as well.

Postwar Unwinding

An attitude of "don't remind me" marked the country's mental state in the years immediately following the war. The lines of the Cold War were beginning to emerge, but the civilians who had fought World War II desired only to be left alone. Hollywood pretty much complied with their wishes—as far as war films were concerned. Battle pictures were abandoned, although a few others were released.

O.S.S. (1946) focused on espionage by American agents. It illustrated the training of American agents, who had to cram years of experience into a few months, and one of the agents advocated the establishment of a professional corps of warriors. "This job takes guts, intelligence, and at the end discipline. We're late, 400 years late. We've only a few months to build a worldwide intelligence agency to beat the enemy at its own game." Thus, he concluded, to protect itself in the future the United States had to give up its leisurely habits; it could not afford to be "too sentimental, too trusting, too easy going, and self centered." The message was to be repeated time after time in future years.

Using a flashback to 1922, The Searching Wind (1946) conveyed a similar message. Responsibility for World War II as far as the

United States was concerned was credited to a foreign service too inept to see the implications of a Fascist takeover in Italy. The point
was that the nation could not afford to curl up and ignore the rest
of the world.

Meanwhile, The Best Years of Our Lives (1946) tackled the readjustment of returning servicemen--the youth without arms, the sergeant
who cannot accept the hypocricy as a loan officer, and an Air Force
captain denied his old job in a drug store. The problems were solved,
but producers probably later regretted the attack on financial institu-
tions when the film caught the attention of HUAC.

By 1947 Hollywood was ready to illustrate the implications of
Hiroshima and Nagasaki--or try to. The Beginning or the End promised
more than it accomplished. The film ostensibly was a questioning of
the morality of the bomb. In reality it was an unreserved praising of
American science and technology. The moral dilemma by the movie's Robert
Oppenheimer was vastly outweighed by the nobility of the end--a quick
and decisive victory over Japan.

Summary

The performance of the film industry from 1939 to 1947 can be
viewed as that of an adjunct institution responding to political and
economic pressure of the American society. Its products--war films--
fit pretty much into the mainstream of American thought, especially
in 1942-1947. The anti-Nazi pictures of 1939-1941 were somewhat of a
deviation from an institutional role, but that may have been only an
apparent deviation because a major portion of society was vocally
isolationist and pacifist.

Comparing the films of the prewar era with Sam Goldwyn's advice, "If you have a message, send it Western Union," one could conclude that Hollywood violated the counsel. But it must be remembered that the anti-Nazi films were relatively few, and they apparently were not regarded with much displeasure by the administration. That the films occasionally exceeded American policy cannot be doubted; that they were more extreme than general American sympathy can be.

Pearl Harbor ended controversy over Hollywood's prewar films. The war provided an excellent example of an economic institution trying to fulfill political functions without relinquishing too much of its profit. Part of Hollywood's willingness to convert to war purposes was a consequence of patriotism, but some might also be traced to pressures from the government and the OWI and WPB in particular, as well as the general mood of the American public.

As the war changed so did Hollywood's efforts. In the beginning the industry released mass-produced war films coinciding with the idea of total war for civilian and soldier alike. Later as it became apparent the war would be won and governmental and public pressure eased, the industry reduced its war-film output. After the war films almost avoided the topic altogether.

CHAPTER II

RED SCARE

Like most American industries Hollywood anxiously awaited the end of World War II and the return of normalcy. The war had treated the movie industry well enough, stabilizing its financial outlook, but postwar promised more--with returning servicemen adding to the market and without the necessity to service the nation's war needs. The script unfolded as expected for two years. Attendance increased and the industry prospered. However, in 1949 prosperity departed (for a number of reasons, the primary of which was television), and the decade of the 1950's was spent trying to recover.

Attempts at recovery were not without complications. Compounding the economic problems was a political purge initiated by HUAC in 1947. The purge had consequences lasting into the 1960's, i.e. a blacklist of artists with leftist connections. In addition the purge resulted in a minor wave of anti-Communist films and for a time the avoidance of controversial social topics.

Most significant of Hollywood's response to political coercion was the blacklist, which reflected an insecurity that gripped the nation and Hollywood. The nation's fear came from an image of the Soviet Union as an enemy ready to devour the country. The industry's insecurity was caused by financial uncertainty. Hollywood's behavior in the face of political persecution can be seen partly as a consequence of national insecurity, but a more viable explanation views its concessions as an attempt to pacify the government while the industry confronted its economic problems.

Purge and Blacklist

If Hollywood intended to resign from national service after
World War II, its plans were cast asunder by HUAC's 1947 publicity-
motivated attack. Relatively quiet during World War II, HUAC was
functioning again by 1945, and the Soviet Union's activities during
1946 and 1947 in Eastern Europe fueled the committee's momentum.
After the 1945-1946 committee turned toward Hollywood only momentarily,
J. Parnell Thomas' (Republican from New Jersey) 1947 group launched a
full scale attack. Other members of the 1947 committee included:
Richard B. Vail of Illinois; Karl E. Mundt of South Dakota; and Richard
M. Nixon, of California, all Republicans; and Democrats John S. Wood of
Georgia; J. Hardin Peterson of Florida; Herbert C. Bonner of North
Carolina; and John C. Rankin of Mississippi.

The bulk of the 1947 hearings were in October in Washington,
but a preview was held in May in Los Angeles. Fourteen "friendly"
witnesses supporting HUAC's attack appeared before the May hearings
(closed although daily news bulletins were issued). Robert Taylor testified that the government (meaning to the committee F.D.R.) had prevented
him from entering the Navy before he had finished Song of Russia in
1943. Lela Rogers, mother of Ginger, said her daughter had refused
to deliver a line of Communist propaganda in Tender Comrade (1943).
The line was "share and share alike--that's democracy."[1] Adolphe
Menjou charged that Hollywood was one of the main centers of Communist

---

[1]Walter Goodman, The Committee (New York: Farrar, Strauss, and
Giroux, 1968), p. 203. Much of the discussion of the HUAC hearings and
the blacklist is based on Goodman's book plus John Cogley, Report on
Blacklisting, Vol. I: Movies (New York: The Fund for the Republic, 1956)
and Gordon Kahn, Hollywood on Trial (New York: Boni & Gaer, 1948).

propaganda in the United States.

> Two weeks after their Los Angeles visit, the Thomas-McDowell
> subcommittee issued an idictment, based on what their fourteen
> friendly witnesses had told them: the N.L.R.B. was abetting the
> effort of Communist organizers to take control of the industry;
> scores of highly paid screen writers were injecting propaganda
> into movies: White House pressure had resulted in the production
> of 'some of the most flagrant Communist propaganda films'; subtle
> techniques were used for glorifying the Communist Party, while the
> Communists prevented the production of films which glorified loyal
> American citizens; the heads of the studios had done nothing to
> prevent all of this. Exposure was essential; public hearings were
> promised. Not one of the above charges would ever be substantiated,
> but the publicity which these coming attractions received bespoke
> high success for the future event.[2]

On October 20, 1947, the Washington hearings opened amid sparkling

lights and live microphones. Plans called for a parade of friendly wit-

nesses before confrontation with nineteen unfriendly witnesses, eight

of whom were never called. The friendly witnesses were to provide evi-

dence that Communists were rampant in Hollywood and Hollywood's films.

The unfriendly witnesses had said they would refuse to answer questions

as a matter of principle.

First witness was Jack Warner, fervent anti-Nazi turned anti-

Communist. He reeled off names of persons he thought to be Communists.

When pressed for evidence, he displayed a not-too-incisive understand-

ing of communism and could not cite any specific examples of Communist

propaganda in Hollywood's films. One film he mentioned was Humoresque

(1946).

> John Garfield played the part of the boy and he was mad at Joan
> Crawford for romantic reasons and said, 'Your father is a banker.'
> He was alluding to the fact that she was rich and had all the
> money. He said, 'My father lives over a grocery store.' That is

---

[2]Goodman, The Committee, p. 203.

very, very subtle, but if you see the film with those lines in it
you will see the reason for it. But it is not in the film. I
eliminated it from the script.[3]

One of the committee's reasons for interrogating Warner was to
credit Roosevelt with instigating the production of Mission to Moscow
(1943), once a patriotic effort praising an American ally but in 1947
blatant Communist propaganda. In the May hearings Warner had said that
Ambassador Davies and the administration had approached him about the
film. This time he credited his brother with the idea.

From each witness HUAC sought support to outlaw the Communist
Party and to blacklist party members. On the stand Warner refused
support for the blacklist, vehemently defending the right of any American to work.

Robert Taylor appeared in order to retract his previous statement
about being forced to make Song of Russia, Louis B. Mayer to defend the
picture, and Ayn Rand to contradict him.

In her view, Louis B. Mayer was not much better than an agent of
a foreign government inasmuch as the film produced showed the
Russians smiling, which Miss Rand said, 'is one of the stock
propaganda tricks of the Communists—to show these people smiling'.
The presence of neat, clean cottages in the picture appalled her.[4]

Lela Rogers repeated her statement about Tender Comrade and then
displayed her knowledge of Communist propaganda. She cited the movie,
None But the Lonely Heart (1944) as a propaganda example because a
review characterized the film as being "pitched in a low key, is moody
and somber throughout in the Russian manner."[5] Then, she described an

---

[3]Quoted in Kahn, Hollywood on Trial, pp. 17–18.

[4]Ibid., p. 33.

[5]Ibid., p. 44.

instance of propaganda.

> I will tell you of one line. The mother in the story runs a
> second-hand store. The son says to her, 'you're not going to'--
> in essence, I am not quoting this exactly, because I can't remember
> it exactly--'You're not going to get me to work here and squeeze
> pennies out of little people who are poorer than we . . .'
> We don't necessarily squeeze pennies from people poorer than we
> are. Many people are poorer and many people are richer.[6]

Other Hollywood notables added similar weight to the evidence,

including Ronald Reagan, president of the Screen Actors Guild, and

George Murphy and Robert Montgomery, his predecessors; Leo McCarey,

producer and director of Going My Way (1944) and Bells of St. Mary's

(1945); screenwriter Richard Macauley; James K. McGuinness, founder of

the Motion Picture Alliance for the Preservation of American Ideals;

critic John Charles Moffitt; director Samuel G. Woods; and Hearst

columnist Rupert Hughes.

Gary Cooper provided the clinching testimony with this descrip-

tion of Communist activity in Hollywood:

> They haven't attempted to use me, I don't think, because, ap-
> parently, they know that I am not very sympathetic to communism.
> Several years ago, when communism was more of a social chit-
> chatter in parties, in offices and so on, when communism didn't
> have the implications that it has now, discussion of communism
> was more open and I remember hearing statements from some folks
> to the effect that the communistic system had a great many
> features that were desirable, one of which would be desirable
> to us in the motion picture business in what it offered the
> actors and artists--in other words, the creative people--a special
> place in government where we would be somewhat immune from the
> ordinary leveling of income. And, as I remember, some actor's name
> was mentioned to me who had a house in Moscow which was very large--
> he had three cars, and stuff, with his house being quite a bit
> larger than my house in Beverly Hills at the time--and it looked
> to me like a pretty phony come-on to us in the picture business.
> From that time on I could never take any of this pinko mouthing
> very seriously, because I didn't feel it was on the level.[7]

---

[6]Quoted in ibid.

[7]Quoted in ibid., p. 57.

The friendly witnesses represented Hollywood's right wing,
which had been put down by the left for years and was now having its
turn. Many were members of the Motion Picture Alliance for the Preservation of American Ideals, founded in 1944 to fight the "growing impression that this industry is made up of, and dominated by, Communists,
radicals, and crackpots."[8] HUAC's stated purpose was to investigate
Communist propaganda in American films. If judged by a "Screen Guide
for Americans," authored by Ayn Rand and published by the Alliance,
movies contained such propaganda. The guide provided the following
advice for moviemakers:[9]

1. Don't smear the Free Enterprise System.

2. Don't deify the Common Man.

3. Don't glorify the Collective.

4. Don't glorify failure.

5. Don't smear success.

6. Don't smear industrialists.

7. It is the moral duty of every decent man in the motion picture industry to throw into the ashcan where it belongs, every story
that smears industrialists as such.

That some Hollywood artists are Communists has never been disputed nor has the claim that some pictures during 1942-1945 praised
the Soviet Union. However, the first week of the trials did not
establish that any Communist propaganda existed in the films. Friendly
witnesses merely were allowed to pursue the subject as they desired

---

[8] Cogley, Report on Blacklisting, p. 11.

[9] Ibid.

without documenting their assertions.

Eight of the nineteen unfriendly witnesses were never called: Richard Collins, Gordon Kahn, Howard Koch, Lewis Milestone, Larry Parks, Irving Pichel, Robert Rossen, and Waldo Salt. Of the eleven who testified, writer Bert Brecht cooperated to a degree. The remaining ten refused to answer any questions. The ten, or the Hollywood Ten as the group was known, included director Edward Dmytryk and writers Alvah Bessie, Herbert Biberman, Lester Cole, Ring Lardner Jr., John Howard Lawson, Albert Maltz, Samuel Ornitz, Adrian Scott, and Dalton Trumbo.

The Ten had numerous movies to their credit, and, if the Thomas committee had followed its stated purpose, those films would have been analyzed for Communist propaganda. Included among the pictures were two which were favorable to Russia during World War II. Action in the North Atlantic (1943) depicted a convoy carrying supplies to the Soviet Union and an American sailor referring to Russian planes as "ours." Counter-Attack (1945) featured a Russian soldier playing mental games with a Nazi in a bombed cellar.

HUAC did not conduct a content study, but Dorothy Jones did for Cogley's book and for the Fund for the Republic.

> 1. It was found that none of the 159 films credited over a period of years to the Hollywood Ten contained Communist propaganda . . . Furthermore, it should be stated that the files of the MPAA, which indicated films which the Code Administrator felt contained possible Communist propaganda, confirm the findings of this study with regard to films of the Ten, in that none of the pictures cited are those on which any members of this group received screen credit.
> 2. The Communist Party has, on occasion, once the picture was released utilized films credited to the Ten for the purposes of propaganda . . .

3. The content of the films of the Hollywood Ten appears to
change in a manner which is in keeping with the changes in the
content of Hollywood films generally, with the exception of the
fact that films of The Ten deals more with social themes.[10]

Two questions were of primary importance to the committee: (1)
Are you a member of the Screen Writers' Guild (whose leftist leanings
were well known) and (2) are you a member of the Communist Party?
Attorneys warned the Ten that answering any questions required a response to others. The committee wanted the Ten to answer only "yes"
or "no" and then to pursue names of other members of the organizations.

Justifying their actions by the First Amendment, the members of
the Ten refused to answer either question. Instead, they played verbal
games with the committee and tried to make personal statements. Dalton
Trumbo explained, "I shall answer 'Yes' or 'No' if I please to answer.
I shall answer in my own words. Very many questions can be answered
'Yes' or 'No' only by a moron or a slave."[11] The appearances of the
Ten were quite theatrical, typified by Lawson's abrasive shouting.
Part of Lawson's appearance is quoted here to indicate the nature of
the Ten's testimony. This particular episode serves the purpose well,
and additional elaboration of the testimony would be superfluous. In
response to whether he was a member of the Screen Writers' Guild,
Lawson said:

> The raising of any question here in regard to membership, politi-
> cal beliefs or affiliation is absolutely beyond the powers of this
> committee.
> Mr. Thomas: I think the witness will be more responsive to the
> questions.
> Mr. Lawson: Mr. Chairman, you permitted--
> Mr. Thomas:· (pounding gavel) Never mind--
> Mr. Lawson: (continuing)--witnesses in this room to make answers

---

[10] Ibid., pp. 226-227.

[11] Quoted in Kahn, Hollywood on Trial, p. 79.

of three or four or five hundred words to questions here . . . I
am not on trial here, Mr. Chairman. This committee is on trial
before the American people. Let us get that straight.
　Mr. Thomas: Mr. Lawson, you will have to stop or you will
leave this witness stand. And you will leave the witness stand
because you are in contempt. That is why you will leave the witness stand. And if you are just trying to force me to put you
in contempt, you won't have to try much harder. You know what
has happened to a lot of people that have been in contempt of this
committee this year, don't you?
　Mr. Lawson: I am glad you have made it perfectly clear that
you are going to threaten and intimidate the witnesses, Mr. Chairman.
　(The chairman pounding gavel.)
　Mr. Lawson: I am an American and I am not at all easy to
intimidate, and don't think I am.[12]

The Ten received backing from Hollywood contemporaries. The

Committee for the First Amendment was formed to help the original

nineteen. Organized by producers William Wyler and John Huston and

screenwriter Philip Dunne, the group issued a petition to the House

of Representatives, placed advertisements, and solicited defense

funds before embarking for Washington and the hearings. The trip was

intended to show solidarity for industry efforts to fight HUAC and

was planned to coincide with the testimony of Eric Johnston, president

of the Motion Picture Producers and Distributors of America.

Unfortunately, the order of witnesses had been changed. The

travelers attended Lawson's show. His behavior surprised, embarrassed,

and demoralized committee members.[13] Two more unfriendly witnesses

appeared the next day and the group departed.

　The complete collapse of the committee was hastened by another
incident growing out of the Hollywood hearings. A Washington newspaper had reported that Sterling Hayden, one of the stars who made
the Washington trip, was a Communist. After William Wyler had

　[12]Quoted in ibid., pp. 69-70.

　[13]Cogley, Report on Blacklisting, pp. 8-9.

called a meeting of committee members to raise funds so Hayden could sue for libel, it was discovered that there was some truth in the story. (Hayden subsequently testified that he had been a Party member for six months in 1946.)[14]

Thus collapsed an industry-wide resistance to the purge. The reality of political battle had disillusioned some of the industry's top liberals. Included were: Robert Ardrey, Humphrey Bogart, Larry Adler, Lauren Bacall, Geraldine Brooks, Jules Block, Richard Conte, Philip Dunne, Melvin Frank, Anne Frank, Ira Gershwin, Sheridan Gibney, Sterling Hayden, Mrs. Sterling Hayden, June Havoc, David Hopkins, Paul Henreid, John Huston, Gene Kelly, Evelyn Keyes, Danny Kaye, Arthur Kober, Marsha Hunt, Robert Presnell Jr., Henry Rogers, Sheppard Strudwick, Joe Distrom, and Jane Wyatt.

The hearings continued. One by one the witnesses refused cooperation, and one by one they were cited for contempt. Congress approved the citations, sending all Ten to prison. Eight received maximum sentences of one year in jail and $1,000 fine while Biberman and Dmytryk got six months and $1,000.

Throughout the hearings, Thomas' attempts to get Hollywood's leaders to approve of a blacklist were rebuffed. Johnston repeatedly reassured the troubled artists. The hearings proved practically nothing about communism in Hollywood. HUAC had no power over the industry. Yet in November in New York the industry capitulated. "It was here, in the words of the Chicago Sun, that the motion picture industry caved in and turned defeat into victory for J. Parnell Thomas."[15] A statement explained:

---

[14]Ibid., p. 9.

[15]Kahn, Hollywood on Trial, pp. 183-184.

Members of the Association of Motion Picture Producers deplore
the action of the ten Hollywood men who have been cited for contempt by the House of Representatives. We do not desire to pre-
judge their legal rights, but their actions have been a disservice
to their employers and have impaired their usefulness to the industry.

We feel forthwith discharge or suspend without compensation
those in our employ, and we will not re-employ any of the ten until
such time as he is acquitted, or has purged himself of contempt,
and declared under oath that he is not a Communist.

On the broader issue of alleged subversive and disloyal elements
in Hollywood, our members are likewise prepared to take positive
action.

We will not knowingly employ a Communist or a member of any
party or group which advocates the overthrow of the Government of
the United States by force, or by any illegal or unconstitutional
method.

In pursuing this policy, we are not going to be swayed by any
hysteria or intimidation from any source.

We are frank to recognize that such a policy involves dangers
and risks. There is the risk of creating an atmosphere of fear.
Creative work at its best cannot be carried on in an atmosphere of
fear. We will guard against this danger, this risk, this fear.
To this end we will invite the Hollywood talent guilds to work with
us to eliminate any subversives, to protect the innocent, and to
safeguard free speech and a free screen wherever threatened.

The absence of a national policy, established by Congress, with
respect to the employment of Communists in private industry makes
our task difficult. Ours is a nation of laws. We request Congress
to enact legislation to assist American industry to rid itself of
subversive disloyal elements.

Nothing subversive or un-American has appeared on the screen,
nor can any number of Hollywood investigations obscure the patriotic
service of 30,000 Americans employed in Hollywood who have given our
government invaluable aid in war and peace.[16]

The Ten were the first to go but only the first. The remainder

of the unfriendly witnesses were asked to sign loyalty oaths. Some

refused and were fired. Also threatened were members of the Committee

for the First Amendment and 208 actors in the Actor's Division of the

Progressive Citizens of America who had taken an advertisement in Daily

Variety to protest the hearings. The list broadened as new hearings

---

[16]Quoted in ibid., pp. 184-185.

ded names in 1951-1952 and such organizations as the American Legion

olunteered assistance to rid the industry of Communists.

The 1951-1952 HUAC hearings took a slightly different approach.

homas was no longer around as he had been convicted of payroll padding

nd sentenced to prison. Georgia's John S. Wood had succeeded Thomas.

is committee moved from charges of propaganda to the claim that Com-

unists had been feeding on the reputations and pocketbooks of

ollywood's inhabitants (an accusation more easily proved than the

947 indictment).

Even in the face of what had happened to the Ten some witnesses

efused to cooperate--this time, though, relying on the Fifth Amendment.

thers cooperated, even admitting party membership. Either action was

nough to join the blacklist, but even cooperation was frowned on.

ogley reported that some of the cooperative witnesses, 1947 and

951-1952, were socially ostracized.[17] Some cooperative witnesses

ound it difficult to find work until members of HUAC and the AFL Film

ouncil leader, Roy Brewer, exerted pressure.[18]

Brewer enabled Dmytryk to return to work in 1951. Unfortunately

or most of the Ten, Brewer was not among their benefactors. In fact,

t has been only within the past ten years that some members of the

en have been acknowledged in screen credits. During the latter half

f the 1950's some of the Ten produced scripts under assumed names,

nd the industry turned its head while paying them less than their

alents would demand. The 1957 Academy Award winning screenplay,

---

[17]Cogley, Report on Blacklisting, p. 113.

[18]Ibid., p. 112.

The Bold Ones, was credited to R. Rich. Rich was Trumbo, who is yet
to receive that Oscar. Trumbo was the first of the Ten after Dmytryk
to be recognized in film credits--Exodous in 1960.

Thus, the political events of 1947-1952 had lasting internal
consequence for the motion picture industry. They also had influence
on the war films of the era, which will be discussed later in the
chapter. The crucial point is that the industry buckled under pressure
of the HUAC when it did not have to, a capitulation in marked contrast
to Hollywood's staunch defense of 1941.

What was the difference? The Red Scare was mounting, and the
industry's left wing was without strong political allies. But a major
part of the explanation is non-political. To a certain extent the
compliance with the wishes of HUAC can be seen as a move to fend off
political interference while the industry attacked a more significant
problem--declining attendance.

Impending Economic Disaster

Swelled by returning servicemen, Hollywood's attendance jumped
by an average of 5 million per week in 1946 and stayed at that level
for three years.[19] However, in 1949 a potentially disastrous decline
began as attendance fell from 90 million per week in 1948 to 70 million
in 1949. The decline hit bottom in 1958 at 39.6 million and stabilized
at 40 million into the 1960's.

A number of reasons have been advanced for the decline. Primary

---

[19]All attendance figures are estimates from Film Daily Yearbook
of Motion Pictures.

was television. Why should an individual pay to see something similar
to what he could see for free on television? The novelty of television
was also contributory. A 1951 survey demonstrated that theaters dropped
1 per cent of their gross income for each 2 per cent of homes within
their market that acquired television receivers.[20]

Television's importance was a manifestation of a broader trend.
Personal disposable income was being diverted from movies to other
items. Just after the war the "marked increase in incomes gave people
extra money when there was still an excess demand for automobiles and
other recreation items. Since movies were the ever present alternative,
large sections of the public were not too selective and attended any
picture that was showing."[21] By 1950, however, money could be spent
on radios, television, cars, houses, and a variety of recreational
equipment.

Parking, especially in larger cities, was also a problem although
the growth of drive-in theaters tended to alleviate this difficulty. In
fact, "48 per cent of the decline in four-wall receipts might be attributed to the expansion of drive-ins, except that obviously a substantial
number of drive-in patrons never or seldom have gone to regular theaters."[22] Drive-ins increased from 300 in 1946 to 4,000 in 1964, while
four-wall theaters were dropping from 18,719 to 9,800 in that same

---

[20]Michael Conant, Antitrust in the Motion Picture Industry
Berkeley, Calif.: University of California Press, 1960), p. 13.

[21]Ibid., p. 10.

[22]Simon N. Whitney, Antitrust Policies, American Experience in
Twenty Industries (New York: Twentieth Century Fund, 1958), Vol. II,
p. 177.

period of time.[23]

The attendance worries were accompanied by government antitrust action that changed the economic structure of the industry. The change was inaugurated by the Paramount Consent Decree in 1948 which forced Paramount to divest itself of its theaters. Traditionally, the industry had been a vertical monopoly with the major companies controlling production, distribution, and exhibition. Such an arrangement allowed studios to dictate rental rates and thus provided an instrument for gaining competitive advantages over independent producers. The structural arrangement gave rise to discriminatory first-run privileges, arbitrary clearance arrangements, and monopolistic influences on sales policies of distributors.[24] Having a manipulatable market also enabled the major studios to mass produce films and market them as a package.

The government's first attack on vertical integration was in 1938. The 1948 Paramount decision culminated the efforts by requiring divestiture of production and distribution from exhibition and prohibiting several other practices including block booking, stipulating admission prices, establishing any fixed system of clearance, and granting to circuits any contract except theater by theater and picture by picture.

Uncertainty is the best way to describe the situation facing Hollywood during the late 1940's and throughout the 1950's. The Paramount Decree threatened the oligarchy that was Hollywood since vertical

[23]Figures are from various issues of Film Daily Yearbook of Motion Pictures.

[24]Ralph Cassady, "Impact of the Paramount Decision on Motion Picture Distribution and Price Making," Southern California Law Review, XXXI (1958), p. 155.

integration had allowed the major studios to dominate the industry. The decree removed the base for vertical integration and left in doubt whether the majors would continue to dominate. A broader and ultimately more important question was whether the industry could continue on a profitable basis. With such issues facing industry leaders, they could not afford to irritate political authority--or, at least, so they thought.

Besides, it did seem that public opinion favored anti-Communist measures, and Louis B. Mayer said that fear of film censorship and the belief that public opinion could be appeased led to the blacklist.[25] The American Legion aided the industry's decision by threatening a national boycott of films and pickets in front of theaters. Some threats were carried out. The Legion was very cooperative in providing lists of supposed Communists and helping Brewer's rehabilitation program.

Other groups demanded changes of all types. It may have seemed to Hollywood that through some quirk everyone had turned enemy of the industry at once. _Variety_ described the situation:

> Real sensitivity to the pressure groups dates back to the J. Parnell Thomas committee investigation last fall . . . that was accompanied by such a fanfare that the charges, although unproved, are believed to have resulted in a considerable bite being taken out of the boxoffice. Ever since, Hollywood's brass has been so busy trying to prove that the picture industry is a right-living, right-thinking and right-producing community that they have gone far out of their way to offend no one--whether it be Thomas, the Catholic Church, the Jews, the Negroes, the President, the American Dental Society, or the Institute of Journeymen Plumbers of America.[26]

---

[25] _New York Times_, Dec. 10, 1948, p. 5.

[26] _Variety_, July 7, 1948, p. 3.

n-Offensive Films for Defense

film response to the Red Scare was explicitly
War pictures although ideological traces slipped
into Kо̣̇   d World War II movies. The Cold War pattern was set in
1948-1953 with emphasis primarily on espionage, Communist promotion
of dissent, and the plight of Communist refugees. The style lasted
into the 1960's. The Korean War movies, which were about a conflict
which might be classified as the military portion of the Cold War,
were generally noncommittal on broader issues. In fact, the Korean
films resembled the World War II pictures produced in 1948-1962 as
much or more than they resembled Cold War productions. Table 4 gives
a hint of this similarity. World War II films of 1948-1962 and the
Korean War pictures put extremely more emphasis on military characters
and war settings than did the Cold War movies.

TABLE 4

PERCENTAGE OF FILMS BY CHARACTER-LOCALE
AND WAR, 1948-1962

Classification	WWII	Cold	Korea	Total
Espionage-War	8.7%	15.4%	- %	9.5%
Soldier-War	65.2	8.6	86.3	49.1
Civilian-War	19.3	26.0	–	18.4
Espionage-Home	1.2	26.0	–	9.2
Soldier-Home	5.0	23.1	9.8	11.7
Civilian-Home	0.6	3.9	3.9	2.2
Total	100.0	100.0	100.0	100.0
Number	161	104	51	316

[a]Data derived from question 21 Form A in Appendix I.

Korea was a military war and the Cold War was non-military as well as military. Thus, films about the two wars should have emphasized different kinds of characters. Also, as the memory of World War II faded, the intensity and urgency of the home front were forgotten and the remembered excitement of the battlefield made combat pictures more marketable than home-front films about the same topic. However, the emphasis on military pictures could also be the consequence of the rise of the military as a political force in American society.[27] A strong military was seen as a necessity for national security during 1948-1962. Hollywood oft repeated this argument, partly induced into this position by the prospect of technical assistance from the Pentagon. The military's involvement in commercial motion pictures hit its peak during 1948-1962.

Cold War

The era's first anti-Communist film resembled Confessions of a Nazi Spy in that both were based on real events. The Iron Curtain (1948) came from an incident in which members of the Canadian Parliament, scientists, and an Army officer were involved in a conspiracy to obtain atomic secrets. The efficiency and intricacies of Soviet espionage are depicted, but the focus is on Igor Gouzenko as Canadian friendliness, freedom, and material comforts (a four-room flat) cause him to defect.

Espionage was not the only Soviet threat. Just as ominous, according to the screen, was the creating and spreading of dissent by

---

[27]For a discussion of the military see Morris Janowitz, The Professional Soldier (Glencoe, Ill.: The Free Press, 1960).

the Communists. <u>The Red Menace</u> (1949) shows Communist exploitation

of a returning serviceman who cannot find a job and is cheated by

housing racketeers. The film also emphasized that Communists exploit

Jews and Negroes and use sex, money, and fear to attain their purpose,

which is to disrupt the day-to-day operation of the United States.

Other films of the first few years were similar to these two.

<u>I Married a Communist</u> (1949) substituted Communists for gangsters in

a style reminiscent of the anti-Nazi films. <u>I Was a Communist for the</u>

<u>FBI</u> (1951) featured Frank Lovejoy infiltrating the party infrastructure

to gather evidence on the Communists' disruptive union activities. His

life is in danger at all times, but his greatest anguish is caused by

being ostracized by family and friends because of his known party

membership. The educational system, or rather its intellectual pro-

duct, was scrutinized in <u>My Son John</u> (1952). The son is depicted as

the typically naive intellectual falling for the Communist line but

ultimately reconsidering, thanks to his mother's advice to "get in the

game . . . on God's side and carry the ball . . . before the clock runs

out."[28]

In the same year Hollywood did its bit for HUAC, using John

Wayne to convey the message. In <u>Big Jim McLain</u> Wayne plays a special

investigator for HUAC whose efforts are continually frustrated. The

culprit is the Fifth Amendment--a portion of the Bill of Rights that

receives concluding criticism from Wayne.

Other films of 1952 and 1953 had strong elements of cops-and-

robbers. <u>The Thief</u> (1952), which interestingly contained no dialog,

---

[28]Quoted in "The New Pictures," <u>Time</u>, April 7, 1952, p. 104.

portrayed a nuclear physicist selling out, but surrendering to the FBI at the end, while the FBI again saved the country in Walk East on Beacon (1952). At the other end of the continuum a pick-pocket turned patriot when confronted with treason in Pickup on South Street (1953).

Hollywood retained the internal-threat theme into the 1960's but at a lower rate than in 1948-1953. Operation Manhunt (1954) added a chapter to the Gouzenko story, and Security Risk (1954) focused on the FBI again.

Trial (1955), Three Brave Men (1957), and The Fearmakers (1958) added twists to the usual story line. Trial attacked racial bigotry by showing that one of its worst evils is its exploitation by Communists. Three . . . highlights some unfairness in the Navy's security bureaucracy but sidesteps the issue by rationalizing the security process as necessary. The Fearmakers cast distrust on public opinion pollsters.

Soviet strategy and methods in Europe appeared on the screen as early as 1948 when The Red Danube depicted the repatriation process of a ballerina who wishes to defect but is forced by regulations to return to Russia. The film features several suicides in an overcrowded train of deportees.

Some of the European-based films were satirical, such as The Iron Petticoat (1956) and Silk Stockings (1957) but most were strictly melodrama. Man on a Tightrope (1953) followed the efforts of a circus owner to escape the intervention of a Communist state while Clark Gable aided the escape of a Russian ballerina in Never Let Me Go (1953). The Secret Ways (1961) had East Europeans escaping with the aid of Richard Widmark. The Girl in the Kremlin (1957 capitalized on Stalin's death and The Beast of Budapest (1958) on the Hungarian Revolt for commercial value.

The most significant of the European group was Night People (1954), not particularly notable for artistic achievement though it was a notch above the usual, but because of its message: civilians should leave international affairs to experts, i.e. the military and other trained agents. In this film the transition from a civilian war of the 1940's to the professionals' Cold War can be observed.

China's threat was acknowledged in 1954 and 1955. The Shanghai Story (1954) and Blood Alley (1955) portrayed European and Chinese refugees trying to escape the Communists. Hell and High Water (1954) featured a team of civilians (mostly scientists and former military men) foiling a plot by the Chinese to bomb Russia in an American plane.

These civilian-oriented, anti-Communist films as a whole were not particularly good. Most were "B" productions although "B" productions were being phased out due to the economic changes already mentioned. The pictures contrasted with the films of World War II, which exumed a degree of positivistic patriotism. The anti-Communist films were formed on a basis of fear and distrust rather than faith. A citizen's loyalty was not assumed; it had to be proved.

The black mood of the anti-Communist films fit nicely with a trend of movie making that characterized some of Hollywood's productions following World War II. Instituted by returning directors who had had experience with documentaries during the war, the style, first used in gangster films, was an attempt to inject more reality into the screen world. The trend did not match the Italians' Neo-Realism, but it borrowed from the documentary by shooting on location and trying to avoid

actorish mannerism. It "was a candid-camera style of photographic
coverage giving a new flexibility to the treatment of action and
authentic revelation of certain processes and techniques in crime-
detection stemming from wartime documentary and pre-war March of
Time magazine series . . ."[29]

New realism stayed with Hollywood into the 1960's but did not
dominate--for economic reasons as much as anything else. Declining
attendance forced the industry to rethink its strategy. Hollywood
had to offer the customer something new, something he could not get
on television. Color was one solution. In 1948 only 16.8 per cent
of the films used color; by 1954 the figure had risen to 58.4 per
cent.[30]

In an attempt to produce an advancement that would compare with
sound, technological experimentation was stepped up. The first revo-
lutionary technique was 3-D, but the new process was not accepted by
the audiences. The glasses were uncomfortable, and few top films were
produced in 3-D. In addition the process was expensive.[31]

Wide screen productions (Cinemascope, Vistavision, Super Scope)
proved more workable. They had disadvantages from an artistic standpoint. Closeups, particularly a facial shot of an individual, looked
distorted because of the extra width. However, the screen width was
perfect for outdoor scenes and shots of soaring planes. Strategic Air
Command (1955) and Bombers B-52 (1957) capitalized on the wide screen

[29]Roger Manvell, New Cinema in the U.S.A. (New York: E. P.
Dutton & Co., 1958), p. 12.

[30]Conant, Antitrust in the Motion Picture Industry, p. 13.

[31]Richard Dyer MacCann, Hollywood in Transition (Boston: Houghton
Mifflin Company, 1962), pp. 20-26.

and American interest in jet planes for market value.

Korean War

To the extent that the enemy in Korea was identified as Communist, these war films were part of the Cold War. Generally, the Korean War films resembled the Cold War style (realistic photography) but not the content. Instead of evolving into ideological diatribes, the Korean pictures more frequently inquired into the nature of man in battle-- superficial in many instances but nevertheless an inquiry.

Samuel Fuller provided two such investigations, The Steel Helmet and Fixed Bayonets, low budget 1951 productions. In each the heroes are soldiers simply doing a dirty, dangerous job in an efficient manner. They lack the noble qualities of the classic hero but nevertheless are experts at their job. Duty was not always pure. In One Minute to Zero (1952) Robert Mitchum's duty forces him to order a column of refugees to be fired upon. The column contained North Korean soldiers.

Some attention was given to justifying the military presence in Korea. Retreat Hell (1952) justified the presence as a matter of duty while praising Marines for a fighting withdrawal from the Chosin Reservoir in December, 1950. Another actual event was the basis for A Yank in Korea (1951), which concluded with the reading of a dead soldier's letter to his two sons. The well publicized letter explained why Americans were fighting another war so soon.

Notable in 1953 (but only in retrospect) was Battle Circus, the story of the Mobile Army Surgical Corps, starring Humphrey Bogart. The hero and the picture present an interesting contrast with 1970's M*A*S*H.

From late 1953 until 1959 the Korean ground war was neglected in favor of the glamorous jet fighters. Sabre Jet (1953), The Bridges at Toko-Ri (1954), Men of the Fighting Lady (1954), The McConnell Story (1955), Battle Hymn (1957), and The Hunters (1958) featured the military's new air corps.

During the same era, the treatment of prisoners of war by the Communists was depicted in Prisoner of War (1954), The Bamboo Prison (1955), and The Rack (1956). Prisoner . . . had Ronald Reagan volunteering to slip into a prison to check reports of brutalities. The Manchurian Candidate (1962) was the best of the prisoner of war pictures, wrapping its story around brainwashing and hypothesizing that it was possible for brainwashing to have hypnotic power over an individual even after he is released (thus giving a false impression of the actual nature of brainwashing).

Korean War films began to decrease in the last part of the 1950's. The survivors focused on the infantry and related problems: face saving by the brass in Pork Chop Hill (1959), racial bigotry in All the Young Men (1960), and war crimes, or at least psychiatric difficulties, in Sniper's Ridge (1961) and War Hunt (1962). These films generally depicted battle in a realistic manner, a mood aided by black-and-white filming. They differed from earlier Korean pictures by presenting a more critical view of the military and circumstance. The criticism was not always explicit but did tend to touch the pocks as well as the beauty marks.

World War II

Until 1949 Hollywood avoided World War II combat topics. A few war films slipped in, such as The Search (1948), dealing with refugee problems, and The Boy with Green Hair (1948), a tale of a war orphan who wakes up with green hair and decides that he is meant to spread a message against war. But it was not until 1949 that Hollywood decided the American public was ready once again for World War II combat stories.[32]

Battleground (1949) was the first large scale battle picture of the period but in a few months followed Command Decision (1949), 12 O'clock High (1949), and Breakthrough (1950). Each featured non-heroic depictions of military organizations and the decision making required for winning a modern war. Command . . . pointedly argued that civilians, meaning Congressmen, did not understand war and should leave it to professionals. Using Sands of Iwo Jima (1949) and Flying Leathernecks (1951) as vehicles, John Wayne made similar points about the necessity of having a professional military leadership.

Battle Cry (1955) continued the professional tradition as did three (naval) submarine pictures of 1958, The Deep Six, Run Silent, Run Deep, and Torpedo Run. The Deep Six presented an argument against pacifism that would have been more appropriate in 1942. Another 1958 picture, The Naked and the Dead, aroused possibilities of an antiwar message but failed to live up to Norman Mailer's novel.

Some combat pictures rose above the professional syndrome. Home of the Brave (1949) wrapped a combat mission around a criticism of racial bigotry while Enemy Below (1958) treated the battle of wits between a German submarine commander and the captain of an American

---

[32]Variety, Oct. 4, 1948, pp. 1, 53.

b chaser with sympathy on both sides. The German as well as the
erican was human.

Four films received some critical acclaim. The Bridge on the
ver Kwai (1957) won the Academy Award with a story about British
d American prisoners of war. The Young Lions (1958) almost matched
at achievement while giving a sympathetic characterization to young
zi officer Marlon Brando. In 1961 The Guns of Navarone was lavishly
aised but in retrospect it must have been solely for its technical
hievement. Finally, The Longest Day (1962) tried to dramatize the
ganization and heroics of Normandy but failed--except in the adver-
sements. Its stars were too famous to be anonymous men doing a
all part in a massive task; they had identities which overshadowed
e event. Besides, the film was artistically poor and naive.

World War II films produced in 1948-1962 sometimes downgraded
litical or military significance and used war as a container for
her types of stories.

Service comedies continued during 1948-1962 but they moved the
medy to combat. Up Front (1951) took Willie and Joe out of print
d put them on the screen, but even these two comics were professionals
 at least experienced fighting men. Imitation General (1958) drew
me ire for its comical treatment of combat but its comedy was
rictly in the line of duty. Glenn Ford imitates a general to carry
t a mission and is careful to be the general in front of his men
t dead when a personal nemesis is around.

Danny Kaye provided two whimsical comments in Me and the Colonel
958) (against prejudice) and On the Double (1961) (against willing
lfillment of duty). Then, in 1959 and 1962 two comedy departures

appeared--Operation Petticoat and The Pigeon that Took Rome. They

deviated from the norm in that their comedy is a slicker variety than

other service films and in the resolution of combat. Chance determines

the outcome, not professional knowledge and execution.

Romance with war on the fringe was a popular topic. From Here

to Eternity (1953) won an Academy Award with its portrayal of an

illicit love affair in an immediately prewar Pearl Harbor army camp.

William Holden in Force of Arms (1951) began the wave of combat romances

this one ending happily with Nancy Olsen. Others did not end in such a

manner--Act of Love (1953), D-Day, the Sixth of June (1956), Gaby (1956)

and Until They Sail (1957).

Three love stories were as important for their treatment of the

Japanese as for the romances. Teahouse of the August Moon (1956),

Sayonara (1957), and Cry for Happy (1961) were set in postwar Japan,

Sayonara as late as the Korean War, and featured romances between

American soldiers and Japanese women. The Japanese traded their former

barbarism for a more docile, almost passive image (all in the tradition

of Madame Butterfly). It was almost as if Hollywood were trying to

correct misconceptions, ten years too late.

The German image also underwent redrawing, at least partly due

to West Germany being an ally not an enemy. Nevertheless, The Desert

Fox (1951), piling accolades on Rommel, was too early for some patriots.

The American Legion threatened boycotts and in some cases carried them

out. James Mason received much praise in the picture, one of 1951's

most heralded. The film sharply contrasts with Richard Basehart's

1962 portrayal in Hitler, another movie more at home in the 1940's.

In 1958 Fraulein and A Time to Love and a Time to Die sympathized

with the plight of German civilians forced into a war in which they did
not believe. Two artistically more competent pictures, The Diary of
Anne Frank and Judgement at Nuremberg gave a bit more realistic depiction of the German situation. The 1959 and 1961 releases were nominated
for Academy Awards but did not win.

Summary

As an institution Hollywood during 1948-1962 had to cope with
strain on two fronts. It was faced with the need to pacify the political
sector while trying to adjust to new economic realities. The industry
did not fight both threats. It accepted political conditions with
which it could live and devoted its major attention to the financial
problems. A check of the pages of Variety, the industry's representative trade publication, supports the conclusion that political harrass-
ment was not considered as grave a threat as the declining market.

The war films of 1948-1962 reflected the political realities of
the period. Cold War pictures conveyed Cold War rhetoric as did Korean
War movies to a limited extent. Even World War II films produced
during 1948-1962 showed evidence of Cold War influences in providing
a redefinition of the character of old enemies.

CHAPTER III

INTERNATIONALIZATION AND DEPOLITICIZATION

Hollywood's movement into 1963-1970 was tranquil and transitional compared with the abrupt clamor of the Red Scare. In fact, it is difficult to pinpoint an exact dividing line between this era and the Red Scare. Nevertheless, differences exist, both in the industry and in war films. The differences are manifestations of an evolution that has tended to internationalize and depoliticize the motion picture industry. This process has had subsequent implications for the war films of the era. The following discussion focuses first on the transformation undergone by the film industry and then on the implications for war films.

Institutional Transformation

It requires no genius to conclude that national feelings about war in general and the Vietnam War in particular have experienced some changes within the past decade. These changes are manifest in practically all of the rumblings of dissent over the Vietnam War that have characterized the country during the past few years.

Polls conducted by Gallup illustrate to a limited extent differences in the state of opinion concerning the Vietnam War compared to past wars. In 1947 Gallup asked: "Do you think it was a mistake for the United States to enter World War II?"[1] Only 24 per cent of

---

[1] The figures cited are from Hazel Erskine, ed., "The Polls: Is War a Mistake?" Public Opinion Quarterly, XXIV (Spring, 1969), pp. 134-150.

those polled thought it was a mistake; 66 per cent felt the United
States should have entered the war. A similar question about the
Korean conflict in 1950 found 65 per cent supporting entry into the
war. Two years later 43 per cent said going into the war was a mistake
while only 37 per cent supported the move.

Opinion about the Vietnam War has undergone a similar evolution.
In 1965 a total of 61 per cent of the people surveyed supported the
war. From that point decline began until by October, 1969 only 32 per
cent agreed with the war. A total of 58 per cent believed the war to
be a mistake.

The figures are presented only to demonstrate the amount of
disagreement with the Vietnam War that has characterized the United
States. Conflict over war has been the context within which war films
have been produced during the past five or six years. Certainly, that
context has had some influence on the way war has been portrayed.

However, other conditions must be considered as well. It would
be easy but simplistic to accept the assertion that movie values directly
reflect audience values. If that were true, shifts in film images would
simply represent changes in audience values. Novel views of war by the
screen would simply mean that the audiences had changed their conceptions of war. Whatever the attraction of such an explanation, it is not
adequate. The other side of the coin is that certain kinds of films
attract certain kinds of audiences.

One must look beyond audience opinion to explain changes in war
films of 1963-1970. One must examine changes in the movie industry for
such an explanation. Alterations in the movie industry have been in
process for two decades although the consequences have only recently

become strongly evident. The changes can be tied directly to the
economic crisis that faced Hollywood in the beginning of the 1950's,
i.e. declining attendance and the Paramount Consent Decree. Attempts
to deal with the crisis brought about three conditions which seem to
be extremely important: the rise of Europe as a major Hollywood
market; increased independent production; and loosened content controls within the industry.

Rise of the European Market

After World War II the American government encouraged Hollywood
to export films to Europe for propaganda purposes. Europe had played
a role in Hollywood's prewar economy but had been closed for nearly a
decade. Thus, more than 2,000 already produced films were available
for export at little added expense. Such exportation allowed the
industry through the overseas branch of the Motion Picture Association to get in on the ground floor of postwar readjustment in Europe.[2]

What began as "gravy" for Hollywood soon became a necessity.
Declining attendance cut more and more into the American market. "Film
being infinitely exportable, and with Hollywood's declining dependence
upon the American market, the American industry was compelled to undertake a program of vigorous exportation so as to spread the amortization
of its investment over more countries."[3] Europe and other foreign
countries have been so good to Hollywood that more than half the industry's

---

[2] For a complete discussion of Hollywood's postwar expansion,
see Guback, The International Film Industry.

[3] Ibid., pp. 348-349.

revenue is now derived from outside the United States.

As American film proved successful in Europe, American companies
found themselves caught in a balance of payments web. European countries froze a portion of the American income, compelling American companies either to leave the money or utilize the funds through local
production. The latter course had advantages: lower labor costs,
important when union wages in the United States were soaring; a better
tax break for stars; the custom of many European governments of sub-
sidizing national productions, even if they were only part-national;
and the glamor and color of locales that could not be matched by
television.

To shorten a long story, Hollywood's move into Europe brought
(1) increased dependence upon European audiences for profit margin and
(2) cross-national film production. Cross-national production tends
to spread effective control of film content, in effect loosening the
strangle hold of a strictly American perspective. What once was the
American film industry is now an international film industry; it has
been internationalized in terms of market and in terms of production
control. This does not mean that American financial control over the
film industry has lessened any, only that it is financially risky to
exercise such control from any one nationalistic viewpoint.

Increased Independent Production

The consent decree made it easier for independent producers to
market their films. Vertical integration had allowed major studios to
produce hundreds of pictures a year of varying quality and sell them
as a package. If the exhibitor wanted to show one, he had to show all.

One independent production among hordes of studio productions had slim chance of being sold to a major exhibitor, especially if the exhibitor was controlled by the studios. The decree required that pictures be rented only theater by theater and picture by picture. Without the automatic market, major studios were reluctant to mass produce pictures.

Even without the decree picture production probably would have declined. Decreasing attendance and fewer theaters lessened the demand for the volume of pictures that was standard during the 1930's and 1940's. Whatever the primary cause, production did decline after the decree, and soon afterwards major studios began to withdraw from production. Withdrawal was gradual, but today the major studios are primarily leasing agencies, if, indeed, they are operating at all.

Someone had to fill the production void, and that someone was actors, directors, and producers formerly under contract to the studios. By forming their own companies, the artists, first of all, could work and, secondly, received a better tax break since income could be taxed as capital gains rather than salary.

Another supposed advantage of independent production—at least for the artist who regarded true independence as a blessing—was that the artist could exercise greater control over his product. Under the old system, Richard Macann said:

> The staff producer had to film the stories the company executives bought. He had to work within the limits of tolerance of the executive in charge of production. He might be hemmed in by the veterans in the art department or the cutting rooms. He had to use players on contract at the studio, and he had no control over advertising or publicity.[4]

---

[4] Richard Dyer Macann, Hollywood in Transition, p. 59.

Increased independence did not lead immediately to a greater range of film topics. The independent found that he still was part of a system. Funding came from the same conservative sources as before, and even the major studios still had a voice through their distribution guarantees. Funding is ready only for very sure bets, i.e. boxoffice stars and proven types of films. The independent must show he can make money and thus relies on the worn path of formula pictures.

> The universal fear of the box office is what makes the red tape bind so tightly for the truly independent producer. The same psychological hurdle faced the staff producer in the studio, but for the independent it is more immediate, more ever present and far more intense.[5]

Hollywood's increasing reliance on the super-spectacular film compounded the financial conservatism during the rise of independent production. The spectacular seemed to attract more of an audience but also required a much larger investment. Thus, costs spiraled upward, pushed by higher salaries for stars, location shooting, and inflation. By 1966 Saturday Review was reporting:

> The cost of movie-making has got out of hand. Movies that traditionally cost under $1,000,000 to make are now requiring budgets of several million. More and more films end up costing two or three times their initial budgets. Hollywood a town that has always admired the 'super-colossal blockbuster' has all but forgotten how to make a more modest film on a more serious theme.[6]

With as much as $30 million (Cleopatra) riding on a particular film financial backers were not apt to be receptive to experimentation.

Out of necessity the trend toward spectaculars has tended to

---

[5]Ibid., p. 61.

[6]Peter Bart, "$upercolossalitis$," Saturday Review, Dec. 24, 1966, p. 12.

dissolve during the past three years. It took only two years for
Saturday Review to turn from the subject of "$upercolossaliti$"[7] to
"The Now Movie . .. . New Approaches to New Audiences."[8] Pictures
like Rachel, Rachel (1968) and Easy Rider (1969) demonstrated that
relatively low-budget pictures could be very lucrative. With less
money risked, the possibility exists that more experimentation might
be permissible.

Whether actual experimentation exists is another question. One
can look at some of today's movies and find examples of content that
could not have been depicted fifteen years ago. One can also examine
films of fifteen years ago that could not find financial backing today.
The point is that independent production does not necessarily lead to
variety of films but may instead simply bring about a different kind
of standardization.

The Production Code

For more than twenty years the Motion Picture Association's
Production Code, based on fundamental American tenets, dictated cor-
rectness for American films. The code originated during the late
1920's in the face of possible governmental censorship and was enforced
cooperatively by the major and minor studios. Penalty for ignoring the
code was refusal of a seal of approval and a $25,000 fine. Vertical
integration made it very difficult for any picture violating the code
to reach the exhibitors.

Conditions changed in the 1950's. The Supreme Court included

---

[7] Ibid.

[8] "The Now Move," Saturday Review, Dec. 12, 1968, pp. 8-23.

motion pictures within the protective confines of the First Amendment for the first time. The Paramount Consent Decree knocked out vertical integration and with it the ultimate sanction against non-code films.[9]

New freedoms allowed by these two changes were not taken advantage of immediately. First, attendance had to continue to decline and the blockbuster had to fail as a drawing card. Then, the industry turned more and more to sex and nudity as an attraction, a maneuver which involved virtually ignoring the production code. A code still exists (as well as a rating system) but provides wide latitude and has very little authority. In seeking larger audiences film producers have taken advantage of the wide latitude not only in sex-related subjects but also by deviating in other areas from what is generally regarded as traditional American tenets.

The three changes in Hollywood just discussed (internationalization, increased independent production, and the decline of the motion picture code) have served to allow a more extreme range of content in films. Partly as a consequence of wider constraints war movies produced in 1963-1970 deviated from the pattern of the previous two periods. The deviation, which will be discussed later, manifested itself mostly in the fact that the films of 1963-1970 largely were apolitical. In general they did not justify one nation's reasons for fighting another. Frequently, they did not even mention such reasons.

War Films, New Directions

An examination of the war films of 1963-1970 immediately hits

---

[9]Macann, Hollywood in Transition, pp. 64-69.

on the fact that only two movies have been produced about the Vietnam War. Other pictures in the past have been situated in Indo-China, but only two have made any mention of the American involvement in Vietnam. The absence of Vietnam pictures, though, only fits into a tendency among war movies of the period to avoid political comment.

In the previous two periods, of course, the lack of activity by Hollywood with a fresh war boiling would have been unforgivable. Some segment of the political spectrum--probably the right--would have tried to force the industry to rectify its oversight. In 1963-1970 there was no outcry, no righteous indignation. It was as if the political sector of American society did not notice, or, if it noticed, it did not care.

The latter alternative is the more probable. Changing conditions in the past twenty years have removed Hollywood from the necessity of having to reaffirm patriotism in times of crises. One change has already been mentioned. Hollywood is an international industry which no longer can afford chauvinistic ties to any single nation. The divisiveness in the United States over the Vietnam War likewise made it doubtful either side of the issue could have mustered enough strength to force the industry to do anything. If coercion had been tried, the dispersion of production internationally and among independents would have acted against gaining the degree of compliance that occurred after 1948. Finally, television's emergence as the nation's favorite mass medium may have been a blessing for Hollywood is so far as political pressure is concerned. In 1948 motion pictures were the nation's visual pastime and were reaching 90 million persons a week. In the 1960's television was reaching that many or more daily.

The attainment by television of status as everyone's habit may have carried with it the distinction of being the polity's scapegoat.

Whatever the causes, war films produced in 1963-1970 differed from those of the past. Those differences will now be discussed, examining first films about each of the four wars and then focusing on some of 1970's pictures that seem to epitomize the direction of the movies of the past eight years.

Vietnam

As early as 1948 Indo-China was an American film topic. Rogues Regiment followed the tracking of a Nazi leader into Indo-China and managed some asides about Russians supplying arms to revolutionaries. Four years later a pair of Americans flew their air freight business into the area and promptly turned the tide against the Communists in A Yank in Indo-China. However, history would not let Hollywood pull victory from defeat. Jump into Hell (1955) depicted the plight of the French at Dien Bien Phu, which, according to the screen, was lost primarily because the rest of the free world did not care or was too involved with diplomatic niceties to help.

Guerrilla activity in other parts of Southeast Asia was portrayed in Brushfire (1962) and The Seventh Dawn (1964). The Seventh Dawn was interesting because it not only depicted the Communists in Malaya as being vicious and conniving but also characterized the British as bungling and stupid.

American diplomatic efforts in Indo-China were treated in The Quiet American (1958) and The Ugly American (1963). In The Quiet American Audie Murphy tried to establish a barrier in Vietnam between communism and French colonialism. Charles Greene's novel contained some criticism of American foreign policy, but the bite was lost in transition to film. Marlon Brando's bull-headed Americanism almost cost the United States the mythical country of Sarkhan in The Ugly American.

All of the films just mentioned were treated as Cold War pictures (as was a minor league production Operation CIA, 1965) because they did not deal with the American episode in Vietnam. The first Vietnam War film was A Yank in Vietnam (1964), released before the peak of American involvement. This low budget location production, filmed by and starring Marshall Thompson, follows a Marine major's adventures as an adviser in Vietnam. He manages to foil the Viet Cong, rescue a doctor, and fall in love with one of the natives.

Green Berets (1968) is the more famous of the two Vietnam War pictures. The film largely resembles any of John Wayne's war endeavors except for more blood, brutality, and nudity. The picture flatly praises the American Special Forces in Vietnam, although Wayne denies propaganda as his intent. "We are making this picture for entertainment value. If I was going to work this hard to get over a point of view, I'd state my opinion rather than try to do it in a piece of entertainment."[10]

However, the message is there, as revealed in dialogue between a former dove reporter (David Janssen) and Major Kirby (Wayne). The discussion takes place as Janssen departs for the United States.

_____

[10]Quoted in Joan Barthel, "John Wayne, Superhawk," New York Times Magazine, Dec. 4, 1967, p. 21.

Kirby: What do you suppose you're going to write for that paper
of yours?
Beckworth: I may be out of a job.
Kirby: We'll give you a job.
Beckworth: I think I can give you more support with a pen.[11]

Despite Wayne's disclaimer, the fact is that until he gained
assistance, the Pentagon seemed unwilling to back a Vietnam War picture. The Pentagon's policy toward such movies was revealed by the
difficulties encountered by author Robin Moore in arranging for the
production of the film version of his novel, The Green Berets. A
former member of the special forces, Moore detailed his problems on
the CBS radio show, "Mike Wallace at Large," on May 5, 1967.[12] Moore
charged the Pentagon had interfered in a contractual arrangement
between him and David Wolper of Universal Studios and later discouraged
Metro-Goldwyn-Mayer from producing the picture. Moore claimed:

> The Pentagon threatened Wolper with reprisals which he could not
> live with if he went ahead and made it; they plain reneged on a
> contract, which I've never heard happening before . . . The deal
> was made in Hollywood between my agent, William Morris, and
> Universal and Wolper and, rather than suffer the consequences
> which were promised them by Arthur Sylvester, then assistant
> secretary of defense for information, they preferred to take a
> chance on a suit, or at least just plain welching. So, then, I
> went to MGM. The president of Metro had me in his office twice
> and they got so excited about it that they actually released
> something to one of the papers.[13]

A check of Moore's story by Variety yielded denials. MGM
production chief Bob Weitman said, "We read the book, but didn't consider going ahead. We were not actively interested because we knew
Columbia had a project with the same title. I know nothing of any

---

[11] Ibid.

[12] Reported in Variety, May 10, 1967, p. 7.

[13] Quoted in ibid.

Defense Department threats."[14] Wolper answered:

> The Defense Department was working with Columbia on its 'Beret'
> property, and Columbia also had the title registered first, so
> I couldn't get its cooperation or guaranteed use of the title.
> They couldn't cooperate because they had already promised coopera-
> tion to Columbia, and under their regulations, they can't cooperate
> on the same subject, at the same time. . . . I think Moore mis-
> understood.[15]

Moore discounted the claims of Weitman and Wolper and pinned
the problem on Defense Department opposition. He said the Pentagon
discouraged the film because eighteen points in his book had been top
secret and "the Department of Defense was also at that time trying to
phase Special Forces out of the United States Army altogether; and
between my book, and, then, my song that I wrote with Barry Sadler,
we so glorified Special Forces that it would be like trying to kill
off the Marines to kill off the Green Berets now."[16]

A more likely explanation of Pentagon reluctance may have
been uncertainty about the orientation of a Vietnam War film. When
the Defense Department found a producer it trusted, full cooperation
was extended. That producer, of course, was John Wayne, "the man who
from Fort Apache to Bataan has never lost a war."[17]

Wayne began seeking approval by appealing through a personal
letter to President Lyndon B. Johnson, and there should have been no
doubt of the outcome. As son Michael Wayne commented, "In Washington

---

[14]Quoted in ibid.

[15]Quoted in ibid., p. 16.

[16]Quoted in ibid., p. 7.

[17]Barthel, "John Wayne, Superhawk," p. 4.

they have known my father for many years, and they had confidence in his part in this."[18]   A statement by John Wayne confirms the faith.

> If you go into depth on it--the war, it has to be almost that you're for it; if you're a decent person you can't let people be so oppressed . . .
>   I think I'm liberal, but under the semantics, the use of the word today, I have to say I'm a conservative. I'm a progressive conservative . . .
>   If they would call this a war, the American people would get behind it, I think. Semantics again. Things that we know would be absolute treason during a war they can do now and get away with, because they can be covered by words in the Supreme Court for any goddam thing they do. I think they oughta shoot 'em if they're carrying the Viet Cong flag. A lot of our boys are getting shot looking at that flag. As far as I'm concerned, it wouldn't bother me a bit to pull the trigger on one of 'em.[19]

Why would a studio require Pentagon assistance in order to produce a film about Vietnam? It would not for a low budget production, but for an undertaking the size of Wayne's outside assistance makes the difference between profit and loss. Assistance, material as well as advisory, is obtained through a long process which amounts to military censorship over the script.

> Before a producer can obtain assistance he needs from the military to make his film, his project is subject of a process of review of the Office of the Assistant Secretary for Public Affairs that in effect makes the Department of Defense an overseer of the production. The producer first must submit in writing to the Assistant Secretary for Public Affairs his proposal for a motion picture or television documentary 'stating the story objectives of the project and the identifiable benefit for the D.O.D., and agreeing to abide by the provision' of pertinent regulations. The Assistant Secretary's office then gives its reaction to the project and if asked will 'give guidance, suggestions, and technical research in the producer's endeavor to prepare a script which might qualify the project ultimately for assistance'. If assistance is desired, four copies of the film's script must be submitted for 'evaluation and review', and an itemized list of the kinds of assistance needed from the military might be provided. Only after the script is

---

[18] Quoted in _Variety_, May 10, 1967, p. 16.

[19] Quoted in Barthel, "John Wayne, Superhawk," p. 4.

approved are arrangements made to provide shooting assistance. This can range from the sale of reels of action film to making a submarine available . . . or to turning over a sizeable part of a military installation to the film maker.[20]

Aid to Wayne included Fort Benning, Georgia, for the filming of Green Berets plus such props as planes, helicopters, soldiers, M-16s, 81-mm mortars, M-60 machine guns, and M-79 grenade launchers.[21] Senator J. William Fulbright reported that Wayne's request ran eight pages and included jeeps and Viet Cong weapons as well as Fort Bragg, North Carolina, and Fort Benning. The request asked for forty days on the post and 359 Army personnel to appear on camera, 143 of whom were to be of Asian extraction. "The Army obligingly found a platoon of such troops, men from Hawaii, training at Fort Devens, Massachusetts, and put them on leave status so that Wayne could bring them to Fort Benning to be in the picture."[22]

The performing troops were paid by Wayne; $1.40 an hour or $100 a week, somewhat below union wages.[23] Troops used in support functions (10th Aviation Group and 197th Infantry Brigade of the Infantry Center) were not paid by Wayne.[24]

Wayne's bill from the Pentagon was $18,623, according to Fulbright and the Government Accounting Office. Fulbright added that

---

[20] J. William Fulbright, The Pentagon Propaganda Machine (New York: Liveright, 1970), p. 112.

[21] Barthel, "John Wayne, Superhawk," p. 22.

[22] Fulbright, The Pentagon Propaganda Machine, p. 118.

[23] Barthel, "John Wayne, Superhawk," p. 22.

[24] Fulbright, The Pentagon Propaganda Machine, p. 119.

to operate a UH-1 helicopter for eighty-seven flying hours, which
Wayne's company Batjac did, cost the government $36,105.[25] It is
obvious that Wayne's $8 million budget would have been considerably
more had he been charged fully for military services, and it is
doubtful that a Vietnam War picture of such scope could have been
profitably produced without such aid.

Cold War

The attitude of Cold War films produced in 1963-1970 toward
ideological comment might be described in the following manner: "We're
the good guys and they're the bad, but let's not waste time telling why.
Get on with the action."

Part of this attitude was manifested in a decline in production
of films about the home front. The home-front film produced in 1948-
1962 carried stronger ideological comment than did war-front pictures.
During the Red Scare home-front films accounted for more than 55 per
cent of the Cold War production. In 1963-1970 that figure dropped to
slightly more than 35 per cent (Table 5). In addition only 4.3 per
cent of the 1963-1970 productions tried to relate the Cold War to
the civilian on the home front. The Cold War had become the property
of professionals, whose primary concern was accomplishing an objective
through whatever means available rather than why they were attempting
the objective.

A Gathering of Eagles (1963) continued the standard practice
of the previous era of praising the efforts and efficiency of the

---

[25]Ibid.

TABLE 5

PERCENTAGE OF FILMS BY CHARACTER-LOCALE AND WAR, 1963-1970

Classification	WWII	Cold	Korea	Vietnam	Total
Espionage-War	7.8%	39.1%	- %	- %	14.9%
Soldiers-War	67.2	13.6	80.0	100.0	55.3
Civilians-War	21.9	13.6	-	-	18.1
Espionage-Home	1.6	13.6	-	-	4.3
Soldiers-Home	1.6	17.4	20.0	-	6.4
Civilians-Home	-	4.3	-	-	-
Total	100.0	100.0	100.0	100.0	100.0
Number	64	23	5	2	94

Strategic Air Command. Rock Hudson risks divorce and loss of friends to get his base in top working order, but no major attempt is made to explain why the base must be in peak condition. That it must be is assumed. Similarly, in Torn Curtain (1966) physicist Paul Newman fakes defection to gain information about an advanced anti-missile device from the other side (East Germany) without really having to justify his actions. One year later in The Venetian Affair Robert Vaughn as a newsman kept a peace conference from being sabotaged. Brainwashing is the method of sabotage but brutality is used by both sides without distinction.

Recent Cold War films inserted gore into their scenes. Ice Station Zebra (1968) twisted the normal ending by having an East-West confrontation finish in stalemate. Meanwhile, Alfred Hitchcock's Topaz (1969) featured blood flowing from the Soviet Union to the United States to Cuba to France.

Major exceptions to the traditional Cold War theme were produced

in 1964, a couple of years following the Cuban missile crisis and at
the same time the militaristic policy of Barry Goldwater met with much
anxiety. Seven Days in May hypothesized the potential internal danger
of an ego-inflated military leader, who disagrees with a disarmament
pact between the United States and the Soviet Union. Two other pictures (Fail Safe and Dr. Strangelove or: How I Learned to Stop Worrying
and Love the Bomb) pointed out for the first time the dangers of too
much hardware and a rigid military perspective.

Interestingly, Columbia released both Fail Safe and Dr.
Strangelove. Fail Safe originally was to be independently produced,
but Columbia filed a federal suit claiming plagiarism. The controversy was settled when Columbia took over financing and distribution,
and the original producers agreed to make the film for the studio.

In 1965 The Bedford Incident posited that human nature could
lead to nuclear warfare even with all the technological safeguards.
The threat in this film is American naval captain Richard Widmark,
who is fond of playing bluff with Soviet submarines.

Included in the Cold War films are some spy dramas or spoofs
of the James Bond genre. The Bond pictures were not included because
the adversaries were not other governments but individuals or groups
of individuals. However, once the 007 movies proved successful,
numerous copies were made—such as Dean Martin as Matt Helm. These
spy heroes possessed similar characteristics: cold professionalism,
innumerable weapon gadgets, physical prowess, and a lot of time for
sexual pursuits but almost no attention to ideological hair splitting.

The spy spoofs typify one portion of war films produced in
1963-1970, possessing little ideology and much activity. Another

symptomatic production was <u>The Russians Are Coming, The Russians Are</u> <u>Coming</u> (1966) which challenges some of the underlying beliefs of the Cold War or any war. The film satirizes American stereotypes of Russians and Russian stereotypes of Americans, pointing out that they are quite similar. The fact that such a movie was made, depicting the blustering of Americans in the face of a national enemy, is significant in itself. Such a satirical stance would have been cause for burning at the stake in the 1950's.

Korea

About all that can be said about Korean War films from 1963 through 1969 is that there were not many of them. <u>The Young and the</u> <u>Brave</u> (1963) and <u>Sergeant Ryker</u> (made originally for television but released to theaters in 1968 after Lee Marvin became a box office attraction) presented fairly standard war stories. <u>The Hook</u> (1963) was unique in that it provided a humanistic view of a North Korean.

World War II

Politically speaking, the World War II films of 1963-1970 were relatively silent. Twenty years after the end of the war it was natural that they would lose their chauvinism. However the lack of some type of political propaganda falls in the pattern of other war films of the era just as in 1948-1962 World War II pictures followed the common practice of advocating the necessity of a professional military.

A large number of World War II films produced in 1963-1970 were made and exploited for action. Some action pictures were elaborate productions with majestic explosions, scenic locations, and big-name stars. The Dirty Dozen (1967) seemed to pave the way for this type of film. In The Dirty Dozen a group of condemned prisoners are offered freedom if they attempt an impossible mission, which they complete with a spectacular explosion. The Devil's Brigade (1968) told a similar story, while Tobruk (1967) portrayed ninety Britishers holding off 50,000 Germans and Italians and blowing up Axis oil tanks.

The Great Escape (1963) and Von Ryan's Express (1965) exploited prisoner of war escapades with emphasis on the danger of a chase. The Great Escape's most memorable episode featured Steve McQueen crashing a motorcycle through a barbed wire fence while he was trying to escape the Germans. His failure was irrelevant to the thrill of the attempt.

The Train (1965) pitted Frenchman and German in another chase. Burt Lancaster stopped the Nazi from confiscating art treasures but not before the German had executed forty civilians, and there had been a gigantic train crash.

Less expensive productions did not have the spectacular explosions but managed to tie sex and violence together. In Cry of Battle (1963), Van Heflin had this philosophy: "You fight when you got to, you get a dame when you can. That's about it."[26] Once Before I Die (1966), an American-Filipino coproduction, featured Ursula Andress giving herself to a virginal soldier before he dies in an attack.

Violence was not always without purpose. Cornel Wilde used it in Beach Red (1967) to present an antiwar message. The film focused on fatigue and boredom of battle as well as showing a severed foot

---

[26] Quoted in Variety, Oct. 16, 1963, p. 16.

floating down stream, an arm blown off, and a thumb shot off. The
Victors (1963) painted war as morally degenerating to victims, heroes,
and aggressors. Depicted in a series of vignettes were the murder of
a black soldier by his fellow Americans and the use of a small dog as
target practice just to spite a naive rookie.

Deviants from the violence syndrome included The Americanization
of Emily (1964) and The Secret War of Harry Friggs (1968). The
Americanization . . . was a sex-filled comedy with a biting message
about service rivalries and the heroic quality, while The Secret . . .
followed a non-heroic or even antiheroic hero on a secret mission. In
their irreverent attitude toward heroism these two films were similar
to some of 1970's releases which rejected traditional bravery altogether.

Current Direction

Three war films of the past year received no small acclaim for
artistic competence--Patton, Catch-22, and M*A*S*H. They are discussed
here, though, along with Kelly's Heroes not because of critical recognition but because of the way they portrayed war--less as a moralistic
quest and more in human and social terms as comedy, grotesqueness,
fear, and self adulation.

Patton could have been a reversion to the days of unqualified
praise of the military. However, George C. Scott's Patton is an
egomaniac more at home in the days when war was military, not political.
He served his purpose well but in some situations Scott as Patton was
dangerous.

M*A*S*H was much publicized as the ultimate antiwar movie.

After viewing it, one is apt to wonder if it is a war movie at all.
It could very well be a satirical, irreverent hospital soap opera except that in this case the hospital is a tent in the middle of the
Korean War. The mixture of sex and football with blood in the scenario
adds to the impression that war is not the topic. There is no shooting
or fighting or bombing on the premises. However, the significance of
the picture lies in its avoidance of the nationalistic hostilities.
The point is that men in war are not always devoted to the activities
of which they are a part. Their actions are not always political;
sometimes they are not even warlike.

Donald Sutherland followed M*A*S*H with another rollicking
appearance. Kelly's Heroes received less acclaim than the other
three films but its ideas were similar. An entire company abandoning
World War II to strive for a more rewarding goal--gold bullion--would
never have happened in films of the previous two periods. Americans
rejecting war as irrelevant and striving for material gain would
have been unthinkable.

Then, late in the year Catch-22 was to have been the ultimate
antiwar statement. It had an excellent novel as a base, and it achieved
a good measure of success--although greeted with mixed, tending toward
unfavorable, reviews. Alan Arkin as Yossarian spends the entire film
yearning for one thing: safety. He cares for nothing else--certainly
not the heroic action required for winning the war nor for the entre-
preneural activities of his superiors. He wants out, the devil with
anything else, as Harper film critic Edward Grossman pointed out:

> Earlier, a popular novel and movie, The Caine Mutiny, had championed
> the idea that civilians finding themselves at the mercy of distaste-
> ful, even dangerous, officers and professional soldiers in wartime
> should swallow their feelings, in the interest of protecting what

civilization there is from the real barbarians. Yossarian, in
this view, is reprehensible because he does not keep his eye on
the Big Picture. But now, in 1970, the director and writer of
a movie like Catch-22 evidently think that the case for saving
one's skin need not be embroidered about with nice distinctions.
There is no Hitler. The only objection to Yossarian's decision
that is used to any effect is based on comradeship: how, he is
asked, can he leave his buddies in the lurch? Yossarian ponders
this, he says, 'Hell, they can do the same thing,' and starts
rowing toward Sweden.[27]

Thus, to Yossarian war is not a national endeavor for the sur-

vival of the country. Its political implications are irrelevant.

For the individual it is only an obstacle to his continued existence.

Summary

Unlike the previous two periods changes in war film directions

during 1963-1970 were not primarily the consequence of political in-

fluence or coercion. In fact, political groups paid little or no

attention to Hollywood during 1963-1970 for a number of reasons. In

the meantime the war films of the era were being depoliticized as

national chauvinism in movies was becoming the exception rather than

the rule. The changes could be attributed to more critical views of

war on the part of national sentiment, but that explanation in itself

is not enough. To fully understand the changes in film content one

must look also at the transformation within the motion picture industry

over the past twenty years. During that time centralized control by

major studios has dissipated as independent production has increased,

strict adherence to the motion picture code has declined, and an

American institution has become an international institution with no

rigid ties to any particular nation.

---

[27]Edward Grossman, "Bloody Popcorn," Harper's, December, 1970,
p. 39.

CONCLUSION

The history of war films produced by the American motion picture
industry since 1939 is very much intertwined with Hollywood's political
and economic relationships. Other influences are also important, such
as the nature of national sentiment, and must be taken into consideration.

In 1939-1941 Hollywood released a number of anti-Nazi pictures
that gathered more than a little criticism from isolationists. However,
Pearl Harbor ended a congressional inquiry into the movie industry and
placed Hollywood in a war role. The part was assumed willingly—or at
least as willingly as the rest of the country—but with cautious
glances at the government's control of raw film. War film production
peaked during the first two years of World War II and declined toward
the end and as governmental pressure lessened.

Coercion by HUAC and surrender by Hollywood's leadership led
to a blacklist of suspected Communists and a rash of Cold War films
in 1948-1962. The Cold War influenced Korean War and World War II
pictures of the same era, manifested in the emphasis such movies placed
on the necessity of having a strong, professional military. Hollywood's
actions during 1948-1962 were not solely the consequence of political
coercion. Popular opinion seemed to support strong action against
Communists, and, more importantly, the movie industry found itself
in an economic bind. Apparently, Hollywood leaders felt they could
not fight political pressure (and it is not certain they wished to)
and contend with declining attendance and the Paramount Consent Decree
at the same time. So, political concessions were made and economic
problems were tackled.

The consequences of the industry's corrective measures became most evident in the 1960's. Independent production increased; the motion picture code lost its authority; and the growing importance of foreign markets tended to denationalize the movie industry. These conditions plus a national divisiveness over the Vietnam War have accompanied a period of time when Hollywood has been relatively free of political interference. Gradually, during 1963-1970 the industry's war films have lost nationalistic perspectives, replacing them with emphasis on action or in some instances a questioning of warfare itself.

Thus, war films are not produced in isolation. They are subject to the institutional influences that act on the motion picture industry. An understanding of why certain kinds of pictures are produced is incomplete without examining those institutional forces.

PART TWO

THE AMERICAN WAR HERO

INTRODUCTION

In the last three chapters some of the characteristics of American war films were mentioned in brief. This section begins an in-depth look at the films. The examination first focuses on Hollywood's portrayal of the American war hero. The hero's aspirations, beliefs, behavior, and demographic characteristics will be discussed in filling out the screen's interpretation of Americans' roles in specific wars and in war in general. The American hero can also serve as a cultural indicator of American sentiment toward war, but it should be re-emphasized that films are not isomorphic reproductions of American opinion. The American war hero as presented by Hollywood is a creation of artists and technicians of that institution and influenced by their own ideas as well as basic American cultural assumptions and relevant political, social, and economic conditions.

CHAPTER IV

CIVILIAN PATRIOTS

Demographically, the American war hero of 1939-1947 is best described as a male WASP with an X substituted for the P. He was characteristically a civilian patriot with some sense of social responsibility, although he underwent some changes during the nine-year period. Before American entry into the war the major American characters belong to the more privileged classes or to a profession apt to be in position to observe the Nazis first hand. The war years leveled the hero as he became a member of all classes and within limits more heterogeneous. Toward the end of the war began an evolution which in future years would transform the composite hero from civilian to professional warrior. Despite the differences the heroes of 1939-1947 were unified by a common belief that the individual by nature must be concerned with others and that there is a time when his egotistical interests must be put aside for the general good.

A statistical composite of the 278 American heroes of 1939-1947 shows that 84.2 per cent were male, 71.2 per cent mature adults, 36.3 per cent middle class and 29.9 per cent outside the class structure, 60.8 per cent never married, and 44.6 per cent having a high school or college degree (Table 6). These Americans were practically 100 per cent native born and were 100 per cent white. Only 1.8 per cent belonged to any discernible minority group although supporting characters frequently had minority backgrounds.

Approximately as many characters had never served in the military as were members (39.6 per cent and 38.1 per cent). More than 28 per

TABLE 6

DEMOGRAPHICS OF AMERICAN HEROES, 1939-1947

	1939–1941	1942	1943	1944	1945	1946–1947	Total
Sex							
Male	89.5%	87.1%	81.8%	78.3%	83.3%	84.6%	84.2%
Female	10.5	13.1	18.1	21.7	16.7	15.4	15.8
Total	100.0	100.0	100.0	100.0	100.0	100.0	100.0
Age							
Youth	–	1.2	–	2.2	–	–	0.7
Young adult	7.9	4.7	5.6	13.0	20.8	–	7.9
Mature adult	86.8	74.1	66.7	80.9	66.7	77.8	71.2
Middle age	–	3.5	6.9	10.9	8.3	7.8	5.8
Old age	–	1.3	–	–	–	–	0.4
No answer	5.3	15.3	20.8	8.7	4.2	15.4	13.3
Total	100.0	100.0	100.0	100.0	100.0	100.0	100.0
Class							
Upper	28.9	15.3	13.9	17.4	20.8	23.1	18.0
Middle	37.8	38.8	40.3	41.3	25.0	7.8	36.3
Lower	7.9	7.1	13.9	10.9	25.0	7.8	11.2
Outside structure	18.4	35.3	30.6	21.7	25.0	61.5	29.9
No answer	7.9	4.7	1.4	8.7	4.2	–	4.7
Total	100.0	100.0	100.0	100.0	100.0	100.0	100.0
Marital Status							
Married	10.5	7.1	18.1	23.9	16.7	30.8	15.1
Never married	65.8	63.5	63.6	60.9	45.8	38.5	60.8
Divorced	–	2.3	–	–	4.2	–	1.1
Other	–	–	–	–	–	–	–
No answer	21.1	24.7	16.7	13.0	33.3	30.8	21.2
Total	100.0	100.0	100.0	100.0	100.0	100.0	100.0
Education							
In school	2.7	1.3	2.8	4.4	–	–	2.2
High school	10.5	27.1	27.8	17.4	12.5	30.8	22.3
Undergraduate	13.2	28.2	19.6	19.6	37.5	7.8	22.3
Higher degree	26.3	2.3	1.4	4.4	4.2	–	5.8
Other	–	–	–	–	–	–	–
No answer	47.4	41.3	48.6	54.4	45.8	61.5	45.3
Total	100.0	100.0	100.0	100.0	100.0	100.0	100.0
Number	38	85	72	46	24	13	278

[a]Data derived from questions 3-6 Form B in Appendix I.

cent of the heroes were in the Army (20.8 per cent in the regular Army and 7.6 per cent in the Army Air Corps). Enlisted men roles had the most frequent depiction (11.9 per cent) followed by Army lieutenants and Navy ensigns (7.2 per cent). (See Table 7 for a complete breakdown.)

The statistical cross-section gives some idea of the composition of major American characters during 1939-1947, but the numbers do not provide the mood of those heroes. That requires an in-depth look at the characters, an examination of their sentiments, their goals, their personalities. The remainder of the chapter attempts such an examination, though, admittedly, with 278 characters it is rather difficult to analyze any particular one very deeply.

1939-1941

The American heroes of the prewar years were men, and less frequently women, with missions. Through some quirk of fate they were thrust into situations that gave them advance knowledge of the German threat to the United States. These prewar characters can be divided into four groups. One, gifted by wealth or occupational assignment, viewed Europe first hand and was inspired to warn unconcerned Americans about the Nazi threat. A second was already fighting the Germans on the home front, a third serving in the Allies' armed forces, and a fourth training for future military action.

The Touring Prophets

These characters were either victims who related the horrors of Nazism through their personal experiences or observers (chiefly

TABLE 7

AMERICAN MILITARY CHARACTERISTICS, 1939–1947

	1939–1941	1942	1943	1944	1945	1946–1947	Total
Military Status							
Member	47.3%	27.1%	36.1%	47.8%	62.5%	15.4%	38.1%
Former member	–	–	–	–	4.2	23.1	1.4
Never member	18.4	40.0	50.0	47.8	25.0	38.5	39.6
No answer	34.2	32.9	13.9	4.4	8.3	23.1	20.9
Total	100.0	100.0	100.0	100.0	100.0	100.0	100.0
Branch							
Army	26.3	17.8	18.2	17.4	41.7	15.4	20.8
Navy	10.5	2.3	4.2	15.2	12.5	7.8	7.2
Army Air Corps	10.5	5.9	9.7	4.4	8.3	7.8	7.6
Marines	–	2.3	4.2	8.7	4.2	7.8	4.0
Coast Guard	–	–	–	–	–	–	–
Other	–	–	–	–	–	–	–
No answer	52.6	71.8	63.9	54.2	33.3	61.5	60.4
Total	100.0	100.0	100.0	100.0	100.0	100.0	100.0
Rank							
Gen.-Adm.	–	–	–	–	–	–	–
Col.-Capt.	–	1.2	1.4	2.2	4.2	–	1.4
Maj.-Cmdr.	–	–	1.4	8.7	8.3	–	2.5
Capt.-Lt.	2.7	3.5	5.6	–	8.3	7.8	4.0
Lt.-Ens.	10.5	3.5	8.5	10.9	8.3	–	7.2
Sgt.-CPO	2.7	4.7	8.5	–	12.5	–	5.0
Non com	2.7	1.2	2.8	2.2	4.2	–	2.2
Enlisted	21.1	9.4	8.5	17.4	12.5	–	11.9
Other	–	–	–	–	–	–	–
No answer	60.5	76.5	63.9	58.7	41.7	92.3	67.3
Total	100.0	100.0	100.0	100.0	100.0	100.0	100.0
Number	38	85	72	46	24	13	278

[a] Data derived from questions 15, 16, and 18 Form B in Appendix I.

journalists) who felt compelled to warn of impending danger. Physical prowess meant little to the success of this group of characters since they met adversity with wit and words. In fact, force was only the third most popular means of striving for goals for all characters in 1939-1941 although it was one of the two favorites for 1939-1947 (Table 8).

TABLE 8

AMERICANS' PRIMARY METHODS, 1939-1947

Primary Method	1939-1941	1942	1943	1944	1945	1946-1947	Total
Hard work	23.7%	14.1%	19.4%	23.9%	12.5%	7.8%	17.9%
Luck	7.9	9.4	11.1	8.7	16.7	23.1	10.8
Trickery	18.4	15.3	16.6	6.5	25.0	-	14.7
Knowledge	10.5	12.9	13.9	10.9	12.5	15.4	12.6
Charm	7.9	5.9	11.1	15.2	4.2	15.4	9.4
Force	15.8	22.3	16.6	15.2	12.5	30.8	17.9
Persuasion	2.7	2.3	5.6	13.0	16.7	-	6.1
No answer	13.2	16.5	6.9	6.5	-	7.8	10.4
Total	100.0	100.0	100.0	100.0	100.0	100.0	100.0
Number	38	85	72	46	24	13	278

[a]Data derived from question 29 Form B in Appendix I.

In Escape (1940) Robert Taylor provided a glimpse of the plight of Nazi victims. His actress mother is detained in Germany, and a frantic search yields no information until he locates some German collaborators. Mother Emmy Ritter finally escapes in a casket after pretending death but not until the horrors of a Nazi prison camp are sharply outlined.

Then, art critic Joan Bennett became a model of attitudinal transformation for American isolationists in The Man I Married (1940).

She is skeptical about what she reads in the newspapers about the Germans. However, a tour of the country changes her mind. Her husband is converted by the mystique and glamor of Nazism; she witnesses Storm Troopers beating elderly Czechs; and her son is almost detained by the regime.

The melodramatic intrigue seems overdone in another time, but apparently the film was quite moving, as reviews indicate: "Prepare for a stirred audience's hisses and boos—and one big laugh, when after hearing much heiling, Joan tells off her husband with 'Heil, Heel'!"[1] "When the newspaperman, at the end, offers a fervid apostrophe to good old American hamburgers and ice cream sodas you will mutter a heartfelt amen."[2]

Liberated journalist Joan Colbert and wire editor Don Ameche underwent similar transformations in Arise My Love (1940) and Confirm or Deny (1941). Both discover that there is more to life than a scoop. They decide they are human beings first and journalists second and that news stories must be tempered by the needs of the moment.

Joel McCrea receives a European assignment in Foreign Correspondent (1940) when his editor decides a pragmatic police reporter can cover the European conflict better than an empty-headed economist, or as the editor phrased it, he wanted a "fresh, unused mind."[3] McCrea loves, thinks, writes, and fights his way to success. "The one thing

---

[1] Philip T. Hartung, "Oh Say Can You," Commonweal, Aug. 16, 1940, p. 352.

[2] New York Times, Aug. 3, 1940, p. 2.

[3] Quoted in Theatre Patrons, 1940, p. 111.

everybody forgets is that I'm a reporter,"[4] he explains. But as
reporter he is not strictly an observer. In the final scene his message from the rooftops of London is: "Ring yourself with steel
America. The lights are going out all over Europe."[5]

Prewar Warriors

While the word about Hitler was being spread, some adventurers,
generally brash (a common American depiction during this era) were
already in the war. Tyrone Power in A Yank in the RAF (1941) and
Ronald Reagan in International Squadron (1941) learned that the
individual must be subjugated to the group in modern war. Power, who
chafes under regulations, finds responsibility, shoots down three
German planes over Dunkirk, and wins Betty Grable away from upper
class Britisher John Sutton. Reagan fails the test of responsibility
twice, once costing the life of his wingman. He finally succeeds by
completing a suicidal bombing mission--taking his pet canary with
him.

There were no brash Americans on the other side of the world,
just Charles Bickford (Burma Convoy, 1941) as a soldier of fortune
from Kansas City. A munitions truck driver, Bickford captures the
enemy in a final chase. The enemy is not labeled Japanese but instead
called Chinese insurrectionists.

---

[4] Quoted in New York Times, March 28, 1940, p. 2.

[5] Quoted in Jacobs, "World War II and the American Film," p. 31.

Home Front Guardians

Unfortunately for the American film audience Edward G. Robinson,
the first major agent-hero of 1939-1941, was unmatched by later guard-
ians, who were in the mold of the strong-arm detective resolving
issues through fisticuffs rather than intelligence. As Turrou in
Confessions of a Nazi Spy (1939) Robinson headed a team of FBI agents
who broke the German-American Bund through modern crime detection
techniques and a bit of mental dexterity by Robinson.

William Henry, Wallace Ford, and Forrest Tucker (Television
Spy, 1939; Here Come the Marines, 1941; and Emergency Landing, 1941)
were inventors, but the inventions were only justifications for whipping
enemy agents. Similar resolutions characterized heroes in The Lone Wolf
Spy Hunt (1939), Sky Murder (1940), Federal Fugitives (1941), The Devil
Pays Off (1941); and International Lady (1941).

Sally Eilers deviated from the pattern in They Made Her a Spy
(1939) but only because she was female. Her compatriot Army intelligence
agents are not repelled by violence.

Military Preparation

A military buildup in 1941 brought on a rash of service pictures, some serious, many comical. Common to most was the necessity
of their major characters proving their patriotism.

In Flight Command (1940) Robert Taylor is a recent college
graduate rejected by Navy veterans because of his brashness, his
education, and an apparent illicit relationship with Commander Walter
Pidgeon's wife. But Taylor proves himself by saving Pidgeon's life

through an impossible landing on Guadelupe, and it turns out that his relationship with Ruth Hussey was strictly platonic.

Errol Flynn's rejection in <u>Dive Bomber</u> (1940) is due to a similar conflict between new and old generation Navy men. Veteran Fred MacMurray ultimately is convinced that a flight surgeon's research is important to the new Navy and sacrifices himself for the good of that research. His only regret, he said, as he left for his deadly mission was that he would miss "the big one that's soon to start over there."

Cocky, debonaire Ray Milland experiences misfortune and misunderstanding, partly as a consequence of his own attitude, in <u>I Wanted Wings</u> (1941). But he ultimately recognizes his individualistic transgressions and achieves the one thing his wealth could not buy: wings in the Army Air Corps.

Of the numerous comic characters, Bob Hope in <u>Caught in the Draft</u> (1941), Dick Powell in <u>In the Navy</u> (1941), and Fred Astaire in <u>You'll Never Get Rich</u> (1941) deserve attention--though not much and not because of their performances. Astaire and Hope play selfish characters not concerned with a national commitment until they experience the love of a good woman. Powell joined to avoid publicity while serving his country. In the end all three find they are no better no worse than anyone else in the service and that service to country supercedes their careers.

If one word could characterize the heroes of the prewar, it would be "burdened"--burdened with the knowledge of the dangers that threatened the world and/or burdened with doing something about it. In the beginning of the films many of the characters were unconcerned individuals, but through personal experiences they came to realize

their dependency on others. They concluded that they could not retain

isolationism without endangering themselves. This conversion to social

responsibility is oft repeated in 1942-1945 and seems to be the unify-

ing element of American heroes during that time period.

1942-1945

In January, 1942, Roosevelt emphasized that victory would depend

as much on civilians at home as on soldiers in battle (see Chapter I).

This was to be a civilian war, and it certainly was that on the screen.

Of 227 American characters during 1942-1945 only 34.4 per cent were

depicted in military roles (Table 9), while 58.6 per cent were portrayed

as civilians. Emphasis on civilians was greater during the first years

of the war. The percentage of characters in military roles started

at a low of 23.5 per cent in 1942 and reached 54.2 per cent by 1945.

TABLE 9

ROLES OF AMERICAN CHARACTERS, 1939-1947

Role	1939-1941	1942	1943	1944	1945	1946	Total
Spy	18.4%	9.5%	4.2%	2.2%	16.7%	38.5%	10.1%
Soldier	42.1	23.5	34.7	43.7	54.2	7.8	34.2
Civilian	39.5	67.1	61.1	54.4	29.2	53.9	55.8
Total	100.0	100.0	100.0	100.0	100.0	100.0	100.0
Number	38	85	72	46	24	13	278

[a]Data derived from question 1 Form B in Appendix I.

A character's identification can be approached in a number of ways. However, the crucial distinction in 1942-1945 was the relationship of the character to the war. Coming from a variety of backgrounds, the characters shared in a common task--the war effort--and were generally dedicated to that task. Concern with the war, though, seemed to lessen in 1945. Table 10 is based on a content analysis question which posed the following situation: there are three possible concerns for any character--(1) the war; (2) romance; and (3) a conflict not related to the war. Table 10 shows that for each of the first three years of the war, the national conflict was most important for about three/fourths of the characters. That figure dropped to 50 per cent in 1945 as the war neared end.

TABLE 10

PRIMARY CONCERNS OF AMERICANS, 1939-1947

Primary Concern	1939-1941	1942	1943	1944	1945	1946	Total
War	76.3%	76.5%	73.6%	71.7%	50.0%	38.5%	70.9%
Romance	10.5	5.9	16.6	17.4	12.5	23.1	12.6
Other	13.2	11.6	8.5	10.9	20.8	15.4	11.9
No answer	-	5.9	1.4	-	16.7	23.1	4.7
Total	100.0	100.0	100.0	100.0	100.0	100.0	100.0
Number	38	85	72	46	24	13	278

[a]Data derived from question 38 Form B in Appendix I.

Characters of 1945 also differed from those of 1942-1944 in the goals they pursued. The earlier characters showed more interest in patriotism (42.9 per cent held patriotism as the primary goal in 1942-1944 compared with 20.8 per cent in 1945) and less in achieving a specific war task (9.8 per cent in 1942-1944 compared to 25.0 per cent in 1945). (See Table 11.) The point is that there seems to be a difference between the characters of 1942-1944 and those of 1945, and for that reason the following discussion deals with each separately.

TABLE 11

PRIMARY GOALS OF AMERICANS, 1939-1947

Primary Goal	1939-1941	1942	1943	1944	1945	1946-1947	Total
Safety	- %	3.5%	1.4%	2.2%	4.2%	- %	2.2%
Escape law	-	-	-	-	-	7.8	0.4
Health	-	-	-	2.2	8.3	-	1.1
Individualism	-	1.2	8.5	2.2	-	-	2.9
Money	2.7	1.2	2.8	2.2	-	7.8	2.2
Comfort	2.7	4.7	1.4	2.2	-	15.4	3.2
Power	-	-	-	-	-	-	-
Adventure	-	1.2	1.4	-	-	-	0.7
Love	13.2	4.7	8.5	17.4	8.3	19.4	9.7
Family	7.9	3.5	2.8	4.4	4.2	-	4.0
Sex	-	1.2	-	-	-	-	0.4
War task	10.5	11.8	6.9	10.9	25.0	-	10.8
Fame	2.7	1.2	5.6	2.2	8.3	-	3.2
Patriotism	36.8	38.8	48.6	41.3	20.8	53.8	40.6
Justice	5.3	4.7	2.8	2.2	4.2	-	3.6
Truth	7.9	2.3	-	4.4	4.2	-	2.9
Revenge	5.3	1.2	1.4	-	8.3	-	2.2
Honesty	-	7.1	4.2	2.2	4.2	-	4.0
No answer	5.3	11.8	4.2	4.4	-	-	6.1
Total	100.0	100.0	100.0	100.0	100.0	100.0	100.0
Number	38	85	72	46	24	13	278

[a]Data derived from question 25 Form B in Appendix I.

An Integrated Effort, 1942-1944

During the first three years (when the issue was in doubt most of the time), each of the heroes contributed in his own way to the war effort, whether he was a high ranking officer, a construction worker, or a criminal. Some fought the enemy as soldiers, agents, or civilians. Others built planes and ships or farmed while still others (meaning females) served by remaining faithful to loved ones.

Women

In general women were relegated to traditional sex roles, although their environments were sometimes abnormal. The overwhelming majority were sexy blondes, brunettes, or redheads filling female occupations--secretary, entertainer, housewife, socialite. However, in keeping with the pattern of American life at that time, some of the heroines worked on assembly lines or as welders, e.g. Paulette Goddard as a shipyard welder in I Love a Soldier (1944), Ann Sothern as an airplane assembly line worker in Swing Shift Maisie (1943), Jane Frazee in a similar role in Rosie the Riveter (1944), and Joan Davis as a factory worker in He's My Guy (1943). These women were not masculine facsimiles of females but attractive young ladies characterized by a comic sense or a sexy singing voice and motivated by romantic desires. They were dedicated to their war roles. For example, Joan Davis put so much value on her job that she threatened to leave her husband if he did not settle down to a war position. The messages were clear but well interspersed with comedy and song.

In Ladies Courageous (1944) Loretta Young, Geraldine Fitzgerald, and Diana Barrymore played flyers in the Women's Auxiliary Ferrying Squadron. Young was the leader, having to push the Pentagon to take her pilots into the regular Army and having to baby her charges at the same time. The women do a good job but are primarily concerned with romance.

Margaret Sullavan and Claudette Colbert portrayed nurses in the Philippines during the Japanese invasion. In Cry Havoc (1944) Sullavan is one of a unique mixture of girls—a strip teaser shot in the leg; a brainless Southern aristocrat stealing other women's men; a fashion writer afraid she will be afraid; a shell-shocked pianist; and an artist who learns to fire an antiaircraft gun. They suffer through the invasion, serve as hospital volunteers, man guns, bicker over the men, and finally surrender to the Japanese. So Proudly We Hail (1943) is much the same kind of picture only in it Colbert and some others escape.

The heroines in battle served a number of purposes. The films were convenient for combining romance and war without stretching too hard for either. Women falling into the hands of Japanese also should have raised some anger. And, as indicated by So Proudly We Hail, the films were an attempt to persuade audiences that "this is our war, and this time it will be our peace."[6]

Back home the loyal wives were keeping the fires burning. In Tender Comrade (1943) Ginger Rogers and five other wives live and work together until their husbands return. They experience the home-front problems of rationing, hoarding, playing both father and mother, working an assembly line, and explaining to baby why the father died. Rogers told her son:

Little guy . . . you two aren't ever going to meet . . . Only through me will you ever know anything about each other . . . He was such a baby himself . . . He went·out, and died so you could

---

[6]Philip T. Hartung, "Hail," Commonweal, Sept. 17, 1943, p. 358.

have a better break when you grow up than he ever had . . . He didn't leave you any money. He only left you the best world a boy could ever grow up in. Don't ever let anybody say he died for nothing . . . Chris boy.[7]

According to Time, the producers thought the ending inappropriate and were changing it when "a letter came from a war widow who had seen the sneak preview. Miss Rogers, wrote the widow, had put into words exactly what she had felt and been unable to say in all the months since her husband was killed. The first ending stayed in."[8]

Claudette Colbert presented the ideal of American motherhood in Since You Went Away (1944)--in a slightly more pleasing form than Kate Smith. When her advertising executive husband is drafted, she is left to manage a home with two daughters, a dog, boarder Monty Woolley, and bachelor friend Joseph Cotten plus working in a defense plant. Vacillating between despair and optimism but always resolute, she and her family survive until the husband returns. Cotten best described the purpose of the film and Colbert's role: "It all added up to a simply corny phrase I couldn't know--Home Sweet Home."

The Workers

The home front was personalized in the blue collar worker and the business executive. Fred MacMurray (So This is Washington, 1943) and John Wayne (Pittsburgh, 1942) provided contrasting portrayals of businessmen. MacMurray plays a toy executive trying to convince Washington's bureaucracy to convert his toy factory into an ordnance plant. Somehow in his fumbling, comical manner, MacMurray succeeds

---

[7] Quoted in "The New Pictures," Time, March 27, 1944, p. 94.

[8] Ibid.

and departs as the earnest, efficient businessman. Then, there is
Wayne, who in any role is John Wayne. As Pittsburgh Markham, he is
forced to fight and bribe his way back to Pennsylvania from Pearl
Harbor in December, 1941. His actions are motivated by one thought:
that he must get back as quickly as possible so that his coal mine
will operate at peak efficiency. Everyone must do his part even if
it requires cutting corners, breaking regulations, and fighting. Wayne
loses the girl to Randolph Scott while accomplishing his job and
delivering occasional lectures on coal and sulphur.

A trio of stereotyped businessmen were Wallace Berry (Rationing,
1944), John Litel (The Boss of Big Town, 1942), and Peter Cookson
(Swingtime Johnny, 1944). Litel as a West Coast wholesaler and
Berry as a butcher turned director of rationing halt black marketeers.
With the help of Harriet Hilliard, Cookson also reverses some hoodlums
who try to take over his pipe-organ-turned-munitions factory. A
stuffy long-hair, Cookson becomes a swinging patriot during the film,
thanks to his secretary and the Andrews sisters.

At the other end of the social ladder, the workers were packed
with swingers, most already patriots but a few who had to be convinced.
The workers generally were younger than the executives and more naively
patriotic. In a comical manner they welded ships, manufactured planes,
invented wondrous formulas, and conducted air raid drills, frequently
with music.

Melodramatically, cowboys initiated the Civil Air Patrol in Texas
(Charles Starrett in Cowboy in the Clouds, 1943); construction companies built the Alcan Road to Alaska (Richard Arlen in Alaskan Highway,
1943); a shiftless farmer captured a spy when he moved to the city

(Barton MacLane in The Underdog, 1943); and a truck driver crashed a plane loaded with nitroglycerine into a plant, extinguishing a fire but killing himself (Chester Morris in High Explosives, 1943).

Many of the characters just described resembled characters in non-war movies. They were lifted in their stereotyped totality and transplanted into a war situation where each found his niche. Common, everyday people (as common and everyday as screen characters can be), they nevertheless distinguished themselves by relinquishing selfish desires for the good of the nation.

If one character typifies this group, it is Robert Young in a film by the likely name of Joe Smith, American (1942). Joe is an aircraft worker, 30, born in Wisconsin of Norwegian and Austrian parents, has a wife and son, owns a house with an FHA mortgage, and makes $1 an hour at Atlas Aircraft Corporation. The war allows Joe some mark of distinction by giving him a chance to work on a bomb-sight.

Naturally, enemy agents learn of his role and kidnap him as the weakest link, a fatal mistake. Blindfolded, he is wisked off to a hideout, where he is tortured and threatened with death. Joe does not give in. He has a secret strength, the memories of his wife and son and how just that very morning his son had told him the story of Nathan Hale.

For some reason Joe is not killed and escapes to lead the police back to the hideout. Despite being blindfolded, he had memorized the direction of the automobile trip, the number of turns, a dip in the pavement, and the sound of a calliope. Thus, Joe, the common work-man, displayed uncommon attributes in resisting the Nazis—not unexpected of Hollywood's war heroes.

The Fighters

Today when one speaks of the American fighting man John Wayne immediately comes to mind. He starred in three films during 1942–1944 (Pittsburgh, 1943; Flying Tigers, 1943; and The Fighting Seabees, 1944) but the era belonged to Humphrey Bogart. Bogart represented the zenith of the screen's image of rugged individualism, the very characteristic that had to be discarded by so many of the film heroes in the face of social responsibility.

As Rick in Casablanca (1943) he epitomized the cynical individualist who had lost zeal for noble causes but who suddenly rediscovers his social concern during the events of the picture. He had been jilted by Ingrid Bergman and had retired within himself as a cafe owner in Casablanca when the story starts. "I stick my neck out for nobody," he says. "The problems of the world are not in my department. I'm a saloon keeper."

Ultimately his actions deny his words. He foregoes fleeing Casablanca with Ingrid Bergman allowing expatriate Paul Henreid to escape instead. Then, Bogart and Vichy Frenchman Claude Raines seek a Free French garrison where they can carry on the fight.

In To Have and Have Not (1944) Bogart is a completely independent fisherman who earns money on the side by aiding the Free French. At the conclusion, though, he and Lauren Bacall are set to storm a Vichy garrison in the interest of freedom, not money. Passage to Marseilles (1944) followed Bogart's fight against appeasement as a French newspaper editor, his arrest and abandonment of ideals, and finally his reclamation as a machine gunner for the Free French Air Force.

In other roles Bogart did not undergo a conversion to responsibility. He already possessed the quality although it might have been hidden. As Gloves Donohue in All Through the Night (1942) Bogart is a gambler, almost but not quite outside the law. He is propositioned by a German agent to join the cause. "It's a pity Mr. Donohue that you and I should oppose each other. We have so much in common. You take what you want and so do we. You have no respect for democracy. Neither do we." Bogart's ire is raised.

> You are screwy . . . I've been a registered Democrat ever since I could vote. I may not be model citizen No. 1 but I pay my taxes, wait for traffic lights, and buy twenty-four tickets regular for the policemen's ball. Brother, don't get me mixed up with no league that rubs out innocent little bakers (Bakers reference is to a neighbor of his mother.)

Bogart played similar self reliant roles in Across the Pacific (1942) and Action in the North Atlantic (1943). In Across . . . he pretends leaving the Army as a cover to snare enemy agents seeking the defense plans of the Panama Canal. As a top merchant seaman in Action . . . he has had his share of flings, women, and fights but has settled down with marriage. He would rather stay home but there is a war to win and supplies to be carried by the merchant fleet. Thus, he leaves his wife temporarily to provide the rugged, superman leadership needed for the mission.

One of Bogart's better performances was as Sergeant Joe Gunn in Sahara (1943). He commands a lone tank, LuluBelle, in the Libyan Desert trying to escape Germans and dehydration. One by one the crew collects six Allied stragglers, a Nazi pilot, a Negro (Sudanese), a Southern bigot, and an Italian prisoner, each a national symbol. The melting pot was a frequent theme during 1942-1944 but not portrayed as well in any other film--except perhaps Hitchcock's _Lifeboat_ (1944). Anyway, the Allied group holds off an entire battalion of parched Germans until word of the British victory at El Alamein seeps through. Bogart demonstrates ingenuity as well as toughness. He offers to trade the water hole for a German surrender and then tantalizes the Nazis with an imaginary bath splashed from an empty bucket.

The tough guy description did not apply to the entire group of fighters. One exception was the journalists, who composed the largest occupational grouping in 1939-1947 (Table 12). The journalists often used words rather than fists for fighting, for example Cary Grant in _Once Upon a Honeymoon_ (1942), who was more concerned, however, in watching Ginger Rogers than the intrigue of Europe.

Some of the more interesting journalists were never involved in direct international conflict. In _Journey for Margaret_ (1942) Robert Taylor was a cynical journalist who had lost his zeal for saving the world. He rediscovers concern while at a British war orphanage and becomes infatuated with two of the orphans. His anxiety over being able to bring only one back to the United States is very touching.

Newsmen Spencer Tracy and Guy Kibbee put the good of the country above journalistic goals in _Keeper of the Flame_ (1942) and _Power of the Press_ (1943). Kibbee is a country newsman who comes to the big city to halt the abuse of freedom of the press by the editors of one of the country's largest papers. Tracy keeps quiet about a murder to protect Katherine Hepburn and the country's morale. It seems the dead man, apparently an unquestionable patriotic leader, was really

TABLE 12

AMERICAN OCCUPATIONS, 1939–1947

Occupation	1939–1941	1942	1943	1944	1945	1946–1947	Total
Journalist	13.2%	12.9%	9.7%	10.9%	8.3%	- %	10.7%
Military	15.8	11.8	6.9	13.0	-	-	9.7
Entertainer	10.5	7.1	12.6	8.7	-	7.8	8.6
Laborer	-	7.1	5.6	6.5	8.3	7.8	5.8
Criminal	-	10.6	4.2	2.2	-	7.8	5.8
Spy	13.2	3.5	-	-	-	30.8	4.3
Medical	-	3.5	2.8	6.5	8.3	-	3.6
Businessman	-	2.3	2.8	8.7	4.2	-	3.2
Private detective	5.3	4.7	1.4	2.2	-	-	3.2
Adventurer	7.9	1.2	5.6	-	-	-	2.8
Scientist	2.7	7.1	-	-	-	7.8	2.8
Student	2.7	1.2	4.2	4.4	-	-	2.5
Self sufficient	-	4.7	2.8	-	4.2	-	2.5
Law enforcement	-	2.2	4.2	2.2	-	-	2.4
Engineer	-	1.2	2.8	2.2	4.2	-	1.8
Farmer	-	2.3	2.8	2.2	-	-	1.8
Seaman	2.7	-	2.8	4.4	-	-	1.8
Housewife	-	1.2	-	6.5	-	-	1.4
Athlete	-	2.3	-	2.2	-	-	1.1
Attorney	-	1.2	1.4	-	4.2	-	1.1
Pilot	5.3	-	1.4	-	-	-	1.1
Secretary	-	-	4.2	-	-	-	1.1
Teacher	-	-	4.2	-	-	-	1.1
Artist	-	-	-	4.4	-	-	0.7
Clerk	2.7	-	1.4	-	-	-	0.7
Cowboy	-	1.2	-	2.2	-	-	0.7
Diplomat	2.7	-	-	-	-	7.8	0.7
Salesman	5.3	-	-	-	-	-	0.7
Servant	2.7	-	-	-	-	-	0.4
No answer	7.9	10.6	16.7	10.9	58.3	30.8	16.9
Total	100.0	100.0	100.0	100.0	100.0	100.0	100.0
Number	38	85	72	46	24	13	278

[a]Data derived from question 7 Form B in Appendix I.

a Fascist plotting to overthrow the government.

Other exceptions to the tough guy hero were provided by usual tough guys, Gary Cooper and Edward G. Robinson. In The Story of Dr. Wassell (1944) Cooper is a former Arkansas country doctor concerned foremost with his medical responsibilities. Hence he refuses to abandon his injured when the Navy evacuates Java. He abstains from violence because his role is healing. His strength comes from inner confidence and an unobtrusive faith in God.

In the beginning of Mr. Winkle Goes to War (1944) Robinson is a timid bank clerk bullied by his wife. He returns from the Army a hero, still reserved but no longer afraid of his wife. He asserts himself, leaving the bank to establish a repair shop in his garage.

The detectives of 1942-1944 were little different than crime-busters of any other time: strong, brave, relatively quick-witted, handsome, and stereotyped. They ranged from cowboys Lee Powell (Texas Man Hunt, 1942) and Bob Livingston (Wild Horse Rustlers, 1943) to Ellery Queen (Enemy Agents Meet Ellery Queen, 1942). One interest-ing exception was Edward Arnold in Eyes in the Night (1942). Arnold is blind and thus without the normal physical capacity for cracking heads. He is forced to depend on wit and a seeing-eye dog.

Gangsters and toughs who if not outside the law were on the fence constituted a Hollywood tradition in the 1930's and into the 1940's. The ways in which this antisocial lot was integrated into the film war typified the conversions of Hollywood's war heroes in 1942-1944. In Chapter 1 it was suggested that the nation felt guilty for having abandoned its role in world affairs after World War I. The reformations experienced by gangsters and other characters seem to correspond quite closely to the guilt and ensuing internationalism that characterized the country during the years of World War II.

An early gangster who turned socially responsible was Alan Ladd, the sullen, babyfaced tough guy of the 1940's. As Danny Raven in This Gun for Hire (1942) Ladd is a hired killer methodically finishing what he starts when he is double crossed by a well known industrialist. Ladd's try for revenge is intensified when he learns the industrialist is a traitor. He kills the industrialist but in turn is shot down by the police in keeping with the Motion Picture Code. After all he was a murderer.

In Lucky Jordan (1942) Ladd has a better fate after going AWOL and returning to find his former mob in the hands of the Nazis. He corrects things before surrendering to the Army.

Cary Grant's conversion in Mister Lucky (1943) is quite visible. A gambler, Grant steals a 4-F draft classification from a dying man. The conversion comes when a priest reads a letter from the mother of the dead man. As Grant kneels to pray, a light on his face changes four times.

Some military heroes experienced similar conversions or at least had to prove their loyalty. A conflict between Chester Morris and Richard Arlen in Aerial Gunner (1943) illustrates conversion and redemption. Victim of slums and hoodlum father, Morris has a running feud with Arlen, the son of a school principal. Morris finally realizes that personal differences must be subordinated to the common welfare during crises. He sacrifices himself so that Arlen can escape the Japanese. Other conversions move Dana Andrews and Tyrone Power in Crash Dive (1943), Arlen in Minesweeper (1943), George Murphy in

The Navy Way (1944).

Many characters dispensed information about the machinery of modern warfare as they trained and went into battle. In Bombardier (1943) Pat O'Brien is a dedicated soldier in a friendly rivalry with pilot Randolph Scott trying to recruit bodies for their respective specialties. The plot is secondary to an explanation of modern precision bombing and the necessity of a reliable bombsight. Similar roles placed Arlen in Aerial Gunner, Power in Crash Dive, and Preston Foster in Thunderbirds (1942).

Although there were few victories to commemorate in the early years of the war, battle heroes were depicted in not infrequent numbers. Some have already been mentioned. Others served as sacrificial symbols of those killed in early battles.

In the actual incidents on which some of the films were based groups rather than individuals provided the heroism. The groups in the films contained every American minority imaginable. In Wake Island (1942) Brian Donlevy leads the hopeless defense of the island immediately before being overrun by Japanese. Much of the action, however, revolves around a mixed collection of supporting characters (featuring as often was the case William Bendix) realizing they were doomed but dedicated to holding out as long as possible.

Bataan (1943) featured Robert Taylor and a group that included jitterbug Desi Arnez, a Filipino, a conscientious objector, a Negro, a former deserter, a gruff veteran, a youthful and rash lieutenant, and a pilot. They defend a bridge until the last man, Taylor, dies over a machine gun in his own freshly dug grave.

A sympathetic but deadly serious Cary Grant leads similar

characters into Tokyo Bay in <u>Destination Tokyo</u> (1944). He is kind but firm and efficient, refusing a youth permission to grow a beard because it might lead to lax discipline. An interesting subplot pits an atheistic pharmacy mate against a young Christian. In the middle of a battle the pharmacist is forced to perform an emergency appendectomy on the boy, who enters the operation without fear and whispering prayers. The operation a success, the pharmacist discards his skepticism and moves toward faith in God and his fellow man.

John Wayne's two combat portrayals presented contrasting images with similar implications. In <u>Flying Tigers</u> (1942) he is a business-minded colonel leading a mixture of volunteers in the air war over China. John Carroll, a smart alec pilot with little respect for regulations, represents a problem, but Wayne's prodding convinces Carroll that the job can only be accomplished if he places the group above himself. Carroll redeems past mistakes by flying a bomber into a Japanese train.

The conversion extends to Wayne in <u>The Fighting Seabees</u> (1944). As a muscular, gruff, but likeable owner of a construction company building airfields in the Pacific, Wayne balks at Navy rules forbidding arming of civilians. He disobeys instructions, arms his men, and leads them to disaster, an experience that convinces him to accept a Navy offer to establish a construction battalion. He absolves himself by exploding large oil tanks, killing hundreds of Japanese as well as himself.

Why should a character so willingly sacrifice himself? A great deal of the motivation is provided by guilt arising after conversion when the individual realizes the selfishness of his egotistical pursuits.

Part of the answer is also given by a character in Thirty Seconds Over
Tokyo (1944). He explained his willingness to risk his life with this
hope: "If we could only fix it so that this would be the last one."[9]

A New View of the Military, 1945

By the end of 1944 and during 1945 the screen's civilian
emphasis began to evaporate. In 1945 a total of 62.5 per cent of
American heroes were in the military, compared with 35.1 per cent
for the previous three years (Table 7). The end of the war was near,
the citizenry tired, and the home-front frenzy diminished. Consequently the OWI and other governmental agencies relaxed demands for
home front films.

A few civilians who made home-front appearances did not resemble
those of the past. The earlier civilians were preoccupied with finding
ways to contribute to the war effort; the civilians of 1945 were trying
to readjust to civilian life.

The best of the portrayals was John Garfield in Pride of the
Marines, the story of Marine hero Al Schmid. After becoming a hero
on Guadalcanal, Garfield loses his sight and is transformed from a
self-confident, carefree optimist to a bitter, self-pitying defeatist.
At home in Philadelphia he rejects his parents, friends, and girl because he "wants nobody to be a seeing eye dog for me."[10] Ultimately
he adjusts.

---

[9]Quoted in Philip T. Hartung, "Hollywood's Reply to Dec. 7,"
Commonweal, Dec. 22, 1944, p. 257.

[10]Quoted in Variety, Aug. 8, 1945, p. 22.

Richard Arlen suffers from war-induced amnesia in _Identity Unknown_. He knows he is one of three persons but is not sure which one. Thus, he travels the country searching for identity and creating the chance to visit a cross-section of Americana and explain the death of a loved one. He finds his identity, his future wife, and a renewed life. He and his future wife emerge, _Variety_ said, "as the embodiment of the hopes of the war generations for a world that will feel the sacrifice made was worthwhile."[11]

In _A Medal for Benny_ elderly Mexican-American J. Carrol Naish reminds home-front Americans that they have not always been model citizens. Local press agents, politicians, and opportunists seek to take advantage of his dead son's medal of honor until they find he was of Mexican descent. The old man corrects things with a monologue explaining the virtues of America and decrying the exploitation of its heroes.

A few civilians on the war front continued to fight the enemy. Selfish playgirl Constance Bennett changes to responsible patriot who runs an underground railway for downed flyers in Paris in _Paris Underground_ and sensitive medical missionary Randolph Scott is transformed into guerilla leader in _China Sky_. In _Blood on the Sun_ James Cagney's prewar experiences as a journalist in Japan brings death and a piece of parting advice: "Forgive your enemies but first get even."[12]

If 1942-1944 was Bogart's era, 1945 with a few exceptions began John Wayne's age. One exception was John Hodiak in _A Bell for Adano_.

---

[11] Quoted in _Variety_, April 4, 1945, p. 10.

[12] Quoted in Philip T. Hartung, "Flow Like Water," _Commonweal_, July 13, 1945, p. 309.

Charged with administering a Sicilian town, Hodiak finds his greatest obstacle is not the enemy but the hunger and thirst of the occupied peoples and the authoritarian bureaucracy of the American military. Hodiak bucks superior officers and goes over their heads to return a city hall bell to his village. His success costs him his job, and in the firing is a criticism of Army procedures which is a significant departure from normal portrayals of 1939-1947.

The typical soldier of 1945 was either a professional or a civilian-turned-hardened-veteran simply trying to do a military assignment. He may have been motivated by patriotism, but idealism was tempered by his first obligation--the job at hand.

Wayne plays a career officer in They Were Expendable who doubts the value of PT boats. The boats prove themselves, and he returns to the United States, unwillingly but understanding that the training of new men takes precedence. In Back to Bataan Wayne trains a group of Filipino guerrillas after he is stranded during the Japanese invasion and leads them until MacArthur returns.

In A Walk in the Sun Dana Andrews and the rest of his squad are ordered to destroy a tank. It is a small job but one of many such jobs that collectively are crucial to the invasion of Sicily. They complain but do the job because it must be done.

Then, of course, there was Robert Mitchum in Story of G.I. Joe. A young lieutenant in the beginning, Mitchum is followed through the eyes of Ernie Pyle as he matures to captain and encourages, scolds, and kicks his men into battle. The war is dirty and uncomfortable but necessary, and even with Mitchum's death it continues. However, hope still glimmers. Pyle concludes, "Surely, something good must

come out of this. I hope we can rejoice in victory so that another
great war can never be possible."

Some characters represented ways to prevent future conflicts.
The answer was a strong professional group of warriors, espionage agents
as well as soldiers. Lloyd Nolan played this kind of agent in House
on 92nd Street. Nolan and the rest of the FBI team use the newest
scientific methods to protect one of the nation's secret weapons, a
formula supposedly similar to the atom bomb. It is the organization
headed by Nolan but not an indispensable Nolan that is responsible for
protecting the secret.

Teamwork is also apparent in Betrayal from the East, a poorly
constructed tale of Japanese espionage starring Lee Tracy as a volunteer aide of Army intelligence. The film was distinguished by a
personal message from Drew Pearson, who warns that the Japanese threat
was compounded by Americans' unconcern for internal security and concludes, "It must not happen again."

1946-1947

No combat pictures were released in the two years following
the war. However, the characters of the few war films that were released presented an interesting tale of the consequences of the war,
an explanation of its causes, and a suggestion for avoiding a future
confrontation.

Three returning servicemen portrayed the non-political consequences of the war in The Best Years of Our Lives (1946). Dana
Andrews plays an Air Force pilot returning home, which has no use for
him. He is untrained, and subordinates who stayed behind are unwilling

to offer him a job--even in his old position as a soda jerk. After

three years of an active life and becoming acquainted with the virtues

of men from the laboring class, banker Frederic March has difficulty

returning to his job as a loan officer--particularly when he has to

refuse a loan to a farmer who has no collateral but wants to buy a

farm. The biggest problem belongs to Harold Russell, who has lost both

arms in a naval battle. His problems of emotional adjustment occupy

much of the film.

The problems of the trio are not completely resolved at the

end, but each has found some degree of hope. However, the significance

of the three was not in their hope but in the honesty with which the

film treated their postwar problems.

Robert Young provides an explanation of the causes of the war

in The Searching Wind (1946). A career diplomat, he recognizes that

foreign policy blunders and appeasement (meaning isolationism) were

responsible for Hitler's initial successes. Young's interpretation

of history was a clear warning, according to Variety.

> The lessons of the first and second World Wars are apparently
> forgotten. By recalling the mistakes agreed on, by calling
> attention . . . to President Roosevelt's words that 'we failed
> once 25 years ago and musn't again', the film may wake the U.S.
> up through its message.[13]

Four espionage agents offered advice by example for avoiding

the mistakes of the 1930's--Alan Ladd in O.S.S. (1946), James Cagney

in 13 Rue Madeleine (1946), Gary Cooper in Cloak and Dagger (1946),

and William Gargan in Rendezvous 24 (1946). Each was either a pro-

fessional or a civilian with professional training. They were not

_____

[13]Variety, May 15, 1946, p. 8.

former private detectives free lancing or civilians trapped by circumstance. They were a trained cadre of warriors, the only hope of countering the enemy's trained corps. As professionals the agents were forerunners of the American war hero of 1948-1962. They embodied the message that the United States had to have a professional corps of warriors to prevent future wars or at least to sound advance warning.

Summary

The American heroes of 1939-1947 were a varied lot. However, as a group they shared two important characteristics. First, they were generally civilians, or civilians-turned-soldiers, each of whom had something to contribute to the war effort. Second, they felt some sense of responsibility for their fellow man and for their country. The feeling might be ingrained in the individual throughout the film or he might have to acquire it. Whatever the case his war contributions are motivated by a sense of social responsibility.

CHAPTER V

PROFESSIONAL WARRIORS

In 1948 the American people turned attention to a different kind
of war. While World War II had been an awakening to international responsibility marked by total civilian participation, the Cold War was
characterized by a division of labor intertwined with deeply embedded
fear. The division of labor put the conduct of war into the hands of
professionals (the military and various intelligence agencies). As the
fear of communism grew so did the belief in the necessity of a strong
military force.

The emphasis on professional warriors shows up among the American
heroes in 1948-1962 war films. It is to be expected that Korean and
Cold War films would manifest increased faith in the military since
the pictures dealt with contemporary wars at a time when the professional philosophy was dominant. That World War II movies made in
1948-1962 would possess the same traits is slightly less predictable
if one expects Hollywood to be true to historical fact. Perhaps that
is an unwarranted expectation. Actually, World War II films produced
in 1948-1962 had more in common with Korean War and Cold War pictures
than with 1939-1947 predecessors.

Content analysis results support the conclusion that films of
1948-1962 placed emphasis on professional warriors--at least to a
greater extent than did those of 1939-1947. In 1939-1947 a total of
55.8 per cent of 278 American heroes played civilian roles, 10.1 per
cent espionage agents, and 34.2 per cent soldiers. Nearly three-
fourths of 244 Americans played military parts in 1948-1962 (Table 13).

TABLE 13

ROLES OF AMERICAN CHARACTERS, 1948-1962

Role	WWII	Cold	Korea	Total
Spy	5.3%	29.6%	- %	12.3%
Soldier	87.7	37.0	100.0	72.5
Civilian	7.1	33.3	-	14.4
Total	100.0	100.0	100.0	100.0
Number	114	81	49	244

[a]Data derived from question 1 Form B in Appendix I.

Only 14.4 per cent were civilians and 12.3 per cent spies. The fact that Korea was strictly a military conflict discouraged anything but military roles for its war film heroes. Also causing the increase in military characters was the fact that as the memories of World War II dimmed, military films were more marketable than civilian pictures. The Cold War offered more possibilities of civilian portrayal, but even its pictures had a higher percentage of soldier heroes.

A further indication of the increase in depiction of the military is provided by the fact that the percentage of Americans in the armed services in 1948-1962 films is twice as high as in 1939-1947 (76.2 per cent to 38.1 per cent). (The percentage of characters in the military is higher than those playing roles of soldiers because characters playing roles of spies may be members of the military.) Not only was there a larger proportion of military characters, but also those who were in were more likely to be career soldiers. In 1948-1962 a total of 25.8 per cent of the characters was career soldiers compared to 6.1 per cent in 1939-1947. (See Table 14.)

TABLE 14

AMERICAN MILITARY CHARACTERISTICS, 1948-1962

	WWII	Cold	Korea	Total
Military Status				
Member	90.4%	42.0%	100.0%	76.2%
Former member	1.8	8.6	–	3.7
Never member	5.3	14.8	–	7.4
No answer	2.6	34.6	–	12.3
Total	100.0	100.0	100.0	100.0
Branch				
Army	42.1	21.0	40.8	34.8
Navy	25.4	7.4	16.3	17.6
Air Force	7.0	14.8	20.4	12.3
Marines	14.0	2.5	10.2	9.4
Coast Guard	1.8	–	–	0.8
Other	0.9	–	–	0.4
No answer	8.8	56.4	12.2	24.2
Total	100.0	100.0	100.0	100.0
Rank				
Gen.-Adm.	4.4	–	–	2.0
Col.-Capt.	7.9	4.9	12.2	7.8
Maj.-Cmdr.	13.2	6.2	14.3	11.1
Capt.-Lt.	13.2	2.5	6.1	8.2
Lt.-Ens.	23.7	3.7	18.4	16.0
Sgt.-CPO	10.5	2.5	20.4	9.8
Non com	1.8	1.2	6.1	2.5
Enlisted	14.9	18.5	10.2	15.2
Other	0.9	–	–	0.4
No answer	9.6	60.5	12.2	27.0
Total	100.0	100.0	100.0	100.0
Membership Reason				
Career	26.3	13.6	44.9	25.8
Draft	30.7	9.9	20.4	21.7
Patriotism	2.6	2.5	2.0	2.5
Personal	3.5	1.2	4.1	2.9
Other	–	4.9	2.0	2.0
No answer	36.8	68.5	26.5	45.1
Total	100.0	100.0	100.0	100.0
Number	114	81	49	244

[a]Data derived from questions 15, 16, 18, and 20 Form B in Appendix I.

Further evidence to the point is provided by the fact that the
military supplanted journalism as the American hero's favorite occupation. The characters of 1939-1947 were journalists 10.7 per cent of
the time and soldiers 9.7 per cent. In 1948-1962 the soldier category
included 31.1 per cent of the heroes and the journalist 2.5 per cent.
Table 15 also shows spies were second highest in occupations, and
entertainers, as in 1939-1947, retained third place.

TABLE 15

AMERICAN OCCUPATIONS, 1948-1962

Occupation	WWII	Cold	Korea	Total
Military	30.7%	18.5%	53.2%	31.1%
Spy	–	18.5	–	6.2
Entertainer	2.6	9.9	2.1	4.9
Adventurer	1.8	9.9	–	4.1
Self sufficient	2.6	6.2	2.0	3.7
Journalist	2.6	2.4	2.0	2.5
Attorney	2.6	1.2	–	1.6
Laborer	1.8	1.2	2.0	1.6
Medical	1.8	2.4	–	1.6
Criminal	1.8	1.2	–	1.2
Engineer	1.8	–	2.0	1.2
Student	0.9	2.4	–	1.2
Businessman	1.8	–	–	0.8
Farmer	–	2.4	–	0.8
Housewife	0.9	1.2	–	0.8
Minister	–	1.2	2.0	0.8
Politician	0.9	1.2	–	0.8
Teacher	1.8	–	–	0.8
Artist	0.9	–	–	0.4
Private detective	–	1.2	–	0.4
Seaman	–	1.2	–	0.4
Scientist	0.9	–	–	0.4
Union leader	–	1.2	–	0.4
White collar	–	1.2	–	0.4
Other non-military	14.9	6.2	14.3	11.9
No answer	26.3	8.6	20.8	19.7
Total	100.0	100.0	100.0	100.0
Number	114	81	49	244

[a]Data derived from question 7 Form B in Appendix I.

With the Americans gaining in professionalism in 1948-1962 their primary goals shifted. In 1939-1947 a total of 40.6 per cent of the characters was primarily motivated by goals of patriotism or public service and only 10.8 per cent by a war task. Task orientation exchanged places with patriotism in 1948-1962 (Table 16). A total of 32.6 per cent of the Americans sought task goals and 17.6 patriotism.

TABLE 16

PRIMARY GOALS OF AMERICANS, 1948-1962

Primary Goal	WWII	Cold	Korea	Total
Safety	1.8%	3.7%	4.1%	2.9%
Escape law	0.9	1.2	2.0	1.2
Health	0.9	2.5	-	1.2
Individualism	1.8	-	-	0.8
Money	1.8	2.5	2.0	2.0
Comfort	0.9	2.5	4.1	2.0
Power	1.8	-	2.0	1.2
Adventure	-	-	-	-
Love	20.2	12.3	12.2	16.0
Family	0.9	3.7	2.0	2.0
Sex	2.6	1.2	4.1	2.4
War task	34.2	25.9	38.8	32.4
Fame	2.6	4.9	-	2.9
Patriotism	14.9	25.9	10.2	17.6
Justice	2.6	4.9	-	2.9
Truth	1.8	3.7	6.1	3.3
Revenge	5.3	-	6.1	3.3
Honesty	3.5	6.2	4.1	4.5
No answer	2.6	2.5	-	2.0
Total	100.0	100.0	100.0	100.0
Number	114	81	49	244

[a]Data derived from question 25 Form B in Appendix I.

The only 1948-1962 characters whose goals resembled 1939-1947 heroes were those in Cold War films. This similarity should not have been too unexpected since the Cold War was current and often demanded a display of faith through action.

The methods used by Americans in 1948-1962 were quite similar to those relied on by their predecessors although force received greater emphasis. Force was the primary method of 17.9 per cent of the characters in 1939-1947 (tied for first) and 28.7 per cent of 1948-1962's heroes (first). Force, of course, is a characteristic method of a professional warrior as are hard work (discipline) and knowledge (specialized knowledge) which were the second and third most popular methods among 1948-1962 Americans (see Table 17).

TABLE 17

AMERICANS' PRIMARY METHODS, 1948-1962

Primary Method	WWII	Cold	Korea	Total
Hard work	25.4%	14.8%	12.2%	19.3%
Luck	8.8	17.3	8.2	11.5
Trickery	7.0	16.0	8.2	10.3
Knowledge	10.5	23.5	20.4	16.8
Charm	9.6	3.7	2.0	6.1
Force	32.5	18.5	36.7	28.7
Persuasion	4.4	4.9	8.2	5.3
No answer	1.8	1.2	4.1	2.0
Total	100.0	100.0	100.0	100.0
Number	114	81	49	244

[a]Data derived from question 29 Form B in Appendix I.

Otherwise, demographic data characterize the American hero of 1948-1962 as a WASP with an X, the same as in 1939-1947 (see Table 18). The crucial distinction of the American hero of 1948-1962, then, is his professionalism. The rest of the chapter discusses the theme of professionalism and its variations among the characters

TABLE 18

DEMOGRAPHICS OF AMERICAN HEROES, 1948-1962

	WWII	Cold	Korea	Total
Sex				
Male	95.6%	96.3%	98.0%	96.3%
Female	4.4	3.7	2.0	3.7
Total	100.0	100.0	100.0	100.0
Age				
Youth	-	-	-	-
Young adult	10.5	11.1	8.2	10.2
Mature adult	80.7	80.2	91.8	82.8
Middle age	3.5	4.9	-	3.3
Old age	-	-	-	-
No answer	5.3	3.7	-	3.7
Total	100.0	100.0	100.0	100.0
Class				
Upper	14.0	25.9	6.1	16.4
Middle	12.3	29.6	12.2	18.0
Lower	8.8	7.4	4.1	7.4
Outside structure	63.2	32.1	71.4	54.5
No answer	1.8	4.9	6.1	3.7
Total	100.0	100.0	100.0	100.0
Marital Status				
Married	14.9	13.6	20.4	15.6
Never married	48.2	61.7	53.1	53.7
Divorced	1.8	1.2	4.1	2.0
Other	0.9	1.2	-	0.8
No answer	7.0	2.5	4.1	4.9
Total	100.0	100.0	100.0	100.0
Education				
In school	2.6	14.8	-	6.1
High school	16.7	16.0	16.3	16.4
Undergraduate	20.2	16.0	22.4	19.3
Higher degree	9.6	13.6	6.1	10.2
Other	0.9	-	-	0.4
No answer	50.0	39.5	55.1	47.5
Total	100.0	100.0	100.0	100.0
Number	114	81	49	244

[a]Data derived from questions 2-6 Form B in Appendix I.

of World War II, the Cold War, and Korean War films.

Cold War

As indicated by Table 13 the heroes of the Cold War included
a higher percentage of civilians than did other American war characters of 1948-1962. These civilians, though, were in sharp contrast
with the civilians of 1939-1947. The earlier civilians frequently
were self-confident to the point of cockiness and in general felt they
could control the influences on their lives. The Cold War civilians
were victims of circumstance, frequently snarled between fear of
physical harm and the demand that they prove their patriotism. Sometimes they managed to find their own way out of the entanglement,
but frequently they needed help--from professional warriors.

Parts played by Ernest Borgnine in two films illustrate the
power of circumstance. As Bernie Goldsmith in Three Brave Men (1957),
a history of liberal activities and a neighbor who considers him a
radical cause him to lose his Navy job of twenty-two years. The
loss of financial security for a family of four is bad enough, but
Borgnine is more concerned because his patriotism was challenged. A
year-long campaign regains his job.

In Man on a String (1960) Borgnine's concern for his father
and brother, still living in the Soviet Union, is exploited by the
Communists to gain access to Hollywood elite. The all knowing Central
Intelligence Bureau is well aware of the Communist plans and confronts
Borgnine with charges of disloyalty. Confessing his foolishness, he
partly volunteers and is partly coerced into serving as a double agent.
Throughout his single mission (West Berlin to Russia to East Berlin and

back to West Berlin) he is a frightened, nervous civilian seeking only to redeem himself. He succeeds, just barely, needing professional agents to save him from Communists who chased him from Russia through East Berlin to his hotel room.

Another victim was Robert Rockwell in The Red Menace (1949). A veteran without job or housing, he is courted by the Communists, whose orders for him or anyone are: "Promise him anything. When we get him into the party, he'll find that it's not so easy to get out."

The film documents what it calls standard operating procedure for the Communists. Finally, Rockwell recognizes his mistake. His reasoning is no more profound than that of a mother of a party member. "I don't even know what communism is but it must be bad if it makes you do things you do." The hero of 1939-1947 would have taken it upon himself to finish off the Communists. When Rockwell finds the wolf, he runs. He and a party agent who regrets her sins flee to Texas where they marry and decide to tell the government. Whether the government will actually do anything about the Communists is left in doubt, but at least it has the resources for action.

Not all civilians were powerless. For example steamer captain John Wayne leads a Chinese village to freedom in Blood Alley (1955); journalist Elliot Reed exposes a Soviet bacteriological warfare lab operating in the United States in The Whip Hand (1951); doctor Edmond O'Brien delivers an important message to British intelligence in The Shanghai Story (1954); and Richard Widmark, a callous adventurer motivated originally only by money, combines with a group of scientists to halt a Chinese plot in Hell and High Water (1954).

Even the civilians who had some measure of control over their destinies differed from civilians of 1939-1947. Unlike their predecessors, the 1948-1962 civilians seemed to have little comprehension of their role in the overall war effort, and their actions (except for Widmark in Hell and High Water) seemed to have little more than short range implications.

In The Secret Ways (1961) Widmark, playing a soldier of fortune without a fortune, illustrates the point. He aids a private group in arranging the escape of an underground Hungarian leader. In 1939-1947 such action might have been depicted as crucial to war strategy. This time, though, the escape was effected solely to protect the safety of the leader.

Earlier the success of the mission would have been the basis of rejoicing and some concluding remarks about a future without war. In The Secret Ways success is only the occasion for relief. Cold War civilians may complete their tasks successfully, but rarely does optimism accompany success. The heroes can see no day when the conflict will be resolved in peace. Their activities are just another episode in a succession of episodes.

Suffering from emotional problems as a result of treatment in a North Korean prisoner of war camp, Dana Andrews returns to Washington to find his polling business in the hands of a stranger (The Fearmakers, 1958). The stranger is a Communist using information gathered by Andrews' organization to manipulate public opinion. Andrews regains control of his business, but his success stops only one probe on one front. As the story ends, he is scheduled to testify before a Senate committee concerning other Communist activity, particularly the Reds' use of a peace organization as a front.

The war, thus, continued with no end in sight. To combat an enemy who could be almost anywhere required more than civilians reacting to individual emergencies. Needed were professionals.

One professional left over from World War II was Tyrone Power in Diplomatic Courier (1952). He is "shot, stabbed, drugged, tossed in the river, down steep steps, and knocked out three times without damage to his time piece,"[1] but accomplishes his mission--the recovery of Russian plans for an invasion of Yugoslavia.

As a group the Cold War agents of 1948-1962 fell somewhat short of Power's flamboyancy. Robert Wagner had all the physical characteristics for such a role, but in Stopover Tokyo (1957) he is quite businesslike. He is moody, sullen, and close-mouthed. He is so devoted to duty that at the end he leaves beautiful Joan Collins because his work comes first.

In I Was a Communist for the FBI (1951) Frank Lovejoy not only ignores romance but also risks loss of his family in order to gather evidence of Communist involvement in American steel unions. He risked so much because the threat was so great, as he told an investigating committee:

> Political action is a front for a Communist spy system composed of American traitors whose only purpose is to hand the American people into the hands of the Soviet Union as a slave colony.

Lovejoy and other agents were not mere individuals fighting communism but were backed by organizations who fed them information and sustained them. Given the proper support, the agents could stop the Communists in a particular situation. They did not always have

---

[1] Motion Picture Review Product Digest, June 21, 1952, p. 1417.

the appropriate support, according to John Wayne, who complained bitterly about the Fifth Amendment in Big Jim McLain (1952). Wayne would
capture Communists and because of their use of the Fifth Amendment they
would be released, according to the film. Yet he continued. Why? "I
don't know the whys. I didn't know the whys in the war. I shot at the
man on the other side of the perimeter because he was the enemy."

Gregory Peck's comments in Night People (1954) explain why a
little more fully. An Army colonel, Peck is reflective, cool, and
patient while trying to effect the release of a corporal kidnaped by
the Russians. His plans are complicated by worried father and wealthy
capitalist Broderick Crawford, who thinks he can buy his son's freedom.

"These are cannibals, Mr. Leatherby . . . head-hunting, blood-
thirsty cannibals out to eat us up," Peck tells Crawford. Therefore,
decisions must not be made by civilians. "Anything that burns me is
an amateur trying to tell a professional what to do," and later, he
adds, "These decisions have to be made by soldiers."

As a soldier Peck was an exception. He could deal with the
enemy more or less directly. Others had to be satisfied with building
an efficient, well equipped armed force and staffing it with dedicated,
experienced professionals.

Rarely were Cold War warriors infantrymen. Big bombers were
more photogenic. However, the Marines' infantry had its advocate in
Jack Webb (The D.I., 1957). Released shortly after public outrage
flared over mistreatment of recruits at Parris Island, the film
rationalized the Marines' rigid training. "The corps is kinda like
a club," Webb explains. "Parris Island is like an initiation, and
we think ours is the best club in the world."

The initiation has two purposes. First, Webb says, "We're the first ones in and we're the best. If we are not the best, we'll be the deadest." Second, a modern army has no room for the non-conformist. As Webb tells his biggest problem child, "You listen to me youngster. Learn to think in terms of the group, your responsibility in and to the group."

Most Cold War military characters were involved in developing and using the technology of modern warfare. Glenn Ford starred in one of the original Cold War service films, The Flying Missile (1950). As a submarine commander he is mystified at the Pentagon's reluctance to mount missiles on subs. He proves his point by developing hardware and testing it.

Later characters had the benefit of an enlightened leadership which provided the technology. All the military had to do was keep it at peak efficiency, a task which included retaining qualified men in the service. The process of convincing men of their proper place of service was personalized by Jimmy Stewart in Strategic Air Command (1955), Karl Malden in Bombers B-52 (1957), and Rex Reason in Thundering Jets (1958).

Malden plays a sergeant and expert mechanic tempted to foresake the Air Force for a lucrative business offer and thus provide his family with the luxuries they have not had. He decides, though, that the satisfaction of doing a job as part of an important team outweighs financial considerations. Reason has to adjust to a new job in the team--teaching rather than flying.

Stewart relinquishes more than the other two to pursue an Air Force career. He gives up the money and fame of major league baseball because, as his commanding officer explains, "This is a new kind of war. We've got to stay ready to fight." Staying ready depends on hardware and maintaining a professional team. After all, the new jet is "a ship and a crew working together to put a bomb on target."

Korean War

One does not have to view too many Korean War movies before concluding that he is watching the same characters over and over. That is not quite true, but it pinpoints a major similarity among nearly all Korean War heroes: they were unified by a professional approach to a necessary task. Some were more satisfied than others; some are career soldiers, others retread civilians or fast maturing rookies; a few fight glamorous air battles, many more constricted mud wars; but together they do what cannot be done individually.

Some Korean War heroes of this era experienced conversions but but quite unlike the conversions of 1939-1947. In the preceding era conversion had been to social responsibility. This time the consequence of transformation was acceptance of the necessity for military discipline and teamwork.

Arthur Franz learned such a lesson in Battle Taxi (1955). Franz is a former jet pilot brooding because he is assigned to Helicopter Rescue Service with no opportunity for fighting. He makes the opportunity by taking unnecessary chances with his helicopter. Only when Franz crashes and is rescued by another helicopter does he realize that fighting is not the only way to contribute to a modern war effort.

Most of the characters did not have to be convinced of the method of fighting although they sometimes wondered why they had to fight at all. The doubt was not ideological, but simply they had had their war in the 1940's and it was now someone else's turn. William Holden expresses this feeling in The Bridges at Toko-Ri (1954). Holden is married with children, a veteran pilot of World War II, and bitter at being recalled to fight a young man's war, but he methodically performs his duty. Admiral Fredric March explains, "It is always the wrong war in the wrong place but you do your job because you are here to do it."

In The McConnell Story (1955) dissatisfaction rests with the wife, June Allyson. She does not understand why Alan Ladd is perfectly content fighting in Korea because he is doing what he loves: flying. He also understands the reason for the police action, as explained by his commanding officer.

> Police action? You're wrong. This is a war. We're good but never underestimate the enemy. Merely holding the enemy is not good enough. Nor is beating him. Your job is to slaughter him. This is a testing ground for the Reds and if we don't stop him here, he'll use his arms somewhere else.

The Korean War needed experienced men with single-minded dedication to military goals. Rock Hudson in Battle Hymn (1957) did not have that degree of dedication. He re-enlisted in an attempt to relieve guilt created by having accidentally bombed an orphanage during World War II. The guild restricts performance of duty.

The true professional, Robert Mitchum in The Hunters (1958), separated his personal and professional lives. As Cleve Savell, a middle-aged ace of World War II, Mitchum requests combat duty, and the "Iceman" has lost none of his efficiency. He quickly becomes an ace, downing the Chinese's top pilot, nicknamed "Casey Jones."

During off-hours visits to Japan, Mitchum develops a near affair

with May Britt, the wife of one of his pilots. The pilot has abandoned
her because he fears not proving himself in combat. Mitchum does not
let his relationship with Britt interfere with the war. He babies the
husband, even crash landing to save the guy. His reward? After it is
over, May Britt returns to her husband. The professional continues
his profession; the civilian goes home.

The characters in the few romances of the Korean War films
managed like Mitchum to separate love and war, e.g. Humphrey Bogart
and June Allyson in Battle Circus (1953), John Hodiak and Linda
Christian in Battle Zone (1952), and Scott Brady and Elaine Edwards in
Battle Flame (1959).

The excitement of the war was conveyed through the air conflict,
but the typical hero was anchored to the ground. He was ordinarily a
sergeant or lower echelon officer confronted with achieving an immediate objective, a task often complicated by his men or other companions.
For example, Mitchum encounters misunderstanding from his girl, Anne
Blyth, in One Minute to Zero (1952). The disagreement is over his
order to fire into a group of refugees. The decision was necessary
because North Koreans were masquerading as refugees. He fired, he
said, because the etiquette of war does not always apply. When one
side breaks the conventions, the other is forced to bend them. He
made a decision worthy of any veteran professional.

Racial bigotry hindered Alan Ladd in All the Young Men (1960).
He feels more qualified than sergeant Sidney Poitier for leadership.
However, a blood transfusion alleviates the tensions, and Ladd and
Poitier die propped against each other during the final enemy attack.

Emotional problems handicapped Richard Basehart in Fixed

Bayonets (1951) and John Goddard in Sniper's Ridge (1961). Basehart
cannot shoot an enemy soldier face-to-face and thus convinces himself
that he is not fit to command. When an emergency thrusts command on
him, he performs admirably. On the other hand, Goddard's cowardice
in World War II turns him into a tyrant and eventually destroys his
control over his men and his effectiveness as a leader.

The shells of three gruff sergeants were softened by their
Korean War experiences. In The Nun and the Sergeant (1962) Robert
Webber, a professional tired of death, finds peace of mind from a
nun who just happens to be leading a group of girls behind enemy lines.
Then, he and his men charge a North Korean position toward certain
death. Callous top sergeant Chuck Henderson happens upon a theatrical
troop behind enemy lines in Operation Dames (1959). He and an egotistical singer fall in love and find happiness together, an ending
worthy of the film's inexpensive budget.

Undoubtedly, the best of the seasoned sergeants was Gene Evans
in The Steel Helmet (1951). His actions presented interesting con-
tradictions. He professes no attachment to anyone but practically
adopts a small Korean orphan who is later killed by the Communists.
He is the complete professional minus emotion but denies his detachment
by reacting irrationally when the boy is killed, i.e. he shoots a North
Korean in cold blood. He disdains religion but gives a hint of faith
when burying the child. He refuses to aid a lost squad but later joins
them because he believes their lieutenant is incompetent. In short, he
is an efficient fighting man, earthy and not averse to killing but is
not the perfect professional. He allows feeling to interfere with
duty.

Seldom were the characters involved in any criticism of the war or the military. Two exceptions were Gregory Peck in <u>Pork Chop Hill</u> (1959) and John Saxon in <u>War Hunt</u> (1962). As Lieutenant Clemons, Peck is ordered to take a hill of no strategic value during the armistice talks. He questions the order but carries it out. The deaths that ensue are clearly depicted as the result of generals' willingness to sacrifice lives for the psychological effect of a final victory.

Saxon plays a psychopath tolerated by his commanding officer because he does best what has to be done: killing. Every night he sneaks past his own guards and slits enemy throats. His behavior is overlooked and rationalized while the war continues. When it is over, it can no longer be excused and he cannot quit. His own army eliminates him.

Saxon differed from the professionals of the Korean War. They were doing a job; he actually enjoyed it. The professionals had a postwar role to which they could adjust. His usefulness ended with the war; he could not adjust.

One group of heroes remain. They represented Americans taken prisoner by the Communists and subjected to torture and brainwashing. Included among them were Ronald Reagan in <u>Prisoner of War</u> (1954), Robert Francis in <u>Bamboo Prison</u> (1955), Paul Newman in <u>The Rack</u> (1956), Richard Basehart in <u>Time Limit</u> (1957), and Frank Sinatra in <u>The Manchurian Candidate</u> (1962). In the characters can be seen an answer to American bewilderment that any patriotic son would collaborate with the enemy under any conditions. A progression of explanations evolves in the films.

Reagan volunteers to be captured and to rid a prison camp of

the very few traitors who do exist. Francis explains that the collaborators are actually intelligence agents. Newman admits cooperating
with a noble purpose--to protect others--but believes that aiding the
enemy is inexcusable under any circumstance. Basehart excuses cooperation because it saves sixteen lives.

Only Sinatra's story accepts the possibility that brainwashing
could break an American. Sinatra is programmed for assassination when
he returns to the United States. Conditioned to perform in a prescribed
manner, he is a far cry from the individualistic hero of 1939-1947 who
was in full control of every action.

One could speculate, though, that Sinatra might not have been
too deviant from the rest of the Korean professionals. The professionals
were trained to perform in a disciplined, efficient way. Sinatra's
orders simply came from another master.

World War II

With some exceptions the World War II heroes of films made in
1948-1962 are much like their Cold War or Korean War contemporaries.
In general they possessed the same distinguishing characteristic as
the other heroes: a recently acquired or already held belief in
discipline as a prerequisite for an effective fighting force. However,
not all 1948-1962 heroes were soldiers first and personalities second.
With the emotional furor of World War II subsided, Hollywood started
to portray characters who were primarily concerned with non-war
activities in a war context.

The prime example of this category of characters was the lovers.
Whatever romances were depicted in 1939-1947 were secondary to the

war itself. During 1948-1962 the romances occur in war environments
without much emphasis on the war. Beginning in 1948 with Clark Gable
and Lana Turner in Homecoming, the romantics pair off: Burt Lancaster
and Deborah Kerr in From Here to Eternity (1953); William Holden and
Nancy Olsen in Force of Arms (1951); Kirk Douglas and Dany Robin in
Act of Love (1953); Robert Taylor and Dana Wynter in D-Day the Sixth
of June (1956); Frank Sinatra and Natalie Wood in Kings Go Forth (1958);
and Holden and Kerr in The Proud and the Profane (1956).

The romances of 1939-1947 frequently were terminated by the
death of the male. The partner could reconcile herself to it, however, as it was a death with purpose. Unsuccessful pairings of 1948-
1962 resulted from other than war deaths and could not be reconciled.

Another difference in romances of the two periods was in the
nature of the physical relationship. Following the Motion Picture
Code, the relationships of 1939-1947 were most of the time romanticized
hand holding. In 1948-1962 the kissing was more passionate, and in
almost all cases it was implied that the couple slept together. There
was no particular effort to depict the sexuality (which was still in
violation of the code) but neither to avoid the suggestion that they
might climb into the same bed.

Changes were evident in the comedy characters of 1948-1962.
Traditional service comics transferred to the Cold War, and their
replacements were more aptly described as comedy actors rather than
comics. The most prolific comedy actor was Glenn Ford, who appeared
in Don't Go Near the Water (1957), Imitation General (1958), and
Teahouse of the August Moon (1956). His performances normally do not
evoke side-splitting laughter but rather chuckles and usually with him

rather than at him.

The same generalization applies to Jack Lemon in The Wackiest Ship in the Army (1961), based on an actual incident in which a naval officer has to teach soldiers to operate a sailing sloop in one week. In On the Double (1961) Danny Kaye slips comedy into an important espionage task.

Among the characters primarily concerned with the war, positive depictions were many and negative few. Some began with personal defects but the war corrected them. Van Johnson in Go for Broke (1951) and Robert Wagner in Between Heaven and Hell (1956) are bigots who learn to appreciate the value of the individual regardless of outward appearances.

On the other hand, in Attack (1956) Eddie Albert plays a complete coward whose indecision causes the death of more than a few men. Tough sergeant Jack Palance warns him, "If you play the gutless wonder, just one more time, I'll get you."[2] He does; Palance does; and his demise is not unrewarding.

The contaminating violence of war condemned Jimmy Stewart in The Mountain Road (1960). An engineer assigned to a demolition team fleeing across China just in front of the Japanese, Stewart in vengeance slaughters a group of Chinese bandits--reacting emotionally to the murder of some of his men. The act is enough to drive away his lover, the widow of a Chinese general.

Steve McQueen in The War Lover (1962) provides an insight into

[2]Quoted in Philip T. Hartung, "Yellow Golden Glorious," Commonweal, Oct. 5, 1956, p. 16.

a reckless, smart alecky pilot who thrives on war. He cares for no
one or nothing except himself. War does not contaminate him. It only
accentuates his characteristics.

As always some of the heroes were virtuous, brave, brutal, and
brilliant. Audie Murphy, whose battlefield exploits were rivaled only
by Alvin York, specialized in these roles--since after all he was merely
playing himself. Rising from private to company commander while serving
in Company B, 15th Infantry Regiment, Third Division, 7th Army in North
Africa and Europe, Murphy killed 240 Germans and was decorated twenty-
five times. So he played the war hero, and when his own story was
dramatized who else would play the role (To Hell and Back, 1959)?

Similar parts were tried by James Garner in Darby's Rangers
(1958), John Derek in Thunderbirds (1953), and Edmond O'Brien in
Fighter Squadron (1948). They fell somewhat short of heroic status,
however, because they were in group situations. For a hero to be
really heroic he must be an individual. At the moment of his exploit
he is not a cog in a machine but self-sufficient. In an era in which
war was depicted as a group project it was difficult to provide a setting
in which the soldier could achieve his individualism.

Thus, Hollywood lifted the military man from his conventional
surroundings. During 1948-1962 such an action normally abandoned the
hero in the Philippines just in front of the invading Japanese. Then,
as liaison between Filipino guerrillas and the United States, he possessed some degree of independence as well as responsibility. This
brand of hero popped up many times--Audie Murphy in Battle at Bloody
Beach (1961), Tyrone Power in American Guerrilla in the Philippines
(1950), George Montgomery in The Steel Claw (1961), Jeffrey Hunter in

No Man Is an Island (1962), and Keith Andes in Surrender Hell (1959).
Providing the proper environment for a hero was not the only reason
for using the Philippines as a locale. The Philippine government
encouraged American companies to make movies in that country with
congenial financial arrangements.

Characterizing 1948-1962's World War II professional is facilitated by John Wayne. He is the premier professional against whom all
others are judged. Of course, his current image is so associated with
the military and conservative America that it is not always easy to
distinguish the screen character from the real man. Wayne provides
examples of three kinds of professionals during 1948-1962. He appeared
in four films: The Wings of Eagles (1957) in which he portrays a
famous military leader; Operation Pacific (1951) in which a combat
decision is misinterpreted; and Sands of Iwo Jima (1949) and Flying
Leathernecks (1951) in which he gives lessons in the disciplined
approach to war.

In The Wings . . . Wayne gives an honest but sympathetic portrayal
of Admiral Frank (Spec) Wead, focusing on his personal problems--a neglected wife and paralysis--as well as his career. Other leaders
received rather unqualified praise: General K. C. Dennis portrayed
in Command Decision (1949); Admiral John M. Hoskins in The Eternal Sea
(1955); Admiral William F. Halsey in The Gallant Hours (1960); and
General Frank Merrill in Merrill's Marauders (1962). Sterling Hayden
as Hoskins overcomes the loss of a leg and traditional Pentagon
resistance to place jets on carriers. Jeff Chandler as Merrill and
James Cagney as Halsey are somber professionals attacking their appointed tasks with dedication and single-mindedness.

Walter Pidgeon as Dennis provides a keen insight into the attitude of the screen's professional warrior toward his job. Commanding
Europe's air war, Dennis is intensely irritated by criticism from
politicians and the press. The film persistently argues that civilians
should leave war to those trained for it and that restraints they might
try to impose on professionals only delay victory.

Propaganda against civilian interference in the decisions of
war was infrequent, perhaps because few films dealt with admirals,
generals, or battle strategy. However, the arguments directed against
civilian recruits about the necessity of discipline were innumerable.
Wayne provided two such arguments in Sands . . . and Flying . . . .

In Sands . . . he is a Marine sergeant, known for his drinking
sprees brought on by his wife's divorce and no letters from his son.
His life is complicated by the son of a former commanding officer who
wants nothing to do with the service. In Flying . . . the problem is
created by a second-in-command who would rather make friends than
decisions. In both cases Wayne finally wins his point that discipline
and cold decisions are more effective tools than are friendship and
fathering.

One of the earliest advocacies of discipline was made by Alan
Ladd in Beyond Glory (1948). He plays an average West Point cadet
charged with malicious treatment of a plebe. To complicate matters
Ladd believes that his own cowardice in battle cost the life of a
friend and commanding officer.

He is acquitted as well as discovering he was not a coward.
Sprinkled through the film are Ladd's remarks about West Point as the
"bulwark of democracy" and the necessity for a standing army. Ladd

says, "I saw and so did you what happens to countries without competent armies," and to have a competent army requires discipline and toughness.

Van Heflin molds a mixture of American youth (an All American football player, a Navajo, a white from the slums, a farmer, a bookworm, a lumber jack, and a practical joker) into a model Marine unit in Battle Cry (1955). His philosophy of training is revealed by this statement: "I don't want one of my men to die because he's a straggler."

Heflin dies during an invasion, a typical ending. Not so typical were the fates of Gregory Peck in 12 O'Clock High (1949) and David Brian in Breakthrough (1950). They suffered emotional disturbances caused by constant decisions sending men into battle and death. Breakthrough follows John Agar's evolution from a naive OCS product into a cooly efficient battlefield commander while at the same time it depicts Brian's gradual deterioration.

These characters seemed to be the only ones who felt the weight of command. Note that they appeared early in 1948-1962 before the impact of the Cold War and the Korean War had elevated the military to peak influence.

Status as a career officer did not imply mindlessness. The heroes of 1948-1962 sometimes broke the letter of orders but always stayed within the intent. Hellcats of the Navy (1957) in the person of submarine commander Ronald Reagan established that it was possible that orders did not always cover everything. Faced with orders to avoid action but also with the possibility of sinking a good portion of the tonnage of Japanese shipping, Reagan chooses the latter over the objection of his second-in-command. "Orders don't say anything about a situation like this and we can't call for new ones," Leslie explains.

A twist to professionals' difficulties was added by extra-military influences. In Operation Pacific (1951), Wayne orders his sub to dive during an emergency, a decision that abandons an officer in the sea. The victim just happened to be a rival for Wayne's former wife. (Three of Wayne's screen marriages during 1948-1962 break up because of his incessant devotion to duty.) The misconception is ultimately clarified but hinders Wayne's pursuit of duty throughout the picture.

In Torpedo Run (1958) Glenn Ford's problem is guilt and revenge. His sub fires a torpedo at a Japanese carrier, which uses a prison ship for a shield. The torpedo sinks the prison ship. Ford's wife and child happened to be on the ship, and he is preoccupied with revenge for the rest of the film.

Finally, Richard Widmark's battle performance is hampered by migraines and drugs. A former high school teacher who has adopted the professional warrior's fighting method, Widmark has one fault: fear of battle. Fear causes migraines which he in turn tries to cure with drugs to which he becomes addicted. Carrying the burdens of supposed cowardness and addiction, he nevertheless performs efficiently and effectively before death. His method is professional even if his attitude is not.

Summary

In one word the war heroes of films produced in 1948-1962 can be described as "professionals." Civilians are sprinkled among the heroes, but in general the Americans are soldiers or spies who are aptly labeled professional warriors, which implies an underlying devo-

tion to duty and an unqualified subscription to a disciplined, unemo-

tional approach to warfare.

CHAPTER VI

THE INDULGENCE OF SELF

At first, epitomizing the major American characters of 1963-1970
seemed no easy task. The heroes of this era appeared more varied, apparently lacking a unifying element of the preceding periods: professionalism in 1948-1962 and social responsibility in 1939-1947. The
variety exists, perhaps typifying the time—a period when the nation
and the movie industry twisted, stretched, and even fragmented under
pressures from external and internal sources. However, what the heroes
of 1963-1970 lacked was not a unifying element, but rather a devotion
to national or military purposes. They were held together not by a
cause but by the pursuit of the pleasures of self.

A small shift in percentages among the primary goals of the
characters reflects the concern with self. As Table 19 shows, the
dominant goals of 1963-1970's heroes were war tasks (35.9 per cent)
and patriotism (11.5 per cent), not greatly different from those of
1948-1962 (32.4 per cent and 12.6 per cent). The difference lies in
the pursuit of some of the less prevalent goals. In 1963-1970 the
percentage of Americans primarily concerned with self-oriented goals
(safety, material success, comfort, and fame) jumped from 9.8 per cent
in 1948-1962 to 21.8 per cent. The heroes still pursued war tasks
foremost but without the inclination to forego pleasure that marked
earlier Americans.

The heroes of 1963-1970 differ in three other ways from those
of the Red Scare: methods, love life, and degree of success in pursuit
of goals.

TABLE 19

PRIMARY GOALS OF AMERICANS, 1963-1970

Primary Goal	WWII	Cold	Korea	Vietnam	Total
Safety	6.0%	- %	20.0%	- %	5.1%
Escape law	2.0	-	-	-	1.3
Health	-	-	-	-	-
Individualism	-	-	-	-	-
Money	4.0	4.8	20.0	-	5.1
Comfort	8.0	-	-	-	5.1
Power	2.0	-	-	-	1.3
Adventure	4.0	-	-	-	2.6
Love	6.0	9.5	-	-	6.4
Family	2.0	-	-	-	1.3
Sex	-	-	-	-	-
War task	36.0	38.1	20.0	50.0	35.9
Fame	6.0	4.8	20.0	-	6.4
Patriotism	8.0	19.0	-	50.0	11.5
Justice	4.0	9.5	-	-	5.1
Truth	4.0	-	-	-	2.6
Revenge	4.0	-	-	-	2.6
Honesty	-	-	20.0	-	1.3
No answer	4.0	14.3	-	-	6.4
Total	100.0	100.0	100.0	100.0	100.0
Number	50	21	5	2	78

[a]Data derived from question 25 Form B in Appendix I.

Force was the primary means of American characters in each of the three eras. Dependency on force increased over time from 17.9 per cent in 1939-1947 to 28.7 per cent in 1948-1962 (the consequence of emphasis on professional warriors) to 38.4 per cent in 1963-1970 (tied to an overall trend of motion pictures to emphasize violence for its sheer adventure). Thus, like goals, little change occurred among American heroes in their dominant methods.

The major change took place in the emphasis given hard work. The drop was from 19.3 per cent of 1948-1962's characters using hard work, or perserverence, to 6.4 per cent in 1963-1970. Perserverence implies pursuit of long range goals rather than the pleasures of the moment, thus losing prominence as short range objectives became more dominant. (See Table 20.)

TABLE 20

AMERICANS' PRIMARY METHODS, 1963-1970

Primary Method	WWII	Cold	Korea	Vietnam	Total
Hard work	10.0%	- %	- %	- %	6.4%
Luck	10.0	-	-	-	6.4
Trickery	18.0	4.8	40.0	-	15.4
Knowledge	16.0	33.3	-	-	19.2
Charm	6.0	4.8	-	-	5.1
Force	30.0	42.9	40.0	100.0	35.9
Persuasion	6.0	-	20.0	-	5.1
No answer	4.0	14.3	-	-	6.4
Total	100.0	100.0	100.0	100.0	100.0
Number	50	21	5	2	78

[a]Data derived from question 29 Form B in Appendix I.

The romantic life of the 1963-1970 American was primarily the pursuit of immediate pleasures. From hand-holding, love-and-marriage romances of 1939-1947 the characters moved to temporary, love-and-implied-sex affairs in 1948-1962. The latter romances were short lived but at least temporarily involved the hero emotionally. The romantic trend during 1963-1970 was toward physical involvement without emotional implications. While no single result of the content analysis directly reflect the emotional detachment, a couple imply it. For example, fewer characters in 1963-1970 pursued love as a primary goal than in 1948-1962 (6.4 per cent compared to 16.0 per cent).

Secondly, fewer romances lasted. Only 51.5 per cent of the romances continued either in or out of marriage beyond the end of stories in 1963-1970 in contrast with 70.1 per cent during the previous era (Table 21).

TABLE 21

AMERICANS' ROMANTIC OUTCOMES, 1939-1970

Outcome	1939-1947	1948-1962	1963-1970	Total
Marriage	32.0%	23.8%	2.8%	25.0%
Romance continues	9.4	12.7	-	10.0
Willing breakup	2.9	2.5	4.3	2.9
Unwilling breakup	9.7	6.6	2.8	7.6
Uncertain	2.9	2.5	8.2	3.4
No answer	43.2	52.0	82.2	51.6
Total	100.0	100.0	100.0	100.0
Number	278	127	73	595

[a]Data derived from question 36 Form B in Appendix I.

The final major difference between the 1963-1970 hero and his immediate predecessor was his degree of success. In 1963-1970 some 64.4 per cent of the Americans achieved their goals, down from 80.7 per cent in 1948-1962. In no way should the American hero be described as an abject failure, but the movement away from success says something about the war films of 1963-1970 (Table 22). In 1939-1947 the characters exhibited some amount of optimism that ultimately peace and happiness would be achieved. This feeling was succeeded by a faith in professionalism as the way to save the nation from destruction. The final group has no confidence that security can be maintained; all that can be done is to meet and survive each emergency, if, indeed, even that is possible. In such a situation, it will be noted later, the hero has two choices if he is to survive: stay and fight using whatever means available or run.

TABLE 22

SUCCESS OF AMERICANS, 1963-1970

Success	WWII	Cold	Korea	Vietnam	Total
Lives, succeeds	58.0%	47.6%	60.0%	100.0%	56.4%
Lives, fails	2.0	19.0	–	–	6.4
Dies, succeeds	12.0	4.8	–	–	9.0
Dies, fails	–	–	20.0	–	1.3
Uncertain	28.0	28.6	20.0	–	26.9
Total	100.0	100.0	100.0	100.0	100.0
Number	50	21	5	2	78

[a]Data derived from question 31 Form B in Appendix I.

Demographically, the 1963-1970 hero was practically the same as the 1948-1962 character (Table 23). The distribution of roles (Table 24) was quite similar as well (spies 10.0 per cent soldiers 66.7 per cent, and civilians 15.4 per cent compared to 12.3 per cent, 72.5 per cent, and 14.4 per cent respectively in 1948-1962). Principal occupations were still soldiering (25.6 per cent) and spying (10.3 per cent) (Table 25).

Military membership declined to 69.2 per cent in 1963-1970 after reaching 76.2 per cent in 1948-1962. Interestingly, the enlisted man practically disappeared, dropping to 3.8 per cent from 19.5 per cent (Table 26).

The distinguishing characteristic of the 1963-1970 American hero,

TABLE 23

DEMOGRAPHICS OF AMERICAN HEROES, 1963-1970

	WWII	Cold	Korea	Vietnam	Total
Sex					
Male	98.0%	95.2%	100.0%	100.0%	97.4%
Female	2.0	4.8	-	-	-
Total	100.0	100.0	100.0	100.0	100.0
Age					
Youth	-	-	-	-	-
Young adult	4.0	-	-	-	-
Mature adult	78.0	90.5	100.0	100.0	83.3
Middle age	2.0	9.5	-	-	3.8
Old age	-	-	-	-	-
No answer	16.0	-	-	-	10.3
Total	100.0	100.0	100.0	100.0	100.0
Class					
Upper	12.0	38.1	20.0	-	19.2
Middle	10.0	14.3	20.0	-	11.5
Lower	10.0	-	40.0	-	9.0
Outside structure	44.0	33.3	20.0	100.0	41.0
No answer	24.0	14.3	-	-	19.2
Total	100.0	100.0	100.0	100.0	100.0
Marital Status					
Married	10.0	14.3	80.0	-	15.4
Never married	36.0	28.6	-	100.0	33.3
Divorced	4.0	9.5	-	-	5.1
Other	-	-	-	-	-
No answer	50.0	47.6	20.0	-	46.2
Total	100.0	100.0	100.0	100.0	100.0
Education					
In school	-	-	-	-	-
High school	8.0	-	40.0	100.0	10.3
Undergraduate	20.0	33.3	-	-	21.8
Higher degree	2.0	14.3	20.0	-	6.4
Other	2.0	-	-	-	1.3
No answer	68.0	52.4	40.0	-	60.3
Total	100.0	100.0	100.0	100.0	100.0
Number	50	21	5	2	78

[a]Data derived from questions 2-6 Form B in Appendix I.

TABLE 24

ROLES OF AMERICAN CHARACTERS, 1948-1972

Role	WWII	Cold	Korea	Vietnam	Total
Spy	10.0%	42.9%	- %	- %	17.9%
Soldier	78.0	28.6	100.0	100.0	66.7
Civilian	12.0	28.6	-	-	15.4
Total	100.0	100.0	100.0	100.0	100.0
Number	50	21	5	2	78

[a]Data derived from question 1 Form B in Appendix I.

TABLE 25

AMERICAN OCCUPATIONS, 1963-1970

Occupation	WWII	Cold	Korea	Vietnam	Total
Military	20.0%	23.9%	60.0%	100.0%	25.6%
Spy	4.0	28.6	-	-	10.3
Artist	4.0	4.8	-	-	3.8
Criminal	6.0	-	-	-	3.8
Journalist	2.0	9.5	-	-	3.8
Self sufficient	2.0	9.5	-	-	3.8
Medical	2.0	-	20.0	-	2.6
Teacher	-	9.5	-	-	2.6
Adventurer	2.0	-	-	-	1.3
Politician	-	4.8	-	-	1.3
Seaman	2.0	-	-	-	1.3
Other non-military	14.0	-	20.0	-	10.3
No answer	42.0	9.5	-	-	28.2
Total	100.0	100.0	100.0	100.0	100.0
Number	50	21	5	2	78

[a]Data derived from question 7 Form B in Appendix I.

TABLE 26

AMERICAN MILITARY CHARACTERISTICS, 1963-1970

	WWII	Cold	Korea	Vietnam	Total
Military Status					
Member	82.0%	28.6%	100.0%	100.0%	69.2%
Former member	2.0	23.8	-	-	7.7
Never member	10.0	9.5	-	-	9.0
No answer	6.0	38.6	-	-	14.1
Total	100.0	100.0	100.0	100.0	100.0
Branch					
Army	50.0	9.5	100.0	50.0	42.3
Navy	12.0	14.3	-	-	11.5
Air Force	8.0	9.5	-	-	7.7
Marines	12.0	-	-	50.0	9.0
Coast Guard	-	-	-	-	-
Other	-	-	-	-	-
No answer	18.0	57.1	-	-	28.2
Total	100.0	100.0	100.0	100.0	100.0
Rank					
Gen.-Adm.	4.0	4.8	-	-	3.8
Col.-Capt.	18.0	9.5	-	50.0	15.4
Maj.-Cmdr.	6.0	4.8	-	50.0	6.4
Capt.-Lt.	24.0	-	20.0	-	16.7
Lt.-Ens.	12.0	-	-	-	7.7
Sgt.-CPO	10.0	4.8	80.0	-	12.8
Non com	4.0	-	-	-	2.6
Enlisted	6.0	-	-	-	3.8
Other	-	-	-	-	-
No answer	16.0	76.2	-	-	30.8
Total	100.0	100.0	100.0	100.0	100.0
Membership Reason					
Career	14.0	14.3	20.0	100.0	16.7
Draft	18.0	-	40.0	-	14.1
Patriotism	2.0	-	-	-	1.3
Personal	-	4.8	-	-	1.3
Other	-	-	-	-	-
No answer	66.0	81.0	40.0	-	66.7
Total	100.0	100.0	100.0	-	100.0
Number	50	21	5	2	78

[a]Data derived from questions 15, 16, 18, and 20 Form B in Appendix I.

thus, is his pursuit of immediate, self-oriented goals sometimes in addition to and sometimes instead of his war task. The following discussion focuses on that distinction.

Vietnam War

The two heroes of the Vietnam War films resemble professional warriors of 1948-1962, but John Wayne pursued his tasks with more sophisticated gimickry and more brutality.

In A Yank in Vietnam (1964) Marshall Thompson possesses the undistinguished personality of the professional warrior of 1948-1962. However, he finds time for a love affair in the middle of the fighting. Incidentally, the film reveals that the Vietnamese welcome Americans as allies.

Wayne and The Green Berets (1968) combine sex, violence, and helicopters to kidnap an important North Vietnamese general and strike a propaganda blow for the American effort in Southeast Asia. Wayne submits a number of times that civilians should leave the war to a military trained for such endeavors.

Korean War

Two of the five Korean War heroes of films made in 1963-1970 deviated from traditional characterizations. The other three were fairly standard portrayals: Lee Marvin trying to prove he did not commit treason in Sergeant Ryker (1968); Rory Calhoun leading his platoon from behind enemy lines in The Young and the Brave (1963); and Tony Russell uncovering a supposed hero who falsified a report and murdered his commanding officer in War Is Hell (1964).

In The Hook (1963) Kirk Douglas plays a career non-com just a few months away from twenty years and retirement. He always follows orders to the letter--until he is told to kill a North Korean prisoner. He wants to, but, first, his companions stop him and then he cannot pull the trigger. Convinced of his failure as a soldier, Douglas is ready to turn himself in and accept the loss of rank and pension.

However, his experiences when the prisoner escapes and is finally killed change his mind. The North Korean was the enemy, but even he could not kill Douglas at a critical moment. The hesitation costs his life and made Douglas realize that his own failure may have been motivated by human concern not human frailty.

Donald Sutherland is anything but a career soldier in M*A*S*H (1970). He manages to ignore and violate the conventions that govern a professional warrior's behavior. He is merely a doctor serving where he does not wish. But he does serve--although with somewhat less reverence than is expected from a normal screen doctor. Psychologically removing himself from the war and its consequences, Sutherland methodically makes his way to surgery, saving what lives he can but emotionally forgetting the many he cannot save. Away from the job, there is no talk of the war, its issues, and its battles.

Cold War

The Cold War film hero of 1963-1970 differed from his 1948-1962 predecessor in two ways. First, the civilian traded his helplessness for a mixture of attributes, punctuated by exposure to professional training. Second, some of the professionals lacked the dedication of their predecessors. They performed the immediate task but attention to duty was somewhat less than single minded.

In The Ugly American (1963) Marlon Brando is one civilian who is rather helpless, but his plight is not exactly sympathetic. His problems are entirely his own making. A famous journalist appointed ambassador to Sarkhan in Southeast Asia, Brando almost wrecks American diplomatic efforts in that country. Not the least of his sins is a shouting match with a former friend who is the opposition leader in Sarkhan. "You are a Judas goat," he tells his friend, "leading your country down the path to destruction."

To a large degree his actions are meant to be a demand for professionalism in the diplomatic corps. However, they likewise serve to demonstrate the foolishness of blind patriotism in a modern world. Patriotism is an anachronism. It does not guarantee Brando's success and in fact hinders his well intentioned pursuit.

Another civilian, lacking Brando's chauvinism, was somewhat more successful. In The Seventh Dawn (1964) William Holden has rejected all nationalistic ties. A plantation owner in Malaya, he condemns both Communist guerrillas and British and only becomes involved in the conflict when the stupidity and stubborness of both sides threatens the woman he loves. He fails and retires once again to neutrality.

Paul Newman in The Prize (1964) and Torn Curtain (1966) definitely was not neutral. In Torn Curtain he feigned defection in order to trick a formula out of an East German physicist, while in The Prize he stops a Communist plot to turn the Nobel prize ceremonies into a propaganda coup. The 1966 production would be worthy of the Red Scare era except for one thing. The characters are good and evil,

and one is sure which is which. However, the film makes no explicit
try at explaining the ideological differences.

As Andrew Craig in The Prize Newman fits the James Bond mold
although he is not the strong man other spy spoofers were. His kinship
is in not allowing his unofficial efforts to stop the Communists to
interfere with pleasure--Elke Sommer in this case.

Not all agents were pleasure seekers. Exceptions included
Howard Duff as a sort of middle-age reincarnation of Frank Lovejoy in
Panic in the City (1968) and Dan Duryea as a peace messenger in Bamboo
Saucer (1968). Many agents, though, were quite adept at mixing sex
and spying.

One of the most adept was Dean Martin as Matt Helm confronting
Chinese agent Victor Bruno in The Silencers (1966). Martin has all
the physical and technological necessities: a gigantic round bed, a
television communicators, a bed that dumps him into a pool, a pistol
that shoots to the rear, a coat button that can blow up the Bank of
England, and a covey of beauties whenever he needs them. His philosophy
is strictly utilitarian. Do the job as quickly as possible with the
least pain and the most pleasure.

Martin's primary means are physical force and technological
gimmickry, a characteristic shared in varying degrees with Blair
Robertson in Agent for H.A.R.M. (1966) and Troy Donahue in Come Spy
with Me (1967). Ultimate dependency on technology belongs to Gregory
Peck in The Chairman (1969). A college professor, Peck is recruited
to return to China, where he had studied before the Communist takeover,
to prevent the Chinese from claiming an enzyme formula critical to
world agriculture. Along the way to success he shoots his way out

of imprisonment and plays table tennis with Mao.

His success is determined solely by his own exploits, but he is more subject to the control of technology than any other agent. Implanted in his brain is a tiny explosive controlled by supervisors in England. Failure on his part to obtain the formula and escape China means death, a fate he avoids by a fraction of a second as he reaches the Russian border just in time.

Technology and professionals continued to play a role in the lives of Cold War soldiers during 1963-1970 but with some radical departures from the 1948-1962 script. Rock Hudson as an Air Force colonel in A Gathering of Eagles (1963) is a fairly standard character from the Red Scare era. He is assigned to firm up a SAC installation that has failed to maintain the fine edge required for Cold War readiness. Nothing interferes with the assignment, not even the bitter criticism of an old friend or threatened loss of his wife. Eventually, of course, he is vindicated.

Hudson displays similar professional dedication in Ice Station Zebra (1968) but without results. He is a submarine commander trying to reach the site of an Arctic expedition before the Russians, an assignment he pursues in strictly professional terms. There, though, his similarity to the Air Force colonel ends.

In Ice . . . the primary obstacles are not the lethargy or unprofessional attitudes of his compatriots as in the Air Force picture. The hindrances are nature and an unknown Russian agent. Unlike in 1948-1962 Hudson's professional, disciplined approach to the task does not guarantee success. The best that can be attained is stalemate. Neither East nor West recovers an important camera and both sulk off to confront each other again.

Other characterizations were not as kind to professional warriors. In Dr. Strangelove (1964) and Fail Safe (1964) the military, if not the complete villain, is portrayed as at least a major contributor to the dire circumstances in which the United States finds itself--i.e. with mistakes launching bombers toward the Soviet Union. Richard Widmark played the villain's role in The Bedford Incident (1965). His calm, disciplined approach to war would have been worthy of praise in 1948-1962 but seemed almost sadistic in 1963-1970.

So does Burt Lancaster as Chief of Staff in Seven Days in May (1964). He is a general with too much stature in right-wing circles and has decided to take over the United States government to stop it from signing a nuclear weapons treaty.

"I think signing of the nuclear pact with the Soviet Union is naive," Lancaster comments, "That piece of paper will substitute for missile sites, and, of course, every twenty years or so we have to pay for our mistakes." To avoid the next payment Lancaster is willing to void the treaty and become dictator. He will destroy the democratic process to preserve security.

In every way Lancaster is the perfect professional--of ten years earlier. He has dedication, patriotism, and conviction that a strong military is the only solution to peace. His statement would have been applauded in 1948-1962 but seems archaic in 1963-1970.

World War II

The Americans of World War II films made in 1963-1970 possessed a variety of characteristics. Among their number were converts to social responsibility and professionals of earlier times as well as the dominant 1963-1970 self-oriented characters.

The few civilians who found themselves in war zones during 1963-1970 might just as well have been left out, judged on their over-all quality. Orchestra leader Charlton Heston in Counterpoint (1967) and adventurer Dennis Weaver in Mission Batangas (1968) underwent minor conversions, drawing Heston away from his artistry and Weaver away from making a fast buck. Hermit Cary Grant experienced a similar but comical transformation in Father Goose (1964), while Van Heflin in Cry of Battle (1963) and Ursula Andress in Once Before I Die (1966) mixed a liberal portion of violence and sex in a war context.

Espionage heroes included Jan Murray in A Man Called Dagger (1967) and Robert Goulet in I Deal in Danger (1966) with nothing dis-tinguishing either except Goulet's possession of gadgetry in advance of its time.

A few standard service comics were portrayed during 1963-1970, e.g. Bob Hope in The Private Navy of Sergeant O'Farrell (1968) and Ernest Borgnine and Tim Conway in McHale's Navy (1964) and McHale's Navy Joins the Air Force (1965). Although the 1963-1970 comics' goof-off ability matched any of their predecessors, one important difference was that the recent characters got away with goofing off. McHale's gang especially did not through some miraculous transformation become ideal, disciplined sailors at the conclusion of their films. In the beginning and at the end they were concerned primarily with comfort and relaxation but soldiering only when absolutely necessary.

Among the fighting men of 1963-1970 were counted a few who experienced conversions to social responsibility. In The Longest

<u>Hundred Miles</u> (1968) Doug McClure escapes a Japanese prison camp in the Philippines with only one objective: leave the islands. Along his escape route, however, he picks up a priest, a busload of children, a lover, and a social conscience. Chad Everitt's had to relearn responsibility in <u>First to Fight</u> (1967). A Marine hero, he freezes in the first battle after marriage and must be shown that he is selfishly interested only in security before he can recover his military productivity.

The practice of lifting the soldier from his military environment and placing him in situations unrestricted enough to allow individual heroism continued during 1963-1970. The Philippines remained a popular locale as Hugh O'Brien and Mickey Rooney attack a Japanese radio center to prevent MacArthur's invasion plans from being released in <u>Ambush Bay</u> (1966), John Saxon and Filipino guerrillas storm a convent to protect the islands' gold in <u>The Ravagers</u> (1965), and Michael Parsons leads Filipinos in battle against the Japanese in <u>The Raiders of Leyte Gulf</u> (1963). In Italy Larry Mann and Rock Hudson play behind-enemy-lines roles in <u>The Quick and the Dead</u> (1963) and <u>Hornet's Nest</u> (1970).

Away from individual heroics John Wayne again managed to portray the peak of professionalism, this time in <u>In Harm's Way</u> (1965). And, as usual, his performance of duty would be hindered by family problems if he were not too much of a professional to allow it. A Navy captain stuck at a desk after Pearl Harbor, Wayne has a son who thinks he abandoned his mother, when in actuality the mother divorced Wayne because of his military career. All ends right, though. The son dies a hero, loving his father, and Wayne finds a Navy wife and admiral's stars.

The professional of professionals could have been George C. Scott in Patton (1970). Scott, as Patton though, was not the normal screen professional. His profession was war not merely soldiering. As was indicated when surveying the results of a blood battle, he admitted, "Oh God, I love it."

Scott's war is not neat and orderly. It is a mad dash toward the enemy. It is not teamwork in which everyone contributes and in turn shares in the glory. Honor belongs only to Scott. Scott is a professional but not one who subjugates self for country. "I want you to remember that no bastard ever won a war by dying for his country. He won by making the other poor dumb bastard die for his country."

As Scott admits during the film, he belongs to another era when war was not quite so devastating and was a field of honor where men achieved manhood. In his dashing and glamor Scott resembles Cliff Robertson as John F. Kennedy in PT 109 (1963), but Robertson's motives were purely patriotic. Scott sought personal recognition and praise before anything else. In that regard Scott differed only slightly from many of 1963-1970's antiheroes who sought not praise but self preservation.

In The Dirty Dozen (1967) Lee Marvin and a band of convicts display a brutal style of warfare while completing a commando mission of extreme importance. The convicts' motives, though, are something less than altruistic. They are promised pardons from death sentences upon completion of the mission.

Marvin is not exactly the typical professional warrior either.

He makes no effort to obey rules or convince his men of the necessity of discipline. Indeed, the mission does not call for discipline or patience. What is required is cold-blooded ruthlessness.

Cliff Robertson leads a similar group of misfits in The Devil's Brigade (1968) although they are slightly more respectable than Marvin's gang. This true story featured a bunch of Americans too rebellious to fit into the regular Army but too brutal to be excluded from the war.

Even the German prison camps failed to tame rowdy Americans in The Great Escape (1963) and Von Ryan's Express (1965). The Germans tried in The Great Escape to "put all (their) rotten eggs in one basket, then watch this basket carefully."[1] It did not work as McQueen leads a partially successful mass escape. Sinatra has more success but shows a quality quite uncharacteristic of past American heroes. He shoots a woman in cold blood--a traitor to be sure but nevertheless in cold blood. She was a threat to the escape.

Ordinarily, the antiheroes were too insensitive to feel emotional consequences of their own brutality or of war in general. Besides, their acts could be rationalized as necessary to their own self preservation. In addition the films apparently were never intended to explore the corruptive nature of war. They were produced to exploit the vicarious adventure of action and violence.

The contaminated nature of war was personalized in two contrasting officers, Cornel Wilde in Beach Red (1967) and George Montgomery in Warkill (1968). Wilde is sensitized rather than narcotized to death and

---

[1]Quoted in Variety, April 17, 1963, p. 6.

suffering by his experiences. He dutifully leads his men into battle despite doubts of ultimate utility. His greatest torture, though, comes after the battle. "I'll have a lot of letters to write (to survivors) . . . I'd rather get shot, I think."[2]

Wilde contrasts sharply with his calloused sergeant Rip Torn, who philosophizes, "That's what we're here for--to kill--and the rest is all crap."[3] Montgomery would agree with Torn. A supposed noble hero, Montgomery is part sadist, part realist as he pursues his duty-- using hungry dogs and rats to flush out the Japanese and then shoots the helpless enemy. An idealistic reporter parachutes into the jungle to write a story about Montgomery and gradually recognizes that his hero has clay feet. However, accompanying this conclusion is his concurrence with Montgomery that battle is for survival and one uses whatever means available in order to survive.

To one degree or another the heroes just mentioned did not show the disregard for self that marked the socially responsible character or the professional warrior. The self-oriented heroes were typified by Keir Duliea's assertion in The Thin Red Line (1964). "Everybody's gonna get killed except me because I'm gonna be thinking of myself."[4] However, these brutal heroes continued to serve political purposes by fighting even though selfish motives may have been primary.

---

[2] Quoted in Variety, Aug. 2, 1967, p. 6.

[3] Quoted in ibid.

[4] Quoted in Film Facts, Dec. 4, 1964, p. 292.

Other characters managed to avoid political or military necessities. In Up from the Beach (1965) Cliff Robertson is an infantry
sergeant who wants to fight but finds himself herding French civilians
from the beach to their hometown. Gradually, he begins to see the war
in new terms--in terms of civilian victims, a congenial German officer,
and the immediacy of death. As an observer of combat rather than a
participant, Robertson comes to view war as more than an either-or
proposition.

Gregory Peck rejects military goals altogether as a maverick
psychiatrist in Captain Newman, M.D. (1964). He is solely concerned
for his patients and fights red tape and military stubbornness to keep
them out of combat as long as possible. His behavior violates military
principle, but as a doctor his primary responsibility is to his patients
not to the Air Force.

Outside of combat situations George Segal in King Rat (1965)
and Lee Marvin in Hell in the Pacific (1969) found that they did not
have to obey the conventions of war. Segal's behavior would have
offended the multitude of prisoner of war heroes who sought only to
escape the enemy. Segal enjoys the Japanese prison camp because the
situation gives him authority not enjoyed in the outside world.
Trained professionals in the camp, especially the British, cannot
forget that they are soldiers. Segal can and does, using bribery,
blackmail, and coercion to become king of the camp.

Marvin and a Japanese soldier are lost on an island in Hell . . . .
They cannot speak each other's language and are antagonistic at first.
However, they need each other, acquiring a respect for one another that
transcends the social convention of war.

Two final characters reject the aims of war altogether without redirecting their efforts toward nobler endeavors, without even un-intentionally aiding the military, and without being removed from the combat situation. Their rejection is willful and complete. Donald Sutherland and his group of thieves fight Germans in Kelly's Heroes (1970) but only to seize a cache of gold the Germans happen to control. In Catch 22 (1970) Alan Arkin finds no political or social significance in war. It is merely a personal threat to avoid by whatever means possible. War could be a matter of kill or be killed—as with the antiheroes—but for Arkin it is simply run or be killed.

Summary

The American war heroes of films produced in 1963-1970 included examples of the socially responsible character of 1939-1947 and the professional warrior of 1948-1962. However, the predominant hero of 1963-1970 was neither of these. His defining characteristic was lack of concern with or even rejection of political or moralistic righteous-ness of either side in warfare. Instead of striving for long range social or military goals, the 1963-1970 American sought immediate personal objectives: sex, money, status, and survival.

CONCLUSION

Hollywood's war hero had three separate identities during 1939–1970. In 1939–1947 when the United States was marked by governmental emphasis on a total war effort and by concern with internationalism, the screen's American was a socially responsible civilian. Frequently, his film experience included a conversion in which he discarded selfish individualism in the realization that his welfare was very much related to what happened to others.

The hero became a professional warrior in 1948–1962 with faith in a disciplined, sometimes technological approach to war. In Cold War films produced in the era the professional had a civilian companion snarled in a crisis he could not handle without the warrior's assistance. The appearance of the screen's professional warrior occurred at a time the military's status and influence were in ascendancy and Hollywood was anxious to pacify HUAC.

Finally, in 1963–1970 Hollywood's American hero rejected long range political, social, and military goals in favor of immediate personal considerations. The rejection manifested itself in a variety of ways. Sometimes it took the form of explicit criticism of Cold War military strategy (such as in 1964's Dr. Strangelove). More frequently the rejection was personified in the behavior of a particular hero—interruption of a mission for personal pleasure, completion of a dangerous assignment as payment for pardons of death sentences, fighting to survive, and fleeing to stay alive. The nonpolitical, non-nationalistic film hero was produced during a period in which American sentiment was examining Cold War assumptions and was split over the Vietnam War, Hollywood was relatively free of political pressure, and the American film industry had become internationalized.

PART THREE

ALLIES AND ENEMIES

INTRODUCTION

The character analysis shifts in this section to the United States' allies and enemies. While the preceding discussion examined the screen's image of Americans' war roles, the next three chapters will focus on the nature of the United States' international companions--as conveyed by Hollywood of course.

In contrast with American heroes the portrayal of allies and enemies sometimes presented problems for movie makers. With the beginning of the Cold War allies and enemies exchanged places. Thus, at the same time some screen wars had Germans and Japanese as enemies while others had them as allies. The ways in which Hollywood handled the changing national identities will be a focal point of the following three chapters. Another major concern will be Hollywood's view of the significance of other nationalities' war contributions.

CHAPTER VII

INTERNATIONALISM AMERICAN STYLE

Even when attention shifts to foreign characters it is difficult to escape Americanism. Of course few films of 1939-1947 did not
include Americans. A total of 81.2 per cent of the pictures of the
era featured Americans in dominant or subordinate roles (Table 27).
In fact only 23.7 per cent of 1939-1947's 405 war pictures had non-
Americans in dominant roles. This percentage might seem rather low
considering the government's urging that the war was an effort of
united nations. However, Hollywood was producing films primarily for
American audiences, and many of the pictures told home-front stories
that automatically excluded foreigners.

Frequently films without Americans had heroes with American
characteristics. Some nationalities did receive distinctive characterizations, but in general they were white Anglo-Saxons (even if the
nationality was not Anglo-Saxon) united in the pursuit of freedom and
democracy. On the other hand, the enemy sometimes had the appearance
of Americans but were usually depicted as totalitarians and barbarians.

Demographically, there were some minor differences between allies
and Americans. For example, fewer allies than Americans were soldiers
(Table 28); they were more likely from the upper class and less from
the middle; and they were more likely married (Table 29).

Both allies and Americans pursued the goal of patriotism foremost, the ally slightly more than the American (51.4 per cent to 40.6
per cent) (Table 30). Greater patriotism by the allies can be attributed to the fact that most were in countries already or about to be
captured by the Germans. Such a situation demanded attention to the

TABLE 27

NATIONALITY OF CHARACTERS, 1939-1947

Nationality	Dominant Roles	Subordinate Roles	Total Roles
American	76.3%	4.9%	81.2%
German--enemy	1.2	44.4	45.6
British	9.1	5.2	14.3
Japanese--enemy	0.5	12.8	13.3
French	2.7	0.8	3.5
Chinese	1.2	2.0	3.2
German--ally	2.5	-	2.5
Russian	1.2	0.8	2.0
Dutch	0.5	0.8	1.2
Norwegian	1.0	0.2	1.2
Czech	1.0	-	1.0
Canadian	0.7	-	0.7
Australian	0.2	0.2	0.5
Burmese	-	0.5	0.5
Filipino	-	0.5	0.5
Italian	-	0.5	0.5
Polish	0.5	-	0.5
Portuguese	-	0.5	0.5
Austrian	0.2	-	0.2
Belgian	-	0.2	0.2
Egyptian	-	0.2	0.2
Roumanian	-	0.2	0.2
Sudanese	-	0.2	0.2
Turk	-	0.2	0.2
Yugoslavian	0.2	-	0.2
Unknown	0.7	1.0	1.7
Total	100.0	76.5	176.5
Number	405	405	405

[a]Data derived from question 20 Form A in Appendix I.

TABLE 28

MILITARY CHARACTERISTICS OF ALLIES, ENEMIES, 1939-1947

	Ally	Enemy
Military Status		
Member	25.7%	56.3%
Former member	8.1	6.3
Never member	48.8	31.3
No answer	17.6	6.3
Total	100.0	100.0
Branch		
Army	16.2	31.3
Navy	1.3	6.3
Air Force	8.1	6.3
Other	1.3	6.3
No answer	73.0	50.0
Total	100.0	100.0
Rank		
Gen.-Adm.	-	-
Col.-Capt.	4.1	6.3
Maj.-Cmdr.	1.3	-
Capt.-Lt.	5.4	6.3
Lt.-Ens.	1.3	6.3
Sgt.-CPO	-	-
Non com	1.3	6.3
Enlisted	6.8	-
Other	-	6.3
No answer	64.9	56.3
Total	100.0	100.0
Membership Reason		
Career	4.1	12.5
Draft	4.1	6.3
Patriotism	6.8	18.8
Personal	1.4	-
Other	-	6.3
No answer	83.8	56.3
Total	100.0	100.0
Number	74	16

[a]Data derived from questions 15, 16, 18, and 20 Form B in Appendix I.

TABLE 29

DEMOGRAPHICS OF ALLIES, ENEMIES, 1939–1947

	Ally	Enemy
Sex		
Male	81.1%	87.5%
Female	18.9	12.5
Total	100.0	100.0
Age		
Youth	-	6.3
Young adult	5.4	12.5
Mature adult	63.5	37.5
Middle age	9.5	18.8
Old age	4.1	-
No answer	17.6	25.0
Total	100.0	100.0
Class		
Upper	29.7	56.3
Middle	25.7	6.3
Lower	10.8	-
Outside structure	22.9	25.0
No answer	10.8	12.5
Total	100.0	100.0
Marital Status		
Married	32.4	18.8
Never married	39.2	31.2
Divorced	-	-
Other	2.7	-
No answer	25.7	50.0
Total	100.0	100.0
Education		
In school	2.7	6.3
High school	17.6	12.5
Undergraduate	20.3	25.0
Higher degree	8.1	18.8
Other	-	-
No answer	51.4	31.3
Total	100.0	100.0

TABLE 29--Continued

	Ally	Enemy
:ionality		
itish	32.5%	- %
ench	9.5	-
:man	9.5	87.5
inese	8.1	-
ssian	6.8	-
ıadian	5.4	-
ech	5.4	-
rwegian	5.4	-
tch	2.7	-
stralian	1.4	-
strian	1.4	-
lish	1.4	-
goslavian	1.4	-
panese	-	6.3
thical	-	6.3
known	9.5	-
Total	100.0	100.0
:upation		
lf sufficient	9.5	-
dical	8.1	6.3
venturer	5.4	-
borer	5.4	-
acher	5.4	-
litary	4.1	16.7
w enforcement	4.1	-
y	4.1	6.3
iminal	2.7	-
gineer	2.7	6.3
tist	1.4	-
torney	1.4	-
tertainer	1.4	-
rmer	1.4	-
usewife	1.4	-
urnalist	1.4	-
litician	1.4	16.7
cretary	1.4	-
udent	1.4	6.3
sinessman	-	6.3
answer	36.5	31.3
Total	100.0	100.0
Number	74	16

[a]Data derived from questions 3-8 Form B in Appendix I.

TABLE 30

PRIMARY GOALS OF ALLIES, ENEMIES, 1939-1947

Primary Goal	Ally	Enemy
Safety	8.1%	6.3%
Escape law	-	6.3
Health	1.3	-
Individualism	1.3	-
Money	-	-
Comfort	1.3	-
Power	1.3	37.5
Adventure	-	-
Love	-	6.3
Family	5.4	-
Sex	-	-
War task	8.1	6.3
Fame	-	-
Patriotism	51.4	18.3
Justice	12.2	-
Truth	2.7	-
Revenge	12.5	1.3
Honesty	-	2.7
No answer	2.7	6.3
Total	100.0	100.0
Number	74	16

[a]Data derived from question 25 Form B in Appendix I.

war. The Americans were safe from invasion and could afford diversions.

Cast into a situation in which their country was occupied and their arms were confiscated, the screen's allies had to depend on means other than force to achieve their objectives. Hence, trickery was the primary means for 21.6 per cent of the allies with force trailing by just a little at 20.3 per cent (Table 31). Americans relied on trickery in 14.7 per cent of the cases.

At the opposite extreme the goals of the enemy in no way resemble those of allies and Americans. The Germans and Japanese (the Italians were never portrayed as major characters) sought power above all else (37.5 per cent compared to none of the Americans and 1.3 per cent of the allies) (Table 30). Force was the primary means to success. A

TABLE 31

PRIMARY METHODS OF ALLIES, ENEMIES, 1939-1947

imary Method	Ally	Enemy
rd work	14.9%	6.3%
ck	5.4	12.5
ickery	21.6	-
owledge	17.6	-
arm	9.5	6.3
rce	20.3	75.0
rsuasion	8.1	-
answer	2.7	-
Total	100.0	100.0
Number	74	16

[a]Data derived from question 29 Form B in Appendix I.

tal of 75.0 per cent of the enemy relied primarily on force compared

the allies' 20.3 per cent and the Americans' 17.9 per cent (Table 31).

Seldom did Hollywood portray the German people as the enemy in

39-1947. The enemy was the Nazis--militaristic leaders who forced

eir way of life on the Germans. Similarly, while the distinction

etween leaders and citizenry was not quite as sharp for the Japanese,

e leaders were military members. Thus, the enemy was more often

rtrayed in the role of soldiers than were allies and Americans (56.3

r cent compared to 21.6 per cent and 34.2 per cent respectively)

able 32).

Allies

Internationalism found increasing subscription in the nation

nd in Hollywood as the war unfolded. The screen's interpretation of

nternationalism emphasized similarities of Americans and allies,

pecifying the allies' desire for freedom and a brand of democracy

esembling that in the United States. Providing such portrayals was

TABLE 32

ROLES OF ALLIES, ENEMIES, 1939-1947

Role	Ally	Enemy
Spy	14.9%	6.3%
Soldier	21.6	56.3
Civilian	63.5	37.5
Total	100.0	100.0
Number	74	16

[a]Data derived from question 1 Form B in Appendix I.

not always easy (particularly for the Russians), but Hollywood managed to weave its way past minor nuisances.

Britain

Hollywood did not face an overly difficult task in finding similarities between Americans and British because of traditional links between the two countries. However, in the past Hollywood had focused on England's monarchy and aristocracy, ingredients hardly compatible with the screen's egalitarian interpretation of the war.[1] A number of war films sought to rechart the British character, or at least to re-interpret it, pointing out democratic and cultural similarity with Americans. Two pictures which did this best were Mrs. Miniver (1942) and This Above All (1942).

In This Above All Tyrone Power plays an English war hero who

---

[1]Siegfried Kracauer, "National Types as Hollywood Presents Them," in Mass Culture, ed. by Bernard Rosenberg and David Manning White (New York: The Free Press, 1957), pp. 257-277.

begins to doubt his country. A product of London slums, he wonders if a better England would not emerge from defeat. His doubt leads to desertion and romance with aristocratic Joan Fontaine. She and a country parson soothe Power's discontent and convince him that a Nazi England would be the worst of all worlds. He still does not accept England as it is, but "it's going to be a different world when this is over. But first we've got to win the war."[2]

Mrs. Miniver admits England's class differences but points out that war affects everyone alike. The Minivers, Walter Pidgeon and Greer Garson, are the typical middle class English family--complete to their large boat, second hand but expensive sports car, son at Oxford, and servants. Their only concern before the war is the good life and whether Dame May Whitty will accept their son as a husband for her niece.

The war changes things. The niece is killed; the Minivers' home is virtually destroyed; Mrs. Miniver captures a German flyer; her husband hauls soldiers from Dunkirk on his small boat; and the community and Dame Whitty draw closer together. In war all classes are one, or as the vicar reminds them it is a "people's war."

The RAF provided a convenient peg on which to hang a plot of cooperation between Americans and British. A Yank in the RAF (1941), International Squadron (1941), and Eagle Squadron (1942) exploited such themes. Most pictures contrasted the brash, overstated American

---

[2] Quoted in Philip T. Hartung, "To Thine Own Self Be True," Commonweal, June 5, 1942.

with the reserved, understated Englishman. The English reserve bothered some American heroes who mistook reserve for unconcern--e.g. Robert Stack in Eagle Squadron. He learns that the English are not unfeeling; they just do not express their emotions.

For example, Monty Woolley in The Pied Piper (1942) is a crusty, stubborn retiree whose behavior belies his words. Fishing in France at the time of the German invasion, he continually feigns distaste for children but nevertheless consents to deliver a pair of Americans to England and along the way picks up three others. "I am occasionally seized with the conviction that I am conveying guinea pigs," he complains, but his irritability is only superficial. Beneath his bellowing is something of a bleeding heart. In fact, he even accepts the niece of Gestapo colonel Otto Preminger as a member of his group.

Walter Pidgeon is one Englishman who in the beginning is genuinely aloof. In Man Hunt (1941) Pidgeon has Hitler in the sights of his high powered rifle but does not kill him. The rifle is not even loaded because the "sport is in the chase not the kill," according to the British aristocrat.[3]

The Nazis could not care less. They capture and torture Pidgeon, planning to use his prewar escapade as an excuse for an international incident. That Pidgeon did not intend to kill irritates Gestapo agent George Sanders. "You are decadent. We do not hesitate to destroy."[4]

Pidgeon escapes, and the hunter is the hunted through the rest of the film. He survives and discards his idealistic views. The last scene shows him parachuting into Germany with his high powered

---

[3]Quoted in Philip T. Hartung, "More War--Different Angle," Commonweal, Dec. 27, 1941, p. 449.

[4]Quoted in ibid.

ifle loaded this time.

Franchot Tone in The Hour Before Dawn (1944) and Wendy Barie
n Women in War (1940) also find they cannot remain aloof from the
vents that surround them. A sometimes promiscuous barmaid forced to
erve as a nurse, Barie's war experiences convert her from selfishness
o social responsibility. Tone is a perfectly respectable pacifist
ho kills his wife when he discovers she is a spy. The point of the
ilm was that violence is sometimes necessary, even for the pacifist.

Canadians

The few Canadians of 1939-1947 so resembled Americans that it
as difficult to differentiate the two. Randolph Scott was a typical
aval commander in Corvette K-225 (1943) and Errol Flynn was the dashing undercover agent in Northern Pursuit (1943). Then, Captains of
the Clouds (1942) featured James Cagney as the brash bush pilot interested only in a fast buck. Ultimately, he undergoes conversion to
social responsibility and sacrifices himself to save a convoy of
bombers on the way to England.

Nazi Europe

The nations of conquered Europe had common screen stories of
groups of patriots antagonizing and dealing moral defeats to their
conquerors. Their weapons were idealism and wit, their ideals American
in origin revolving around liberty and democracy, and their customs and
clothes all too frequently American.

This Land is Mine (1943) was typical of the partisan films.
Situated "somewhere in Europe," its characters had no accent and wore
American costumes. The plot had sniveling Charles Laughton propelled

into court for the murder of a "quisling," who actually committed
suicide.[5] Throughout the picture Laughton is timidity personified
but at the climax he meets the challenge. Quoting from The Rights
of Man, he tells the Nazis that chains cannot enslave and that death
is no defeat. A German commander overrules the jury's verdict of
innocent and sentences Laughton to death.

France, Norway, and Czechoslavakia were the conquered countries
most frequently depicted during 1939-1947, and the following discussion
will focus on characters of those three countries.

Norway

British commando raids plus John Steinbeck's novel, The Moon
Is Down thrust the Norwegians into public view and made their plight
a common Hollywood tale. The predominant theme in the films was that
one must resist or die. A gentle, middle-age meteorologist, Paul
Muni discovered this truth in The Commandos Strike at Dawn (1943).
He found that "there is only one regulation--kill or be killed. I am
ready to observe that regulation. I have come to ask you how we can
change over in this jungle from the murdered Norwegian people to the
murdering Norwegian people."[6]

Walter Huston made such a transition in Edge of Darkness (1943).
His philosophy is to exist neither cooperating nor resisting--until
his daughter is raped. Then, he goes berserk.

---

[5]Quisling was a term applied during World War II to anyone who
cooperated with the conquerors of his country. The term was derived
from Major Vidkun Quisling, head of the Norwegian Nazi Party who became
chief of the Nazi-sponsored government after the 1940 invasion.

[6]Quoted in Senior Scholastic, Feb. 15, 1943, p. 17.

The best resistance was not necessarily violent. Merle Oberon exploits her feminine charms in First Comes Courage (1943) so that she can wangle information from a Nazi colonel. She even marries the colonel--in a civil ceremony featuring Nazi flags, a number of heil hitlers, and Mein Kampf as the Bible. In The Moon is Down (1943) German colonel Sir Cedric Hardwick finds his men's morale disintegrating simply because of the ill will of the conquered. The little village in which the story is set is decimated, but its spirit survives because, according to Steinbeck, "it is always the herd men who win battles and the free men who win wars."[7]

Czechoslovakia

The victimized Czechs were victorious in two films whose heroes, Brian Donlevy and William Bendix, offer interesting contrasts. In Hangmen Also Die (1943) Donlevy plays a doctor who murders Heydrich, a German hatchetman. Donlevy wants to surrender to save hostages who are to be shot. However, his compatriots refuse because of the psychological importance of his remaining free. Through intricate maneuvers and another murder, Donlevy survives and frames a quisling. The Nazis realize the quisling's innocence but accept the evidence as a convenient way out of the situation--a demoralizing alternative nevertheless.

Bendix's Czech in Hostages (1943) is more American than Czech, but perhaps that was due to Bendix. Playing the role he did best, a bumbling washroom attendant, Bendix's bumbling is only pretense. Actually, he is the cunning leader of the Czech underground.

---

[7]Quoted in "Brighter 'Moon'," Newsweek, April 5, 1943, p. 88.

Bendix is captured although the Nazis do not realize his true
identity. They seek the murderer of a German officer, who actually
committed suicide. Unlike Donlevy, Bendix gives no thought to sacrificing himself for the others. He is vital to the underground, and the
twenty-five who are executed are necessary sacrifices.

France

Nearly every French hero experienced some sort of conversion
to social responsibility. Perhaps Hollywood was forcing French heroes
to do penance for the capitulation of the Vichy regime to the Nazis,
but whatever the case conversion is a recurrent theme. For example,
Errol Flynn in Uncertain Glory (1944) sacrifices his criminal life
by surrendering to the Nazis falsely as a saboteur in order to save
100 hostages. Another criminal, Jean Gabin, in The Imposter (1944)
escapes the guillotine due to the explosion of a bomb and after assuming a dead man's identity becomes a patriotic soldier.

Other conversions salvaged the lives of Joan Crawford in Reunion
in France (1942) and Elisabeth Bergner in Paris Calling (1941). Crawford turns to underground activities because her fiance is an apparent
quisling and Bergner because her privileged status is despised by the
common people of France.

Two Frenchmen who did not convert were John Sutton in Tonight
We Raid Calais (1943) and Humphrey Bogart in Passage to Marseilles
(1944). Bogart had to rekindle his enthusiasm, but his opposition to
Nazism stretched back to prewar appeasement. He was framed for his
opposition and sentenced to a prison from which there was no escape.
But he and a group of prisoners escape and wholeheartedly join the Free
French after Vichy France surrenders.

Russia

Redrawing the Russian image after twenty years of suspicion of Lenin, Stalin, and the rest of the "atheistic Commies" was no simple task. Faced with the antithesis of capitalism and communism Hollywood typically chose to ignore the issue. The usual film about the Soviets in 1939-1947 pictured a Russian village populated by simple, occasionally God-fearing peasants. The proletariat and the Soviet political leadership with one exception were notably absent.

The one exception was <u>Mission to Moscow</u> (1943), a semi-documentary starring Walter Huston as Joseph Davies, ambassador to Russia in the 1930's. The film's purpose was to demonstrate the tenacity and intelligence of the Russians in general and the Soviet leaders in particular. In Russia Davies finds a prosperous country, productive factories, warm people not too different from Americans, and even ladies' cosmetics. The victims of the 1938 purge are labeled Hitler's representatives.

Above all Davies is impressed by the Soviet's military preparations. "At least one European nation is ready for anything that comes and I say, thank God," he tells a May Day gathering. Returning to the United States, Davies tries in vain to obtain help for the Russians. Roosevelt listens sympathetically but an isolationist and conservative Congress cannot forgive the Soviets' style of government. Huston's answer to that criticism is: "How they keep their house is none of our business. What matters is what kind of neighbors they will be in case of fire."

According to <u>Song of Russia</u> (1944), <u>North Star</u> (1943), and <u>Days of Glory</u> (1944) the Soviet Union was the right kind of neighbor.

Taylor's subsequently much regretted role in Song . . . placed him opposite Susan Peters, a beautiful peasant girl with a talent for piano. They fall in love, and when war breaks out she must choose her country or the American. She chooses Russia--but ultimately gets her lover too. After her village is burned as a result of the scorched earth policy, the government sends her and Taylor to the United States on a propaganda tour.

About the informational content of the film, Commonweal concluded, "You will learn practically nothing about the Russians from this movie--except they like music, are good fighters, are putting in an all out fight and they will burn their wheat rather than let the Germans get it."[8]

Similar images were projected in North . . ., which featured a confrontation of Russian doctor Walter Huston and German doctor Erich Von Stroheim. The story of a small farming village, the film makes it evident that the Russians, as Von Stroheim noted, are "a strong people, a hard nation to conquer."

Von Stroheim apologizes to Huston for his aid to the Nazis. "I do not like much what I have done for the past nine years," he tells Huston, who answers: "I have heard about men like you. The civilized men who are sorry. Men who do the work of Fascists and pretend to themselves they are better than those for whom they work. It is men like you who have sold your people to men like Hitler." Then, Huston shoots Von Stroheim in cold blood.

A ballerina joins the front lines in Days . . . but is rejected by the guerrillas at first because she is too soft. She gradually falls

---

[8]Philip T. Hartung, "Off Among the Roosians," Commonweal, Feb. 18, 1944, p. 449.

love with leader Gregory Peck and proves herself--enough to die with
m in a futile defense against German tanks. The characters emphasize
d re-emphasize that they are fighting for "Mother Russia" and con-
rsely by omission not the government of the Soviet Union.

Asians

In nearly every case Asian ally meant either Chinese or Filipino--
imarily Chinese. The films generally served to uphold the myth of
e valiant Chinese fighting stubbornly against imperialistic Japan.
equently, though, the pictures' stars were Americans playing super-
en among Orientals, e.g. Randolph Scott in China Sky (1945), John
ayne in Flying Tigers (1942) and Back to Bataan (1945), and Alan Ladd
n China (1943). The lack of availability of Asian actors or boxoffice
ttractions could explain the absence of Oriental heroes. It also
ould be attributed to racism, perhaps, or simply that Americans were
laying the major role in Asia. Besides, Hollywood's Americans domi-
ated all nationalities without regard to race, creed, or color.

Major Chinese characters were either women, children, or Charlie
han. Sidney Toler played Chan in Charlie Chan in Panama (1940) and
harlie Chan in the Secret Service (1944) as the usual wise, patient
etective specializing in murder mysteries. The brutal antics of smaller
hinese were portrayed in China's Little Devils (1945) while feminine
eadership was provided by Gene Tierney, Anna May Wong, and Katherine
epburn in China Girl (1942), Lady from Chungking (1942), and Pearl
uck's Dragon Seed (1944). A Vassar graduate, Tierney falls in love
ith American adventurer George Montgomery and they both die in a
apanese attack. Wong is much more successful in farming, serving as

a guerrilla fighter, and using feminine mystique to extract information from a Japanese officer.

Dragon . . . was intended to depict the goodness of the Chinese people and to demonstrate, according to Walter Huston as Ling Tan, that "all men are brothers and they should not kill each other."[9] Whether Hollywood actually included the Nazis and Japanese in the brotherhood of man is questionable. Variety described the Chinese as "a beacon of hope and courage for all the civilized peoples."[10] The key word is "civilized."

Enemy

Despite some distinctions, the allies of 1939-1947 were very similar in that they were peace loving, democratic, egalitarian, and foes of tyranny and fascism. The enemy (Germany and Japan since Italy was never portrayed as a primary foe) possessed such attributes as immorality, tyranny, and sadism but differed in one crucial respect. In Europe the enemy was a system—fascism and Nazism—while in Asia it was a country and its people and leaders.

Germany

There were two kinds of Germans: the people and the Nazis. Stories about the German people were used to explain the plight of victims of Nazism and to raise hope that there was an active opposition in the country. Movies about the leaders provided little information and often evolved into mere adventures.

---

[9] Quoted in Variety, July 19, 1944, p. 18.

[10] Ibid.

From Hollywood's prewar presentations it appeared that some Germans strongly opposed Hitler but were generally overmatched at least in immediate battles, e.g. such heroes as Alan Ladd, who was imprisoned and tortured in Beasts of Berlin (1939), Jeffrey Lynn who was converted from Nazi to democrat in a few minutes in Underground (1941), and Fredric March who commits suicide to avoid informing on his fellow conspirators in So Ends Our Night (1940).

Opposition to the Nazis demanded in some cases use of their brutal tactics. In Watch on the Rhine (1943) Paul Lukas murders in cold blood to stop Roumanian count George Coulouris from informing. Lukas regrets his action, "I do not like to kill this way, but I have done it before and will do it again--whenever it must be done."

Why extreme action was called for was explained in Hitler's Children (1943), starring Tim Holt and Bonita Granville. In this description of life in Nazi Germany, Granville is a German-American studying in Berlin while the Nazis are consolidating their power. Holt is a future S.S. officer, who asserts, "Today we rule Germany. Tomorrow we rule the world . . . It is our birthright to rule."

Holt and Granville fall in love, and a series of events unfolds leading ultimately to their double execution. Meanwhile Granville refuses Nazi indoctrination and rejects giving birth for the state. "Each generation must look after the one that comes after it . . . If to live for what I think is to die for what I think then let me die."

Instead, she is first threatened with sterilization, and the film explores a camp set up for such projects. "There's no room for the weak, the sick, the unstable," says a Nazi official. Weaknesses include color blindness and improper political beliefs, explains the film.

    <u>Hitler's . . .</u> leaves the impression that some older Germans oppose Hitler but are afraid to put their opposition into action. Besides, explains a German journalist, "the will to obey (is) in us Germans. How easy to march in step once you are started."

    The Hollywood Nazi was varied. He was cultured, appreciated art, and followed proper etiquette in polite company. On the other hand, he was vulgar, sadistic, and arrogant. He was strong against the defenseless, intelligent but a buffoon.

    Paul Lukas began the image of the cultured, educated Nazi in <u>Confessions of a Nazi Spy</u> (1939). An engineer, Lukas runs an intricate espionage and propaganda network in the German-American Bund. The organization is built around propaganda but its success is dependent on force and coercion. Another example of the cultured German was provided by Von Stroheim in <u>North Star</u>. He is no Nazi and disclaims any approval of the Nazis' activities. Yet he bleeds young children to provide blood transfusions for German soldiers. As Huston tells him, Von Stroheim is no better than those he belittles.

    Most Nazis were not as hypocritical as Von Stroheim. Most were plainly despicable beasts. In <u>Hitler's Hangman</u> (or <u>Hitler's Madman</u>) (1943) John Carradine plays German hatchetman Heydrich who on his deathbed supposedly repudiates Hitler. In response to Heydrich's assassination, the Nazis and Himmler wipe out the village of Lidice. <u>Hostages</u> (1943) depicts the execution of twenty-five innocent Czechs by Nazis seeking control over coal mines.

    Nazi crimes were basically against humanity and God. The portrayal of Nazi barbarism seemed to be intended to offend and outrage.

In <u>Women in Bondage</u> (1943) the Nazis shockingly order Gail Patrick to have children by her brother-in-law since her husband was paralyzed. The film explains Nazi rules of marriage, baptism, racial discrimination, sterilization, and regimentation. The theme is continued in <u>Enemy of Women</u> (1944) in which Paul Andor as Goebbels persecutes an actress because she once rejected him. Finally, in <u>The Hitler Gang</u> (1944) Robert Watson raves as Hitler, evoking terror against churches and religion, women, and even children. Through it all Watson is guided by astrology.

The barbaric image of the Nazis was in some cases carefully projected by writers, actors, and directors. Two Germans pursuing Brian Donlevy in <u>Hangmen Also Die</u> were deliberately constructed by German refugee director Fritz Lang. One who cracks his knuckles all the time was, according to Lang,

> a portrait of a very sadistic teacher I had once. With the one who has a pimple, I wanted to show that the depraved Nazi official (a) has syphilis, (b) doesn't give a damn what he's doing in the presence of this woman because probably he is a homosexual. (In principle, I have nothing against homosexual--I mean it very honestly--as long as they don't do damage to children or anybody.) Third, I wanted to show his disregard for the lives of the hostages; she is there pleading for the life of her folks and he is much more interested in this damn pimple.[11]

Nazis were portrayed as poor losers and unbearable victors. Their bloated ego even after capture or near death seemed to be calculated to infuriate loyal Americans. In <u>Nazi Agent</u> (1942) Conrad Veidt plays twin brothers, one a German consul and spy, the other an American citizen. "I hope you don't think you have put an end to our work,"[12]

---

[11] Quoted in Peter Bogdanovich, <u>Fritz Lang in America</u> (New York: Praeger, 1969), p. 62.

[12] Quoted in Philip T. Hartung, "To Be Or Not To Be Laughed At," <u>Commonweal</u>, March 13, 1942, p. 515.

the bad brother sneers just before death to which the twin answers,
"No, but I am only one of 130 million Americans who would do all they
can for their country."[13]

The highest Nazi, Hitler, was a frequent target of slap stick
and ridicule. The premier satire was Chaplin's The Great Dictator
(1940). Others were strictly slap stick, portraying the enemy leaders
as sheer idiots, e.g. Bobby Watson as Hitler, Joe Devlin as Mussolini,
and Johnny Arthur as Suki Yaki in That Natzy Nuisance (1943) and
Watson, Devlin, and Alan Mowbray as the devil in The Devil with Hitler
(1942).

Few of the films addressed the question of how to punish the
Nazis. In The Master Race (1944) Nazi junker George Coulouris pre-
dicted the allies would not be able to handle victory. "You (will)
fall out among yourselves . . . Victory is a nightmare to you."[14]
Lifeboat (1944) observed that strength was required to put an end to
people like the Nazis but that the rest of the world was too compassionate not to make the same mistakes again. Finally, None Shall
Escape (1944) called for strong vengeance, and North Star (1943) with
Walter Huston as executor said that all Germans--not just Nazis--who
participated in the Third Reich were equally guilty.

Japan

Compared to the Nazi villains, the Japanese were a molehill.
Hollywood's image of a Japanese was Sessue Hayakawa (or perhaps

---

[13]Ibid.

[14]Quoted in "The New Pictures," Time, Nov. 13, 1944, p. 94.

Richard Loo) peering through hornrimmed spectacles and commenting how much he liked UCLA before the war. Four pictures went somewhat beyond this simplistic stereotype and tried to demonstrate the alien and supposedly corrupt Japanese culture.

Behind the Rising Sun (1943) starred Tom Neal and provided the first extended look at Japan, and the picture of the country was less than inviting. Modeled·after Hitler's Children the movie featured Neal as a formerly democratic Japanese educated at an Ivy League school. He returns to Japan, at first refusing to cooperate. Ultimately, though, he is caught up in the emotion of military victory, leading to his complete depravation.

The Doolittle raids provided The Purple Heart (1944) with an excuse to hypothesize the Japanese's disregard for Western legal conventions. Four of the Doolittle raiders are shown being tried for so-called civil crimes, tortured, and finally axed to death when they will not reveal the location of their air base. Washington banned films about Japanese treatment of prisoners of war during the early war years for fear of reprisals.[15] The Purple . . . left no doubt of Hollywood's interpretation of such treatment.

In Blood on the Sun (1945) American newsman James Cagney's experiences were used to reiterate the barbarism of the Japanese. Cagney learns in advance of Japanese plans to attack Pearl Harbor but cannot leak them in the press because he is framed on a charge of murder. Most of the film is a chase with Cagney evading the Japanese until being shot in the street at the pictures conclusion.

---

[15]"Movies," Newsweek, March 20, 1944, p. 90.

On fair terms, according to the movie, an American will best a Japanese as Cagney proves by boxing his way to victory over a ju-jitsu champion.

Tom Neal's disgust at the Japanese appearance was highlighted in First Yank into Tokyo (1945). Neal plays an American volunteering to undergo plastic surgery so that he can undertake a mission to Japan. The surgery makes him look Japanese and can never be corrected, but he agrees because he believes his fiancee has been killed. Naturally, he finds her in Japan as well as the scientist he is looking for plus old school chum and Japanese colonel Richard Loo.

Neal completes his mission but refuses to return to the United States despite the pleadings of his fiancee. He dies at a machine gun, covering the others' escape. He could not live the rest of his life with a Japanese appearance. "It would be a fateful reminder of her (his fiancee) experiences at Bataan and Corregidor."

Interestingly, First . . . portrays an active underground in Japan. Its members, however, are predominantly Chinese or Korean, not Japanese.

Italy

The Italians made few appearances in the films of 1939-1947. They were never seriously regarded as an enemy, being portrayed either as buffoons or pathetic weaklings or both (e.g. Five Graves to Cairo, 1943, and Sahara, 1943).

The only film to treat the Italians extensively gave a sympathetic portrayal. A Bell for Adano (1945) depicted the Italians as undeserving victims of war. They are shown as an optimistic, cheerful people with malice toward no one. Even in this film, though, the Italians are comically pathetic participants in a war which the Germans controlled. Early in the picture one is tempted to laugh at the Italians rather than with them.

Summary

Hollywood's depiction of enemy and ally during 1939-1947 was a process of emphasizing similarities between Americans and allies and differences between Americans and enemies. The war films of 1939-1947 portrayed the allies as being united by belief in democracy, individual liberties, and equality. In some cases the screen image violated traditional film portrayals such as England's aristocratic and Russia's communistic stereotypes. Such obstacles were bypassed, however, by stressing that the link between Americans and others was with the people not necessarily the government in Russia's case or that the class system really was not so rigid in England.

The enemy tortured, brutalized, and murdered their victims, but in most cases the allies managed to achieve some sort of satisfaction--moral or otherwise. The chief weapons of the European partisans were wit, belief in freedom, and the knowledge that they were right.

The enemy on both fronts was barbarous, but there was a distinction between Germany and Japan. In Europe the opposition was a system of fascism and Nazism not the German people. In Asia the enemy was Japan, including the Japanese people as well as their leaders. The Japanese culture was frequently depicted as innately barbaric while the Germans supposedly were deceived and coerced into following Hitler.

CHAPTER VIII

DECLINE OF THE ALLIES

Americans and American characteristics dominated the allies in films produced in 1939-1947, but at least there were allies. The allies in films produced in 1948-1962 were notable by their absence from dominant roles. In 1939-1947 allies played dominant roles in 19.6 per cent of the films. That share dropped to 7.9 per cent during 1948-1962. (For nationalities of characters in 1948-1962 films see Table 33.) The decline in emphasis on allies largely can be attributed to a dominant feeling that the United States was solely responsible for the defense of the Free World. During 1948-1962 the early 1940's theory of international cooperation deteriorated into a reality of confrontation between the United States and the Soviet Union. Allies seemed relatively unimportant--at least from a military viewpoint--in such a situation.

The isolated responsibility of the United States manifested itself in war films produced in 1948-1962 qualitatively as well as quantitatively. Quantitatively, as already mentioned, a lower per-centage of allies was portrayed in dominant roles. Qualitatively, the allies did not resemble Americans as much in 1948-1962 as they had in 1939-1947. American heroes of 1948-1962 were characterized by their professional approach to war. The professionalism was not quite so dominant among the allies in 1948-1962's films about the Cold War or World War II. (The generalization applies to films about the Korean War also. However, since all Korean War film heroes were American, the results of the character analyses provide no basis for comparison.)

TABLE 33

NATIONALITY OF CHARACTERS, 1948-1962

Nationality	Dominant Roles	Subordinate Roles	Total Roles
Cold War			
American	85.9%	2.9%	88.5%
Russian	1.0	34.6	35.5
Red Chinese	-	5.8	5.8
British	1.9	1.9	3.8
East German	1.9	1.0	2.9
French	1.0	1.9	2.9
Hungarian	1.9	1.0	2.9
Canadian	1.0	1.0	1.9
Czech	-	1.9	1.9
Japanese	-	1.9	1.9
Nationalist Chinese	-	1.9	1.9
West German	1.0	1.0	1.9
Albanian	-	1.0	1.0
Australian	-	1.0	1.0
Cuban	1.0	-	1.0
Dutch	-	1.0	1.0
Greek	-	1.0	1.0
Vietnamese	-	1.0	1.0
Uncertain	1.0	1.9	2.9
Total	100.0	100.0	100.0
Number	104	104	104
World War II			
American	82.6%	5.0%	87.6%
German	5.6	23.6	30.4
Japanese	1.2	19.3	20.5
British	4.3	5.0	9.3
French	0.6	5.6	6.2
Filipino	-	5.0	5.0
Italian	-	2.5	2.5
Chinese	-	1.9	1.9
Argentine	0.6	-	0.6
Australian	-	0.6	0.6
Burmese	-	0.6	0.6
Canadian	-	0.6	0.6
Czech	-	0.6	0.6
Dutch	0.6	-	0.6
Greek	-	0.6	0.6

TABLE 33--Continued

Nationality	Dominant Roles	Subordinate Roles	Total Roles
Irish	- %	0.6%	0.6%
Israeli	0.6%	-	0.6
Malayan	-	0.6	0.6
Mongolian	-	0.6	0.6
New Zealander	0.6	-	0.6
Polish	0.6	-	0.6
Roumanian	-	0.6	0.6
Russian	-	0.6	0.6
Swedish	0.6	-	0.6
Yugoslavian	0.6	-	0.6
Uncertain	1.2	0.6	1.9
Total	100.0	100.0	100.0
Number	161	161	161

[a]Data derived from question 20 Form A in Appendix I.

In World War II films produced in 1948-1962 the allies and Americans differ in roles, occupations, military membership, primary goals, and primary methods. In each category the American tends more toward professional warriorship than does the ally. (Perhaps one should be cautious about drawing quick conclusions from the character analyses of allies and enemies during 1948-1962 because there were so few of them--six allies and seven enemies in Cold War pictures, seventeen allies and sixteen enemies in World War II films. However, some implications may be gathered from the results.)

Few allies were in warrior roles in World War II movies produced in 1948-1962. Only 41.2 per cent of the allies were either spies or soldiers compared to 93.0 per cent of the Americans of the same era (Table 34), and many of the ally civilians were in non-combat situations. The difference also shows up in military status as 90.4 per

TABLE 34

ROLES OF ALLIES, ENEMIES, 1948-1962

Role	World War II		Cold War	
	Ally	Enemy	Ally	Enemy
Spy	23.5%	6.3%	- %	28.6%
Soldier	17.6	58.3	33.3	-
Civilian	58.8	37.5	66.7	71.4
Total	100.0	100.0	100.0	100.0
Number	17	16	6	7

[a]Data derived from question 1 Form B in Appendix I.

cent of 1948-1962's World War II Americans are soldiers compared to 35.3 per cent of the allies (Table 35).

The allies also were lower in categories indicating war professionalism. Just a little more than one-third as many allies as Americans were professional warriors (11.8 per cent compared to 30.7 per cent) (Table 36). The allies were motivated less by professional military goals than the Americans. A total of 23.5 per cent of the allies pursued war-task goals compared to 34.2 per cent of the Americans while the allies sought to meet patriotic demands more often than Americans (23.5 per cent to 14.9 per cent). Perhaps the most revealing difference in primary goals is that allies had safety as the major objective in 17.6 per cent of the time compared to the Americans' 1.8 per cent. Concern for oneself was not allowed the professional warrior. (See Table 37.)

As a consequence of emphasis on professional warriors the primary methods of American characters of World War II films produced in

TABLE 35

MILITARY CHARACTERISTICS OF ALLIES, ENEMIES, 1948-1962

Role	World War II		Cold War	
	Ally	Enemy	Ally	Enemy
Military Status				
Member	35.3%	50.0%	33.3%	- %
Former member	-	6.3	-	14.3
Never member	52.9	37.5	66.7	28.6
No answer	11.8	6.3	-	57.1
Total	100.0	100.0	100.0	100.0
Branch				
Army	35.3	31.3	33.3	-
Navy	-	12.5	-	-
Air Force	-	-	-	-
Other	-	6.3	-	-
No answer	64.7	50.0	66.7	100.0
Total	100.0	100.0	100.0	100.0
Rank				
Gen.-Adm.	-	6.3	-	-
Col.-Capt.	11.8	12.5	16.7	-
Maj.-Cmdr.	-	6.3	-	-
Capt.-Lt.	11.8	-	16.7	-
Lt.-Ens.	-	12.5	-	-
Sgt.-CPO	-	-	-	-
Non com	-	-	-	-
Enlisted	5.9	6.3	-	-
Other	-	6.3	-	-
No answer	70.6	50.0	66.7	100.0
Total	100.0	100.0	100.0	100.0
Membership Reason				
Career	17.6	25.0	16.7	-
Draft	5.9	6.3	-	-
Patriotism	-	6.3	-	-
Personal	5.9	-	-	-
Other	-	-	-	-
No answer	70.6	62.5	83.3	100.0
Total	100.0	100.0	100.0	100.0
Number	17	16	6	7

[a]Data derived from questions 15, 16, 18, and 20 Form B in Appendix I.

TABLE 36

DEMOGRAPHICS OF ALLIES, ENEMIES, 1948-1962

	World War II		Cold War	
	Ally	Enemy	Ally	Enemy
Sex				
Male	88.2%	81.3%	100.0%	71.4%
Female	11.8	18.7	-	28.6
Total	100.0	100.0	100.0	100.0
Age				
Youth	11.8	6.3	-	-
Young adult	5.9	12.5	16.7	-
Mature adult	70.6	31.3	66.7	85.7
Middle age	5.9	43.8	16.7	14.3
Old age	-	6.3	-	-
No answer	5.9	-	-	-
Total	100.0	100.0	100.0	100.0
Class				
Upper	41.2	50.0	16.7	14.3
Middle	11.8	25.0	16.7	28.6
Lower	17.6	6.3	33.3	57.1
Outside structure	23.5	13.3	33.3	-
No answer	5.9	-	-	-
Total	100.0	100.0	100.0	100.0
Marital Status				
Married	11.8	37.5	16.7	42.9
Never married	47.1	46.7	50.0	42.9
Divorced	-	-	16.7	-
Other	11.8	12.5	-	-
No answer	29.4	6.3	16.7	14.3
Total	100.0	100.0	100.0	100.0
Education				
In school	5.9	6.3	16.7	-
High school	-	12.5	33.3	28.6
Undergraduate	47.1	31.3	16.7	42.9
Higher degree	5.9	12.5	-	-
Other	5.9	-	-	-
No answer	35.3	12.5	16.7	28.6
Total	100.0	100.0	100.0	100.0

TABLE 36--Continued

	World War II		Cold War	
	Ally	Enemy	Ally	Enemy
Nationality				
British	35.3%	6.3%	16.7%	14.3%
German	5.9	87.5	-	-
East German	-	-	-	14.3
West German	-	-	16.7	-
French	11.8	-	16.7	-
Czech	5.9	-	-	28.6
Hungarian	-	-	-	28.6
Argentine	5.9	-	-	-
Canadian	-	-	16.7	-
Dutch	5.9	-	-	-
Japanese	-	6.3	-	-
Polish	5.9	-	-	-
Roumanian	5.9	-	-	-
Russian	-	-	-	14.3
Swedish	5.9	-	-	-
Yugoslavian	5.9	-	-	-
Unknown	5.9	6.3	33.3	-
Total	100.0	100.0	100.0	100.0
Occupation				
Military	11.8	31.3	33.3	-
Student	5.9	12.5	16.7	-
Entertainer	-	6.3	16.7	14.3
Spy	-	-	-	28.6
Teacher	5.9	-	-	14.3
Adventurer	5.9	-	-	-
Attorney	-	6.3	-	-
Businessman	5.9	-	-	-
Butler	-	6.3	-	-
Criminal	-	6.3	-	-
Engineer	5.9	-	-	-
Housewife	5.9	-	-	-
Mechanic	-	-	-	14.3
Planter	5.9	-	-	-
Police	-	-	-	14.3
Secretary	-	-	-	14.3
Seaman	-	6.3	-	-
No answer	47.1	25.0	33.3	-
Total	100.0	100.0	100.0	100.0
Number	17	16	6	7

[a]Data derived from questions 3-8 Form B in Appendix I.

TABLE 37

PRIMARY GOALS OF ALLIES, ENEMIES, 1948–1962

Primary Goal	World War II		Cold War	
	Ally	Enemy	Ally	Enemy
Safety	17.6%	12.5%	16.7%	28.6%
Escape law	-	6.3	-	-
Health	-	-	-	-
Individualism	-	-	-	28.6
Money	-	6.3	-	-
Comfort	-	-	-	14.3
Power	-	6.3	-	14.3
Adventure	-	-	-	-
Love	17.6	6.3	-	-
Family	5.9	-	16.7	-
Sex	-	-	-	-
War task	23.5	-	-	-
Fame	-	-	-	-
Patriotism	23.5	6.3	33.3	-
Justice	11.8	6.3	16.7	-
Truth	-	6.3	-	-
Revenge	-	6.3	-	-
Honesty	-	6.3	-	-
No answer	11.8	-	16.7	14.3
Total	100.0	100.0	100.0	100.0
Number	17	16	6	7

[a]Data derived from question 25 Form B in Appendix I.

1948–1962 were force (32.5 per cent) and hard work or discipline (25.4 per·cent). The allies used force almost as often (29.4 per cent), but, lacking professionalism, they depended on hard work in only one case (5.9 per cent) (Table 38).

Similar differences exist between the allies and Americans in Cold War films produced in 1948–1962. Allies were more apt to be civilians and Americans more likely to be warriors of some kind. One-third of the allies were warriors compared to two-thirds of the Americans.

TABLE 38

PRIMARY METHODS OF ALLIES, ENEMIES, 1948-1962

Primary Method	World War II		Cold War	
	Ally	Enemy	Ally	Enemy
Hard work	5.9%	6.3%	16.7%	14.3%
Luck	11.8	6.3	-	-
Trickery	-	25.0	-	14.3
Knowledge	47.1	37.5	-	14.3
Charm	5.9	12.5	-	14.3
Force	29.4	12.5	16.7	14.3
Persuasion	-	-	50.0	28.6
No answer	-	-	16.7	-
Total	100.0	100.0	100.0	100.0
Number	17	16	6	7

aData derived from question 29 Form B in Appendix I.

Allies had slightly fewer career soldiers and agents (33.3 per cent
against 37.0 per cent) and slightly less military membership (33.3 per
cent and 42.0 per cent). None of the Cold War allies pursued war task
as the primary goal (compared to the Americans' 25.9 per cent) while
50.0 per cent relied primarily on persuasion to achieve success--hardly
the tool of a professional warrior. In contrast only 4.9 per cent of
the Americans depended on persuasion.

The enemies in Cold War films produced in 1948-1962 tended to
resemble allies of the same films in civilian membership (71.4 per cent
of the enemies compared to 66.7 per cent of the allies), occupation
(28.6 per cent as career warriors to 33.3 per cent), and method (28.6
per cent used persuasion compared to 50.0 per cent). The only major
difference between enemies and allies was primary goal. Seeking to

escape Communist oppression, many of the enemies had safety (28.6 per cent), individualism (28.6 per cent), and comfort (14.3 per cent) as goals while patriotism was foremost (33.3 per cent) for the allies.

On the other hand, the 1948-1962 World War II films had enemies showing more similarity to Americans than allies insofar as professional warriorship was concerned. The percentage of roles, occupations, and goals was practically the same: 66.7 per cent of the enemies were in warrior roles compared to 93.0 per cent of the Americans; 33.3 per cent as career soldiers compared to 30.7 per cent; and 33.3 per cent seeking war-task goals compared to 34.2 per cent. The enemies displayed slightly less military membership (53.3 per cent compared to 90.4 per cent) and their primary means was knowledge (37.5 per cent), which resembled the allies more than the Americans.

Thus, the following discussion will focus on the absence of professionalism among the film allies of 1948-1962 and thus their dissimilarity with Americans and on a redefinition of enemies which in some cases made them more like the rest of the world.

Cold War

Hollywood's attitude toward the Cold War in general and the Russians in particular was epitomized in I Was a Communist for the FBI (1951), which referred to the Soviet Union as a "dark and dangerous force" whose purpose was to "soften up the people, demoralize and weaken the will of the American people to fight." At various times in the picture nearly all of the ills of the United States were attributed to the Russians. "Communists are striking at steel mills in Pittsburgh," on the one hand was added to charges that the Soviet Union was responsible for race riots in Detroit and Harlem in 1943.

"Dark and dangerous force" was an apt description of Hollywood's image of communism--particularly that which existed in the United States. The Communists were portrayed as a threatening, ominous element always striking at Americanism, but the party members seldom had any individual characteristics.

In many ways the Communists in the United States were depicted as only slightly removed from gangsterism. It was difficult at times to differentiate Russian Communist from American mobster. The Communists had a gangster mentality and gangster methods, just hooligans out for a fast buck only this time the fast buck was the United States. The ideological nature of communism was not detailed. That the Communists threatened democracy, capitalism, and God was condemning enough. The gangster image was perpetuated in Spy Hunt (1950), I Was a Communist for the FBI (1951), Pickup on South Street (1955), and Man on a String (1960).

Trial (1955) went somewhat beyond the gangster syndrome. Trial explained how Communists exploited local racial troubles for their own benefit. According to Variety, the film was effective. "The phony showmanship, the greedy cut-ins of the participating committee chairmen, the cold cynicism of the publicity machine will hit America like a body blow against those who turn obscure victims of local injustice into party pets."[1]

Outside the United States, the Communists were sometimes more than gangsters, although they were occasionally labeled criminals--e.g.

---

[1]Variety, Aug. 3, 1955, p. 10.

by Gregory Peck in <u>Night People</u> (1954). In <u>Night</u> . . . the Communists
are Russians and East Germans, who kidnap for little reason, murder
their own agents for suspicion, and take a ransom and kill the victim.

Generally, though, stories of Communists in Europe revolved
around their lack of regard for individual freedoms and desires. <u>Guilty</u>
<u>of Treason</u> (1950), apparently patterned after <u>Hitler's Children</u> (1943),
exploited this theme. Bonita Granville, star of <u>Hitler's</u> . . ., this
time is a holdout against communism and falls in love with Soviet
colonel Richard Derr. A sweeping condemnation of communism centers on
Russian persecution of the church in general and Charles Bickford as
Cardinal Mindszenty in particular.

Intellectual oppression drove Roddy McDowell from his native
country in <u>The Steel Fist</u> (1952). He flees only after instigating a
student protest and riot against labor controls and discovering his
efforts were futile. Michael Mills and Violet Rensig come to the
opposite conclusion in <u>The Beast of Budapest</u> (1958), a film which
exalted the spirit of Hungary's Freedom Fighters. Mills is originally
a pacifist and Rensig a party member but seeing the Freedom Fighters
shot down helplessly convinces the pair that they must fight.

On the whole the East Europeans of 1948-1962 did not resemble
the partisans of 1939-1947. Mills and Rensig were exceptions. The
opposition of the 1948-1962 East Europeans was not nearly as open or
positive as that of their 1939-1947 predecessors. In fact the major form
of opposition was defection rather than some violent form of underground
activity. Neither were their motives tied to the democratic ideals of
earlier partisans. Instead, they were motivated by personal concern--
usually manifested in desire for material goods and occasionally in
seeking individual freedom.

The first espionage film of the era, The Iron Curtain (1948), used both material benefits and personal freedom to lure Russian agent Dana Andrews into defection. The material benefit was a small flat and the freedom was found in lack of fear among his neighbors. The agent, Igor Gouzenko, returned in Operation Manhunt (1954) when his assassin defected.

Desire for individual freedom dictated a daring escape by former circus owner Fredric March in Man on a Tightrope (1953). A veteran performer, he is now permitted by "the people and the state" to supervise. He escapes by barreling through border gates with his circus vehicles.

Many comedies portrayed defections motivated by materialism, e.g. The Iron Petticoat (1956), Silk Stockings (1957), and No Time for Flowers (1953). In The Iron . . . Katherine Hepburn is a Russian military captain succumbing to Bob Hope, black lace lingerie, strapless evening gowns, and vintage champagne. Cyd Charisse falls for the same goods and Hollywood producer Fred Astaire in Silk . . . after she (as a Russian commissar) comes to Paris to collect three other agents who have already fallen prey to "decadent capitalism." The Communists create their own downfall in No Time . . ., starring Viveca Lindfors as a Czech secretary bound for the Czech embassy in the United States. The Communists decide to test her susceptibility to materialism, flooding her with gowns, hose, and champagne. Lindfors and her tempter both defect.

Other reasons for escape included love in Never Let Me Go (1953) and safety from brutal East Germans in Escape from East Berlin (1962). However, the lot of civilians under Communist rule was depicted as

materialistically deprived, and consequently the civilians sought
materialism more than other goals. The typical characterization was
demonstrated by a scene in The Secret Ways (1961). Adventurer Richard
Widmark is supposedly a touring manufacturer being given prestige
treatment in Hungary. He happens to ask one of the underlings about
his job. "I'm an assistant to the minister," answers the Hungarian and
in the same breath adds, "I have a telephone and a desk."

Communism in Asia meant China. The Chinese Communists were typically brutal and barbaric--almost like the Japanese of 1939-1947. The
Shanghai Story (1954) and Satan Never Sleeps (1962) typify the portrayal
of Chinese Communists.

In Shanghai . . . Communist police chief Marvin Miller imprisons
a group of Europeans after the revolution. Every action by Miller and
his men violates what might be called traditional standards of American
propriety--from manhandling old men and women to spying on young married,
shooting a dog, ridiculing religion, cold blooded shooting in the back
of the head, cutting food rations, and a threat to the astonished
Europeans: "property owners in the New China don't live long."

Robert Lee represents the New China in Satan . . . . A church-
educated youth, he throws away his faith to become a village leader for
the Communists. He persecutes the priests, including an old friend,
tortures, and rapes. However, a Russian adviser moves in and displaces
Lee, who reverts to humanity.

The Vietnamese were portrayed in A Yank in Indo-China (1952),
Jump into Hell (1955), and The Quiet American (1958). They were pre-
sented in stereotypes with chief attention to Americans and French.
The French are one of the few allies of the Cold War who are active

fighters against the Communists, but that portrayal occurred only in Jump . . . . Many of the other allies were mere pawns seeking release from Communist domination, such as Ruth Roman in Five Steps to Danger (1957) and McDowell in The Steel Fist. Walter Pidgeon was a more or less passive British observer of Russian refugee policy in The Red Danube (1949), but forceful opposition--to a minimal degree--was depicted in Guerrilla Girl (1953) and We Shall Return (1959).

Korean War

South Korean allies and North Korean and Chinese enemies were abundant without distinction in 1948-1962's films. In most cases the allies were soldiers under American guidance or refugees. The enemy was the enemy in all its notoriety but with only hazy exposure.

The North Koreans and Chinese were barbarians (in the manner of the "yellow hordes" of 1939-1947) only recently passing out of the stone age. Prisoner of war films--such as Prisoner of War (1954) and The Bamboo Prison (1955)--reinforced the barbaric image. Otherwise, it was not essential to delve deeply into the character of the enemy. The fact that it was the enemy and communistic was enough.

The refugees essentially were helpless animals responsive to the dangers of the moment. In One Minute to Zero (1952), they are used by the Communists to cover their infiltrations and are caught in the fire of American planes trying to stop the enemy. In The Steel Helmet (1951) an orphan cracks the cynicism of an Army sergeant before being killed. In War Hunt (1962) a small boy is corrupted by an American psychopath.

Two Koreans in Battle Hymn (1957) are self sacrificing philosophers, one a Christian the other a Buddhist. Together they help an American minister, haunted by guilt from accidentally bombing an orphanage during World War II, find peace. They demonstrate to Rock Hudson that no man can control his destiny; he must be prepared to take whatever is bestowed.

World War II

Allies

In a screen era dominated by the American professional warrior it is nearly impossible to find professionals among the allies. The British, however, do provide a few. In attitude and behavior Richard Burton (Desert Rats, 1953) came close to matching the disciplined, unemotional model of warriorship. Burton is not a career officer, but he has learned that discipline is the key to victory.

In Bridge on the River Kwai (1957) Alec Guinness' initial behavior would have made any American officer proud as he fights to maintain morale and discipline in a Japanese prison camp. However, his preoccupation with his men supercedes reason, and he eventually aids the enemy.

Kurt Jurgens is a career soldier but not a warrior in Bitter Victory (1958). Fear restricts his taking charge of a mission to steal German documents. His life is complicated by Richard Burton, his second in command who threatens to steal his wife. Even without Burton's interference, though, Jurgens likely would have muffed the mission. He was by no definition a professional, as an accusation by Burton indicates: "You're not the sort of man to kill for a woman but would murder to keep her from finding out you're a coward. You're not a man . . . but an empty uniform starched by authority so it can stand by itself."

The underground tradition carried over into World War II films produced in 1948-1962 but with some variation. The new partisan pictures were mere action stories with some internal conflict among the guerrillas, a little sex, and a lot of violence but with no eloquent defense of liberty or democracy. In many of the films Americans were central figures complemented by natives. Examples of nationalities as helpers included: Filipinos in American Guerrilla in the Philippines (1950), Surrender Hell (1959), and No Man Is an Island (1962); Roumanians in Heroes Die Young (1961); and Italians in Fighter Attack (1953).

Deviations from the American-as-savior theme included The Angry Hills (1959) in which Greek partisans saved an American reporter, Robert Mitchum, and Betrayed (1954) in which Dutch agent Clark Gable uncovers a Dutch traitor, Victor Mature as "the Scarf."

Five Branded Women (1960) was a major exception among partisan films of the era. No American or other major ally was mentioned anywhere in the picture. The Yugoslavians had to survive with help from no one.

They survive by adopting a professional approach to war. The film follows four young women who are convicted of fraternization of the most extreme form with the enemy and banished from their village. They learn to kill and distrust before finally joining the underground. They are told that sex and emotion have to be suppressed. Everyone is equal and sexless so that petty jealousies will not interfere with fighting the Germans. The reason for the rule is evident once they ignore it. A few minutes devoted to sex rather than war almost destroy the partisans.

Many other allies found their time occupied more by love than

by war, e.g. Britishers Dana Wynter (<u>D-Day the Sixth of June</u>, 1956)
and Leslie Caron (<u>Gaby</u>, 1956), and Frenchwoman Dana Robin (<u>Act of Love</u>,
1953). Each affair was with an American, and each ended unhappily.
Wynter loses her American when he decides to return to his wife at the
end of the war; Robin falls victim to Army regulations; and Caron cannot make up her mind. She refuses to give herself to John Kerr, turns
prostitute when she learns of his death, and kills herself when she
learns he is alive.

Enemy

Redefinition of the two major World War II enemies took two
directions in 1948-1962. The Germans' image was remolded in a war context. The Nazi's and the non-Nazi's behavior was made to seem less
condemnable through a rationalization of his motivation. The rebuilding
of the Japanese's characterization abandoned the war years for postwar
Japan in which "yellow monkeys" of 1939-1947 became tranquil pacifists.

Not every World War II film produced in 1948-1962 contained the
enemies' new image. In some the enemy was still to be hated but nevertheless was not quite as gruesome or sadistic as in earlier years.

Nearly all of the movies with a new Japanese image appeared just
after the conclusion of the Korean War. <u>Three Stripes in the Sun</u> (1955)
initiated the trend, followed shortly by <u>Teahouse of the August Moon</u>
(1956), <u>Joe Butterfly</u> (1957), <u>Sayonara</u> (1957), <u>Cry for Happy</u> (1961),
and <u>Bridge to the Sun</u> (1962). Nearly every film revolved around a love
story and most of them around children, and somewhere along the line
each American hero learned that geisha girls were not prostitutes.

The romances generally paired American male with Japanese female, but Bridge . . . matched Tennessean Carol Baker with Japanese diplomat James Shigeta. Married before Pearl Harbor, Baker chooses deportation in order to stay with her husband. The picture does not rationalize Japan's war actions but stresses by Shigeta's example that the Japanese people are genuinely polite and compassionate.

The other films took place after the war. Immediate postwar problems were explored in Joe . . . , Three Stripes . . . , and Teahouse . . . . As Joe Butterfly Burgess Meredith is a lovable small-time hoodlum using the blackmarket to care for his people. He and a group of American magazine writers get along beautifully. Meredith picked up his "hoodlum" habits in prewar United States—quite different from the Ivy League or West Coast education of Sessue Hayakawa or Richard Loo in 1939-1947 pictures.

Glen Ford's problems in Teahouse . . . are mostly comical, arising to a large extent from military bureaucracy. He is sent to a Japanese village to build a schoolhouse in the shape of the Pentagon and to democratize the villagers. Instead, he is assimilated into the Japanese life style, much to the chagrin of commanding officer Paul Ford. Also, Glen Ford learns the correct meaning of geisha.

Ford relearns the meaning of geisha in Cry . . ., in which he and his men fall in love with the girls of a geisha house and quite unwittingly aid a group of orphans.

Probably the most moving and best of the Japanese films was Sayonara (1957). Marlon Brando plays an ace pilot, a redneck southerner, who learns that Americans have no reason whatsoever to feel superior to the Japanese. Military short-sightedness conspires to keep him and dancer Miko Taka apart and leads to Red Buttons' death.

In each of these films the Japanese were proud, cultured, polite, and sincere. It is they who teach Americans, not the reverse. And the biggest lesson learned by Americans was racial tolerance.

It is interesting to note that the postwar films about Japan never focused on any of the destruction of the war. Joe . . . mentioned people starving, but none of the films ever depicted ruined cities or any of the other consequences of the atomic bomb. On the other hand the films of Europe and particularly of Germany made by Hollywood in 1948-1962 emphasized and advertised portrayal of the ruin of Europe. Japanese children were depicted as lovable innocents. Frequently, movies that included postwar German children featured adolescents running in neo-Nazi gangs, e.g. Verboten (1959). Why there should have been a difference in the portrayal of Germany and Japan is no easy question to answer. Perhaps it was related to a conscious or sub-conscious maneuver by Hollywood to avoid reminders of the dropping of the atomic bomb. Perhaps it was related to East Germany being a foe in the Cold War or West Germany being an ally. Or, perhaps Japanese children are just naturally more appealing than German.

Some of the Nazi characteristics stayed with Germans in films produced in 1948-1962 but the label was missing. Hitler was featured in two pictures (The Magic Face, 1951, and Hitler, 1962) and Nazi renegades in Verboten, Sealed Verdict (1948), and The Devil Makes Three (1952). Stalag 17 (1953) continued the tradition of the fumbling German-- an image carried on in television by Hogan's Heroes.[2]

The new German was presented by the screen in three versions.

---

[2]Hogan's Heroes has recently been sued for plagiarism by the authors of Stalag 17. For details see Variety, May 12, 1971, p. 1.

First was the veteran soldier who fought because Germany was his country, and only as the war evolved did he begin to doubt Hitler. Second, young soldiers, originally ardent Nazis, experienced disillusion in the latter stages of the war and attempted to rectify their mistakes. Finally, civilians and some soldiers were battered and punished by the Nazis and the war itself.

James Mason in The Desert Fox (1951) and Kurt Jurgens in The Enemy Below (1958) provided memorable performances as veteran soldiers while John Wayne in The Sea Chase (1955) and Van Heflin in Under Ten Flags (1960) played similar roles with less competence.

As Rommel, Mason is the perfect career soldier who believes, "A soldier has just one purpose--to carry out the orders of his superiors. All else is politics." Even in the face of inept interference from Hitler and the compounding evidence of impending defeat, Mason remains loyal to the leaders of his country. He cannot ignore the evidence, but he is a soldier. An old friend asks him to aid a plot against Hitler because "we prefer to be defeated as human beings." Still Mason refuses, "I'm a soldier not a politician."

In Enemy . . . Jurgens engages in an unforgettable battle of wits with submarine chaser commander Robert Mitchum. Jurgens is noble in defeat. He is skeptical of Hitler's "race of supermen," who shake at the explosion of depth charges. Despite open doubt about the success of the war he pursues his duty to the utmost.

Two of the young Germans experience abrupt reformation before turning against their former buddies. Oskar Warner in Decision Before Dawn (1951) and Van Johnson in The Last Blitzkrieg (1959) at one time enthusiastically supported the Third Reich. In prison camp, however,

Warner concludes that defeat is inevitable and must be hastened so
that reconstruction can begin and lives can be saved. He returns to
Germany as a spy and serves admirably before death. Johnson plays
the son of a renowned German general and is entrusted with leading a
squad of English-speaking Germans behind American lines during the
last days of the war. The plan raises havoc for a time, but the
group members are mostly killed and Johnson gradually repudiates his
Nazi ideals. The compassion of American soldiers leads him to condemnation of his leaders.

Marlon Brando's disenchantment in The Young Lions (1958) does
not turn him into a raving anti-Nazi. In fact, Brando throughout the
film is passive as events gradually defuse his faith in Hitler. He
falters to utter despair through involvement with the wife of a commanding officer and a French girl with whom he cannot maintain a relationship and when he refuses to shoot a prisoner and learns the secrets of
a concentration camp. His agony is ended by an American rifleman who
in many ways displays more Fascist characteristics than Brando.

The victims of the war were trapped by circumstances which they
could not escape. For Millie Perkins in The Diary of Anne Frank (1959)
the circumstance is that she is Jewish. The Diary . . . effectively
conveys the social relationships and emotions of the hunted rather than
the violence of the hunter.

In A Time to Love and a Time to Die (1958) John Gavin returns
home from the Russian front to find no home and no parents. He is
amazed by the suffering of the home front but ignores it when he falls
in love. The couple finds happiness for a few days, and when Gavin
returns to the front one is certain he will not return.

Finally, <u>Fraulein</u> (1958) described deprivation of postwar
Germany through the story of Dana Wynter. The daughter of a college
professor, Wynter has to deal with poverty and hardship after the
death of her father. She barely escapes a Russian colonel who wants
to make her his mistress and other acquaintances who want her to
become a prostitute. She picks up bricks for a living while continu-
ing to believe her fiance will find her and they will be happy once
again.

Throughout, she bitterly rejects the romantic advances of
Mel Ferrer. He finds her fiance living with another woman, handicapped,
and minus a will to live. Finally, Ferrer corrects the situation by
marrying her and taking her to the States. Wynter represented a group
of Germans who did not necessarily want the war nor did they necessarily
support it, but they suffered the consequences.

Probably the best known picture about postwar Germany was
<u>Judgment at Nuremberg</u> (1961), which spotlighted the anguish and monu-
mental implications of the Nuremberg decisions. The principals were
Spencer Tracy, a gentle and compassionate judge, and Burt Lancaster,
a noted German jurist on trial for complicity in Nazi atrocities.
Lancaster defends himself before finally admitting guilt, which serves
as a reminder that even those who served Hitler only to avoid death
had to be punished. However, the film makes the point that many Germans
repented, and that those Germans surviving the war and punishment were
not the totalitarian Fascists who started the conflict.

Summary

During 1948-1962 Hollywood largely ignored the contributions

of allies in its war movies. Some allies were featured--though not
as large a proportion as in 1939-1947--but in roles that frequently
had little significance in war efforts or did not require the characters
to devote full attention to war. For the screen, then, 1948-1962 was
a period of confrontation between the United States and the enemy in
whatever war was being depicted.

The enemy was presented in a variety of poses. The Korean War
pictures of 1948-1962 portrayed the North Koreans and the Chinese as
hazy ogres. The Cold War enemy was primarily the Russians, which in
most cases were synonymous with Communists. Russians, especially as
agents in the United States, were gangster-like while East European
Communists generally sought escape from communism in order to gain
material satisfaction.

The Germans and Japanese underwent character alterations in
the World War II films produced in 1948-1962. The four-eyed barbaric
image of the Japanese was replaced in many instances by sensitive,
sincerely polite characters while the association of Germany with
fascism faded. Instead, the Germans were true patriots who recognized
the mistakes of Hitler by the conclusion of the films, or civilians
victimized by the war. The transformations of character for Germans
and Japanese seemed to be related to dimmed emotions and national
realignments brought on by the Cold War.

CHAPTER IX

SELFISHNESS AND NON-AMERICANS

American heroes of 1963-1970 tended to brush aside nationalistic
goals and to discard moralistic rationalizations of warfare. The
American characters became denationalized insofar as they substituted
self endeavors for nationalistic behavior. Allies and enemies of 1963-
1970 displayed the same characteristic of pursuing self first and other
goals second. Thus, by nationality becoming less important in the
characters' motivations, a blurring of national distinctions occurred
in 1963-1970's war films.

The blurring of nationalities by Hollywood seems to be related
to a number of conditions, which were mentioned first in Chapter III.
First, it may be reflective of a recognition that atomic warfare affects
everyone equally disastrously regardless of nationality. It may also be
a partial consequence of a recognition that war intrinsically involves
violence on the part of either side. Finally, the decline of nationality
as a significant criterion of identification may be the result of the
growing internationalization of the movie industry. A film packed with
American chauvinism would be rather difficult to market outside the
United States.

It was suspected that smoothing of national distinctions would
be accompanied by an increase in the proportion of allies and enemies
in dominant roles. A small shift was evident in the war films of 1963-
1970. Non-Americans held dominant roles in 17.0 per cent of the pictures, compared to 13.3 per cent in 1948-1962--an indication of what
was happening in 1963-1970 but in itself no more than that. (For

distribution of dominant and secondary roles according to nationality in 1963-1970 see Table 39.)

Because there were few allies and enemies in 1963-1970, the results of the content analysis are rather inconclusive. World War II films produced in 1963-1970 included ten allies and four enemies in featured roles while Cold War pictures had one of each. However, the analysis results are included, and a brief comparison of 1963-1970's World War II allies, enemies, and Americans follows.

Demographically, allies, enemies, and Americans were quite similar. (See Table 40 for demographics of allies and enemies.) The only major differences were that the enemy characters were older, more likely married, and more likely to have military positions as occupations.

These differences were probably related to the fact that two of the four enemies were a general and an admiral, who by the time they achieved such positions had probably advanced in age and established a family (Table 41). Actually, American and enemy military membership was about the same (82.0 per cent for Americans, 75.0 per cent for enemies) while Americans were more often portrayed in warrior roles. Some 88.0 per cent of Americans were either soldiers or spies, compared to 75.0 per cent of the enemy and 60.0 per cent of the allies (Table 42).

Patriotism occupied half of the ten allies as a primary goal while 20.0 pursued primarily war tasks. Enemies' goals were just reversed (50.0 seeking achievement of war tasks and 25.0 patriotism) (Table 43). The American figures were 36.0 per cent for war tasks and 8.0 per cent

TABLE 39

NATIONALITY OF CHARACTERS, 1963-1970

Nationality	Dominant Roles	Subordinate Roles	Total Roles
Cold War			
American	91.3%	8.7%	100.0%
Russian	-	34.7	34.7
Chinese	-	13.0	13.0
East German	4.3	8.7	13.0
Indo-Chinese	-	8.7	8.7
British	-	4.3	4.3
French	4.3	-	4.3
Malayan	-	4.3	4.3
Swedish	-	4.3	4.3
Uncertain	-	8.7	8.7
Total	100.0	95.6	195.6
Number	23	23	23
World War II			
American	78.1	3.1	81.3
German	3.1	39.1	42.2
Japanese	1.6	28.1	29.7
British	7.8	10.9	18.7
Filipino	1.6	12.6	14.2
Italian	1.6	9.4	10.9
French	4.7	3.1	7.8
Belgian	-	3.1	3.1
Norwegian	1.6	1.6	3.1
Canadian	-	1.6	1.6
Greek	-	1.6	1.6
Total	100.0	117.2	217.2
Number	64	64	64

[a]Data derived from question 20 Form A in Appendix I.

TABLE 40

DEMOGRAPHICS OF ALLIES, ENEMIES, 1963–1970

	World War II		Cold War	
	Ally	Enemy	Ally	Enemy
Sex				
Male	80.0%	100.0%	100.0%	– %
Female	20.0	–	–	100.0
Total	100.0	100.0	100.0	100.0
Age				
Youth	10.0	–	–	–
Young adult	20.0	–	–	100.0
Mature adult	50.0	–	100.0	–
Middle age	–	100.0	–	–
Old age	–	–	–	–
No answer	20.0	–	–	–
Total	100.0	100.0	100.0	100.0
Class				
Upper	20.0	25.0	100.0	–
Middle	40.0	25.0	–	–
Lower	–	–	–	–
Outside structure	20.0	50.0	–	100.0
No answer	20.0	–	–	–
Total	100.0	100.0	100.0	100.0
Marital Status				
Married	–	75.0	100.0	–
Never married	50.0	–	–	100.0
Divorced	–	–	–	–
Other	20.0	–	–	–
No answer	30.0	25.0	–	–
Total	100.0	100.0	100.0	100.0
Education				
In school	20.0	–	–	–
High school	–	–	–	–
Undergraduate	20.0	25.0	–	100.0
Higher degree	10.0	–	100.0	–
Other	–	–	–	–
No answer	50.0	75.0	–	–
Total	100.0	100.0	100.0	100.0

TABLE 40--Continued

| | World War II | | Cold War | |
	Ally	Enemy	Ally	Enemy
Nationality				
British	60.0%	- %	- %	- %
French	20.0	-	100.0	-
German	10.0	50.0	-	-
East German	-	-	-	100.0
Italian	-	25.0	-	-
Japanese	-	25.0	-	-
Norwegian	10.0	-	-	-
Total	100.0	100.0	100.0	100.0
Occupation				
Military	10.0	75.0	-	-
Criminal	20.0	-	-	-
Athlete	-	-	-	100.0
Journalist	10.0	-	-	-
Laborer	10.0	-	-	-
Politician	-	25.0	-	-
Self sufficient	10.0	-	-	-
Spy	-	-	100.0	-
Student	10.0	-	-	-
No answer	30.0	-	-	-
Total	100.0	100.0	100.0	100.0
Number	10	4	1	1

[a]Data derived from questions 2-8 Form B in Appendix I.

TABLE 41

MILITARY CHARACTERISTICS OF ALLIES, ENEMIES, 1963-1970

	World War II		Cold War	
	Ally	Enemy	Ally	Enemy
Military Status				
Member	50.0%	75.0%	- %	- %
Former member	10.0	-	-	-
Never member	30.0	-	-	100.0
No answer	10.0	25.0	100.0	-
Total	100.0	100.0	100.0	100.0
Branch				
Army	40.0	50.0	-	-
Navy	-	25.0	-	-
Air force	-	-	-	-
Other	10.0	-	-	-
No answer	50.0	25.0	100.0	100.0
Total	100.0	100.0	100.0	100.0
Rank				
Gen.-Arm.	-	50.0	-	-
Col.-Capt.	20.0	-	-	-
Maj.-Cmdr.	10.0	25.0	-	-
Capt.-Lt.	10.0	-	-	-
Lt.-Ens.	-	-	-	-
Sgt.-CPO	-	-	-	-
Non com	-	-	-	-
Enlisted	-	-	-	-
Other	10.0	-	-	-
No answer	50.0	25.0	100.0	100.0
Total	100.0	100.0	100.0	100.0
Membership Reason				
Career	-	50.0	-	-
Draft	10.0	-	-	-
Patriotism	10.0	-	-	-
Personal	-	-	-	-
Other	-	-	-	-
No answer	80.0	50.0	100.0	100.0
Total	100.0	100.0	100.0	100.0
Number	10	4	1	1

[a]Data derived from questions 15, 16, 18, and 20 Form B
in Appendix I.

TABLE 42

ROLES OF ALLIES, ENEMIES, 1963–1970

Role	World War II		Cold War	
	Ally	Enemy	Ally	Enemy
Spy	20.0%	- %	100.0%	- %
Soldier	40.0	75.0	-	-
Civilian	40.0	25.0	-	100.0
Total	100.0	100.0	100.0	100.0
Number	10	4	1	1

[a]Data derived from question 1 Form B in Appendix I.

for patriotism, but the American hero's distinguishing characteristic was his pursuit of self-oriented goals (21.8 per cent). The allies subscribed to such goals 10.0 per cent of the time and the enemies 25.0 per cent (in other words one character of each).

Finally, both allies and enemies were less dependent than Americans on force as a primary method (allies 20.0 per cent, enemies 25.0 per cent, and Americans 30.0 per cent). The allies depended primarily on trickery (30 per cent), the enemies on knowledge (50.0 per cent) (Table 44).

Differences do exist between allies and enemies and Americans in World War II films of 1963–1970. However, the differences might be the result simply of the number of allies and enemies being so few. They also might be the consequence of the fact that there was one group of allies who had no American counterparts. That group was the "victims" of World War II—civilians who suffered through the war without taking an active part in it. Whatever the causes of the quantitative differences

TABLE 43

PRIMARY GOALS OF ALLIES, ENEMIES, 1963–1970

Primary Goal	World War II		Cold War	
	Ally	Enemy	Ally	Enemy
Safety	10.0%	– %	– %	– %
Escape law	10.0	–	–	–
Health	–	–	–	–
Individualism	–	–	–	100.0
Money	–	–	–	–
Comfort	–	25.0	–	–
Power	–	–	–	–
Adventure	–	–	–	–
Love	10.0	–	–	–
Family	–	–	–	–
Sex	–	–	–	–
War task	20.0	50.0	–	–
Fame	–	–	–	–
Patriotism	50.0	25.0	100.0	–
Justice	–	–	–	–
Truth	–	–	–	–
Revenge	–	–	–	–
Honesty	–	–	–	–
No answer	–	–	–	–
Total	100.0	100.0	100.0	100.0
Number	10	4	1	1

[a]Data derived from question 25 Form B in Appendix I.

the following discussion will focus on qualitative similarities and differences between the 1963–1970 allies and enemies and the self-oriented Americans.

Vietnam War

The Vietnamese resembled the Koreans--North and South--of 1948-1962. The South Vietnamese were portrayed as requiring American aid to maintain freedom from the invading North Vietnamese, a situation resembling South Korea's in 1948-1962.

TABLE 44

PRIMARY METHODS OF ALLIES, ENEMIES, 1963–1970

Primary Method	World War II		Cold War	
	Ally	Enemy	Ally	Enemy
Hard work	- %	- %	- %	- %
Luck	-	-	-	-
Trickery	30.0	25.0	-	-
Knowledge	20.0	50.0	-	-
Charm	20.0	-	100.0	100.0
Force	20.0	25.0	-	-
Persuasion	-	-	-	-
No answer	10.0	-	-	-
Total	100.0	100.0	100.0	100.0
Number	10	4	1	1

[a]Data derived from question 29 Form B in Appendix I.

The Green Berets (1968) gave a standard picture of the evil enemy and the good allies complete with a homeless orphan. The orphan naturally attaches himself to one of the Americans, who is snared in a North Vietnamese trap and thrust against a bed of spikes. The movie shows the influence of the decline of the Motion Picture Code by portraying the sex life of an enemy leader, who is trapped by using an ally agent as sex bait—a departure from 1948–1962 Korean War films but in keeping with 1963–1970 trends.

The standard characterizations are presented by A Yank in Vietnam (1964) with one significant deviation. Marshall Thompson, an American adviser, falls in love with Vietnamese Kieu Nahn. The closest thing to a romance between American and Korean in 1948–1962 was Rock Hudson's platonic relationship with a Korean teacher in Battle Hymn (1957).

Korean War

Of the five Korean War films of 1963-1970, only one departed
greatly from previous portrayals. War Is Hell (1964) and The Young
and the Brave (1963) featured homeless youth, hunger stricken and
frightened. Even M*A*S*H with all its irreverency included an ailing
waif, but, of course, M*A*S*H was an exception because it avoided depictions of military activity--allied, enemy, or American.

The Hook (1963) portrayed a North Korean for the first time
as a human, rather than as a monster whose fulfillment comes through
killing or torture. Enrique Magalona, who appropriately is called
"Gook" throughout the picture, is a frightened young North Korean
soldier, captured by Kirk Douglas and two other Americans. He senses
(since he does not understand English) that he is to be killed. However, his passivity converts the two underlings, and they strive to
prevent Douglas from carrying out orders.

Magalona ultimately is killed--because of his own pacifism.
He cannot bring himself to attack Douglas even with possible death confronting him. His final words are, "Halsuppda" which means "I can't."
But, Douglas, not understanding, shoots him. Magalona had come to view
the enemy as individuals and so did Douglas after shooting him.

Cold War

Representatives of nations replaced communism as the enemy in
1963-1970, but in many cases one East German looked just like another
Chinese. The East Germans were featured in three films and the Chinese
in a pair.

The most unusual of the five starred Ronata Adler in The Wicked

Dreams of Paula Schultz (1968), a second rate, "sexual perils of Pauline."
Adler is a top East German athlete who rebels at wearing drab costumes
during the Olympics. Before the conclusion of the film she has defected
twice, once via pole vault over the Berlin Wall, in a "vast conspiracy
to get people undressed, as clumsily and joylessly as possible."[1]

Standard villain images were projected in The Prize (1963) and
Torn Curtain (1966). In each the East Germans were completely evil
Communists with designs on the world, but both times Paul Newman managed
to foil them. Torn Curtain's brutal but clumsy villainy and resource-
ful underground resembled some of 1939-1947's films.

Except that the audience is told he is a Chinese agent, Victor
Bruno in The Silencers (1966) could be of any nationality. His bald--
or clean shaven--head connotes his bad-guy role, but he is something
more than the typical villain. He has something of an intellect--
though he is not as cunning as Dean Martin in the role of Matt Helm--and
a sophisticated array of technology. He meets a typical end, however,
as his technology cannot protect him from Martin's enslaughts.

In The Chairman (1969) the Chinese are clearly Chinese--of the
Red Guard variety. Ranting and raving, the stereotyped mobs wave Thoughts
of Mao against revisionists through most of the picture. The sinister
Reds are ready to subjugate the world if they can "persuade" one of
their own scientists to relinquish the secret of an enzyme.

The East Germans and Chinese were easily identifiable--with one
exception--in the pictures just mentioned. The villains were villainous
and united through violence. (Of course, one must wonder if there was
a villain in The Wicked . . . .) However, in one group of films the
distinction between hero and villain was not quite so evident (Venetian

---

[1] New York Times, Jan. 4, 1968, p. 5.

Affair (1967), _Ice Station Zebra_ (1968), and _Topaz_ (1969).

In _Venetian . . ._ villain Karl Boehm has no particular nationality. He just happens to be working at the moment for the Russians.
He murders and tortures without feeling and has incorporated behavioristic
theories into his arsenal. American agents similarly lack feeling, merely
trying to accomplish their job in any way possible. Nothing differentiates
the agents of the two powers. They have no strong ideology; they would use
any means available to do their job.

The sides are more distinct in _Topaz_ and _Ice . . ._ but no one is
sure who is on which side. _Ice . . ._ has Ernest Borgnine as a native
Russian turned anti-Communist who is suspected of being a double agent,
Jim Brown as an American Negro and hardcore Marine sergeant with potential
for treason, and Patrick McGoohan as a British agent actually working for
the Russians. Their tactics are so ruthlessly similar that no distinction can be made on the basis of behavior. _Topaz_ also hides the double
agent, who through some quirk is an American, a white Anglo-Saxon (maybe
Protestant) who for no reason other than money works for the other side.
Uncovering him is a French agent in a twist from traditional spy hunts
in which the American spots the traitor among other nationalities.

Some Southeast Asians became individual characters in 1963-1970,
one of which was Elji Okada cofeatured with Marlon Brando in _The Ugly_
American (1963). The story is a tale of mistakes by an American as well
as an Oriental. Okada is a patriotic Sarkhanian who places his country
above the friendship of ambassador Brando. He wants his country to be
neutral. "We do not want to be in the Cold War," he argues, which
Brando misconstrues as "we are Communists." Okada makes mistakes--such
as being deceived by Communists--but at least in this film an Oriental

makes honest, intellectual errors. He is an individual rather than part of a yellow horde.

Russians were also presented in a more human form during 1963-1970, particularly in The Bamboo Saucer (1968) and The Russians Are Coming, The Russians Are Coming (1966). In The Bamboo . . . characterizations are secondary to a simplistic message, i.e. live together or die together. The message of cooperation applies primarily to Americans and Russians as Chinese are still cast in roles of villains.

In The Russians . . . collective characterizations are primary. Stereotyped preconceptions of each other cause Russians and Americans alike a great deal of trouble until they discover that each nationality is similar to the other.

World War II

The American hero of World War II films produced in 1963-1970 was a cold professional whose specialty is violence; a flamboyant secret agent; an unwilling warrior trying to escape war; or an unwilling warrior fighting for personal gain. The allies had no spies and only a few who openly regarded war as irrelevant. However, they included a number of patriots and an additional group of characters, victims, to whom the political purposes of the war had no meaning.

The 1948-1962 era also included victims, who suffered primarily from material discomfort or loss of loved ones. The 1963-1970 victims experienced the same deprivations, but to these problems was added moral depravity, e.g. in The Victors, and loss of timeless values, e.g. in Castle Keep.

The Victors (1963) traces the movement of American soldiers through

Europe: Sicily, Rome, Paris, Belgium, Germany. Hunger, poverty, sexual immorality occur uniformly throughout the continent. Episodes focus on an 11-year-old French boy, a homosexual camp follower; girls sleeping with Americans, Russians, or whomever can provide food, while their parents are in the next room; a young woman indifferent to a decent young American but not to a hoodlum who showers her with clothes; and Melina Mercouri as chief of the Belgium black market begging an American to desert and run her business. The war affects everyone in the same immoral way regardless of nationality.

In Castle Keep (1969) the Belgians who care for a castle are temporary occupants and over time will be replaced. The castle, however, belongs to the ages and cannot be replaced. It is destroyed, and,thus, the picture

> accentuate(s) war's destruction of ideals of art and of human being. There is an added innuendo that war is timeless, that this same destructiveness has accompanied wars past and present . . . (and that) the essential horror of war is its indiscriminate disposition of a cultural heritage in the name of expediency.[2]

Other Europeans experienced the destruction of war in less depressing--for the audience--ways. In The Americanization of Emily (1964) Julie Andrews receives a jolt to her stubborn British patriotism. The young widow, devoutly serving her country as a motor pool driver, is puzzled by James Garner, who instead of passionately rushing to battle tries to avoid combat and live as comfortably as possible. Love overcomes her misgivings. "I fall in love too easily. I shatter too easily."

She also picks up her shattered pieces easily. After Garner's apparent death she realizes she loved him more than country. Thus, when

---

[2]Arthur Knight, "Little Lulus," Saturday Review, Aug. 9, 1969, p. 32.

he returns to a hero's role he did not want nor deserve, she joins him in living a lie she would have haughtily rejected earlier.

The miseries of the old, the young, and the women form the background for Up from the Beach (1965). The light story focuses on bureaucratic inefficiency of an advancing American army which has better things to do than care for French civilians. In a comical but pointed sort of way, Cliff Robertson as the American shepherd learns why the citizenry of a French town can hate the Germans but in apparent contradiction love its German commandant.

It would be stretching reality to call the Italians victims in What Did You Do in the War Daddy? (1966) and Secret of Santa Victoria (1969). (Perhaps Italy was the enemy, but screen Italians were rarely enemies and thus are treated as victims.) The pictures treat the Italians as fun loving, impish, unconcerned. In What . . . Americans march into an Italian village expecting strong resistance but instead find only a soccer match. The war becomes a perpetual orgy for Americans as well as Italians. Italians resist invaders in Secret . . . but only to save a wine supply. Political motivations exist nowhere among the Italians. They may or may not be buffoons, but they continue to survive.

The victims were more interesting characters, the warriors more typical. Many of the warriors were mere supporters of American heroes, for example, the seemingly endless line of Filipino guerrillas (The Raiders of Leyte Gulf, 1963; Cry of Battle, 1963; The Walls of Hell, 1964; The Ravagers, 1965; Ambush Bay (1966); The Longest Hundred Miles, 1968; and Warkill, (1968) and the Italians in The Quick and the Dead (1963). Variations on the partisans theme allowed Norwegian and Italian children to clobber the Germans in <u>Snow Treasure</u> (1968) and <u>Hornet's Nest</u> (1970). Both films emphasized violence for its own sake, sort of a juvenile Dirty Dozen.

An older duplicate of <u>The Dirty Dozen</u> (1967) was provided by a group of criminals in <u>The Secret Invasion</u> (1964). British Intelligence frees five condemned criminals so they might rescue an Italian general held prisoner by the Nazis. Out of the five only Roberto Rocca survives, but the mission is somewhat successful after a pitched battle and dozens of deaths.

Counted among the allies of 1963-1970 were some descendants of professionals of 1948-1962 and socially responsible heroes of 1939-1947. In <u>Tobruk</u> (1967) Rock Hudson and George Peppard lead a group of British soldiers into Rommel's stronghold and blow up the German fuel tanks. Ninety Englishmen hold off 50,000 Germans in completing the mission. Their attitude and method is professional and highlights violence, but the group is largely non-career soldiers and silently patriotic.

An extreme example of the patriotic professional was found in Tony Franciosa as a French intelligence colonel in <u>In Enemy Country</u> (1968). Coldly ruthless devotion to duty is Franciosa's only concern as he betrays an old friend and persuades a lady admirer to marry a Nazi colonel for the good of France. The girl, Anjanette Comer, is something less of a professional. She falls in love with her husband.

Patriotism was also a major motivation of some socially responsible civilians. In <u>The Train</u> (1965) Burt Lancaster is an underground leader tired of fighting and wanting only to relax until the allies drive the Germans out of France. The prospect of France losing great art treasures, however, spurs him to action. <u>The Naked Brigade</u> (1965)

spotlights British aristocrat Shirley Eaton, who is left alone on Crete after her father is killed by the Germans. She is interested only in leaving Crete until at the climactic moment she decides to aid an attack on a Nazi port.

American Dennis Weaver is converted from money-grubbing adventurer to responsibility in Mission Batangas (1968). The interesting twist in this plot is that the source of rehabilitation is Filipino guerrillas, who get along fine without American assistance.

George Chakiris makes the ultimate patriotic sacrifice in 633 Squadron (1964). A Norwegian resistance leader, Chakiris embarks on a mission to demolish antiaircraft guns guarding a German rocket fuel installation. He fails and is tortured severely before dying in the bombs of a raid. Chakiris is interesting because he is a patriot who failed. Perhaps he would have been more successful if he had been less idealistic and more brutal.

Among the enemy characters in World War II films produced in 1963-1970 some of the older stereotypes continued. The greedy, slant-eyed, yellow monkey of 1939-1947 was perpetuated in King Rat (1965) and Ambush Bay (1966). The cultured but sadistic Nazi surfaced in The Train (1965) and Counterpoint (1967). The Train's Paul Schofield is determined to confiscate France's art treasures and shoots forty hostages before being stopped. In Counterpoint Maximillian Schell's tastes run to fine music, and he happens to capture an entire American orchestra during the Battle of the Bulge. His efforts to force the musicians to play for him delays a retreat and brings ultimate defeat.

Other pictures presented significant departures from the stereotypes. In None But the Brave (1965) Matsuya Mihashi plays a Japanese lieutenant, a writer in an uncomfortable role of soldier. He doubts

the worthiness of fighting but is driven by honor to continue. More
humane than the Americans he encounters on an isolated island, he
agrees with the Americans to cooperate in order to survive. However, when
the Americans are rescued, the conventions of war exist again, and he must
fight and die. A similar human relationships were portrayed between
Toshito Mifune and Lee Marvin in Hell in the Pacific (1968).

A Japanese soldier in combat received sympathetic portrayal in
Fox's financial fiasco, Tora Tora Tora (1970). Soh Yamamura as Admiral
Yamamoto doubts the wisdom of attacking Pearl Harbor but carries out his
orders because he is a soldier. The movie does not criticize him or
even the Japanese for attacking Pearl Harbor but treats the act as a
political maneuver full of mistakes on both sides.

A member of the German command disobeyed orders in Is Paris
Burning (1966) in contrast with Yamamura's obedience. As General Von
Choltiz, Gert Froebe is the general responsible for bombing Rotterdam
and Sebastopol but balks at burning Paris. He disobeys orders and lets
the allies take Paris unharmed. His action was not entirely prompted
by nobility. If he had thought burning Paris would have aided the war
effort, he would have obeyed the order. He already knew the war was
lost.

Marlon Brando has the potential in Morituri (1965) to become a
resurrected Nazi like the Germans of 1948-1962. However, his behavior
is motivated by concern for his own safety rather than for Germany's
future. A deserter, he is threatened by the British of being returned
to the Nazis if he does not become a spy. Thus, he is placed aboard
a German blockade runner in an attempt to sabotage 7,000 tons of rubber.

Money moved German guards in Kelly's Heroes (1970) to abandon their post and join the Americans in confiscating gold bullion. German psychiatrist Rod Taylor's motives were only a little more pure in 36 Hours (1964). He uses psychological conditioning in trying to pry D-Day information from James Garner. Taylor is a patriot but is also looking forward to recognition due him upon completion of his assignment.

Helmut Griem was a near stereotype in The McKenzie Break (1970). He has the physical characteristics of the Nazi youth--blonde hair, handsome, a perfect physical specimen, and ruthless. However, he is also intelligent and definitely not bungling. In fact, he organizes fellow prisoners through gymnastics, drills, singing, and skits and practically has British guards looking like the Germans of Stalag 17. Thus, Griem has the physical characteristics of the Nazi and the resourcefulness of previous Americans. His high jinks are entertaining regardless of nationality.

Summary

The allies and enemies of 1963-1970 possessed a variety of characteristics. They included in their ranks some patriots, some professional warriors, some socially responsible heroes, and some stereotyped villains. However, they also included a large number of major characters to whom the political or ideological aspects of war were unimportant--such as the victims damaged by either side, the Italians who learn to exist under whatever master, or the adventurers forced to participate in the wars by coercion or promise of gain. This group of characters were concerned primarily with self and had much in common with the dominant American hero of 1963-1970. In the sharing

of concern with self, the allies, enemies, and Americans underwent a
blurring of national distinctions. Nationality became less important
to the characters personally and less crucial to their war behavior.

CONCLUSION

Throughout 1939–1970 the allies and enemies of Hollywood's war films have been characterized by their differences and similarities to American heroes. During 1939–1947 the allies displayed some of the attributes of social responsibility and affirmed belief in many of the political traditions characteristic of film Americans. At the same time the enemy--Nazis and Japanese--gained at least part of its notoriety by violating traditional American precepts. Thus, the war films produced in 1939–1947 advocated to varying degrees internationalism, but it was an American internationalism--or polynationalism.

The 1948–1962 era of war pictures practically ignored allies of the United States, at least partly reflecting Hollywood understanding of America's isolated responsibility in the Cold War. Cold War enemies were rather shadowy and collective--unlike the Nazis and Japanese of 1939–1947. However, enemies in World War II pictures made in the same era were humanized, a process that seemed at least partially the consequence of the Cold War realignment.

Finally, during 1963–1970 the allies and enemies tended to converge with American in displaying violent characters or rejecting moralistic pursuit of war. In either case nationality became a less crucial distinction of identity. Thus, as in 1939–1947 allies and Americans resembled each other but this time not on uniquely American terms.

PART FOUR

MOTIVES, METHODS, AND CONSEQUENCES

INTRODUCTION

The two preceding sections explored war film characters in an effort to define Hollywood's view of the role of Americans in wars of the past thirty-two years and its conceptions of the contributions of other nationalities in those same wars. Included in Parts Two and Three was some attention to the films' presentation of the justifications, methods, and consequences of war insofar as they were conveyed by major characters. This section will examine these three aspects of war in greater depth, will discuss the influence of Defense Department assistance on war film content, and will explore antiwar pictures of the past thirty-two years.

CHAPTER X

MORALLY RIGHT

On the screen, war as an appropriate instrument of international
policy was not an issue in 1939-1947. Whatever sacrifices, sufferings,
and harm accompanied war were necessary to rid the world of totalitarian
evil. In a situation in which the question is how rather than whether,
it would have been difficult to have produced an antiwar picture--
especially since such a production probably would have been labeled
treason. Thus, 1939-1947's films included no antiwar pictures, restrict-
ing the focus of the analysis of this period to prowar aspects of movies.
Neither does the discussion examine in any great detail relationships
between the Pentagon and Hollywood because in effect Hollywood operated
under the direction of the government during 1942-1945 and it is difficult to differentiate Defense Department and other governmental influences.

Justifications

In an easily forgettable release, Sundown (1941), British bishop
Cedric Hardwicke asserts, "The Church and the Army are the bases of
civilization; the church holds it together and the Army defends it."[1]
This simplistic statement does not completely reflect Hollywood's view
of war in 1939-1947, but it does point to the moralistic base of World
War II. The films of the era evoked most symbols of morality known to
Americans--from mother to family, democracy, apple pie, and even pumpkin
pie. The traditional symbols, though, were mere rationalizations compared

---

[1]Quoted in Motion Picture Herald Product Digest, Nov. 11, 1941,
p. 318.

to the screen's argument of the absolute necessity of ridding the world
of totalitarian evil, i.e. the Nazis in Europe and the Japanese in Asia.

As Table 45 indicates, Hollywood did not delve into the underlying causes of World War II. Only 2.7 per cent of the 405 1939-1947
films examined the causes of the war to any major extent. That contrasts with 52.6 per cent that focused on conduct of the war and 37.5
per cent that featured life during war. Generally, when causes were
mentioned they were blamed on the enemy. The rest of Table 45 indicates
that the enemy's warlike nature was the most frequent cause mentioned by
1939-1947's films (9.1 per cent) and that the enemy and its leaders were
credited with responsibility for the war in 34.8 per cent of the pictures.

Some caution should be used in interpreting the two parts of Table
45 just mentioned because in each of the cases no answer was recorded for
more than 50 per cent of the films. The scarcity of results is partial
evidence that Hollywood did not depict the causes of the war. However,
the scarcity also could be due to the fact that the kind of information
called for might not be ascertained from reviews. Reviews were the
source of 85.5 per cent of the analyses of 1939-1947 movies.

The Nazis and Japanese possessed a number of despicable characteristics, but their greatest sins, according to Hollywood, were their
threats to the American way of life. That assertion in itself was not
enough for Hollywood; the war films also conveyed references to a
multitude of symbols meant to inspire and legitimate the war effort. Most
of the symbols were derived from what is usually considered traditional
Americanism (such as the most frequent symbols, patriotism which was
counted in 12.8 per cent of the 1939-1947 films). Some, however, seemed
to arise from the World War II situation (such as responsibility 6.9 per

TABLE 45

FILMS' VIEW OF WAR'S CAUSES, 1939–1947

	1939–1941	1942	1943	1944	1945	1946–1947	Total
Featured Aspects							
Causes	– %	0.8%	0.9%	9.2%	– %	13.3%	2.7%
Preparations	28.0	10.7	9.6	6.6	7.1	–	9.9
Prevention	–	–	–	–	3.6	–	0.2
Life in war	28.0	25.6	64.3	61.8	39.3	13.3	37.5
Conduct	48.0	67.8	47.0	40.7	50.0	53.3	52.6
Consequences	–	–	0.9	11.8	28.6	20.0	5.2
Total	104.0	104.9	122.6	130.0	128.6	100.0	107.2
War's Causes							
Enemy's nature	16.0	11.6	1.7	14.5	7.1	–	9.1
Territory	8.0	5.0	3.5	–	–	–	3.4
Economic	–	0.8	–	–	–	–	0.2
Religious	–	–	–	–	–	–	–
Ideals	–	0.8	0.9	–	–	–	0.5
Military	–	–	–	–	–	–	–
Political	–	–	–	–	–	–	–
Other	–	–	–	–	–	–	–
No answer	76.0	81.0	91.3	85.5	92.1	93.3	85.4
Total	100.0	100.0	100.0	100.0	100.0	100.0	100.0
Persons Blamed							
Mankind	–	–	–	–	–	–	–
No one	–	0.8	–	1.3	–	6.7	0.7
Enemy	8.0	23.1	10.4	10.5	28.6	–	14.8
Enemy leaders	34.0	23.1	12.2	18.4	17.9	20.0	20.0
Allies	–	–	–	–	–	–	–
Ally leaders	–	–	0.9	2.6	–	6.7	1.0
Other	–	0.8	–	–	–	–	0.2
No answer	58.0	52.1	76.5	67.1	39.3	53.3	53.0
Total	100.0	100.0	100.0	100.0	100.0	100.0	100.0
Number	50	121	115	76	28	15	405

[a]Data derived from questions 12, 31, and 33 Form A in Appendix I.

cent and war task 3.4 per cent) (Table 46).

Table 46 does not differentiate between symbols attached primarily to Americans and symbols attached primarily to allies. If it did, the results would probably show that symbols for Americans were primarily individual and personal including family, love, personal responsibility, and even retribution. The allies' major symbols were collective and generally related to political ideals.

TABLE 46

SYMBOLS OF LEGITIMATION, 1939-1947

Symbol	1939-1941	1942	1943	1944	1945	1946-1947	Total
Patriotism	20.0%	16.5%	1.7%	23.7%	3.6%	6.7%	12.8%
Responsibility	10.0	4.1	7.0	9.2	7.1	–	6.9
Freedom	6.0	5.8	4.3	2.6	3.6	6.7	4.7
War task	2.0	3.3	1.7	5.3	10.7	–	3.4
Democracy	4.0	–	7.0	2.6	3.6	–	3.2
Family, home	4.0	1.7	1.7	5.3	–	–	2.5
Revenge	2.0	–	1.7	5.3	–	6.7	2.5
Journalism	–	5.6	–	–	–	–	1.7
Love	2.0	2.4	1.7	–	3.6	–	1.7
Nat. security	–	1.7	–	–	3.6	13.3	1.2
Materialism	–	2.4	–	1.3	–	–	1.0
Better world	–	–	–	–	10.7	–	0.7
Situation	2.0	–	–	–	3.6	–	0.5
Religion	2.0	–	–	–	–	–	0.2
No answer	46.0	56.1	73.0	44.7	39.3	60.0	56.5
Total	100.0	100.0	100.0	100.0	100.0	100.0	100.0
Number	50	121	115	76	28	15	405

[a]Data derived from question 32 Form A in Appendix I.

The differences arise because justifications were adapted to locale and situation. In Europe war was being waged to stop totalitarianism, which had already enveloped the continent and was threatening Britain and Russia. The Asian enemy threatened liberty also but

in the Pacific revenge was as great or greater a motive as idealism.
The home-front rationalizations were more uniquely American. Americans
were fighting for normalcy--home, family, small towns, financial security,
Americana. Normalcy had to be suspended in order to protect it, but the
screen constantly reminded home-front Americans what normalcy was like--
Hollywood variety.

Thus, each of the war fronts (Europe, Pacific, and home) was given
different kinds of justifications by Hollywood. The differences will be
explored further in the following discussion. First, however, it should
be noted that the justifications provided by war films often occur on
two partially overlapping levels. One level consists of those platitudes
muttered by characters as reasons for fighting--democracy, God, life,
home, love, humanity, etc. Those verbalizations are often just lip
service. For example, it is difficult to believe William Bendix as a
Polish-American in Wake Island (1942) as he asserts, "There are no
atheists in foxholes." The other kind of justification arises from an
impression of the film as a whole. The following discussion focuses on
the second variety of justification with occasional side comments about
the verbalizations.

In the Pacific war films, revenge seemed to be a primary motive.
Pearl Harbor could have been exploited for such a battle cry but was
not--with some evidence that the government discouraged such inclinations.
Instead, Hollywood before the first American victories in the Pacific
focused on early defeats, presenting the American military valiantly
holding out against overwhelming odds. Wake Island was the first such
dramatization--a tale of 377 Marines fending off thousands of Japanese
for sixteen days before final defeat. Bataan (1943) had thirteen

Americans fighting off an entire Japanese army. In both films an underlying theme was that the Americans' defeat was only a matter of numbers;
on more equal footing the result would be different.

The Americans were fighting "to destroy destruction," according
to Brian Donlevy in Wake Island. Destruction included havoc raised among
the Filipinos and Chinese, but perhaps even more importantly destruction
meant death and torture of American soldiers and sexual assault of American
women. In an era of rigid compliance with the Motion Picture Production
Code, films about nurses during the invasion of the Philippines were
quite daring in implication if not depiction. Cry Havoc (1944) featured
a large group of nurses including Joan Blondell as "an easy going strip-
teaser (who) shows her roommates how she used to do her act."[2] The
girls surrender to the Japanese at the conclusion with implication that
more is to follow. (Time said the stage play included offstage screams
of nurses surrendering to the Japanese, but this tidbit was excluded
from the movie.)[3] So Proudly We Hail (1943) pictured Veronica Lake
killing herself and a bunch of Japanese with a grenade--hidden in her
brassiere.[4]

Besides the sexual implications So Proudly . . . portrayed the
Japanese strafing a Red Cross base. Hollywood's Japanese were nationally
barbaric, representing every uncivilized characteristic known to man.
Fighting such an enemy--especially since he struck the first blow in an

---

[2]Philip T. Hartung, "Shall We Join the Ladies?" Commonweal, Dec.
10, 1943, p. 206.

[3]"The New Pictures," Time, Dec. 6, 1943, p. 56.

[4]Variety, June 23, 1943, p. 24.

underhanded fashion--was the only alternative, according to the screen.
Thus, most screen Americans would have agreed with the radioman in Wake
Island who when asked if the hopelessly outnumbered Marines needed any-
thing replied, "Send more Japs."

While the primary confrontation in Europe was political (between
democracy and totalitarianism, fascism, and Nazism) the Nazis' wrong-
doings were not limited to politics. They more than matched the
Japanese in violating human ethics. The highest number of violations
per minute probably came in Hitler's Children (1943). The picture had
the Nazis transgressing against individual freedom, motherhood, true
love, religion, free expression, family, bodily integrity, and life.

The infringement of the Nazis on individual freedom was a recurrent theme in 1939-1941. A Jewish college professor felt the oppression in The Mortal Storm (1940) while physical torture and emotional
agony followed Fredric March as he tried to stay out of reach of the
Nazis. March was a former soldier who could not obey his new superiors.
He fled Germany but his travels only delayed an ultimate confrontation,
which he was destined to lose. Putting the Nazis out of sight did not
eliminate the problem.

Hollywood's justifications of the European war effort shifted
slightly after the United States entered the war. The enemy no longer
infringed merely on individual liberties but became the antithesis of
Hollywood's version of democracy and national liberties. The thesis
that Europeans were rabid democrats was repeated several times by the
screen, e.g. This Land Is Mine (1943), North Star (1943), Edge of
Darkness (1943), Hangmen Also Die (1943), and The Moon Is Down (1943).
Patriotism played no small part in any of these films but seemed tightly

intertwined with democratic ideals.

On the home front the threat of immediate danger was not imminent. However, repaying the Japanese and aiding democracy in Europe were acceptable goals for Hollywood's Americans. Only a few rebelled, and they were quickly converted to the proper viewpoint, e.g. The War Against Mrs. Hadley (1942).

Most went to war quite willingly. They were not warmongers since many had momentary doubts. For example, Since You Went Away (1944) addressed the emotional question of "what right has an over-38 father got to leave his family and a good advertising agency post to fight a young man's war."[5] The reason, according to the film, is to insure his family's future happiness and security. To put it more simply, as Ginger Rogers did in Tender Comrade (1943) while explaining her husband's death to her infant son, "He did it for you--Chris boy."[6]

Another version of the rationale was found in Happy Land (1943), which traces the boyhood of an American casualty. Grandfather's ghost emphasizes that "as long as American kids can be Boy Scouts and aim to do a good turn every day--as long as they can eat ice cream--go to high school . . . play football--have a picnic in Brigg's Woods--then it'll be worthwhile."[7]

On all three fronts motivations for war during 1939-1947 assumed the cloak of righteousness. The American could take his choice: defeat a barbaric almost inhuman people in Asia and at the same time repay

[5]Variety, July 19, 1944, p. 18.

[6]Quoted in "The New Pictures," Time, March 27, 1944, p. 94.

[7]Philip T. Hartung, "Of Thee I Sing," Commonweal, Dec. 24, 1943, p. 253.

treachery; defend democracy in Europe; or relinquish normalcy temporarily in order to insure its permanency. Once these goals were achieved, the future seemed promising, as expressed by a Russian peasant in North Star (1943): "All people will learn and see that wars do not have to be . . . We will make a free world for all men."

Methods

As mentioned in Chapters I and IV, the war movies made in 1939-1947 told stories of the entire war-making process--from manufacturing to battlefield. A total of 47.9 per cent of the era's pictures was about the home front, and about 40 per cent of those focused on civilian activities (Table 2). Consequently, a substantial portion of war pictures did not examine the violent implications of war as a method. In fact, only 23.5 per cent of the films had war or violence as a dominant theme (Table 47). War, then, included such non-violent activities as growing food, building ships and planes, conserving natural resources, waiting loyally for loved ones, and entertaining the troops.

The top civilian activities on the home front included one with the potential for violence: being alert for espionage (found in 12.2 per cent of 1939-1947's films). Other top activities included producing goods (7.4 per cent) and remaining faithful to loved ones (6.7 per cent) (Table 48). Hindrances to the war effort that were emphasized most were unconcern with the war (12.6 per cent) and economic opportunism (4.7 per cent).

Being alert for espionage often forced the American on the home front into violence as he personally stopped the spies. Whether such violence contributed to the image of war is doubtful, however. The

TABLE 47

DOMINANT FILM THEMES, 1939–1947

Dominant Theme	1939–1941	1942	1943	1944	1945	1946–1947	Total
Patriotism	24.0%	19.0%	15.7%	5.3%	14.3%	20.0%	15.5%
War	4.0	12.4	18.3	18.4	21.4	13.3	14.8
Law enforcement	14.0	14.0	3.5	10.5	7.1	–	9.1
Violence	10.0	9.9	7.8	6.6	7.1	13.3	8.6
Love	4.0	2.5	11.3	9.2	–	13.3	6.7
Inner conflict	6.0	8.3	4.3	3.9	7.1	6.7	5.9
Armed forces	34.0	3.3	0.9	10.5	10.7	–	5.7
Foreigners	8.0	3.3	5.2	7.9	10.7	–	5.7
Entertainment	6.0	3.3	7.8	6.6	–	–	5.2
Comraderie	2.0	–	–	3.9	10.7	–	2.7
Family	–	4.1	2.6	3.9	–	–	2.7
Public affairs	–	0.8	3.5	1.3	–	13.3	2.2
Business	–	0.8	4.3	2.6	–	–	2.0
Science	4.0	0.8	2.6	–	–	13.3	2.0
Nature	–	2.5	–	1.3	–	6.7	1.2
Health	2.0	–	–	1.3	3.6	–	0.7
Press	–	1.7	0.9	–	–	–	0.7
Religion	–	–	1.7	–	–	–	0.5
Mental health	–	–	–	2.6	–	–	0.5
Superstition	–	0.8	–	–	3.6	–	0.5
Materialism	–	–	–	1.3	–	–	0.2
Minorities	–	0.8	–	–	–	–	0.2
Alcoholism	–	–	–	–	–	–	–
Domestics	–	–	–	–	–	–	–
Education	–	–	–	–	–	–	–
Fine Arts	–	–	–	–	–	–	–
Accidents	–	–	–	–	–	–	–
Total	100.0	100.0	100.0	100.0	100.0	100.0	100.0
Number	50	121	115	76	28	15	405

[a]Data derived from question 43 Form A in Appendix I.

TABLE 48

DOMINANT CIVILIAN WAR ACTIVITIES, 1939-1947

	1939-1941	1942	1943	1944	1945	1946-1947	Total
H. F. Contribution							
Spy alertness	12.0%	19.8%	12.2%	3.9%	7.1%	- %	12.2%
Production	2.0	5.8	12.2	10.5	-	-	7.4
Faithfulness	8.0	1.7	6.1	10.5	14.3	13.3	6.7
Entertainment	8.0	4.1	6.1	7.9	-	-	5.4
Arms development	8.0	7.4	1.7	1.3	3.6	13.3	4.7
Patriotism	-	0.8	4.3	5.3	-	13.3	3.0
Civil defense	4.0	2.5	1.7	-	-	-	1.7
Buy bonds	-	-	2.6	-	-	-	0.7
Conservation	-	0.8	-	2.6	-	-	0.7
Avoid gossip	-	-	-	-	-	-	-
No answer	58.0	57.0	53.0	57.9	75.0	60.0	57.5
Total	100.0	100.0	100.0	100.0	100.0	100.0	100.0
H. F. Hindrance							
Apathy	6.0	10.7	20.9	14.4	-	6.7	12.6
Opportunism	2.0	2.5	7.8	5.3	-	13.3	4.7
Not patriotic	-	6.8	2.6	1.3	-	-	3.0
Reject war aims	-	-	1.7	1.3	10.7	-	1.7
Unfaithfulness	-	0.8	1.7	-	-	-	0.7
Extravagance	-	-	-	-	-	-	-
Other	-	0.8	-	1.3	-	-	0.5
No answer	92.0	78.5	65.2	76.3	89.3	80.0	76.8
Total	100.0	100.0	100.0	100.0	100.0	100.0	100.0
W. F. Activity							
Underground	8.0	6.6	14.8	9.2	7.1	6.7	9.6
Patriotism	2.0	0.8	3.5	22.4	3.6	-	5.9
Spy alertness	-	11.6	-	1.3	3.6	-	4.0
Para-military	-	2.5	3.5	5.3	14.3	-	3.7
Existing	10.0	3.3	-	2.6	7.1	-	3.2
Treason	2.0	4.1	2.6	2.6	3.6	-	3.0
Civil defense	6.0	2.5	-	2.6	-	-	2.0
Normalcy	2.0	3.3	1.7	-	-	-	1.7
Entertainment	-	1.6	0.9	2.6	-	-	1.2
Arms development	2.0	0.8	-	1.3	-	6.7	1.0
Faithfulness	-	0.8	-	2.6	-	-	0.7
Production	-	-	1.7	1.3	-	-	0.7
Avoid gossip	-	0.8	-	-	-	-	0.2
Conservation	-	-	-	-	-	-	
No answer	68.0	61.2	71.3	46.1	60.7	86.7	61.5
Number	50	121	115	76	28	15	405

[a]Data derived from questions 26-28 Form A in Appendix I.

[b]H.F.--Home Front; W.F.--War Front

espionage stories so often closely resembled past gangster movies that
it was difficult at times to remain aware of their war implications,
e.g. This Gun for Hire (1942).

Table 47 also summarizes the activities of war-front civilians,
who found direct ways to engage the enemy. Their primary activities
were the underground (9.6 per cent) and patriotism (5.9), which was
often expressed by participation in para-military groups (3.7 per cent).
In war-front situations civilians often had to resort to force as a
last resort to defend themselves. However, they frequently relied on
less violent means--and often quite successfully--such as faith, knowledge, idealism, righteousness, and wit.

While 34.3 per cent of 1939-1947's pictures were specifically about
espionage, relatively few pictures featured American and allied spies
(17.8 per cent) (Table 49). Nearly twice as many (33.3 per cent) depicted
enemy agents. Enemy agents frequently were confronted by civilians during
1939-1947 in keeping with the civilian emphasis during the era. By portraying enemy agents and not ally or American spies, the enemy could be
cast in the role of aggressor and the allies as victims acting only in
self defense.

Even military pictures did not concentrate extensively on the
violent aspects of war. Fighting was the primary military activity in
1939-1947 films (featured by 11.1 per cent of the pictures) but almost
as much attention was given to the preliminaries (9.9 per cent focused
on training) (Table 50). The relatively low amount of attention to
military combat is partly due to the fact that the military was not a
predominant film topic during 1939-1947 (featured in 25.7 per cent of
the movies), which in turn was partially the result of governmental
casting of the war as a civilian as well as a military effort.

TABLE 49

DOMINANT SPY ACTIVITIES, 1939-1947

Dominant Activity	1939-1941	1942	1943	1944	1945	1946-1947	Total
Ally and American Spies							
Counterespionage	20.0%	18.2%	2.6%	2.6%	3.6%	13.3%	9.9%
Get information	–	4.3	3.5	1.3	7.1	6.7	3.0
Protect secrets	2.0	4.1	0.9	1.3	–	–	1.7
Sabotage	–	1.7	0.9	–	–	6.7	1.0
Assassination	–	0.8	–	1.3	–	–	0.5
Protect people	–	1.7	–	–	–	–	0.5
Stop sabotage	–	0.8	–	–	–	–	0.2
Other	–	–	1.7	–	–	–	1.0
No answer	78.0	68.6	90.4	93.4	92.1	13.3	82.2
Total	100.0	100.0	100.0	100.0	100.0	60.0	100.0
						100.0	
Enemy Spies							
Sabotage	6.0	20.7	15.7	7.9	–	–	12.8
Get information	12.0	9.9	5.2	3.9	3.6	20.0	7.6
Assassination	6.0	8.3	2.6	1.3	10.7	–	4.9
Protect secrets	4.0	1.7	–	–	–	–	1.0
Counterespionage	–	0.8	0.9	–	–	–	0.5
Protect people	–	–	–	–	–	–	–
Stop sabotage	–	–	–	–	–	–	–
Other	6.0	11.6	3.5	2.6	–	13.3	6.2
No answer	66.0	47.1	72.2	84.2	85.7	66.7	66.7
Total	100.0	100.0	100.0	100.0	100.0	100.0	100.0
Number	50	121	115	76	28	15	405

[a]Data derived from question 29 Form A in Appendix I.

[b]"Other" for enemy spies consists mostly of trying to steal secrets.

TABLE 50

DEPICTION OF MILITARY, 1939-1947

	1939-1941	1942	1943	1944	1945	1946-1947	Total
American Branch							
Army	20.0%	14.9%	8.7%	10.5%	25.0%	20.0%	13.6%
Navy	10.0	5.0	3.5	10.5	7.1	6.7	6.4
Air Corps	-	1.7	4.3	6.6	-	6.7	3.2
Marines	2.0	2.4	2.6	1.3	3.6	-	2.2
Coast Guard	-	-	-	-	-	-	-
Other	-	-	-	1.3	-	-	0.2
No answer	68.0	76.0	80.9	69.7	64.3	66.7	74.3
Total	100.0	100.0	100.0	100.0	100.0	100.0	100.0
Specialty							
Infantry	8.0	6.6	7.0	6.6	7.1	-	6.7
Bomber	-	1.7	2.6	3.9	-	6.7	2.2
Fighter plane	6.0	1.7	1.7	1.3	-	-	2.0
Intelligence	4.0	2.5	-	-	3.6	13.3	2.0
Artillery	-	-	1.7	1.3	71.	-	1.2
Medical	2.0	-	1.7	2.6	-	-	1.2
Submarine	-	0.8	0.9	2.6	-	6.7	1.2
Tanks	2.0	0.8	0.9	-	-	-	1.2
Engineers	-	-	-	1.3	3.6	-	1.0
Warship	4.0	0.8	0.9	-	-	-	1.0
Commandos	-	1.7	0.9	-	-	-	0.7
Canine	-	0.8	-	1.3	-	6.7	0.7
Paratroops	4.0	-	-	-	3.6	-	0.7
Small ships	-	-	1.7	-	3.6	-	0.7
Women's corps	-	0.8	-	2.6	-	-	0.7
Blimps	-	-	-	-	3.6	-	0.2
Carriers	-	-	-	1.3	-	-	0.2
High command	-	-	-	-	3.6	-	0.2
Prison camps	-	-	-	1.3	-	-	0.2
Radio	-	0.8	-	-	-	-	0.2
Supply	-	-	-	1.3	-	-	0.2
Test planes	2.0	-	-	-	-	-	0.2
No answer	68.0	81.0	80.0	72.3	64.3	66.7	75.5
Total	100.0	100.0	100.0	100.0	100.0	100.0	100.0
Activity							
Combat	4.0	9.1	11.1	9.2	25.0	33.0	11.1
Training	24.0	9.9	7.0	9.2	3.6	-	9.9
Intelligence	4.0	3.3	-	1.3	3.6	-	2.0
Medical	4.0	0.8	1.7	2.6	-	-	1.7
Transportation	-	-	1.7	3.9	3.6	-	1.5
Occupation	-	-	1.7	1.3	3.6	-	1.0

TABLE 50--Continued

	1939–1941	1942	1943	1944	1945	1946–1947	Total
Supply	– %	– %	0.9%	2.6%	3.6%	– %	1.0%
Strategy	–	–	–	–	–	–	–
Other	–	–	–	1.3	3.6	–	0.5
Total	100.0	100.0	100.0	100.0	100.0	100.0	100.0

Military Image

Americans and Allies							
Favorable	38.0	31.4	35.7	36.8	50.0	33.3	35.5
Unfavorable	–	0.8	–	–	3.6	–	0.5
Mixed	8.0	3.3	–	2.6	3.6	6.7	3.0
Not applicable	54.0	64.4	64.3	60.5	42.9	60.0	60.7
Total	100.0	100.0	100.0	100.0	100.0	100.0	100.0

Enemy							
Favorable	–	–	–	–	–	–	–
Unfavorable	28.0	31.4	41.7	31.6	39.3	20.0	34.1
Mixed	–	–	–	1.3	7.1	–	3.0
Not applicable	72.0	68.7	58.3	67.1	53.6	80.0	63.0
Total	100.0	100.0	100.0	100.0	100.0	100.0	100.0
Number	50	121	115	76	28	15	405

[a] Data derived from questions 22-25 Form A in Appendix I.

For American and ally characters the methods of war belonged
to anyone who would use them. They were not restricted to a warrior
elite. Hence the individual citizen could and did participate in
actually fighting the war. In fact, the individual was the most important
factor in victory in 26.2 per cent of 1939-1947's films (Table 51). The
second most important reason was material resources (arms, food, manufactured goods, raw materials, etc.) which were mentioned in 15.1 per
cent of the films.

TABLE 51

REASONS FOR VICTORIES, 1939-1947

Victory Reason	1939-1941	1942	1943	1944	1945	1946-1947	Total
Individuals	28.0%	39.7%	20.0%	18.4%	17.9%	13.3%	26.2%
Resources	14.0	11.6	21.7	9.2	10.7	26.7	15.1
Methods	6.0	9.9	11.3	14.4	17.9	33.3	12.2
Goals	10.0	6.6	13.0	13.1	3.6	–	9.6
Circumstance	–	6.9	5.2	6.5	3.6	6.7	5.2
Supreme being	–	–	–	–	–	–	–
No answer	42.0	25.6	28.7	38.2	46.4	20.0	31.5
Total	100.0	100.0	100.0	100.0	100.0	100.0	100.0
Number	50	121	115	76	28	15	405

[a]Data derived from question 41 Form A in Appendix I.

Throughout 1939-1947 numerous heroes fought fascism single
handedly. In Foreign Correspondent (1940) Joel McCrea exploits his
police-reporter pragmatism to reveal Nazi activities, while in Watch on
the Rhine (1943) Paul Lukas is a firm opponent of Nazism. When his
American mother-in-law questions him about his occupation, he replies
that he is an anti-Fascist. His mother-in-law says, "We're all anti-
Fascists," bringing a quick retort from daughter Bette Davis: "But he

does something about it."

Civilians were sometimes successful, sometimes not, and sometimes as in Lukas' case the outcome was in doubt. In fact, fewer than three-fourths of the 1939-1947 films had an unequivocally happy-successful ending (Table 52).

TABLE 52

OUTCOME OF FILMS, 1939-1947

Outcome	1939-1941	1942	1943	1944	1945	1946-1947	Total
Happy-success	74.0%	80.2%	67.8%	68.4%	57.1%	80.0%	72.1%
Unhappy-success	8.0	10.7	18.3	10.5	17.9	13.3	13.0
Mixed-success	6.0	0.8	0.9	1.3	7.1	–	2.0
Happy-failure	–	0.8	–	–	–	–	0.2
Unhappy-failure	2.0	1.7	3.5	3.9	3.6	–	2.7
Mixed-failure	–	0.8	0.9	–	–	–	0.5
Happy-mixed	2.0	0.8	–	–	–	–	0.5
Unhappy-mixed	–	0.8	1.7	1.3	–	–	1.0
Mixed-mixed	8.0	3.3	7.0	14.4	14.3	6.7	7.9
Total	100.0	100.0	100.0	100.0	100.0	100.0	100.0
Number	50	121	115	76	28	15	405

[a]Data derived from question 42 Form A in Appendix I.

In the years before the United States began to win military battles, American soldiers were little more than individual civilians. They were not cogs in a military machine as they were destined to become. The soldiers fought in groups but groups composed of individuals rather than groups that fought as a whole. The individuals in the groups were often ethnic stereotypes representing different minorities within the United States or various nations of the world. These stereotyped collectivities have since become something of a joke (such as jovial but ignorant William Bendix in Wake . . .) but at the time of their release the films carried implicit messages of cooperation. One such picture was Sahara with Humphrey Bogart as an American sergeant leading a collection that included a Southern bigot, a Black Sudanese, an Italian, an Englishman, and a German.

The point is that the stereotyped groups were not units. They were formed by individuals, who after experience or reflection had relinquished some of their own rights and pleasures for the welfare of the whole.

After American victories were gained in the Pacific and after the invasion of Europe, the society in microcosm continued (as in Gung Ho, 1943), but the military unit started to assume some of the collective characteristics it would take on completely during 1948-1962. Hollywood replaced war as a cooperative exercise with war as a collective exercise. As such war fell less to the civilian and more to the soldier. Fighting Seabees (1944) portrays this transition through John Wayne's realization that the military knows more than civilians about war. The Story of G.I. Joe (1945) avoids the typical heroics of early battle films while conveying the competence of the American soldier. However, an impression from the film is that while the individual soldier is a good fighter, he is not irreplaceable. The war goes on even after the death of experienced, disciplined captain Robert Mitchum. He did his duty well but others are ready to take his place.

An intense curiosity with the technology of war expressed itself in 1939-1947's films. Stories about submarines, bomb sights, bombers, fighter planes, carriers were quite prevalent (Table 50). However, the technology was seldom portrayed as better than the man who used it. Air Force (1943) followed a bomber through a host of problems in the

Philippines and Pacific just after the attack on Pearl Harbor. The plane remained aloft--seemingly with some will of its own--but it was pieced together and flown by its crew. The crew provided the means to keep the plane together and in combat. In other pictures the technology was useless until its masters assumed the cloak of responsibility (Chapter IV).

Technology was depicted as a neutral means by which the responsible nations could defeat the irresponsible. War also was neutral, its beneficial or harmful consequences depending on its user. On the side of the allies war was beneficial because they had moral righteousness on their side. In the hands of the enemy war was catastrophic.

Consequences

A commonly accepted supposition is that an antiwar film must elucidate the consequences of war to be truly effective. Director Francois Truffaut told Robert Hughes, "The effective war film is often the one in which the action begins AFTER the war, when there is nothing but ruins and desolation everywhere."[8] The pictures made in 1939-1947 portrayed ruin and destruction. (An idea of the kind of desolation is conveyed by Table 53, which also lists positive consequences of the war.) However, the tendency of such portrayals was to encourage rather than discourage war feelings.

The reasons feelings were flamed rather than calmed can be traced first to the fact that the war films blamed the enemy rather than war per se for the harm. Secondly, the situations depicted did not represent

---

[8] Quoted in Hughes, *Film: Book II*, p. 189.

TABLE 53

CONSEQUENCES OF WAR, 1939-1947

Consequence	1939-1941	1942	1943	1944	1945	1946-1947	Total
Harmful							
Deprivation	16.0%	2.5%	4.4%	11.8%	- %	- %	6.1%
Depravation	2.0	-	0.9	9.2	10.7	6.7	3.2
Freedom loss	-	3.3	7.8	-	-	-	3.2
Physical harm	-	2.5	6.1	1.3	14.3	20.0	3.2
Family loss	-	1.6	-	1.3	7.1	-	1.2
Lose tradition	2.0	0.8	-	1.3	-	6.7	1.0
Upset routine	-	2.5	-	-	-	-	-
Fear	2.0	-	0.9	-	-	-	0.5
Nat. disunity	-	-	-	-	3.6	-	0.2
Pol. instability	-	-	-	1.3	-	-	0.2
No answer	78.0	86.0	80.0	73.7	64.3	66.7	80.5
Total	100.0	100.0	100.0	100.0	100.0	100.0	100.0
Beneficial							
Heroism	-	7.4	6.1	2.6	3.6	-	4.4
Maturity	2.0	-	0.9	3.9	-	-	1.2
Soc. Respon.	-	-	2.6	3.9	-	-	1.2
Moral reform	2.0	0.8	0.9	-	3.6	-	1.0
No answer	96.0	91.8	89.5	89.6	92.9	100.0	93.1
Total	100.0	100.0	100.0	100.0	100.0	100.0	100.0
Number	50	121	115	76	28	15	405

[a]Data derived from question 39 Form A in Appendix I.

utter despair. In all of them, hope existed in the form of opposition
to the conquerors. Finally, the war did not always cause harm. In
many cases war brought out the nobility of Americans and allies; such
films could hardly have leveled criticism at war.

All of these explanations are related to the idea expressed
earlier that war per se was not an issue in American films during 1939-
1947. War was simply a neutral instrument whose morality depended on
who used it. Even when the enemy was not openly blamed for his various
sins, the audience could make such value judgments on its own. For
example, Journey for Margaret (1943) depicts a group of children
orphaned by the war. The film is not an implicit condemnation of the
Germans, but the audience can attach blame regardless of the film's
position.

Only in the waning years of the war and during the postwar were
some of the detrimental aspects attached to war rather than the enemy.
The unpleasantness of death, injury, and handicap which accompanied
many veterans home was not portrayed during the early parts of the war.
The subject would have been poor for morale. However, as the war's
outcome became fairly certain, Pride of Marines (1945), Till the End
of Time (1946), and The Best Years of Our Lives (1946) focused on
emotional problems and readjustments, an adult returning to a student's
world, and family difficulties. The problems were solved, and the
resolution cast such problems as necessary evils in pursuit of a better
world.

Summary

In war films made in 1939-1947 the nobility of purpose of World

War II tended to overshadow whatever criticism of war as a method that might have arisen. Blame for the war rested with the enemy. War as a method of settling international disputes had neutral connotations; in the hands of the enemy it was evil but a legitimate tool for Americans and allies. Any harmful consequences of World War II were attributed to the enemy not to the war itself. Thus, the films made in 1939-1947 were prowar in the sense that they promoted the American effort without critically examining war. In a situation in which the war purpose is regarded as absolutely moral it is difficult to imagine an antiwar picture.

CHAPTER XI

THE SECURITY OF METHOD

As the reality of the Cold War unfolded and the implications of nuclear warfare became apparent, the United States entrusted its security more and more to a growing military establishment. World War II had caught the country with a minimal professional military force and a deficiency of equipment. Belief that such embarrassment a second time would be fatal to the nation launched an unprecedented peacetime buildup. That buildup had its counterpart in Hollywood's 1948-1962 films.

During 1939-1947 the screen's presentation of war had placed overriding significance on World War II's morality of purpose. Purpose became more pragmatic in 1948-1962 as Hollywood shifted emphasis to the planned specialization of a professional corps of warriors. The screen, thus, spent less time justifying war activities and more on the best way to pursue them.

Justifications

The causes of war were a no more popular film topic in 1948-1962 than they had been in the preceding era. As Table 54 shows, only 1.3 per cent of 1948-1962's 316 films examined the causes of war more than in passing. (In 1939-1947 a total of 2.7 per cent of the pictures focused on causes.) Correspondingly, Hollywood blamed something or someone for starting the wars at a rate even lower in 1948-1962 than in 1939-1947. As in the previous era, the low frequency of response might be attributed to lack of information in reviews, although 37.7

TABLE 54

FILMS' VIEW OF WAR'S CAUSES, 1939-1947

	WWII	Cold	Korea	Total
Featured Aspects				
Causes	2.5%	- %	- %	1.3%
Preparations	3.7	17.0	5.9	8.5
Prevention	-	2.9	-	0.9
Life in war	34.2	36.5	37.3	35.4
Conduct	59.0	51.0	76.5	59.5
Consequences	11.0	4.9	13.7	9.8
Total	113.7	112.5	133.3	115.2
War's Causes				
Enemy's nature	1.2	3.8	2.0	2.2
Territory	-	1.0	3.9	0.9
Economic	-	1.0	-	0.3
Religious	-	-	-	-
Ideals	1.2	1.0	2.0	1.3
Military	0.6	1.9	-	0.9
Political	0.6	9.6	-	3.5
Other	-	-	-	-
No answer	96.2	81.7	92.2	90.8
Total	100.0	100.0	100.0	100.0
Persons Blamed				
Mankind	0.6	1.9	-	0.9
No one	-	-	-	-
Enemy	8.1	4.6	13.7	7.9
Enemy leaders	11.2	15.4	3.9	11.4
Allies	-	-	-	-
Ally leaders	-	-	-	-
Other	-	1.0	-	0.3
No answer	80.1	76.9	80.4	79.4
Total	100.0	100.0	100.0	100.0
Number	161	104	51	316

[a]Data derived from questions 12, 31, and 33 Form A in Appendix I.

per cent of the analyses were based on screenings compared to 14.5 per cent in 1939-1947.

However, it is quite possible that 1948-1962's movies did not place explicit blame for the wars. World War II's emotions had faded, and thus it was not fashionable in 1948-1962 to lambast the Germans and Japanese. Neither was much attention devoted to explaining the origins of the Cold War. Hollywood seemed to assume that everyone knew the ingredients of communism, and that the fact that the enemy was communistic was enough justification.

Of course, many of the traditional American symbols were invoked to legitimize action (Table 55), but frequently those symbols were mere lip service. The top two symbols, though, do reveal something about the dominant justifications of the era.

References to war tasks reflected the predominant concern with the methods of war during 1948-1962. Concern with methods arose out of the fear of the Communists undermining the morale of the United States or destroying it by force. If the proper method were not used, the Communists surely would win.

The threat of the Communists was the subject of many films during the early years of 1948-1962. The threat manifested itself in traditional forms of espionage or military activities, but the greatest danger, according to Hollywood, was the Communists' initiation and exploitation of internal dissension. Practically any contemporary American controversy was identified with communism, e.g. union activities in I Married a Communist (1949) and I Was a Communist for the FBI (1951), dissatisfied veterans in The Red Menace (1949), minorities in Trial (1955), and the possibility of opinion manipulation in The Fearmakers

TABLE 55

SYMBOLS OF LEGITIMATION, 1948-1962

Symbol	WWII	Cold	Korea	Total
Patriotism	8.7%	21.2%	2.0%	12.0%
War task	14.3	1.9	19.6	11.1
Love	5.6	-	2.0	3.2
Better world	2.5	4.6	-	2.8
Freedom	-	5.8	5.9	2.8
Situation	3.7	1.0	3.9	2.8
Family, home	3.1	1.9	2.0	2.5
Nat. security	0.6	5.8	2.0	2.5
Materialism	1.2	4.6	-	2.2
Democracy	-	1.9	5.9	1.6
Religion	0.6	2.9	-	1.3
Responsibility	1.2	1.0	-	0.9
Revenge	1.9	-	-	0.9
Authority	1.2	-	-	0.6
Honor	1.2	-	-	0.6
Pol. necessity	-	1.0	-	0.3
Survival	0.6	-	-	0.3
No answer	53.4	46.9	54.9	51.4
Total	100.0	100.0	100.0	100.0
Number	161	104	51	316

[a]Data derived from question 32 Form A in Appendix I.

(1958).

The underlying motivation in the Cold War films made in 1948-1962 was the fear of Communist takeover or destruction of the United States. This contrasts with the more unselfish purpose that dominated 1939-1947 films--i.e. ridding the world of evil with the idea that a better life would result. The Cold War films made in 1948-1962 did not project a better future; seldom did they look beyond stopping the Communists' immediate thrust.

Likewise, Korean War and World War II pictures produced in 1948-1962 had an orientation toward the immediate. Korean War films

occasionally chastised the North Korean and Chinese Communists for
starting the war and sometimes depicted them in sadistic behavior.
On a whole, though, the act of confronting the Communists took precedence over explaining the origins of the confrontation. The issues of
World War II had faded by 1948-1962, also placing emphasis on how
rather than why.

As Table 55 indicated, patriotism was the most frequent symbol
of legitimation during 1948-1962, thanks primarily to its prevalence
in Cold War films. Patriotism in films of this era, however, was not
the positive, inspirational brand of 1939-1947. Some of the earlier
variety filtered through in 1948-1962 but more often in other nationalities than in Americans and particularly among the new breed of
Germans (Chapter VIII).

American patriotism did not lead to great and noble deeds. Such
deeds—characterized neither as great nor noble—were left to professionals. Instead, patriotism was something that had to be proved.
Loyalty to one's country was a test to meet, e.g. Ernest Borgnine
in Three Brave Men (1957) and Man on a String (1960), and suspicion
of disloyalty was enough to condemn a man.

This rather dreary version of patriotism fit well into the Red
Scare era and reflected to some extent a loss of confidence in noble
causes—by Hollywood if not the real world. The lack of confidence
manifested itself on the screen in a phobia over communism, the trusting of war to professional warriors, and a general incapacity to con-
ceptualize goals beyond an immediate task.

Methods

As Hollywood placed less and less emphasis on the goals of war, the actual conduct of war gained in screen time. Nearly half of 1948-1962's films (48.6 per cent) had war or the armed forces as dominant themes (Table 56). In 1939-1947 the figure was 20.5 per cent. With increased emphasis on fighting, the locale of the films naturally shifted (77.9 per cent of 1948-1962 films occurred in war zones compared to 52.1 per cent in 1939-1947; see Tables 2 and 3). Films about World War II and Korea were largely responsible for the shift since Cold War locales were closer to those of 1939-1947 (46.2 per cent in war zones).

With greater emphasis on combat, civilians--even those in war zones--played less important roles in the fighting. Even Cold War civilians, whose locales more closely resembled those of 1939-1947's civilian warriors, played relatively non-violent war roles. Assuming major responsibility for war-making--as has been stated previously-- was the professional warrior as a spy and a soldier.

The home-front contributions of civilians during 1948-1962 were depicted primarily in Cold War films. Only eleven World War II and Korean War films of the era mentioned civilian contributions. The Cold War civilian made the largest contributions by developing weapons and by remaining faithful to loved ones (each 7.7 per cent). Being alert for spies, which was the leading home-front activity in 1939-1947, dropped to third in 1948-1962 (6.7 per cent compared to the previous era's 12.2 per cent). (See Table 57.)

In war-front pictures during 1948-1962 Hollywood allowed

TABLE 56

DOMINANT FILM THEMES, 1948–1962

Dominant Theme	WWII	Cold	Korea	Total
War	38.6%	26.0%	35.3%	33.8%
Armed forces	13.7	11.5	23.5	14.6
Love	7.8	5.8	3.9	7.0
Law enforcement	5.0	12.5	–	6.6
Violence	4.3	5.7	2.0	4.7
Science	2.5	8.7	–	4.1
Comradeship	3.7	1.9	5.9	3.5
Foreigners	3.1	5.8	2.0	3.8
Patriotism	2.5	3.9	5.9	3.5
Minorities	2.5	–	2.0	1.6
Nature	1.9	1.0	2.0	1.6
Entertainment	0.6	1.9	–	0.9
Family	0.6	1.0	–	0.6
Medical	0.6	–	2.0	0.6
Mental health	0.6	–	2.0	0.6
Accidents	–	–	–	–
Alcoholism	–	–	–	–
Business	–	–	–	–
Domestics	–	–	–	–
Education	–	–	–	–
Fine arts	–	–	–	–
Materialism	–	–	–	–
Press	–	–	–	–
Religion	–	–	–	–
Superstition	–	–	–	–
No answer	0.6	1.0	–	0.6
Total	100.0	100.0	100.0	100.0
Number	161	104	51	316

[a]Data derived from question 43 Form A in Appendix I.

TABLE 57

DOMINANT CIVILIAN WAR ACTIVITIES, 1948-1962

	WWII	Cold	Korea	Total
H.F. Contribution				
Faithfulness	2.5%	7.7%	5.9%	5.1%
Spy alertness	0.6	6.7	2.0	2.8
Arms development	-	7.7	-	2.5
Entertainment	-	5.8	-	1.3
Patriotism	-	3.8	-	1.3
Production	0.6	2.9	-	1.3
Buy bonds	0.6	1.0	-	0.6
Avoid gossip	-	-	-	-
Civil defense	-	-	-	-
Conservation	-	-	-	-
No answer	95.9	64.5	92.2	85.2
Total	100.0	100.0	100.0	100.0
H.F. Hindrance				
Not patriotic	0.6	6.7	2.0	2.8
Apathy	-	6.7	-	2.2
Unfaithfulness	1.2	-	-	0.6
Extravagance	-	-	-	-
Opportunism	-	-	-	-
Reject war aims	-	-	-	-
Other	-	1.0	-	0.3
No answer	98.4	85.6	98.0	94.0
Total	100.0	100.0	100.0	100.0
W.F. Activity				
Existing	11.8	4.6	9.8	9.2
Underground	9.3	10.6	2.0	8.4
Faithfulness	5.6	-	5.9	3.8
Para-military	6.2	1.0	-	3.5
Entertainment	3.1	-	2.0	1.9
Normalcy	1.9	1.0	-	1.3
Civil defense	0.6	1.9	-	0.9
Treason	1.2	1.0	-	0.9
Patriotism	0.6	1.0	-	0.6
Production	0.6	1.0	-	0.6
Spy alertness	-	1.0	-	0.3
Avoid talk	-	-	2.0	0.3
Arms development	-	1.0	-	0.3
Conservation	-	-	-	-
Other	2.5	2.9	2.0	2.5
No answer	56.5	73.1	76.5	65.2
Total	100.0	100.0	100.0	100.0
Number	161	104	51	316

[a]Data derived from questions 26-28 Form A in Appendix I

[b]H.F.--Home Front; W.F.--War Front

civilians the possibility of non-political action--at least in World
War II and Korean War movies. In World War II and Korean War films
of 1948-1962 the most frequent activity of civilians was mere survival
(11.8 per cent for World War II and 9.8 per cent for Korean War). The
underground continued to be important activity for World War II civilians (9.3 per cent) and was the most important action of Cold War
civilians (10.6 per cent).

As in the case of civilians espionage agents were the subject
of fewer films in 1948-1962 than in 1939-1947. Ally and American spies
were in only 12.0 per cent of the films compared to 17.8 per cent in
1939-1947, and enemy agents dropped from 33.3 per cent to 17.4 per cent.
Actually, Cold War films' percentages more closely matched the earlier
figures (19.2 per cent for ally and American agents and 40.4 per cent
for enemy agents).

The nature of espionage activity in the Cold War, however, differed somewhat for enemy agents, compared with 1939-1947. Ally spying
was practically the same. Nazi and Japanese agents in 1939-1947 had
sabotage as their prime activity (12.8 per cent of enemy agents in
1939-1947 films). The Communists' actions generally took the form of
subversion, trying to undermine the morale and efficiency of the
American home front (21.2 per cent in 1948-1962). (See Table 58 for
espionage activity.)

Thus, civilian and spy war activities underwent some minor
changes in 1948-1962 films. The changes, though, probably were less
reflective of the era than was the decrease in portrayal of civilians
and spies. Assuming prime importance during 1948-1962 were soldiers
and military activities.

TABLE 58

DOMINANT SPY ACTIVITY, 1948–1962

Dominant Activity	WWII	Cold	Korea	Total
		Ally and American Spies		
Counterespionage	3.7%	8.6%	– %	4.7%
Get information	3.7	5.8	2.0	4.1
Sabotage	1.2	1.0	–	0.9
Protect secrets	–	1.0	–	0.3
Assassination	–	–	–	–
Protect people	–	–	–	–
Stop sabotage	–	–	–	–
Other	1.9	2.9	–	1.9
No answer	89.5	80.8	98.0	88.0
Total	100.0	100.0	100.0	100.0
		Enemy Spies		
Subversion	1.9	21.2	2.0	8.2
Get information	3.1	6.7	–	3.8
Assassination	0.6	6.7	–	2.5
Sabotage	0.6	3.8	–	1.6
Counterespionage	1.2	1.0	–	0.9
Protect secrets	–	1.0	–	0.3
Protect people	–	–	–	–
Stop sabotage	–	–	–	–
No answer	92.8	59.6	98.0	82.6
Total	100.0	100.0	100.0	100.0
Number	161	104	51	316

[a]Data derived from question 29 Form A in Appendix I.

The results of the content analysis reveal little about the differences in military activity in 1948-1962 compared to 1939-1947. In
1948-1962 films the allies and Americans were still depicted predominantly
favorably and the enemy unfavorably (Table 59). The Army was still the
service most frequently portrayed, and combat continued as the most
prevalent activity.

Yet the military in 1948-1962's films differed from its 1939-1947
counterpart. The difference was its methods. In 1939-1947 the waging
of war, even in the military, was basically individualistic and technology was a useful but not absolutely necessary tool. During 1948-
1962 war became a collective activity, carried out deliberately and
with discipline. Thus, the frequent reason for victory in 1948-1962's
pictures was methods (23.1 per cent). The top reason during 1939-
1947 was men as individuals (26.2 per cent). (See Tables 51 and 60.)

The advocacy of a professional approach to warfare was made in
numerous films. John Wayne in Sands of Iwo Jima (1949) and Flying
Leathernecks (1951) probably is the most renowned film exponent of
professionalism. The message was also presented in many other pictures,
including Command Decision (1949), which criticized congressional
interference in military affairs; Battle Cry (1955), which depicted
the molding of a variety of selfish civilians into a hard professional
team; Night People (1954), which ridiculed civilian ineptness in dealing with the Communists; and Retreat Hell (1952), which re-profession-
alized a former Marine recalled to the Korean War.

Hollywood's advocacy of professional militarism fit quite well
into what sometimes seemed an unquestioning acceptance of the Pentagon's
version of national security during the 1950's. In other words, it was

TABLE 59

DEPICTION OF MILITARY, 1948-1962

	WWII	Cold	Korea	Total
American Branch				
Army	31.7%	12.5%	47.1%	31.0%
Navy	17.4	7.7	11.8	13.3
Air Force (Corps)	7.4	8.6	19.6	9.9
Marines	9.3	1.9	9.8	7.0
Coast Guard	1.2	-	-	0.6
Other	1.2	-	-	0.6
No answer	31.7	69.2	11.8	40.8
Total	100.0	100.0	100.0	100.0
Specialty				
Infantry	21.7	3.8	39.2	18.7
Submarines	5.6	2.9	2.0	4.1
Bombers	3.7	2.9	2.0	3.2
Fighter planes	-	2.9	9.8	2.5
Carriers	3.1	-	5.9	2.5
Intelligence	3.1	2.9	-	2.5
Women's corps	-	4.8	2.0	1.9
Law	1.9	-	3.9	1.6
Prison camp	1.9	-	3.9	1.6
Medical	1.2	-	3.9	1.3
Paratroops	1.2	1.9	-	1.3
Tanks	1.9	-	2.0	1.3
Commandos	1.9	-	-	0.9
Demolition	1.2	-	2.0	0.9
Engineers	1.2	-	2.0	0.9
Warship	1.9	-	-	0.9
Frogmen	0.6	-	2.0	0.6
Photography	0.6	-	2.0	0.6
Public relations	1.2	-	-	0.6
Tankers	1.2	-	-	0.6
Supply	0.6	1.0	-	0.6
Air recon.	-	-	2.0	0.3
Entertainment	-	1.0	-	0.3
Helicopter	-	-	2.0	0.3
High command	0.6	-	-	0.3
Missile	-	1.0	-	0.3
National guard	0.6	-	-	0.3
Radar	-	1.0	-	0.3
Ski troops	0.6	-	-	0.3
Weather	0.6	-	-	0.3
No answer	31.6	74.0	13.7	47.8
Total	100.0	100.0	100.0	100.0

TABLE 59--Continued

	WWII	Cold	Korea	Total
Activity				
Combat	41.2%	- %	66.7%	31.6%
Training	4.3	20.2	5.9	9.9
Intelligence	6.8	6.7	3.9	6.3
Strategy	4.3	-	2.0	2.5
Supply	2.5	1.9	2.0	2.2
Medical	1.9	-	3.9	1.6
Occupation	1.9	-	2.0	1.3
Transportation	0.6	-	-	0.3
Other	5.6	1.9	3.9	4.1
No answer	31.1	69.2	9.8	40.2
Total	100.0	100.0	100.0	100.0

Military Image

Americans and Allies				
Favorable	57.8	27.8	82.4	51.9
Unfavorable	1.9	-	-	0.9
Mixed	15.5	4.6	13.7	11.7
Not applicable	24.8	67.3	3.9	35.4
Total	100.0	100.0	100.0	100.0

Enemy				
Favorable	3.1	-	-	1.6
Unfavorable	26.1	18.3	43.1	26.3
Mixed	5.0	-	2.8	2.8
Not applicable	65.8	81.7	54.9	69.3
Total	100.0	100.0	100.0	100.0
Number	161	104	51	316

[a]Data derived from questions 22-25 Form A in Appendix I.

TABLE 60

REASONS FOR VICTORIES, 1948-1962

Victory Reason	WWII	Cold	Korea	Total
Methods	26.7%	15.4%	27.5%	23.1%
Resources	11.2	19.2	15.7	14.5
Individuals	9.9	15.4	5.9	11.2
Circumstance	3.7	3.8	2.0	3.5
Goals	1.2	3.8	5.9	2.8
Supreme being	-	-	-	-
Other	2.5	2.9	5.9	3.2
No answer	44.6	39.4	37.3	41.8
Total	100.0	100.0	100.0	100.0
Number	161	104	51	316

[a]Data derived from question 41 Form A in Appendix I.

fashionable for Hollywood to advocate a professional military. Considering the economic status of the industry and the coercive eye of HUAC, it also might have been dangerous for Hollywood not to promote the military.

However, a major portion of the responsibility for the professional military propaganda in 1948-1962's films can also be traced to the Department of Defense's wide scale assistance of war movies. During 1948-1962 the Pentagon gave aid to nearly half of all war pictures made by Hollywood. More than half of all World War II and Korean War films released during that era received assistance of some kind from the military (Table 61).[1]

---

[1]Information about military assistance to motion pictures came from two sources. The Department of Defense provided a list of pictures which it said had received aid since 1949. The Defense Department said the list was incomplete because some records had been discarded and thus that list was supplemented by information from reviews. A film was added to the list only if a review said it was made with the cooperation of the military. Therefore, the estimates given in Tables 60 and 69 are probably low.

TABLE 61

FILMS RECEIVING PENTAGON ASSISTANCE, 1948-1962

	WWII	Cold	Korea	Total
Assistance Given				
Yes	54.7%	28.8%	58.8%	46.8%
No	45.3	71.2	41.2	53.2
Total	100.0	100.0	100.0	100.0
Services Featured				
Army	20.5	7.7	29.8	17.7
Navy	16.2	7.7	9.8	12.3
Air Force (Corps)	8.6	7.7	13.5	7.6
Marines	8.6	1.0	3.9	3.8
Coast Guard	0.6	1.0	–	0.6
More than one	9.6	3.8	2.0	4.7
Not assisted	45.3	71.2	41.2	53.2
Total	100.0	100.0	100.0	100.0
Number	161	104	51	316

[a]Data derived from list provided by Department of Defense and from reviews. See question 1 Form A in Appendix I.

Assistance varied from providing access to film clips to allowing studios the use of military bases and equipment. The Pentagon allowed Hollywood to shoot portions of movies at such bases as Fort Knox, Fort Benning, Fort Bliss, Fort Leonard Wood, Fort Bragg, Randolph Field, Williams Field, Edwards, Great Lakes, New London, and West Point.[2] In addition Hollywood sometimes was given the opportunity to film jets and big bombers, submarines, carriers, and other technological hardware. Portions of films were made aboard the carrier U.S.S. Essex and the submarine U.S.S. Grayfish.[3]

---

[2]The list of bases was compiled from information carried in various reviews.

[3]Ibid.

Sometimes the military helped promote the war pictures. For example, <u>Variety's</u> review of <u>Strategic Air Command</u> (1955) carried this message to exhibitors: "Gen. Curtis LeMay, four-star commander of SAC, has given the film his endorsement to the extent that his outfit will join in exhibitor promotion--providing military bands or equipment displays for the bally."[4]

Most assistance was not as extensive as that provided by LeMay. However, regardless of the extent of assistance the Defense Department had great control over the content of the films it aided. As Senator Fulbright indicates, the Pentagon had to approve the content of the films before it agreed to lend assistance.[5] When the content was not acceptable the producers changed it or made the film without assistance. For example, <u>Attack</u>, which showed "some very unattractive details of army life and as such . . . met with disapproval of U. S. Army officials."[6]

The monetary value of Pentagon assistance varied. In some cases it was quite high, although probably not at the level cited by the producer of <u>Berlin Express</u> (1948), which was filmed in occupied Germany by the grace of the military. RKO producer Bert Granet said about <u>Berlin</u> . . ., "We could never have made this picture if we'd had to duplicate the ruins and devastation of Germany. I figure we got about

---

[4] <u>Variety</u>, March 30, 1955, p. 8.

[5] Fulbright, <u>The Pentagon Propaganda Machine</u>, p. 112.

[6] "New Films from Books," <u>Library Journal</u>, LXXXI (Oct. 15, 1956), p. 2315.

$65 million worth of free sets."[7]

Certainly, the economic value of some assistance was substantial.
In the middle 1950's Hollywood released a number of films about jet
fighters and bombers, e.g. Strategic Air Command (1955), Air Strike
(1955), Battle Taxi (1955), Bridges at Toko Ri (1954), The McConnell
Story (1955), and The Hunters (1958). It is doubtful that without
Pentagon assistance Hollywood would have been able to produce so many
pictures about war's advanced technology. Consider that in the past
few years Battle of Britain (1968) with primary emphasis on air battles
cost $20 million and Tora Tora Tora (1970) and its large cast of ships
ran $28 million. The 1950's films would not have cost so much, but
what they would have cost--without Defense Department assistance--
probably would have been prohibitive.

Thus, Pentagon aid probably meant that the services depending
on expensive technology--the Navy and the Air Force--received more
frequent exposure on the nation's screens than would have otherwise
been the case. Assistance probably encourage other kinds of war films
as well.

Consequences

In the films made in 1939-1947 the consequences of war were
either harmful and blamed on the enemy or inspired nobility. In 1948-
1962 neither consequence appeared in such exact form. The destructive
aspects of war were depicted more frequently and with more detail but
minus attribution of blame. Secondly, nobility as a consequence was

---

[7]Quoted in "The New Pictures," Time, May 3, 1948, p. 93.

replaced by a new form of ideal behavior--that which was expected of

a professional warrior: maturity and discipline. (As in the previous

chapter the results of the content analysis concerning consequences of

war with rather minimal; see Table 62.)

TABLE 62

CONSEQUENCES OF WAR, 1948-1962

Consequence	WWII	Cold	Korea	Total
Harmful				
Depravation	8.1%	7.7%	3.9%	7.2%
Physical harm	3.7	6.7	3.9	5.1
Freedom loss	2.5	10.6	–	4.7
Deprivation	7.5	–	2.0	4.1
Emotional harm	3.7	1.9	9.8	4.1
Upset routine	–	1.0	–	0.3
No answer	75.2	72.1	78.4	74.0
Total	100.0	100.0	100.0	100.0
Beneficial				
Heroism	5.0	1.0	5.9	3.8
Maturity	3.1	1.9	7.8	3.5
Freedom	–	2.9	–	0.9
Equality	1.9	–	–	0.9
Humanization	0.6	–	–	0.3
No answer	79.4	94.2	86.3	90.5
Total	100.0	100.0	100.0	100.0
Number	161	104	51	316

[a]Data derived from question 39 Form A in Appendix I.

In general the consequences of war according to 1948-1962's

films were qualitatively of three varieties: those arising from normal

pursuit of duty; those arising from mistakes and stupidity of man; and

those arising as natural consequences of war. The latter two categories

included some antiwar implications; the first did not.

The effects arising from normal pursuit of duty were not always harmful, and those which were could be rationalized as necessary to accomplishing the war task. For example, in Breakthrough (1950) and 12 O'Clock High (1949) David Brian and Gregory Peck experience emotional problems as a consequence of their detached pursuit of duty. They make emotionless decisions, but those decisions gradually break them. The decisions had to be made, though, in order to win the war.

Such examples of mental breakdowns as a result of professionalism were few. The normal consequence of professional leadership was conversion to that same professional attitude, such as in Sands of Iwo Jima and Battle Cry.

Although antiwar statements were not presented by films praising the professional method, such portrayals did tend to soil the noble image of war that had arisen during 1939-1947. Infantry pictures, regardless of whether they were antiwar or jingoistic, especially gave a more drab and thus more realistic image of war. The crusade of 1939-1947 was abandoned in favor of an impression of battle almost like that portrayed by Mauldin's Willie and Joe but without the humor.

When war became just another job to be approached in a planned, disciplined manner, its adventure was lost and its appeal was just a little less. Nevertheless it was still a justifiable exercise as a last resort. Two Samuel Fuller productions presented accounts of battle as dreariness rather than pursuit of the Grail. Steel Helmet (1951) and Fixed Bayonets (1951) followed professionals doing their jobs, complicated by not only the enemy but also fog, frozen ground, wet feet, and mental and physical strain.

When a dreary account of battle was combined with a depiction

of military mistakes, a more critical picture of war emerged. Such
a movie was <u>Pork Chop Hill</u> (1959), based on a true account of troops
trapped between peace talk strategy and Chinese forces in the closing
days of the Korean War. The picture combined a needless but face-
saving assignment with allies turning a spotlight accidentally on an
American attack, the American high command's refusal of reinforcements
or permission to retreat, and an ordered abandonment of a hill after
victory for a none too pleasant view of war.

However, whatever criticism that emerges is diluted by the
fact that war itself is never challenged. The immediate task may have
been foolhardy, but the enemy was still the enemy and had started the
war by invading South Korea. Whether stated or not, that interpretation of reality was ever present providing a legitimizing cover. Besides, regardless of disagreement with the task the soldiers of <u>Pork . .</u>
carried out their orders.

To escape the snare of legitimation some films dealt solely with
consequences of war—with deprivation and depravation. One of the
earliest antiwar pictures was <u>The Boy with Green Hair</u> (1948), which
advocated tolerance as well as pacifism. A war orphan awakens one
morning to find himself with green hair, a characteristic others will
not accept. As he attempts to regain acceptance, a message of pacifism
emerges, made explicit in a dream sequence in which children on war
posters materialize. The picture made its point fairly successfully—
a message much criticized by HUAC.

<u>The Search</u> (1948) and <u>Fraulein</u> (1958) examined the desolation
of the aftermath of war. In both, postwar Germany abounds with hunger,
prostitution, rubble, and general despair. Either film could have been

quite effective in presenting an antiwar message, but both fell somewhat short. The Search leaves the impression that the Germans are
miserable, but perhaps it is a misery at least partly deserved. There
would have been no war if the Germans' Nazis had not started it. Fraulein
falters by providing escape from the deprivation. Dana Wynter finally
realizes that the end of the rainbow lies with Mel Ferrer in the United
States, a happy ending that wipes out the war's despair.

Complete destruction was hypothesized by two films about possible nuclear war--The World, the Flesh, and the Devil (1959) and On
the Beach (1960). In the former war seems almost inbred into man while
the latter posits that once in operation a nuclear arms race must continue to a fatal conclusion. A happy ending negates some of the effect
of The World . . . as a black and two whites conquer their natural
animosities and attempt to begin a better world. On . . . ends in a
fashion slightly more faithful to its beginning as everyone dies, but
its final scene is a bit contrived--i.e. silence with the slogan "There
Is Still Time, Brother" proclaimed from a banner waving in a radioactive
breeze.

War Hunt (1962), The Mountain Road (1960) and Bitter Victory (1958)
portrayed the depravity that man can achieve. In War . . . John Saxon
kills for pleasure while James Stewart's savagery in The Mountain . . .
is strictly in vengeance. One is never sure, though, whether Saxon's
sickness was caused by the war or whether he brought the illness into
the war. This unresolved doubt dilutes any antiwar message in the
film. The Mountain . . . reneges by allowing Stewart to arise from
his sins a better man with a more thorough knowledge of himself.

Bitter . . . pits Richard Burton and Curt Jurgens in a personal conflict in a war context. Burton is a civilian soldier with the manners of a professional and Jurgens a professional interested in promotion more than war. Jurgens' jealousies of Burton's competence are intensified by a supposed rivalry for Jurgens' wife.

Jurgens bungles the mission when his personal hatred of Burton interferes with pursuit of duty. Burton's reminders to Jurgens about his failures are no more commendable. Jurgens allows Burton to be killed by a scorpion but fails the mission when an unguarded prisoner burns a sachel of secret documents. Despite his failure Jurgens receives a medal, but he loses his wife and is certain to be haunted by the memory of his deed.

Bitter . . . presented an utterly disgusting view of men in war. However, it falls short of being an ultimate antiwar picture because its culprit is not war but man. War merely serves as a container for man's failings.

Thus, some of 1948-1962's war films attempted antiwar statements by focusing on the harmful results of war. However, most of the pictures fell short of challenging war as a legitimate means of solving international disputes, and their artistic effectiveness was frequently hindered by allowing escape from the detrimental effects of war.

Summary

Hollywood's presentation of war in 1948-1962 was somewhat different than its view in 1939-1947. Purposes and motivations were less noble and generally more task oriented. War became a specialized job allocated to the professional warrior, and the films tended to emphasize method more than purpose or consequence in keeping with the stress on professionalism. Detrimental side effects of war were presented more often in 1948-1962 than they had been in 1939-1947, but most attempts at antiwar statements fell short of success. On the whole, however, war was presented as a necessary task, which could be carried out successfully only by a professional force. The necessity of war rationalized whatever harm evolved from international conflict.

CHAPTER XII

DENIAL OF MOTIVE, CRITIQUE OF METHOD

The films produced in 1939-1947 and those made in 1948-1962 were dissimilar in the relative emphasis placed on justifications and methods and in the way they portrayed approaches to war. They were alike in one critical respect: both confirmed the legitimacy of war as a means to settle international disputes. In some cases war may have been portrayed as a last resort but nevertheless necessary.

During 1963-1970 some Hollywood products began to challenge the traditional views of war, first by critically examining the super-sophisticated technological procedures of the Cold War and later by featuring characters who denied the relevance of war aims. Not all war films produced in 1963-1970 departed from tradition, but enough did to distinguish the recent era from the first two.

The new treatments of war occurred in an environment that had released Hollywood from its traditional role of American institution and had cast it as an international industry. The new economic reality allowed Hollywood--or perhaps forced the industry--to discard its remnants of American chauvinism. A significant disenchantment with war in general and the Vietnam War in particular in the United States facilitated the discard.

Justifications

As in 1939-1947 and 1948-1962 Hollywood's films devoted little attention to the causes of war during 1963-1970 (Table 63). Neither did preparations for war occupy much screen time, decreasing from 8.5

TABLE 63

SYMBOLS OF LEGITIMATION, 1963-1970

Symbol	WWII	Cold	Korea	Vietnam	Total
Patriotism	12.5%	21.7%	20.0%	– %	14.9%
War task	18.8	4.3	–	–	13.8
Personal gain	14.1	–	40.0	–	11.7
Situation	10.9	8.7	–	–	9.6
Nat. security	–	13.6	–	–	3.2
Pol. necessity	–	13.6	–	–	3.2
Responsibility	4.7	–	–	–	3.2
Sex	4.7	–	–	–	3.2
Fairness	–	–	40.0	–	2.1
Freedom	–	–	–	100.0	2.1
Revenge	1.6	–	–	–	1.1
No answer	32.8	39.1	–	–	31.9
Total	100.0	100.0	100.0	100.0	100.0
Number	64	23	5	2	94

[a]Data derived from question 32 Form A in Appendix I.

per cent in 1948-1962 to 3.2 per cent in 1963-1970. Instead of discussing causes or preliminaries Hollywood put more emphasis on war situations independent of the causes. The situation and the characters' reactions to it came to be more important than either justification or the proper (professional) approach.

Although Table 63's information about things or persons blamed for war has shortcomings similar to the previous two periods, some interesting trends emerge. Responsibility for war was still awarded to the enemy (23.4 per cent of the films), but, from a qualitative standpoint, without the enthusiasm of 1939-1947 or the fear of 1948-1962. To a limited extent the films of 1963-1970 humanized the enemy, thus denationalizing him and making him somewhat less hateful (Chapter IX).

Indications of the denationalization process in 1963-1970's movies are given by the symbols used to legitimize war activities. As in the earlier eras war task (13.8 per cent) and patriotism (14.9 per cent) received greatest subscription. However, of emerging significance were situation (9.6 per cent) and personal gain (9.6 per cent) (Table 64). Reference to the situation meant that the characters had no greater goal than reacting to crisis, and personal gain meant simply that the characters had been bribed (in a variety of ways) into participating in the war. Neither group of characters had higher goals nor nobler purposes beyond their immediate needs. Actually, what is indicated by the symbols is a fragmentation over the purposes of war. Some of the nationalistic and humanitarian rationalizations still existed, but the films produced in 1963-1970 allowed non-righteous motivations as well.

Moralistic preachment about the necessity of war was provided in Green Berets (1968) and A Yank in Vietnam (1964). Both stressed the need for American help to enable the South Vietnamese to maintain their independence. Green . . . also argues against civilian interference in military affairs. Repetition of arguments about the need for professional warriors was made in A Gathering of Eagles (1964), which was another laudatory production about the Strategic Air Command, and In Harm's Way (1965), in which John Wayne outperforms a muddling congressman. Other remnants of the past included PT 109 (1963), a story about the heroism of John F. Kennedy, and First to Fight (1967), featuring a heroic Marine who has to be reconverted to social responsibility. Each hero in his own way ultimately became a part of the overall war task and accepted the broader war aims.

TABLE 64

FILMS' VIEW OF WAR'S CAUSES, 1963–1970

	WWII	Cold	Korea	Vietnam	Total
Featured Aspects					
Causes	1.6%	– %	– %	– %	1.1%
Preparations	1.6	8.7	–	–	3.2
Prevention	–	4.3	–	–	2.1
Life in war	34.4	21.7	20.0	–	29.8
Conduct	71.9	69.6	60.0	100.0	71.3
Consequences	14.1	8.7	40.0	–	13.8
Total	125.0	113.0	100.0	100.0	120.2
War's Causes					
Enemy's nature	3.1	8.7	–	–	4.3
Territory	–	–	–	–	–
Economic	–	–	–	–	–
Religious	–	–	–	–	–
Ideals	–	–	–	–	–
Military	4.7	4.3	–	–	4.3
Political	1.6	21.7	–	50.0	7.4
Other	–	–	–	–	–
No answer	90.6	65.2	100.0	50.0	84.0
Total	100.0	100.0	100.0	100.0	100.0
Persons Blamed					
Mankind	3.1	–	–	–	2.1
No one	1.6	–	–	–	1.1
Enemy	7.8	–	–	50.0	6.4
Enemy leaders	17.2	17.4	–	50.0	17.0
Allies	–	–	–	–	–
Ally leaders	–	4.3	–	–	1.1
Other	–	8.7	–	–	2.1
No answer	70.3	69.6	100.0	–	70.2
Total	100.0	100.0	100.0	100.0	100.0
Number	64	23	5	2	94

[a]Data derived from questions 12, 31, and 33 Form A in Appendix I.

Other characters, though, served the war cause without accepting the aims. Their objectives were self-oriented as they were coerced into fighting. They fought to benefit themselves--often through pardon from prison or a death sentence--in such films as Morituri (1965), The Secret Invasion (1964), and The Dirty Dozen (1967).

Regardless of the goal--moralistic, professional, or selfish-- the behavior of the characters frequently led to the same conclusion: achievement of war objectives. The characters may have been motivated by different goals in the beginning, but once in the situation they accepted war's conventions and pursued the normal end.

However, another group of characters rejected the conventions and goals, thus avoiding participation in war. American and Japanese soldiers in None But the Brave (1965) and Hell in the Pacific (1968) accidentally escaped battlefield conventions and thus found that they could cooperate peacefully. In None . . . the social reality of war infringed again at the conclusion and once again the soldiers were enemies.

The influence of social myths on war behavior was also depicted in The Russians Are Coming, The Russians Are Coming (1966), which examined unfounded fears of Russians and Americans after a Russian submarine run aground off New England. The fears and animosities of the two nationalities were shown to be based on stereotypes that had no correspondence to either American or Russian.

None . . . , Hell . . . , and The Russians . . . portrayed the possibility of accident removing characters from the necessity of pursuing wartime goals. Three 1970 releases eliminated fate and gave the choice to fight or not to fight to the characters themselves. Each of

the films (M*A*S*H, Catch 22, and Kelly's Heroes) comically discarded
the idea that the individual, either willingly or unwillingly, must
participate in war. Thus, rejection took the form of mental dis-
countenance in M*A*S*H, pursuit of gold in Kelly's . . ., and physical
flight in Catch 22.

By allowing the possibility of rejecting the political ends
of war and of avoiding participation in war, Hollywood was making antiwar statements unmatched by its previous emphases on the deprivation of
war. When a film focuses on the consequences of war and portrays suffering of innocent bystanders, there still remains the possibility that
the war itself was necessary and thus justified. If the end is moral
and good, it is very difficult to condemn the means. If the end is
illegitimate, it is rather difficult to justify the means.

Methods

Hollywood's treatment of the methods of war in films produced
in 1963-1970 took a variety of directions. Some fairly traditional
views were presented, but two new slants were evident. In one the
physical, brutal aspects of methods of war were eulogized with emphasis
on violence for entertainment's sake. The other new direction found
Hollywood challenging some of the traditional faiths in Cold War
policy.

The results of the content analyses partially indicated the
trend toward violence. As Table 4 (Chapter III) shows, 88.3 per cent
of films made in 1963-1970 were located in war zones (up from 77.9 per
cent in 1948-1962; see Table 3, Chapter II), thus opening the possibility

of more violent activities to occur. An examination of the themes of
1963-1970's films reveals a substantial increase in emphasis on
violence. A total of 19.1 per cent of the films produced in 1963-
1970 had violence as the primary theme, compared to 4.7 per cent in
1948-1962. When violence is linked with harmful consequences, the
result often is an antiwar statement. Such statements were few in
1963-1970 because violence was not tied to deprivation of war. Instead, violence was purely an entertainment device. (See Table 65 for
distribution of themes among 1963-1970's movies.)

An examination of activities of civilians, espionage agents,
and soldiers reveals an emphasis on violence--though not to a much
greater extent than in the past (Table 66). War zone civilians
practiced underground and para-military activities more than all other
forms of behavior combined (23.4 per cent compared to 19.2 per cent
for the others). The home-front civilian was not involved in any
kind of violent activity, but, then, he was almost not portrayed.
The home-front civilian's appearance in only 8.5 per cent of the war
films released in 1963-1970 is at least partial consequence of increased
emphasis on the war front and violence.

Significant among the results of the content analysis of dominant
spy activities (Table 67) was the fact that allies' and Americans' spying rate equaled that of the enemy. In 1939-1947 and again in 1948-
1962 the enemy engaged in more spy activity than allies and Americans--
perhaps a result of Hollywood casting the enemy as aggressor. Equaliz-
ing the rate of spy activity was perhaps a consequence of recognizing
that the enemy was not always the aggressor.

Table 68's summary of the depiction of the military in 1963-1970

TABLE 65

DOMINANT FILM THEMES, 1963-1970

Dominant Theme	WWII	Cold	Korea	Vietnam	Total
War	40.6%	21.7%	20.0%	100.0%	36.2%
Violence	20.3	21.7	-	-	19.1
Public affairs	-	34.8	20.0	-	9.6
Armed forces	10.9	4.3	-	-	8.5
Inner conflict	6.3	-	40.0	-	6.4
Comradeship	4.7	4.3	-	-	4.3
Love	4.7	4.3	-	-	4.3
Law enforcement	3.1	4.3	-	-	3.2
Mental health	4.7	-	-	-	3.2
Patriotism	3.1	-	-	-	2.1
Family	1.6	-	-	-	1.1
Science	-	4.3	-	-	1.1
Medical	-	-	20.0	-	1.1
Alcoholism	-	-	-	-	-
Accidents	-	-	-	-	-
Business	-	-	-	-	-
Domestics	-	-	-	-	-
Education	-	-	-	-	-
Fine arts	-	-	-	-	-
Entertainment	-	-	-	-	-
Foreigners	-	-	-	-	-
Materialism	-	-	-	-	-
Minorities	-	-	-	-	-
Nature	-	-	-	-	-
Press	-	-	-	-	-
Religion	-	-	-	-	-
No answer	-	-	-	-	-
Total	100.0	100.0	100.0	100.0	100.0
Number	64	23	5	2	94

[a]Data derived from question 43 Form A in Appendix I.

TABLE 66

DOMINANT CIVILIAN WAR ACTIVITIES, 1963-1970

	WWII	Cold	Korea	Vietnam	Total
H.F. Contribution					
Faithfulness	1.6%	8.7%	20.0%	- %	4.3%
Arms development	-	13.6	-	-	3.2
Entertainment	-	4.3	-	-	1.1
Avoid gossip	-	-	-	-	-
Civil defense	-	-	-	-	-
Conservation	-	-	-	-	-
Patriotism	-	-	-	-	-
Buy bonds	-	-	-	-	-
Production	-	-	-	-	-
Spy alertness	-	-	-	-	-
No answer	98.4	73.9	80.0	100.0	91.6
Total	100.0	100.0	100.0	100.0	100.0
H.F. Hindrance					
Not patriotic	-	4.3	-	-	1.1
Unfaithfulness	-	4.3	-	-	1.1
Apathy	-	-	-	-	-
Extravagence	-	-	-	-	-
Opportunism	-	-	-	-	-
Reject war aims	-	-	-	-	-
No answer	100.0	91.3	100.0	100.0	97.9
Total	100.0	100.0	100.0	100.0	100.0
W.F. Activity					
Para-military	20.3	-	-	50.0	14.9
Underground	7.8	13.6	-	-	8.5
Existing	6.3	-	20.0	-	5.3
Normalcy	1.6	8.7	-	-	3.2
Arms development	1.6	-	20.0	-	2.1
Faithfulness	3.1	-	-	-	2.1
Civil defense	1.6	-	-	-	1.1
Entertainment	1.6	-	-	-	1.1
Spy alertness	-	4.3	-	-	1.1
Avoid gossip	-	-	-	-	-
Conservation	-	-	-	-	-
Patriotism	-	-	-	-	-
Production	-	-	-	-	-
Treason	-	-	-	-	-
Other	3.1	4.3	-	-	3.2
No answer	53.1	69.6	60.0	50.0	57.4
Total	100.0	100.0	100.0	100.0	100.0
Number	64	23	5	2	94

[a]Data derived from questions 26-28 Form A in Appendix I.

[b]H.F.--Home Front; W.F.--War Front

TABLE 67

DOMINANT SPY ACTIVITY, 1963-1970

Dominant Activity	WWII	Cold	Korea	Vietnam	Total

Ally and American Spies

Dominant Activity	WWII	Cold	Korea	Vietnam	Total
Counterespionage	- %	30.4%	- %	- %	7.4%
Get information	1.6	8.7	-	-	3.2
Sabotage	1.6	-	-	-	1.1
Assassination	-	-	-	-	-
Protect people	-	-	-	-	-
Protect secrets	-	-	-	-	-
Stop sabotage	-	-	-	-	-
Other	4.7	4.3	-	-	6.4
No answer	92.2	47.8	100.0	100.0	85.1
Total	100.0	100.0	100.0	100.0	100.0

Enemy Spies

Dominant Activity	WWII	Cold	Korea	Vietnam	Total
Assassination	-	13.6	-	-	3.2
Protect people	-	13.6	-	-	3.2
Sabotage	-	13.6	-	-	3.2
Get information	-	8.7	-	-	2.1
Protect secrets	-	8.7	-	-	2.1
Counterespionage	-	-	-	-	-
Prevent sabotage	-	-	-	-	-
Other	3.1	4.3	-	-	3.2
No answer	96.9	47.8	100.0	100.0	85.1
Total	100.0	100.0	100.0	100.0	100.0
Number	64	23	5	2	94

[a]Data derived from question 29 Form A in Appendix I.

TABLE 68

DEPICTION OF MILITARY, 1963-1970

	WWII	Cold	Korea	Vietnam	Total
American Branch					
Army	25.0%	4.3%	100.0%	50.0%	24.5%
Navy	10.9	8.7	–	–	9.6
Air Force (Corps)	6.3	13.6	–	–	7.4
Marines	7.8	–	–	50.0	6.4
Coast Guard	–	–	–	–	–
Other	–	4.3	–	–	1.1
No answer	50.0	69.6	–	–	51.1
Total	100.0	100.0	100.0	100.0	100.0
Specialty					
Infantry	14.1	–	60.0	100.0	14.9
Bombers	6.3	13.6	–	–	7.4
Commandos	6.3	–	–	–	4.3
Law	3.1	–	20.0	–	3.2
Medical	1.6	–	20.0	–	2.1
Small ships	3.1	–	–	–	2.1
Submarines	1.6	4.3	–	–	2.1
Tanks	3.1	–	–	–	2.1
High command	–	4.3	–	–	1.1
Intelligence	1.6	–	–	–	1.1
Public relations	1.6	–	–	–	1.1
Tankers	1.6	–	–	–	1.1
Warships	–	4.3	–	–	1.1
No answer	56.3	73.9	–	–	56.1
Total	100.0	100.0	100.0	100.0	100.0
Activity					
Combat	43.8	4.3	40.0	100.0	35.1
Intelligence	3.1	8.7	–	–	4.3
Medical	1.6	–	20.0	–	2.1
Strategy	1.6	4.3	–	–	2.1
Supply	1.6	–	20.0	–	2.1
Training	–	8.7	–	–	2.1
Transportation	–	4.3	–	–	1.1
Occupation	–	–	–	–	–
Other	14.1	–	20.0	–	10.6
No answer	34.4	69.6	–	–	59.4
Total	100.0	100.0	100.0	100.0	100.0

TABLE 68--Continued

	WWII	Cold	Korea	Vietnam	Total
Military Image					
Americans and Allies					
Favorable	35.9%	13.6%	40.0%	100.0%	31.9%
Unfavorable	6.3	8.7	20.0	-	7.4
Mixed	25.0	8.7	40.0	-	21.3
Not applicable	32.8	69.6	-	-	39.4
Total	100.0	100.0	100.0	100.0	100.0
Enemy					
Favorable	-	-	-	-	-
Unfavorable	40.6	13.6	20.0	50.0	33.0
Mixed	23.4	-	-	-	16.0
Not applicable	35.9	86.9	80.0	50.0	51.1
Total	100.0	100.0	100.0	100.0	100.0
Number	64	23	5	2	94

[a]Data derived from questions 22-25 Form A in Appendix I.

indicates a slight increase in portrayal of combat in comparison with 1948-1962 (35.1 per cent compared to 31.6 per cent). The real difference does not appear in the quantified results. The difference is in the character of the violence and its users.

In 1948-1962's films the violence was perpetrated collectively through an organized military's disciplined teamwork. Violence in the pictures made in 1963-1970 was often return to the individual--not the socially responsible individual of 1939-1947 but the brutal antihero familiarized in the James Bond and other spy spoof movies. Thus, Table 69 which summarizes the principal reasons for war victories given by

TABLE 69

REASONS FOR VICTORIES, 1963–1970

Victory Reason	WWII	Cold	Korea	Vietnam	Total
Methods	31.3%	17.4%	- %	50.0%	26.6%
Individuals	14.1	30.4	-	50.0	18.1
Resources	14.1	4.3	-	-	10.6
Circumstance	9.4	13.6	-	-	9.6
Goals	3.1	4.3	-	-	3.2
Supreme being	-	-	-	-	-
Other	1.6	-	-	-	1.1
No answer	26.6	30.4	100.0	-	30.9
Total	100.0	100.0	100.0	100.0	100.0
Number	64	23	5	2	94

[a]Data derived from question 41 Form A in Appendix I.

films in 1963–1970 quantitatively does not differ too much from Table 60 which provides the same information for 1948–1962. In both eras methods were the primary determinant of victory (23.1 per cent in 1948–1962 and 26.6 per cent in 1963–1970). However, the character of the method is vastly different--discriminate brutality in 1963–1970, disciplined teamwork in 1948–1962. One need only look at the entertaining devastation prevalent in The Dirty Dozen (1967), Tobruk (1968), The Devil's Brigade, The Venetian Affair (1967), and The Silencers (1966) to understand the method characteristic of 1963–1970's films.

Part of the emphasis on brutality came from the entertainment attraction of screen violence. Part of it is also indicative of recognition that violence is not restricted to the enemy; it is an integral part of the good guys' arsenal as well. Warkill (1968) states that point rather explicitly. A naive reporter travels to the Philippines to write a story about a semi-legendary hero, whose cruelty and viciousness disappoints the reporter. When the hero dies, however, the reporter has become convinced of the need to fight brutality with brutality and thus allows the hero's image to remain unscarred as an attempt to maintain morale.

Hollywood's escalation of the brutality of film wars in some cases may have been intended as a criticism of war but in other instances the intent probably was entertainment. Whatever the intent, a frequent effect was to isolate method from purpose and thus to judge method on its own merits rather than by its achievements.

Explicit criticism was leveled at super-sophisticated methods of war during 1963-1970. In 1963 Hollywood released A Gathering of Eagles, which did little more than duplicate praise of the military and technology given by a multitude of pictures in 1948-1962. One year later the military's honeymoon with Hollywood ended with the distribution of Dr. Strangelove, Fail Safe, and Seven Days in May. Dr. . . . portrayed the dangers involved in too much reliance on sophisticated technology, and Fail . . . did the same thing but rationalized the mistake with some hope that it would lead to world peace. Seven . . . explored the potential dangers of an ego-inflated military.

Hollywood's criticism of the military would have been impossible a decade earlier in the midst of the Red Scare, HUAC coercion, and Pentagon assistance. The first two elements had practically disappeared in importance by 1963, and the third declined in significance. As Table 70 shows, the Department of Defense assisted only 29.0 per cent of the war films in 1963-1970 compared to 46.8 per cent in 1948-1962. For some producers the level of assistance for some films matched that provided in 1948-1962. Lavish aid was provided John Wayne and The

TABLE 70

FILMS RECEIVING PENTAGON ASSISTANCE, 1963-1970

	WWII	Cold	Korea	Vietnam	Total
Assistance Given					
Yes	28.3%	34.8%	- %	50.0%	28.7%
No	71.9	65.2	100.0	50.0	71.2
Total	100.0	100.0	100.0	100.0	100.0
Services Featured					
Army	7.8	4.3	-	50.0	7.4
Navy	7.8	8.7	-	-	7.4
Air Force (Corps)	3.1	4.3	-	-	3.1
Marines	4.7	-	-	-	3.1
Coast Guard	-	-	-	-	-
None featured	4.7	17.4	-	-	7.4
Not assisted	71.9	65.4	100.0	50.0	71.2
Total	100.0	100.0	100.0	100.0	100.0
Number	64	23	5	2	94

[a]Data derived from list provided by Department of Defense and from reviews. See question 10 Form A in Appendix I.

Green Berets (1968). (See Chapter III for details.) Similar assistance was intended for Tora Tora Tora (1970), but Twentieth Century Fox received a bill after congressional uproar over the project.[1]

It is possible that the Pentagon's decline in involvement with Hollywood in 1963-1970 was due to the nature of war movies rather than intent. The war films produced in 1963-1970 were not as blatantly complimentary to the military as they had been during 1948-1962. Thus, Hollywood may not have approached the Defense Department for assistance, believing the likelihood of such aid small. On the other hand some film films were denied assistance, e.g. Bridge at Remagen (1969). "A

---

[1]Fulbright, The Pentagon Propaganda Machine, pp. 122-124.

soldier's robbing dead Germans and an officer threatening another with
a pistol and an enlisted man knocking an officer into a bomb crater
were among the reasons for . . . 'turn down'."[2]

Consequences

Hollywood's portrayal of the consequences of war in the films
made in 1963-1970 departed dramatically from the past--mostly as the
result of de-emphasis on purpose and increasing concentration on the
brutality of war methods. Deprived of the legitimation of moralistic
purposes, the war films released in 1963-1970 were able to present the
harmful consequences of war without rationalization. They did not
always do that, but the potential was there. In fact, the consequences
portrayed were a mixture of good and bad (Table 71).

Consequences reminiscent of 1939-1947 were provided by noble
heroes in PT 109 (1963), Father Goose (1964), and First to Fight (1967)
and similar to 1948-1962 in A Gathering of Eagles (1963), In Harm's
Way (1967), and The Green Berets (1968), all three expounding victory
as the consequence of professionalism.

Other films were not so conventional in portraying the consequences of war. The group of pictures focusing on the adventure and
entertaining violence of war ended in conventional manners--with the
Americans or allies defeating the enemy, e.g. The Silencers (1966),
The Dirty Dozen (1967), Tobruk (1967), and The Devil's Brigade (1968).
In the march toward victory the heroes (or antiheroes) left dozens of
bodies behind them as well as mass destruction. It was difficult,
though, to attach much significance to the deaths and destruction. The

---

[2]Fulbright, The Pentagon Propaganda Machine, p. 116.

TABLE 71

CONSEQUENCES OF WAR, 1963-1970

Consequence	WWII	Cold	Korea	Vietnam	Total
Harmful					
Physical harm	17.2%	8.7%	- %	- %	13.8%
Depravation	9.4	-	20.0	-	7.4
Devastation	4.7	8.7	-	-	5.3
Deprivation	1.6	-	60.0	-	4.3
Freedom loss	1.6	-	-	50.0	2.1
Dehumanization	-	-	20.0	-	1.1
Emotional harm	1.6	-	-	-	1.1
No answer	64.1	82.6	-	50.0	64.9
Total	100.0	100.0	100.0	100.0	100.0
Beneficial					
Heroism	15.6	-	-	-	10.6
Maturity	7.8	-	-	-	5.3
Friendship	1.6	-	-	-	1.1
Profit	1.6	-	-	-	1.1
No answer	73.4	100.0	100.0	100.0	81.9
Total	100.0	100.0	100.0	100.0	100.0
Number	64	23	5	2	94

[a]Data derived from question 39 Form A in Appendix I.

films apparently were designed to highlight the thrill of violence as the bodies were simply a byproduct of an exciting moment. In other words, the consequences--good or bad--were practically irrelevant in relation to the exhilaration of the method.

The Victors (1963) was reminiscent of the attempts at antiwar statements in the 1950's, i.e. focusing on the desolation of war. However, it overcame the handicaps of the earlier films--which had provided hope or had rationalized the consequences as deserved--by leaving no hint of future happiness. Nearly every character in The Victors displayed

at least traces of depravity, and despair pervaded every vignette.
The destruction and depravation arose from the war and from human nature.
While the Americans were fighting Germans over an unstated cause, the
Americans seemed no better morally than their foe. War corrupts with
a little help from human nature.

A few films focused on the destructive results of battle--in
relation to the fighters, e.g. Bridge at Remagen (1969), Beach Red
(1967), and Warkill (1968). The death and suffering was depicted with
more explicit realism than in the past, but antiwar sentiment is
partially neutralized by rationalization that the violence of war is
necessary.

Finally, a group of pictures critically examined war as a method
and decided that its costs were too extreme. From that conclusion the
characters move in a variety of directions. None But the Brave (1965)
puts Americans and Japanese back into a war situation in which they
must fight to the death while Cliff Robertson in Up from the Beach
(1965) learns first hand the experience of helpless civilians and then
returns to battle albeit reluctantly. Characters in The Russians Are
Coming, The Russians Are Coming (1966) and The Hook (1963) also learn
of the human individuality of enemies, but as in the other two pictures
just mentioned the war continues.

For Americans in Catch 22 (1970) and M*A*S*H (1970) war continues,
but not for certain individuals. Alan Arkin in Catch 22 dissociates
himself from the war by deserting while the doctors in M*A*S*H achieve
the same thing mentally. The Korean war rages around the doctors and
the casualties come in daily, but neither infringes on the doctors once
they leave the operating tent.

One exception to the normal depiction of the consequences of war was Patton (1970). Victory is achieved and praise heaped on George C. Scott, but his vigor for life is ended. He gained his meaning in life from war itself. He drove for victory over the Germans in order to fulfill himself, but once the war ended the goal of victory was deflating. Scott thrived on the method, not on the goal or the consequences.

Many pictures portrayed the detrimental consequences of war. These films released in 1963-1970 had a variety of conclusions, some even hypothesizing the possibility of individuals avoiding involvement in wars. Only one presented the possibility that war, or rather the consequences of war, would lead nations to avoiding the method as a means of settling disagreement. Even that picture (Fail Safe, 1964) was somewhat unrealistic. In the film the president, Henry Fonda, exchanges destruction of New York for the accidental demolishment of Moscow, and out of the ruins of the two cities comes a promised negotiated disarmament of the two major powers.

Summary

The films produced by Hollywood during 1963-1970 presented a varied view of the purposes, methods, and consequences of war. However, some significant new trends in the portrayal of war appeared in the era. First, the purposes of war lost their moralistic and nationalistic importance. Purposes were de-emphasized either by ignoring them in the films or by the characters rejecting them as irrelevant. Second, methods were dissociated from purposes as the brutality of war's methods was shown to belong to either side, and some critical examination focused on the

United States' elaborate Cold War defenses. Finally, the consequences

of war portrayed by the films of 1963-1970 ranged from conversions to

social responsibility or to professionalism to complete rejection of

war by individuals. In only a few cases did the movies produced in

1963-1970 show the idealism of purpose of the films made in 1939-1947

or the necessity of purpose of those released in 1948-1962. But,

neither did Hollywood move idealistically in the other direction; no

starry-eyed proclamations of how to end war were issued (with the

possible exception of Fail Safe). Thus, the image of war projected by

Hollywood during 1963-1970 tended in most instances to be either neutral

or critical but accepting war as inevitable.

CONCLUSION

Hollywood's treatment of the general nature of war has undergone a vast transformation in the past thirty-two years. The depiction of methods has moved from individualistic spontaneity to disciplined professionalism to a moral violence. Meanwhile the characterization of the consequences of warfare has gradually begun to show the harmful effects as a result of war itself rather than of the enemy. At the same time the justifications of war have moved in an almost complete circle as far as the individual character is concerned. In 1939-1947 the hero began as a selfish individual but through the course of a film quickly was converted to social responsibility and became inspired by the moral necessity of World War II. Security was the motivating factor during 1948-1962, but the justification moved back toward selfish individualism during 1963-1970.

Since 1948 some attempts have been made by Hollywood to produce antiwar films. During 1948-1962 the attempts focused on the detrimental consequences of war. The antiwar message failed because the harm was portrayed as an inevitable effect of a good cause. It was only when the films made in 1963-1970 began to deny the nationalistic morality of war that the antiwar message could survive. The righteousness of purpose had to be denied before criticism of method or elucidation of consequence could be effective.

SUMMARY

The bulk of this thesis has focused on the content of American war movies. An attempt has been made to give the content meaning in relation to its social environment. These concluding remarks are intended to draw together the earlier discussions, particularly as they relate to the role of war films in the social process. The task will be attempted in three parts. First, conclusions about war film content will be summarized. Then, the social, political, and economic influences on war films will be explored and finally some brief suggestions about the possible consequences of war films will be presented.

Summary of Content

During the past thirty-two years American war films passed through three stages: 1939-1947, which included the preliminaries, conduct, and aftermath of World War II; 1948-1962, the most intense years of the Cold War; and 1963-1970, an era during which Americans became divided over Vietnam and began to examine traditional Cold War and nationalistic assumptions.

Within each epoch the war pictures resembled each other, regardless of the war they portrayed, more than they did movies of previous epochs. In other words the war movies were characteristic of their time of production, and an examination of their content yielded an insight--albeit stereotyped--into American views of war during the particular period of film production.

1939-1947

The war films made in 1939-1947 were built around the themes of civilian patriotism and social responsibility. The government had pronounced World War II to be a total war involving civilians as deeply as soldiers. Nearly half of Hollywood's war pictures released during 1939-1947 featured civilians, sometimes fighting the enemy in a war zone but frequently producing goods and besting enemy spies on the home front.

American heroes of this era were distinguished by their frequent conversion to social responsibility during the course of a film. The conversion caused the hero to relinquish his individualistic selfishness and to assume a role of brother's keeper regardless of nationality. The theme fit quite well with growing internationalism within the United States and with what some observers had concluded was a feeling of collective guilt among Americans for having abandoned the nation's international responsibility after World War I.

Despite conversion to social responsibility the hero remained an individual in method--capable of using violent or non-violent means to defeat the Nazis or the Japanese. His strength was derived from his purpose: to prepare the way for a cooperative world devoid of totalitarianism and packed with democracy. His righteousness allowed him moral victory even if physically defeated.

Moral fortitude was shared by American and ally alike in a poly-national era. The Allies were prominent in many films and displayed national peculiarities. However, in political terms American and ally were virtually alike in their complete devotion to political democracy, egalitarianism, and the freedoms of the Bill of Rights.

1948-1962

Militaristic necessity replaced socially responsible obligation
in war pictures produced by Hollywood during 1948-1962. Cold War movies
released during this era generally reinforced the dread of communism
that gripped the country and especially the right wing beginning in the
late 1940's. To counteract the Communists, the government, the country,
and Hollywood placed their faith in a strong military and other professional warriors.

Hollywood's version of the militaristic necessity emphasized the
virtues of professional war making and the futility of civilian efforts.
The Korean War and World War II pictures of the era extolled discipline
and collectivization as the key to military victory. The Cold War films
made in the same era painted the dangers of communism to America's
internal security, the helplessness of civilians, and the superiority
of professional spy organizations. Frequent secondary themes argued
against civilian control of military or espionage decisions and advocated
benefits of advanced weapon technology.

The allies of 1948-1962 were practically non-existent, probably
reflecting Hollywood's interpretation of Americans' sense of isolated
responsibility at that time. All wars were depicted as the bailiwick
of Americans who were really Americans and not just foreigners who
behaved and believed like Americans.

Interestingly, World War II enemies received almost favorable
portrayals during 1948-1962. Both German and Japanese became less
barbaric and more compatible with Cold War realignments. The Germans,
previously uncivilized Fascists, became mistaken patriots who ultimately
paid for their transgressions. The Japanese were rebuilt as well

mannered, cultured, and intelligent pacifists.

1963-1970

In a period of internationalization and depoliticization of the movie industry, Hollywood presented a number of films during 1963-1970 which tended to deny the morality or the necessity of war. Of course, many films produced during this era did include arguments resembling the socially responsible presentations of 1939-1947 or the professional advocacies of 1948-1962. However, many more productions removed war directly or indirectly from its base of nationalistic or militaristic morality and treated it more as a personal matter.

Admittedly, one group of 1963-1970 movies exploited brutality and violence for entertainment purposes and thus on the surface seemed to glorify war, especially since many of the films tended to ignore the harmful consequences of war. However, by dissociating the act of war from noble purpose or by portraying purpose as self-oriented, the pictures removed the base of righteousness from war.

Another group of films produced in 1963-1970 removed its heroes from the necessity of participation in war. The removal was either accidental or intentional on the part of the characters, who in effect substituted concern for self for social responsibility. In some instances the characters represented a complete reversion to 1939-1947's selfish individual before conversion. While the 1939-1947 war hero has been characterized as responding to the war situation with "I'm not fighting for myself anymore,"[1] the 1963-1970 stalwart simply asserted, "I'm not fighting."

---

[1] Barbara Deming, Running Away from Myself . . . , pp. 9-38.

Impact of the Social Process

The following explanation of the social conditioning of war film content is based on observations about the derivations of war films. The generalizations may be unique to the production of war pictures. However, since war film production often is not very different from the making of other movies, it is believed that the following discussion is also a valid description of the broader institutional workings of the film industry.

Both the beginning and end of the film production process can be conceived of as an image of reality. Between the first and final stages occurs a molding operation in which the original idea is judged, reformulated, altered, and translated before release in film form. In this intermediary process institutional control as well as artistic and technical skills are brought to bear on the idea to transform it into film.

Movie production occurs in a variety of environments. The ultimate environment of course is physical reality, but physical reality is experienced by few people first hand. Thus, more important in influencing war film content is pseudo-reality--i.e. second hand information, communicated knowledge, images of people, places, and events--and the assortment of social, cultural, and personal values and beliefs through which reality is interpreted.[2]

The other major environment is institutional in scope. Hollywood, as American or international institution, is a capitalistic enterprise functioning primarily to turn a profit. The production process occurs

---

[2] For more complete discussion of pseudo-reality, see Introduction.

under the constant concern of whether a particular film will be profitable. Any idea thus is subjected to determination of its commercial
potential and is likely to be rejected if it is not promising.

Commercial potential is judged by reference to a number of
criteria, including stars, locale, producers, directors, and timeliness,
in relation to cost. Tradition plays a major role in the decision.
Notorious for sequels, Hollywood exploits proven money makers to the
limit. Experimentation is discouraged and conformity is the rule
with few exceptions.[3]

Film ideas are derived from the prevailing societal environment,
primarily from pseudo-reality. The ideas are an abstraction of some
part of reality but do not have to be intended to correspond to reality.
Idea selection is not independent of institutional control, which is
exerted through dictation, suggestion, implication, and deduction.

For war films, the direction of institutional control was primarily determined by an interaction of political and economic considerations. Other minor influences might be noted, but by and large
control over content of war pictures has been determined by the economic
stability of the movie industry measured against the power, influence,
and inclinations of political forces.

Political interference has seldom focused on one or a few films.
The consequence of such interference, if successful, has been to
establish general patterns of acceptability. However, in some cases
Hollywood has voluntarily relinquished control over at least part of
its product in exchange for financial benefits. In such cases prior

---

[3]MacCann, Hollywood in Transition, pp. 59-61.

censorship insured movie content favorable to the benefactor. The most active practitioner of prior censorship has been the Department of Defense, which assisted about half of the war pictures produced during 1948-1962 and about 30 per cent during 1963-1970. The FBI also has been involved in such endeavors.

It is probably true that Hollywood's cooperation in the war effort during 1942-1945 and its participation in Cold War propaganda were partially the result of patriotism. However, without pressure from the political sector in both 1942-1945 and 1948-1962 Hollywood's level of war film production would have been less. And, economic conditions were conducive to cooperation on Hollywood's part.

In 1942 Hollywood probably was as willing as other industries to participate in the war effort--i.e. participation without sacrifice of too much profit. However, the government's influence and badgering administered by the OWI prompted the movie industry into more complete participation, and possible economic sanctions insured it. Non-cooperation could have led Hollywood to lose its raw film supply, take over of the industry by the government, or a rebellious boycott from the public. These threats may never have been verbalized, but Hollywood's leaders were aware of them, as evidenced by any number of issues of _Variety_ during 1942-1944. Greatest anxiety was over the raw film supply, probably the most likely of the threats to materialize.

Furthermore, compliance with HUAC's wishes in the late 1940's was encouraged by the shaky economic foundation of the movie industry. Television was slashing attendance, and the Justice Department was attacking and destroying the industry's vertical integration. Despite the vocal persecution of HUAC, Hollywood's leaders were more concerned with the economic problem. Without income Hollywood could not exist; with income it could exist even if shackled by right-wing restrictions.

Cooperation with the Defense Department in so many films since 1948 can be seen as an effort to be patriotic or to please the political establishment. It can also be traced to the desire to cut costs on some films.

Finally, Hollywood has not been under political pressure to produce patriotic war movies during 1963-1970, and the economic situation has internationalized the movie industry, thus discouraging nationalistic biases. Political factions did not seem seriously interested in Hollywood's output during 1963-1970. Perhaps television had become a more convenient target. However, the fact that the movie industry had internationalized, gaining half or more of its income from foreign markets, probably would have meant greater resistance to political interference, especially if such interference led to chauvinistic films that would not have been marketable in other countries.

Internationalization led to a lessening of nationality as an important aspect of character identity in war movies. One character consequently was much like another, regardless of nationality. Freed from political coercion and serving economic considerations, Hollywood recently has produced war films appealing to international audiences without offending any particular nationality.

Institutional pressures, thus, have operated over the past thirty-two years to keep war film content generally within the limits of societal and institutional acceptability. Deviations can be pointed out, but normally they occurred only if the films were produced outside establishment control or if their producers had enough status in the establishment to gain approval for deviation.

Possible Consequences of War Movies

The effects of mass communication have been discussed and re-discussed down through the years. This final section will not rehash the issues but is intended to mention possible consequences of war movies for individuals and for society.

One can usually assume that a person attends a film to be entertained—in one way or another. What happens during that entertainment may have other implications. Those other implications are of concern here.

The audience experience is basically emotional, tempered by reflection. It is one in which the audience member identifies—more or less—with what is happening on the screen. Such identification may be accompanied by catharsis or wish fulfillment as the individual receives some degree of satisfaction from the portrayal of good over evil or American over enemy. The individual may also vent his anger and frustration through identification with the violence on the screen. Pauline Kael has asserted that war movies serve nations as modern morality plays.[4]

All of these suggestions seem to have some validity, depending on audience, film, and situation. However, the suggestions are microscopic on the whole and do not deal with the implications of war film for society's view of reality.

In discussing the consequences of war films for a nation's images,

---

[4]Pauline Kael, I Lost It at the Movies (New York: Bantam Books, 1966), pp. 288-311.

it should be emphasized that the focal point is not just one or a few pictures but hundreds of movies over more than twenty years. It should also be recognized that the particular viewpoint of war pictures was reinforced by and reinforced other forms of social communication.

The ideas presented in motion pictures seemed to fit quite well with what generally was taken to be prevailing American feelings during 1942-1964. Prevailing, however, does not mean monolithic. Other opinions existed, but one would be hard pressed to demonstrate that from the war films—or at some time periods even by examining other media. The point is that the ideas of war films—particularly from 1939-1962— received near monopolistic treatment and were of such a nature as to take advantage of existing opinions. In other words, the conditions in which war films operated nationally—in combination with other media— were conducive to successful propaganda.

Thus, war films as propaganda could have had two major effects in the United States. First, the films in combination with other influences could have fostered a view of the international situation leading to only one course of action—further dependency on force as a tool of national policy. Secondly, the war pictures could have con- tributed to the military's ascendancy in political favor during the 1950's by promoting force as the tool of peace and the military as the benevolent users of that tool. Certainly, few political groups in the United States have had the massive unqualified praise bestowed on the military by motion pictures. War films may have contributed to the situations just mentioned, but, on the other hand, they may have merely reflected those situations. Actually, they probably did a little of both.

Internationally, the monolithic views of war films may have fostered a somewhat false impression among foreigners. There are examples of foreigners conceiving of the United States solely in terms of cowboys and Indians and in terms of gangsters—images perpetrated by Hollywood. Certainly, war films may have led to similar misimpressions.

It is difficult to pinpoint exact consequences of war films as with the effects of any mass communication. War films are only one portion of the social process and their consequences cannot be understood outside that process. Perhaps this is the point that has guided this investigation of motion pictures about war: movies are a part of the social process and to dissociate them from that context is to distort their meaning.

BIBLIOGRAPHY

ARTICLES

"Brighter 'Moon'." Newsweek, April 5, 1943, p. 86.

"Film War," Current History, L (March, 1939), pp. 46-47.

"Movies." Newsweek, March 20, 1944, p. 90.

"Movies." Senior Scholastic, Feb. 15, 1943, p. 17.

"New Films from Books." Library Journal, LXXXI (Oct. 15, 1956), p. 2315.

"The New Pictures." Time, Sept. 28, 1942, p. 82.

"The New Pictures." Time, May 10, 1943, pp. 23-24.

"The New Pictures." Time, Dec. 6, 1943, p. 54.

"The New Pictures." Time, March 27, 1944, p. 94.

"The New Pictures." Time, Nov. 13, 1944, p. 96.

"The New Pictures." Time, May 3, 1948, p. 93.

"The New Pictures." Time, April 7, 1952, p. 104.

"The Novels of the Second World War." Publishers' Weekly, CLIV (Oct. 23, 1948), pp. 1802-1808.

"The Now Movie." Saturday Review, Dec. 12, 1968, pp. 8-23.

"Totem and Taboo." Time. May 15, 1939, pp. 58-59.

"Winning His Navy Cross." Newsweek, June 12, 1944, p. 72.

Bart, Peter, "$upercolossaliti$." Saturday Review, Dec. 24, 1966, pp. 14-16.

Barthel, Joan, "John Wayne, Superhawk." New York Times Magazine, Dec. 4, 1967, pp. 4, 22.

Behlmer, Rudy, "World War I Aviation Films." Films in Review, XVIII (August-September, 1967), pp. 413-440.

Cassady, Ralph, "Impact of the Paramount Decision on Motion Picture Distribution and Price Making." Southern California Law Review, XXXI (1958), pp. 12-13.

Erskine, Hazel, ed., "The Polls: Is War a Mistake?" Public Opinion Quarterly, XXIV (Spring, 1968), pp. 134-150.

Ferguson, Otis, "They're Down! They're Up!" The New Republic,
    May 10, 1939, p. 20.

Ferguson, Otis, "Three for the Show." The New Republic, Oct. 18,
    1939, p. 301.

Gerbner, George, "Cultural Indicators: The Case of Violence in
    Television Drama." The Annals of the American Academy of
    Political and Social Science, CCCLXXXVIII (March, 1970),
    pp. 69-81.

Gerbner, George, "Toward 'Cultural Indicators': The Analysis of
    Mass Mediated Public Message Systems." The Analysis of
    Communication Content. Edited by George Gerbner et al. New
    York: Wiley & Sons, 1969, pp. 123-132.

Grossman, Edward, "Bloody Popcorn." Harper's, December, 1970,
    pp. 32-40.

Hartung, Philip T., "Flow Like Water." Commonweal, July 13, 1945,
    p. 309.

Hartung, Philip T., "Hail." Commonweal, Sept. 17, 1943, p. 538.

Hartung, Philip T., "Hollywood's Reply to Dec. 7." Commonweal,
    Dec. 22, 1944, p. 25.

Hartung, Philip T., "More War--Different Angle." Commonweal, July
    27, 1941, p. 233.

Hartung, Philip T., "Off Among the Roosians." Commonweal, Feb.
    18, 1944, p. 448.

Hartung, Philip T., "Oh Say Can You." Commonweal, Aug. 16, 1940,
    p. 352.

Hartung, Philip T., "Shall We Join the Ladies?" Commonweal, Dec.
    10, 1943, p. 206.

Hartung, Philip T., "To Be Or Not To Be Laughed At." Commonweal,
    March 13, 1942, p. 514.

Hartung, Philip T., "To Thine Own Self Be True." Commonweal, June
    5, 1942, p. 160.

Hulett, J. Edward, Jr., "A Symbolic Interactionist Model of Human
    Communication. Part I." AV Communication Review, XIV (Spring,
    1966), pp. 5-31.

Jacobs, Lewis, "World War II and the American Film." Film Culture,
    Fall, 1969, pp. 28-42.

Jones, Dorothy B., "Hollywood Goes to War." Nation, Jan. 27, 1945, pp. 93-95.

Jones, Dorothy B., "Hollywood's War Films, 1942-1944." Hollywood Quarterly, I (October, 1945), pp. 1-19.

Knight, Arthur, "Little Lulus." Saturday Review, Aug. 9, 1969, p. 32.

Larson, Cedric, "The Domestic Motion Pictures Work of the Office of War Information." Hollywood Quarterly, III (Summer, 1968), pp. 434-443.

Leab, Daniel J., "Cold War Comics." Columbia Journalism Review, III (Winter, 1965), pp. 42-47.

McDonald, John, "Films." Public Opinion Quarterly, V (March, 1941), pp. 127-129.

McKenzie, Vernon, "Treatment of War Themes in Magazine Fiction." Public Opinion Quarterly, V (June, 1941), pp. 227-232.

Nugent, Frank S., "Hollywood Counts the Pennies." New York Times Magazine, Aug. 30, 1942, pp. 14-15.

Sanders, Clinton R., "The Portrayal of War and the Fighting Man in Novels of the Vietnam War." Journal of Popular Culture, III (Winter, 1969), pp. 553-564.

Sinclair, Upton, "The Movies and Political Propaganda." The Movies of Trial. Edited by William J. Perlman. New York: The Macmillan Company, 1936, pp. 189-195.

Smith, William J., "The War Novel." Commonweal, May 11, 1956, pp. 146-149.

Soderbergh, Peter A., "On War and the Movies: A Reappraisal." Centennial Review, XI (Summer, 1967), pp. 405-418.

Spears, Jack, "World War I on the Screen." Films in Review, XVII (May and June-July, 1966), pp. 274-292 and 347-365.

Waldemeir, Joseph, "Novelists of Two Wars." Nation, Nov. 1, 1958, pp. 304-307.

Wanger, Walter, "The Role of Movies in Morale." American Journal of Sociology, XLVII (November, 1941), pp. 378-383.

Young, Colin, "Nobody Dies." Film: Book 2. Edited by Robert Hughes. New York: Grove Press Inc., 1962, pp. 87-110.

BOOKS

America Organizes to Win the War. New York: Harcourt, Brace and Co., 1942.

Bogdanovich, Peter. Fritz Lang in America. New York: Praeger, 1969.

Boulding, Kenneth. The Image. Ann Arbor: The University of Michigan Press, 1966.

Cassirer, Ernst. An Essay on Man. New Haven, Conn.: Yale University Press, 1966.

Cogley, John. Report on Blacklisting, Vol. I: Movies. New York: The Fund for the Republic, 1956.

Conant, Michael. Antitrust in the Motion Picture Industry. Berkeley: University of California Press, 1960.

Deming, Barbara. Running Away from Myself: A Dream Portrait of America Drawn from the Films of the Forties. New York: Grossman, 1969.

Durgnat, Raymond. The Crazy Mirror: Hollywood Comedy and the American Image. London: Faber and Faber Limited, 1969.

Fulbright, J. William. The Pentagon Propaganda Machine. New York: Liveright, 1970.

Gerbner, George. Mass Communications and Popular Conceptions of Education: A Cross-Cultural Study. Cooperative Research Project No. 876. Urbana: Institute of Communication Research, University of Illinois, 1964.

Gerbner, George. "The Film Hero: A Cross-Cultural Study." Journalism Monographs, no. 13. Lexington: University of Kentucky, 1969.

Gerbner, George, et al, eds. The Analysis of Communication Content. New York: Wiley & Sons, 1969.

Goodman, Walter. The Committee. New York: Farrar, Strauss, and Giroux, 1968.

Guback, Thomas H. The International Film Industry. Bloomington: The Indiana University Press, 1969.

Handel, Leo A. Hollywood Looks at Its Audience. Urbana: University of Illinois Press, 1950.

Highman, Charles, and Greenberg, Joel. Hollywood in the Forties. New York: A. S. Barnes and Co., 1968.

Hoehling, A. A. Home Front U.S.A. New York: Thomas Y. Cromwell Company, 1966.

Hughes, Robert, ed. Film: Book 2. New York: Grove Press Inc., 1962.

Janowitz, Morris. The Professional Soldier. Glencoe, Ill.: The Free Press, 1960.

Jarvie, I. C. Movies and Society. New York: Basic Books, Inc., 1970.

Kael, Pauline. I Lost It at the Movies. New York: Bantam Books, 1966.

Kahn, Gordon. Hollywood on Trial. New York: Boni & Gaer, 1948.

Knight, Arthur. The Liveliest Art. New York: The New American Library, 1957.

Kracauer, Siegfried. From Calgari to Hitler: A Psychological History of the German Film. Princeton, N. J.: Princeton University Press, 1947.

Lawson, John Howard. Film: The Creative Process. New York: Hill & Wang, 1964.

Lerche, Charles O. The Cold War...and After. Englewood Cliffs, N. J.: Prentice Hall, 1965.

Limbacher, James L., ed. A Directory of 8 mm and 16 mm Feature Films Available for Rental, Sale, and Lease in the United States. New York: Educational Film Library Association, Inc., 1968.

Lippmann,Walter. Public Opinion. New York: The Free Press, 1965.

MacCann, Richard Dyer. Hollywood in Transition. Boston: Houghton Mifflin Company, 1962.

Manis, Jerome G., and Meltzer, Bernard N., eds. Symbolic Interaction: A Reader in Social Psychology. Boston: Allyn and Bacon, 1967.

Manvell, Roger. New Cinema in the U.S.A. New York: E. P. Dutton & Co., 1958.

Morris, Charles W., ed., Mind, Self and Society. Chicago: University of Chicago Press, 1967.

Ogden, August Raymond. The Dies Committee. Washington: The Catholic University of America Press, 1945.

Perlman, William J., ed. The Movies on Trial. New York: The Macmillan Company, 1936.

Peterson, Theodore, Jay W. Jensen, and William L. Rivers. The Mass Media and Modern Society. New York: Holt, Rinehart and Winston, Inc., 1966.

Powdermaker, Hortense. Hollywood, the Dream Factory. Boston: Brown and Co., 1950.

Rosten, Leo. Hollywood: The Movie Colony and Movie Makers. New York: Harcourt, Brace, and Co., 1941.

Schwartz, Jack. "The Portrayal of Education in American Motion Pictures, 1931-1961." Unpublished Ph.D. dissertation, University of Illinois, 1964.

Summers, Harrison B. Radio Programs Carried on National Networks, 1926-1956. Columbus: Ohio State University, 1958.

Warner, Jack. My First Hundred Years in Hollywood. New York: Random House, 1965.

Whitney, Simon N. Antitrust Policies, American Experience in Twenty Industries. Vol. II. New York: Twentieth Century Fund, 1958.

Williams, Raymond. The Long Revolution. New York: Harper & Row, 1966.

PERIODICALS

Film Daily

Film Facts

The Green Sheet

Hollywood Spectator

Motion Picture Herald

Motion Picture Review Digest

The New York Times

Theatre Patrons

Variety

APPENDIX I

CONTENT ANALYSIS FORM

FORM A

Write legibly in ink or type. Fill in separate FORM A for each
film. Answer all questions on the basis of evidence or clear
inference. Explain if necessary.

TOP OF FORM. A: Write in your name. B: Write in date of filling
out form. C: Write in place of filling out form.

1. Title

2. Releasing company

3. Year released

4. Producer

5. Director

6. Author of screenplay

7. Story source

8. Stars

9. Are you using film reviews or a screening of the film as a
   basis for filling out the form? If the basis is film reviews,
   indicate how many reviews and specify the sources. Write in:
   (1) film reviews
   (2) screening

10. Did the film receive assistance of any kind from the Pentagon
    or any other governmental agency? Specify the agency and the
    nature of the assistance. Write in:
    (1) yes
    (2) no
    (3) uncertain

11. Does the film clearly belong to any of the following tradi-
    tional format categories? Write in the most appropriate number.
    Explain if necessary.
    (1) comedy, humor, situation comedy
    (2) musical
    (3) romance, domestic, family situation
    (4) general drama
    (5) fantasy, horror, science fiction
    (6) crime, gangster, detective, mystery
    (7) western
    (8) adventure, action
    (9) expose, sex exploitation
    (10) other

12. What aspects of war does the film examine? If one of the following, write in the appropriate number. If more than one, write in the sum of all appropriate numbers.
    (1) causes of war
    (2) preparation for war
    (4) prevention of war
    (8) life during war
    (16) conduct of war
    (32) consequences, aftermath of war

13. What war does the film examine? Write in the most appropriate number.
    (1) World War II
    (2) Korea
    (3) Vietnam
    (4) Cold War
    (5) other; explain

14. What is the locale of the story? Specify. Leave parenthesis blank.

15. What is the date of the story? Specify. Leave parenthesis blank.

16. How does the film relate to historical fact? Specify. Write in:
    (1) if film is true story in dramatized form
    (2) if film is fictitious with no claim to represent actual events or persons
    (3) if film is fictitious although given hint of authenticity through use of actual dates, events, persons

17. The film is presented from a point of view sympathetic to what country, if any--i.e., who are the "good guys"? Specify. Leave parenthesis blank.

18. What country is the enemy? Specify. Leave parenthesis blank.

19. How is the enemy labeled? Specify. Write in the most appropriate number.
    (1) country or its people
    (2) political leader
    (3) creeds or their followers, e.g. Fascism, Communism, Nazism
    (4) other; specify; explain
    (5) not applicable
    (6) insufficient evidence to judge

20. Consider the following character classification. Rank in order of importance all groups of characters represented in the film. Explain. Determine the characters' classification by their personal allegiance rather than by their country's official diplomatic stance.

agents	soldiers	civilians	
(1)	(2)	(3)	allies
(4)	(5)	(6)	Americans
(7)	(8)	(9)	enemy
(10)	(11)	(12)	neutrals

21. The following classifies war films according to location and primary characters. Into which category does this picture fit? Write in the most appropriate number.

agents	soldiers	civilians	
(1)	(2)	(3)	war zone
(4)	(5)	(6)	home front

22. What American military branch is featured in the film?
    (1) Army
    (2) Navy
    (3) Air Force or Army Air Corps
    (4) Marine Corps
    (5) Coast Guard
    (6) other; specify
    (7) not applicable

23. What military specialty is featured--e.g. submarines, bombers, tanks, etc.? Specify. Leave parenthesis blank.

24. What military activity is featured? Specify.
    (1) training
    (2) supply, maintenance
    (3) transportation
    (4) tactics
    (5) fighting
    (6) medical
    (7) occupation of conquered countries
    (8) intelligence
    (9) other; specify
    (10) not applicable

25. How does the film depict the role of military organizations (excluding underground and para-military groups) in the modern world? Does the military receive generally favorable or unfavorable treatment? Explain. Write in one number for allied and American military and one for enemy military.

allied	enemy	
(1)	(2)	favorable
(3)	(4)	unfavorable
(5)	(6)	mixed; uncertain
(7)	(8)	not applicable

26. How do American civilians on the home fron contribute to the
war effort? Specify; explain. Write in the three most appropriate numbers in order of importance.
    (1) production of supplies, weapons
    (2) development of supplies, weapons
    (3) providing entertainment
    (4) conserving scarce materials
    (5) buying bonds
    (6) remaining faithful to loved ones in the war
    (7) avoiding loose talk
    (8) being alert for spies, espionage
    (9) civil defense
    (10) remaining loyal to the country
    (11) other; explain
    (12) not applicable

27. How do American civilians on the home front hinder the war
effort: Specify; explain. Write in the three most appropriate numbers in order of importance.
    (1) extravagent consumption
    (2) economic opportunism
    (3) disloyalty to loved ones
    (4) disloyalty to country
    (5) disagreement with the war
    (6) unconcern with the war
    (7) other; explain
    (8) not applicable

28. What are the activities of civilians in war zones (areas in
which combat--ground, naval, or aerial--will take, is taking,
or has taken place)? Specify; explain. Write in the three
most appropriate numbers in order of importance.
    (1) production of supplies, weapons
    (2) development of supplies, weapons
    (3) providing entertainment
    (4) conserving scarce materials
    (5) remaining faithful to loved ones in the war
    (6) avoiding loose talk
    (7) being alert for spies, espionage
    (8) civil defense
    (9) remaining loyal to the country
    (10) life as usual
    (11) surviving, existing
    (12) cooperation with the enemy
    (13) underground activities, cooperation as well as
         active participation
    (14) fighting in para-military groups
    (15) other
    (16) not applicable

29. What are the activities of espionage agents? Specify;
explain. List the three most appropriate numbers in order
of importance. Write in three each for the allied (and

American) and for the enemy agents.

allied	enemy	
(1)	(2)	stopping sabotage
(3)	(4)	protecting secrets against theft, destruction
(5)	(6)	protecting individuals against assassination, harm
(7)	(8)	sabotage
(9)	(10)	assassination
(11)	(12)	counterespionage
(13)	(14)	information collection
(15)	(16)	other; explain
(17)	(18)	not applicable

30. Does the film convey a political message? What is that message? Write in:
    (1) yes
    (2) no
    (3) uncertain

31. What does the film say are the causes of war? Specify; explain. Write in the two most appropriate numbers in order of importance.
    (1) enemy's warlike nature
    (2) territorial
    (3) economic
    (4) religious
    (5) ideals
    (6) military
    (7) political
    (8) other; explain
    (9) not applicable

32. What are the dominant symbols of justification in the film? Explain. Leave parenthesis blank.

33. Who does the film say is responsible for the occurrence of war? Specify; explain. Write in the most appropriate number.
    (1) mankind
    (2) no one
    (3) the enemy in general
    (4) the enemy's leaders
    (5) the allies in general
    (6) the allies' leaders
    (7) other; explain
    (8) not applicable

34. According to the film, what are the reasons for victory or defeat in war? Write in the three most appropriate numbers in order of importance. Specify; explain.
    (1) goals, ideals
    (2) men as individuals
    (3) material resources, including manpower as numbers
    (4) methods

    (5)   nature, circumstance
    (6)   supreme being
    (7)   other; explain
    (8)   not applicable

35. Do battle scenes play a significant role in the film? Des-
    cribe the scenes. Write in:
    (1)   yes
    (2)   no
    (3)   uncertain

36. Describe the behavior of soldiers under battle conditions.
    Differentiate American, ally, and enemy.

37. Does death as a consequence of war play a significant role in
    the film? Explain. Write in:
    (1)   yes
    (2)   no
    (3)   uncertain

38. For whom is death in the film more frequent? Specify; explain.
    Write in the most appropriate number.

agents	soldiers	civilians	
(1)	(2)	(3)	allies
(4)	(5)	(6)	Americans
(7)	(8)	(9)	enemy
(10)	(11)	(12)	neutrals

39. Whom does the war affect most and what is the nature of that
    effect? Specify; explain. Write in the most appropriate
    number from question 38.

40. What are the immediate and ultimate results of the fighting
    from the viewpoint of the United States and its allies and
    friends? Explain.

immediate	ultimate	
(1)	(2)	victory
(3)	(4)	defeat
(5)	(6)	deadlock
(7)	(8)	undeterminable
(9)	(10)	not applicable

41. Of what consequence to the success or failure of the war
    effort (i.e., to the success or failure within the war
    arena depicted in the film as well as to the overall war
    effort) are the events in the film? Explain.

limited	overall	
(1)	(2)	major consequence
(3)	(4)	minor consequence
(5)	(6)	unrelated

limited	overall	
(7)	(8)	undeterminable
(9)	(10)	not applicable

42. What is the general outcome of events? List the most appropriate number. State "moral" or implicit lesson, if any.

happy	unhappy	mixed	
(1)	(2)	(3)	success
(4)	(5)	(6)	failure
(7)	(8)	(9)	mixed

43. Examine the following list of themes and aspects of life. On the sheet, mark the one or two numbers that correspond to the major themes. Mark the most dominant theme as D1 and the second most dominant as D2. Next, mark, at the most, three numbers that correspond to themes and aspects playing any significant part. Mark those numbers, if any, with a circle.

   (1) domestic arts, crafts, hobbies; home and garden; fashions; collection
   (2) religion; religious customs, rituals
   (3) superstition, supernatural, occult, mystical
   (4) animals, nature (jungle, mountains, oceans, rivers); exploration, discovery; natural catastrophies; conservation
   (5) financial success; prize, inheritance; financial hardship, poverty
   (6) injury, illness, deformity--physical and organic; medicine, treatment
   (7) mental illness, deficiency, abnormality; serious mental disorder; amnesia, phobias; cure, therapy, rehabilitation
   (8) alcoholism, heavy drinking; narcotics, drug addiction, cure
   (9) science and scientist (including social science); technology
   (10) entertainment; amusements, sports, show business
   (11) the press; journalism--radio, television, movies, newspapers
   (12) minority groups and people; non-whites; religious and ethnic minorities
   (13) foreign countries and people
   (14) mechanical accidents, catastrophies; explosion, wreck, crash; mechanical failure
   (15) armed forces
   (16) intimate or close relationship between the sexes whether cooperative or hostile; love, sex, prostitution
   (17) home, family, marriage; domestic problems; parent, children, youth, old age
   (18) physical violence, murder, suicide
   (19) war
   (20) public affairs, agencies; courts, prisons; legislation, politics

(21)   crime, corruption, rackets; crime detection, law
       enforcement, investigation
(22)   patriotism; public duty
(23)   inner conflict; maturity; guilt
(24)   business, industry, labor; production, consumption
(25)   school, education, training; study, self development
(26)   literature, fine arts, music, classics, humanities
(27)   friendship; comradrie; esperit de corps

FORM B

Fill out a separate FORM B sheet for the major character of each
film.

TOP OF FORM. A: Write in the name of the character. B: Write in
the title of the movie. C: Write in your name.

1. Write in the number corresponding to the major relevant role
   of the character. State others. Determine his position in
   the war by his personal stance rather than by the official
   policy of the country of his citizenship.

agent	soldier	civilian	
(1)	(2)	(3)	ally (of the United States)
(4)	(5)	(6)	American
(7)	(8)	(9)	enemy (of the United States)
(10)	(11)	(12)	neutral

2. Sex of character. Write in:
   (1) male
   (2) female
   (3) unidentifiable

3. Specify age of character if known. Estimate if unknown.
   Write in:
   (1) youth
   (2) young adult
   (3) mature adult
   (4) middle age
   (5) elderly
   (6) insufficient evidence

4. What is the character's social-economic status? Write in
   the most appropriate number. Indicate actual status of the
   character for the most part (not ambition, destination, or
   ultimate achievement). Base the judgment on the standards
   cf the social system of which the character is a part, not
   just on American standards.
   (1) cannot classify; ambiguous; insufficient evidence
   (2) upper class; title or wealth; great power or prestige
   (3) middle class; moderate or comfortable income; white
       collar
   (4) lower class; manual labor; meager income; little
       power or prestige
   (5) outside class structure; illegal occupation; member
       of armed forces or other service with no indication
       of status

5. Marital status. Write in:
   (1) never been married
   (2) married
   (3) divorced

      (4) other; explain
      (5) unknown

6. Indicate highest schooling or professional training achieved.
    Name degree, if any, college, if known.
      (1) still in school (indicate primary, secondary, college)
      (2) out of school, no more than a high school education
      (3) out of school, no more than an undergraduate college
           education
      (4) higher degree (indicate degree)
      (5) other; explain
      (6) unknown

7. Specify the character's normal occupation. If he is in the
    armed forces for other than career duration, give his civilian
    vocation. Leave parenthesis blank.

8. State nationality (citizenship, not national origin). Leave
    parenthesis blank.

9. State national origin (based on information provided in the
    film or upon inference on basis of name, accent, etc.). Leave
    parenthesis blank.

10. State race. Leave parenthesis blank.

11. State religion. Leave parenthesis blank.

12. Is the person considered a member of a minority (based on
    national origin, ethnic, racial, religious background) in the
    country of his citizenship? Explain. Write in:
      (1) not a member of minority
      (2) national origin different from citizenship, or inferred
           to be different on the basis of name, accent
      (3) non-white
      (4) native born ethnic minority in country of citizenship;
           white
      (5) member of religious minority in country of citizenship
      (6) other; explain
      (7) more than one; explain
      (8) insufficient evidence

13. What is the official policy of the character's country of
    citizenship in the relevant war? Write in:
      (1) American
      (2) ally of the United States
      (3) enemy of the United States
      (4) neutral
      (5) other; explain

14. How does the character's personal position relate to that of
    his country? Explain. Write in:

(1) if he opposes the policy but keeps his opposition within the prescribed legal framework
(2) if he opposes the policy but operates outside the legal framework
(3) if he supports the policy
(4) if he is neutral; non-commital; resigned to policy
(5) other; explain
(6) undeterminable

15. Character's military status. Write in:
    (1) member of military
    (2) former member of military
    (3) never member of military
    (4) unknown

16. If the character is, or was, in the military, what branch?
    (1) Army
    (2) Navy
    (3) Air Force or Army Air Corps
    (4) Marines
    (5) Coast Guard
    (6) other; explain
    (7) unknown
    (8) not applicable

17. What is, or was, the character's military specialty (e.g. Green Berets, fighter pilot, etc.)? Leave parenthesis blank.

18. Specify the character's military rank. Write in:
    (1) general, admiral
    (2) colonel, captain (Navy)
    (3) major, commander
    (4) captain (Army), lieutenant (Navy)
    (5) lieutenant (Army), ensign
    (6) sergeant, chief petty officer
    (7) other non-commissioned officer; explain
    (8) enlisted man
    (9) other; explain
   (10) unknown
   (11) not applicable

19. If an American officer, how was the rank obtained? Specify. Write in:
    (1) service academy
    (2) R.O.T.C.
    (3) officer candidate school
    (4) direct commission
    (5) advancement through the ranks
    (6) battlefield commission
    (7) unknown
    (8) not applicable

20. Why is, or was, the character in the military? Explain.
    Write in:
    (1) career
    (2) drafted or enlisted under threat of draft
    (3) patriotism
    (4) personal reasons; security
    (5) other; explain
    (6) unknown
    (7) not applicable

21. If the character is male and not in the military, why not?
    Explain. Write in:
    (1) physically unfit
    (2) mentally unfit
    (3) illegal draft evasion
    (4) occupational, student deferment
    (5) age, family deferment
    (6) completed obligation
    (7) chose not to join and service not required
    (8) other, explain
    (9) unknown
    (10) not applicable

22. Health, physical and mental. If only one of the following is
    applicable, write in the appropriate number. If more than
    one, write in the sum of all appropriate numbers. Specify
    illness or injury and explanation of illness or injury.
    (0) none of the following
    (1) non-fatal physical injury or illness, not war or
        military related
    (2) non-fatal physical injury or illness, war or military
        related
    (4) mental illness or emotional disturbance, not war or
        military related
    (8) mental illness or emotional disturbance, war or
        military related
    (16) bodily handicap, deformity, abnormality, not war or
        military related
    (32) bodily handicap, deformity, abnormality, war or
        military related

23. Does the character live throughout the picture? Write in:
    (1) lives throughout the picture
    (2) dies, not war or military related
    (3) dies, war or military related

24. Does the character undergo a change as a result of his war
    or military experience? Explain. If one of the following
    is applicable, write in the appropriate number. If more
    than one, write in the sum of all appropriate numbers.
    (0) no change
    (1) change in behavior

(2) change in knowledge
(4) change in attitude

25. Indicate primary goal or value held by character. Write in
the number of the most appropriate category. State specific
goal or value. Explain.
    (1) safety, self preservation
    (2) escape from law, concealment of guilt, evasion of
        consequences of crime
    (3) health, adjustment, bodily or mental integrity
    (4) freedom of expression, individualism
    (5) material success, wealth, financial security, making
        a living
    (6) comfort, leisure, pleasure, self-indulgence
    (7) power, domination, mastery over other
    (8) adventure, thrill, satisfaction of impulse
    (9) love, friendship, affection
    (10) home, family, children
    (11) sex but without love or romance
    (12) accomplishing a task; doing a job
    (13) fame, popularity, prestige
    (14) public service, patriotism
    (15) justice, idealism, a better world
    (16) truth, beauty, knowledge; art, science, professional
         goals
    (17) hatred, revenge, defiance, destruction, spite, brutality
    (18) honesty, honor
    (19) other

26. Indicate the second major goal or value, if any, held by the
character. Write in the number of the appropriate category
from the list above. State specific goal or value. Explain.

27. What barrier, difficulty, or problem does the character
encounter in seeking goals and values? Write in the number
of the major barrier from the list below. Note the exact
nature of the barrier, difficulty, or problem.
    (1) legal conventions; impersonal authority of any kind;
        officials acting as representatives of authority
        (employer, administrator, government, military); law
    (2) social conventions; society, norms, customs, tradition
    (3) nature or the elements
    (4) illness, injury, physical hardship
    (5) other people acting as individuals; personal conflict,
        trickery, hatred, jealousy, rivalry, ignorance
    (6) self; mental or emotional block; fear, phobia,
        obsession; lack of knowledge, training, care, courage

28. Write in the number of the second major barrier. Explain.

29. What is the principal means typical of the character's
actions striving toward goals? Write in the most appropriate

number from the list below. Specify. Explain.
  (1) hard work, industriousness, perserverence
  (2) luck, chance, fate, accident, coincidence
  (3) trickery, deceit, cunning
  (4) knowledge, intellect, information
  (5) charm, attractiveness, kindness
  (6) force, power, firmness, discipline, strength
  (7) persuasion, argument

30. What is the second major means used by the character?
     Specify. Explain. Write in the appropriate number from
     the list above.

31. Indicate the final outcome in terms of the character's own
     goals. Specify. Explain. Write in:
       (1) character is expected to live and achieves goals
       (2) character lives but does not achieve goals, fails
       (3) character dies or is expected to die, but achieves
            goals
       (4) character dies or is expected to die, but does not
            achieve goals, fails
       (5) if more than one, unclear, not indicated

In the following series of questions, describe the relationship
between the character and his principal romantic partner. If he
has other romantic partners, specify those relationships. If
there are no romantic relationships, write 0 in answer to the
questions. Write in the most appropriate numbers to the following
five questions. Describe the nature and outsome of the relationship.

32. Write in the name of the most significant romantic partner
     and the role which the partner occupies. Note if the character
     has other romantic or sexual relationships or attractions.
     Write in:

agent	soldier	civilian	
(1)	(2)	(3)	ally of the United States
(4)	(5)	(6)	American
(7)	(8)	(9)	enemy of the United States
(10)	(11)	(12)	neutral

33. Write in:
       (1) if the other person is of lower status or standing
            than the major character (in terms of social class,
            power, authority)
       (2) if the other person is of higher status
       (3) if the other person is of equal status
       (4) if unclear, or if relative status changes

34. Classify the relationship according to the character's motiva-
     tion and the partner's marital status. Write in:

love and sex	sex without love	
(1)	(2)	unmarried
(3)	(4)	married to someone else
(5)	(6)	character's spouse

35. How is the physical relationship between the pair depicted? Describe. Write in:
    (1) no physical contact
    (2) hand holding
    (3) light kissing, embracing (as in greeting)
    (4) petting, heavy kissing, passionate embracing
    (5) implied that sex will or did take place
    (6) couple shown in sex
    (7) other

36. What is the outcome of the relationship? Specify. Write in the most appropriate number.
    (1) culminates in marriage, marriage continues, marriage implied
    (2) romance continues
    (3) marriage or romance breaks up in accordance with the wishes of either or both partners
    (4) marriage or romance breaks up against the wishes of both partners; explain
    (5) uncertain

37. One of the character's concerns supposedly is the war, i.e., the conflict between American or ally and the enemy. Is the character involved in any other conflicts? Specify the nature, origin, participants, and outcome of the most significant of any other conflicts. Leave parenthesis blank.

38. Consider the three possible concerns of the character: war, romance, or the other conflict. On the sheet rank the three in order of importance to the character by placing 1 beside the one given primary importance, 2 by the one second in importance, and 3 by the one of least importance. If any of the three are unimportant, write C. Explain.

APPENDIX II

WAR FILM TITLES

FILM TITLE	REALEASING COMPANY	WAR
1939		
Beasts of Berlin	PRC	WWII
Confessions of a Nazi Spy	WB	WWII
Espionage Agent	Col	WWII
The Lone Wolf Spy Hunt	Col	WWII
Television Spy	Par	WWII
They Made Her a Spy	RKO	WWII
1940		
Arise My Love	Par	WWII
*Charlie Chan in Panama	20th	WWII
Escape	MGM	WWII
Flight Command	MGM	WWII
Foreign Correspondent	UA	WWII
The Great Dictator	UA	WWII
The Man I Married	20th	WWII
The Mortal Storm	MGM	WWII
Mystery Sea Raider	Par	WWII
Sailor's Lady	20th	WWII
Sky Murder	MGM	WWII
Women in War	Rep	WWII
1941		
Air Devils	Mono	WWII
*Buck Privates	Univ	WWII
Burma Convoy	Univ	WWII
*Caught in the Draft	Par	WWII
Confirm or Deny	20th	WWII
The Devil Pays Off	Rep	WWII
*Dive Bomber	WB	WWII
Emergency Landing	PRC	WWII
Federal Fugitive	PRC	WWII
*Great Guns	20th	WWII
Here Come the Marines	Mono	WWII
*International Lady	UA	WWII
International Squadron	WB	WWII
In the Navy	Univ	WWII
*I Wanted Wings	Par	WWII
Man at Large	20th	WWII
Man Hunt	20th	WWII
*One Night in Lisbon	Par	WWII
Parachute Battalion	RKO	WWII
Paris Calling	Univ	WWII
Rookies on Parade	Rep	WWII
Scotland Yard	20th	WWII
So Ends Our Night	UA	WWII
Submarine Zone	Col	WWII
Sundown	UA	WWII
Tanks a Million	UA	WWII
Three Sons O'Guns	WB	WWII

FILM TITLE	RELEASING COMPANY	WAR
Top Sergeant Mulligan	MGM	WWII
Underground	WB	WWII
A Yank in the RAF	20th	WWII
You'll Never Get Rich	Col	WWII
You're in the Army Now	WB	WWII

1942

About Face	UA	WWII
*Across the Pacific	WB	WWII
*All Through the Night	WB	WWII
Atlantic Convoy	Col	WWII
Berlin Correspondent	20th	WWII
Black Dragons	Mono	WWII
Blondie for Victory	Col	WWII
Blue, White, and Perfect	20th	WWII
Bombay Clipper	Univ	WWII
Bombs over Burma	PRC	WWII
The Boss of Big Town	PRC	WWII
The Bugle Sounds	MGM	WWII
Busses Roar	WB	WWII
Cairo	MGM	WWII
Call out the Marines	RKO	WWII
Canal Zone	Col	WWII
*Captains of the Clouds	WB	WWII
Careful, Soft Shoulders	20th	WWII
China Girl	20th	WWII
Clear for Action	MGM	WWII
Counter Espionage	Col	WWII
Danger in the Pacific	Univ	WWII
Dangerously They Live	WB	WWII
The Daring Young Man	Col	WWII
*The Dawn Express	PRC	WWII
*Desperate Journey	WB	WWII
Destination Unknown	Univ	WWII
The Devil with Hitler	UA	WWII
Drums of the Congo	Univ	WWII
Eagle Squadron	Univ	WWII
Enemy Agents Meet Ellery Queen	Col	WWII
Escape from Hong Kong	Univ	WWII
Eyes in the Night	MGM	WWII
The Falcon's Brother	RKO	WWII
Fall In	UA	WWII
Fly by Night	Par	WWII
*Flying Tigers	Rep	WWII
Foreign Agents	Mono	WWII
Gorilla Man	WB	WWII
The Great Impersonation	Univ	WWII
Halfway to Shaghai	Univ	WWII
Hay Foot	UA	WWII
Hillbilly Blitzkrieg	Mono	WWII

FILM TITLE	RELEASING COMPANY	WAR
Hitler--Dead or Alive	SR	WWII
Invisible Agent	Univ	WWII
Joan of Ozark	Rep	WWII
Joe Smith, American	MGM	WWII
Journey for Margaret	MGM	WWII
*Journey into Fear	RKO	WWII
Jungle Siren	PRC	WWII
Junior Army	Col	WWII
Keeper of the Flame	MGM	WWII
Lady from Chungking	PRC	WWII
The Lady Has Plans	Par	WWII
Let's Get Tough	Mono	WWII
Little Tokyo, USA	20th	WWII
Lucky Jordan	Par	WWII
Madame Spy	Univ	WWII
Manila Calling	20th	WWII
Maxwell Archer, Detective	Mono	WWII
Miss V from Moscow	PRC	WWII
*Mrs. Miniver	MGM	WWII
*My Favorite Blonde	Par	WWII
My Favorite Spy	RKO	WWII
The Navy Comes Through	RKO	WWII
Nazi Agent	MGM	WWII
Nightmare	Univ	WWII
Once Upon a Honeymoon	RKO	WWII
Pacific Blackout	Par	WWII
Pacific Rendezvous	MGM	WWII
Panama Hattie	MGM	WWII
Parachute Nurse	Col	WWII
*The Pied Piper	20th	WWII
Pittsburgh	Univ	WWII
Powder Town	RKO	WWII
Pride of the Army	Mono	WWII
Priorities on Parade	Par	WWII
Prisoner of Japan	PRC	WWII
Quiet Please, Murder	20th	WWII
Remember Pearl Harbor	Rep	WWII
Reunion in France	MGM	WWII
Riders of the Northland	Col	WWII
Rubber Racketeers	Mono	WWII
Sabotage Squad	Col	WWII
*Saboteur	Univ	WWII
Secret Agent of Japan	20th	WWII
Secret Enemies	WB	WWII
Sherlock Holmes and the Secret Weapon	Univ	WWII
*Sherlock Holmes and the Voice of Terror	Univ	WWII
She's in the Army	Mono	WWII
Ship Ahoy	MGM	WWII
Snuffy Smith, the Yard Bird	Mono	WWII
Somewhere I'll Find You	MGM	WWII

FILM TITLE	RELEASING COMPANY	WAR
Spy Ship	WB	WWII
Stand By, All Networks	Col	WWII
Stand by for Action	MGM	WWII
Submarine Raider	Col	WWII
Texas Man Hunt	PRC	WWII
Texas to Bataan	Mono	WWII
They Raid by Night	PRC	WWII
This Above All	20th	WWII
*This Gun for Hire	Par	WWII
This Was Paris	WB	WWII
Thunder Birds	20th	WWII
Timber	Univ	WWII
To Be Or Not To Be	UA	WWII
Torpedo Boat	Par	WWII
To the Shores of Tripoli	20th	WWII
Tramp, Tramp, Tramp	Col	WWII
Treat'em Rough	Univ	WWII
True to the Army	Par	WWII
Two Yanks in Trinidad	Col	WWII
Underground Agent	Col	WWII
Unseen Enemy	Univ	WWII
*Wake Island	Par	WWII
The War Against Mrs. Hadley	MGM	WWII
The Wife Takes a Flyer	Col	WWII
Wings for the Eagle	WB	WWII
A Yank in Libya	PRC	WWII
A Yank on the Burma Road	MGM	WWII

1943

FILM TITLE	RELEASING COMPANY	WAR
Above Suspicion	MGM	WWII
*Action in the North Atlantic	WB	WWII
Adventures in Iraq	WB	WWII
Adventures of a Rookie	RKO	WWII
Aerial Gunner	Par	WWII
Air Force	WB	WWII
Air Raid Wardens	MGM	WWII
Alaska Highway	Par	WWII
The Amazing Mrs. Holiday	Univ	WWII
Appointment in Berlin	Col	WWII
Around the World	RKO	WWII
Assignment in Brittany	MGM	WWII
Background to Danger	WB	WWII
Bataan	MGM	WWII
Behind the Rising Sun	RKO	WWII
Black Market Rustlers	Mono	WWII
Bombardier	RKO	WWII
Bomber's Moon	20th	WWII
The Boy from Stalingrad	Col	WWII
*Casablanca	WB	WWII
Chetniks	20th	WWII

FILM TITLE	RELEASING COMPANY	WAR
*China	Par	WWII
The Commandos Strike at Dawn	Col	WWII
Corregidor	PRC	WWII
Corvette K-225	Univ	WWII
Cowboy Commandos	Mono	WWII
Cowboy in the Clouds	Col	WWII
Crash Dive	20th	WWII
The Desert Song	WB	WWII
Destroyer	Col	WWII
Dixie Dugan	20th	WWII
Doughboys in Ireland	Col	WWII
Edge of Darkness	WB	WWII
The Fallen Sparrow	RKO	WWII
First Comes Courage	Col	WWII
*Five Graves to Cairo	Par	WWII
Flight for Freedom	RKO	WWII
The Gang's All Here	20th	WWII
Gangway for Tomorrow	RKO	WWII
Good Luck, Mr. Yates	Col	WWII
Government Girl	RKO	WWII
*Guadalcanal Diary	20th	WWII
Gung Ho	Univ	WWII
*Hangmen Also Die	UA	WWII
Happy Land	20th	WWII
Harvest Melody	PRC	WWII
Headin' for God's Country	Rep	WWII
He Hired the Boss	20th	WWII
Hers to Hold	Univ	WWII
He's My Guy	Univ	WWII
High Explosive	Par	WWII
*Hitler's Children	RKO	WWII
Hitler's Madman (or Hangman)	MGM	WWII
Hoosier Holiday	Rep	WWII
*Hostages	Par	WWll
I Escaped from the Gestapo	Mono	WWII
The Immortal Sergeant	20th	WWII
The Jive Junction	PRC	WWII
Let's Face It	Par	WWII
London Blackout Murders	Rep	WWII
The Man from Down Under	MGM	WWII
Margin for Error	20th	WWII
Mine Sweeper	Par	WWII
*Mission to Moscow	WB	WWII
Mister Lucky	RKO	WWII
The Moon Is Down	20th	WWII
The More the Merrier	Col	WWII
Mountain Rhythm	Rep	WWII
Murder on the Waterfront	WB	WWII
Night Plane from Chungking	Par	WWII
*Northern Pursuit	WB	WWII

FILM TITLE	RELEASING COMPANY	WAR
*North Star	UA	WWII
Paris after Dark	20th	WWII
Passport to Suez	Col	WWII
Pilot No. 5	MGM	WWII
Power of the Press	Col	WWII
The Purple V	Rep	WWII
Reveille with Beverly	Col	WWII
Rookies in Burma	RKO	WWII
Sahara	Col	WWII
Salute for Three	Par	WWII
Salute to the Marines	MGM	WWII
Secrets of the Underground	Rep	WWII
Seven Miles from Alcatraz	RKO	WWII
*Sherlock Holmes in Washington	Univ	WWII
The Sky's the Limit	RKO	WWII
So Proudly We Hail	Par	WWII
So This Is Washington	RKO	WWII
Spy Train	Mono	WWII
*Stage Door Canteen	UA	WWII
The Strange Death of Adolph Hitler	Univ	WWII
Submarine Alert	Par	WWII
Submarine Base	PRC	WWII
Swing Shift Maisie	MGM	WWII
Tarzan Triumphs	RKO	WWII
Tender Comrade	RKO	WWII
That Natzy Nuisance	UA	WWII
There's Something About a Soldier	Col	WWII
They Came to Blow Up American	20th	WWII
They Got Me Covered	RKO	WWII
This Is the Army	WB	WWII
*This Land Is Mine	RKO	WWII
Thousands Cheer	MGM	WWII
Tiger Fangs	PRC	WWII
Tonight We Raid Calais	20th	WWII
Top Man	Univ	WWII
Two Tickets to London	Univ	WWII
The Underdog	PRC	WWII
*Watch on the Rhine	WB	WWII
We've Never Been Licked	Univ	WWII
Wild Horse Rustler	PRC	WWII
Wings over the Pacific	Mono	WWII
Women in Bondage	Mono	WWII
Yanks Ahoy	UA	WWII
The Yanks Are Coming	PRC	WWII

1944

*Action in Arabia	RKO	WWII
Address Unknown	Col	WWII
The Black Parachuet	Col	WWII
The Canterville Ghost	MGM	WWII

FILM TITLE	RELEASING COMPANY	WAR
Charlie Chan in the Secret Service	Mono	WWII
*The Consipirators	WB	WWII
Crime by Night	WB	WWII
The Cross of Lorraine	MGM	WWII
Cry Havoc	MGM	WWII
*Days of Glory	RKO	WWII
*Destination Tokyo	WB	WWII
Dragon Seed	MGM	WWII
Enemy of Women	Mono	WWII
The Eve of St. Mark	20th	WWII
*The Fighting Seabees	Rep	WWII
Follow the Boys	Univ	WWII
Four Jills in a Jeep	20th	WWII
A Guy Named Joe	MGM	WWII
Hail the Conquering Hero	Par	WWII
*Here Come the Waves	Par	WWII
Hey Rookie	Col	WWII
The Hitler Gang	Par	WWII
Hollywood Canteen	WB	WWII
The Hour Before Dawn	Par	WWII
I Love a Soldier	Par	WWII
The Imposter	Univ	WWII
In Our Time	WB	WWII
In the Meantime Darling	20th	WWII
Janie	WB	WWII
Ladies Courageous	Univ	WWII
Ladies of Washington	20th	WWII
*Lifeboat	20th	WWII
Make Your Own Bed	WB	WWII
Man from Frisco	Rep	WWII
*Marine Raiders	RKO	WWII
The Master Race	RKO	WWII
Meet the People	MGM	WWII
*Mr. Winkle Goes to War	Col	WWII
The Navy Way	Par	WWII
None Shall Escape	Col	WWII
*Passage to Marseilles	WB	WWII
Passport to Destiny (or Adventure)	RKO	WWII
Practically Yours	Par	WWII
The Purple Heart	20th	WWII
Rationing	Col	WWII
Rosie the Riveter	Rep	WWII
Secret Command	Col	WWII
Secrets of Scotland Yard	Rep	WWII
See Here, Private Hargrove	MGM	WWII
Sergeant Mike	Col	WWII
The Seventh Cross	MGM	WWII
*Since You Went Away	UA	WWII
Something for the Boys	20th	WWII
Song of Russia	MGM	WWII

FILM TITLE	RELEASING COMPANY	WAR
Standing Room Only	Par	WWII
Storm over Lisbon	Rep	WWII
*Story of Dr. Wassell	Par	WWII
The Sullivans	20th	WWII
Sundown Valley	Col	WWII
Swingtime Johnny	Univ	WWII
Tampico	20th	WWII
They Live in Fear	Col	WWII
Thirty Seconds over Tokyo	MGM	WWII
Three Russian Girls	UA	WWII
Til We Meet Again	Par	WWII
To Have and Have Not	WB	WWII
Tomorrow the World	UA	WWII
Two Man Submarine	Col	WWII
U Boat Prisoner	Col	WWII
*Uncertain Glory	WB	WWII
The Unwritten Code	Col	WWII
Up in Arms	RKO	WWII
Voice in the Wind	UA	WWII
Waterfront	WB	WWII
Wing and a Prayer	20th	WWII
Winged Victory	20th	WWII

1945

FILM TITLE	RELEASING COMPANY	WAR
Back to Bataan	RKO	WWII
*A Bell for Adano	20th	WWII
*Betrayal from the East	RKO	WWII
Blood on the Sun	UA	WWII
China Sky	RKO	WWII
China's Little Devils	Mono	WWII
Counter-Attack	Col	WWII
Escape in the Desert	WB	WWII
Escape in the Fog	Col	WWII
*First Yank into Tokyo	RKO	WWII
Hotel Berlin	WB	WWII
The House on 92nd Street	20th	WWII
Identity Unknown	Rep	WWII
A Medal for Benny	Par	WWII
Ministry of Fear	Par	WWII
*Objective Burma	WB	WWII
Over 21	Col	WWII
*Paris Underground	UA	WWII
Pride of Marines	WB	WWII
Prison Ship	Col	WWII
Rough, Tough, and Ready	Col	WWII
*Story of G.I. Joe	UA	WWII
Strange Holiday	Elite	WWII
They Were Expendable	MGM	WWII
This Man's Navy	MGM	WWII
Tokyo Rose	Par	WWII
A Walk in the Sun	20th	WWII

FILM TITLE	RELEASING COMPANY	WAR
What Next, Corporal Hargrove	MGM	WWII
1946		
The Bamboo Blonde	RKO	WWII
*The Best Years of Our Lives	RKO	WWII
A Boy, a Girl, and a Dog	FC	WWII
Cloak and Dagger	WB	WWII
Notorious	RKO	WWII
*O.S.S.	Par	WWII
Out of the Depths	Col	WWII
Rendezvous 24	20th	WWII
The Searching Wind	Par	WWII
Step by Step	RKO	WWII
Strange Journey	20th	WWII
*The Stranger	RKO	WWII
Til the End of Time	RKO	WWII
1947		
*The Beginning or the End	MGM	WWII
13 Rue Madeleine	20th	WWII
1948		
*Berlin Express	RKO	WWII
*Beyond Glory	Par	WWII
*The Boy with Green Hair	RKO	WWII
Closeup	EL	WWII
#Fighter Squadron	WB	WWII
Homecoming	MGM	WWII
Jungle Patrol	20th	WWII
Rogues' Regiment	Univ	WWII
Sealed Verdict	Par	WWII
#The Search	MGM	WWII
Women in the Night	FC	WWII
*The Iron Curtain	20th	Cold
1949		
*#Battleground	MGM	WWII
#Command Decision	MGM	WWII
Francis	Univ	WWII
*Home of the Brave	UA	WWII
*#Sands of Iwo Jima	Rep	WWII
#Task Force	WB	WWII
#Tokyo Joe	Col	WWII
*#12 O'Clock High	20th	WWII
I Married a Communist	RKO	Cold
Project X	FC	Cold
The Red Danube	MGM	Cold
*The Red Menace	Rep	Cold
Sky Liner	SG	Cold

FILM TITLE	RELEASING COMPANY	WAR
Sofia	N.A.	Cold

1950

*#American Guerrilla in the Philippines	20th	WWII
*#Breakthrough	WB	WWII
David Harding, Counterspy	Col	WWII
Malaya	MGM	WWII
#Mystery Submarine	Univ	WWII
*Three Came Home	20th	WWII
*#The Big Lift	20th	Cold
The Conspirator	MGM	Cold
Counterspy Meets Scotland Yard	Col	Cold
#The Flying Missile	Col	Cold
The Flying Saucer	FC	Cold
Guilty of Treason	EL	Cold
Spy Hunt	Univ	Cold

1951

#Decision Before Dawn	20th	WWII
*The Desert Fox	20th	WWII
The Fighting Coast Guard	Rep	WWII
*#Flying Leathernecks	RKO	WWII
*Force of Arms	WB	WWII
#The Frogman	20th	WWII
*#Go for Broke	MGM	WWII
#Halls of Montezuma	20th	WWII
#I was an American Spy	AA	WWII
The Magic Face	Col	WWII
Operation Pacific	WB	WWII
Purple Heart Diary	Col	WWII
#The Tanks are Coming	WB	WWII
Target Unknown	Univ	WWII
*Up Front	Univ	WWII
*U.S.S. Teakettle	20th	WWII
*#The Wild Blue Yonder	Rep	WWII
#Air Cadet	Univ	Cold
#At War with the Army	Par	Cold
Bowery Battalion	Mono	Cold
Four in a Jeep	UA	Cold
*I Was a Communist for the F.B.I.	WB	Cold
My Favorite Spy	Par	Cold
One Minute to Twelve	EL	Cold
Peking Express	Par	Cold
#Sailor Beware	Par	Cold
Sky High	Lip	Cold
Tokyo File 212	RKO	Cold
The Whip Hand	RKO	Cold

FILM TITLE	RELEASING COMPANY	WAR
#Fixed Bayonets	20th	Korea
Korea Patrol	EL	Korea
Leave It to the Marines	Lip	Korea
*The Steel Helmet	Lip	Korea
A Yank in Korea	Col	Korea

1952

*#Above and Beyond	MGM	WWII
The Devil Makes Three	MGM	WWII
Eight Iron Men	Col	WWII
Five Fingers	20th	WWII
#Flat Top	Mono	WWII
*#Okinawa	Col	WWII
Operation Secret	WB	WWII
#Red Ball Express	Univ	WWII
Arctic Flight	Mono	Cold
Assignment--Paris	Col	Cold
The Atomic City	Par	Cold
*Big Jim McLain	WB	Cold
Diplomatic Courier	20th	Cold
Fearless Fagon	MGM	Cold
*Invasion U.S.A.	Col	Cold
*#Jumping Jacks	Par	Cold
My Son John	Par	Cold
Red Snow	Col	Cold
*Skirts Ahoy	MGM	Cold
#Sound Off	Col	Cold
The Steel Fist	Mono	Cold
The Thief	UA	Cold
Wac from Walla	Rep	Cold
Walk East on Beacon	Col	Cold
A Yank in Indo-China	Col	Cold
*#Back at the Front	Univ	Korea
#Battle Zone	AA	Korea
Mr. Walkie Talkie	Lip	Korea
#One Minute to Zero	RKO	Korea
*#Retreat Hell	WB	Korea

1953

Act of Love	UA	WWII
China Venture	Col	WWII
*Desert Rats	20th	WWII
Destination Gobi	20th	WWII
El Alamein	Col	WWII
*#Fighter Attack	AA	WWII
*#From Here to Eternity	Col	WWII
#Girls of Pleasure Island	Par	WWII
Sky Commando	Col	WWII

FILM TITLE	RELEASING COMPANY	WAR
South Sea Woman	WB	WWII
*#Stalag 17	Par	WWII
*Thunderbirds	Rep	WWII
Clipped Wings	AA	Cold
The 49th Man	Col	Cold
Guerrilla Girl	UA	Cold
Ma and Pa Kettle on Vacation	Univ	Cold
Man on a Tightrope	20th	Cold
Never Let Me Go	MGM	Cold
#Never Wave at a WAC	RKO	Cold
No Time for Flowers	RKO	Cold
Pickup on South Street	20th	Cold
Tangier Incident	AA	Cold
Target Hong Kong	Col	Cold
#Torpedo Alley	AA	Cold
*#Battle Circus	MGM	Korea
#Combat Squad	Col	Korea
Fear and Desire	Burstyn	Korea
#Flight Nurse	Rep	Korea
*#The Glory Brigade	20th	Korea
*Mission over Korea	Col	Korea
#Sabre Jet	UA	Korea
#Take the High Ground	MGM	Korea

1954

*#Beachhead	UA	WWII
*Betrayed	MGM	WWII
*#The Caine Mutiny	Col	WWII
#Francis Joins the WACS	Univ	Cold
*Hell and High Water	20th	Cold
*Night People	20th	Cold
Operation Manhunt	UA	Cold
Security Risk	AA	Cold
*The Shanghai Story	Rep	Cold
*#The Bridges at Toko Ri	Par	Korea
Dragonfly Squadron	AA	Korea
#Men of the Fighting Lady	MGM	Korea
Prisoner of War	MGM	Korea
Return from the Sea	AA	Korea
Cease Fire		Korea

1955

*#Battle Cry	WB	WWII
#The Eternal Sea	Rep	WWII
#Mister Roberts	WB	WWII
The Sea Chase	WB	WWII
Three Stripes in the Sun	Col	WWII

FILM TITLE	RELEASING COMPANY	WAR
#To Hell and Back	Univ	WWII
*#Blood Alley	WB	Cold
#Francis in the Navy	Univ	Cold
*#Jump into Hell	WB	Cold
Shack out on 101	AA	Cold
Special Delivery	Col	Cold
*#Strategic Air Command	Par	Cold
Trial	MGM	Cold
Air Strike	Lip	Korea
*#An Annapolis Story	AA	Korea
The Bamboo Prison	Col	Korea
#Battle Taxi	UA	Korea
Hell's Horizon	Col	Korea
*#The McConnell Story	WB	Korea
*#Target Zero	WB	Korea

1956

Attack	UA	WWII
*#Away All Boats	Univ	WWII
#Battle Stations	Col	WWII
#Between Heaven and Hell	20th	WWII
#The Bold and the Brave	RKO	WWII
*#D-Day the Sixth of June	20th	WWII
*Gaby	MGM	WWII
The Man Who Never Was	20th	WWII
*#The Proud and the Profane	Par	WWII
#Screaming Eagles	AA	WWII
*#Teahouse of the August Moon	MGM	WWII
The Girl He Left Behind	WB	Cold
The Iron Petticoat	MGM	Cold
*#The Lieutenant Wore Skirts	20th	Cold
Toward the Unknown	WB	Cold
Hold Back the Night	AA	Korea
*#The Rack	MGM	Korea

1957

*The Bridge on the River Kwai	Col	WWII
*#Don't Go Near the Water	MGM	WWII
#Heaven Knows Mr. Allison	20th	WWII
*#Hellcats of the Navy	Col	WWII
*#Joe Butterfly	Univ	WWII
*Operation Mad Ball	Col	WWII
*Sayonara	WB	WWII
Under Fire	20th	WWII
*Until They Sail	MGM.	WWII
*#The Wings of Eagles	MGM	WWII

FILM TITLE	RELEASING COMPANY	WAR
Action of the Tiger	MGM	Cold
*#Bombers B-52	WB	Cold
China Gate	20th	Cold
*#The D.I.	WB	Cold
Five Steps to Danger	UA	Cold
*The Girl in the Kremlin	Univ	Cold
#Jet Pilot	Univ	Cold
#The Sad Sack	Par	Cold
*Silk Stockings	MGM	Cold
*Stopover Tokyo	20th	Cold
*#Three Brave Men	20th	Cold
*#Battle Hymn	Univ	Korea
Men in War	UA	Korea
#Time Limit	UA	Korea

1958

FILM TITLE	RELEASING COMPANY	WAR
*Bitter Victory	Col	WWII
China Doll	UA	WWII
Count Five and Die	20th	WWII
#Darby's Rangers	WB	WWII
*#The Deep Six	WB	WWII
*#The Enemy Below	20th	WWII
*#Fraulein	20th	WWII
Ghost of the China Sea	Col	WWII
Hell Squad	AI	WWII
Imitation General	MGM	WWII
*#In Love and War	20th	WWII
*#Kings Go Forth	UA	WWII
*Me and the Colonel	Col	WWII
*#The Naked and the Dead	WB	WWII
*#Onionhead	WB	WWII
#Run Silent, Run Deep	UA	WWII
#South Pacific	20th	WWII
*Suicide Battalion	AI	WWII
#Tarawa Beachhead	Col	WWII
*A Time to Love and a Time to Die	Univ	WWII
#Torpedo Run	MGM	WWII
When Hell Broke Loose	Par	WWII
*#The Young Lions	20th	WWII
#The Beast of Budapest	AA	Cold
*The Fearmakers	UA	Cold
Hong Kong Confidential	UA	Cold
*No Time for Sergeants	WB	Cold
The Quiet American	UA	Cold
Spy in the Sky	AA	Cold
Thundering Jets	20th	Cold

FILM TITLE	RELEASING COMPANY	WAR
*#The Hunters	20th	Korea
Jet Attack	AI	Korea
Tank Battalion	AI	Korea
Underwater Warrior	MGM	Korea

1959

*The Angry Hills	MGM	WWII
#Battle of the Coral Sea	Col	WWII
Blood and Steel	20ch	WWII
*The Diary of Anne Frank	20th	WWII
#Don't Give up the Ship	Par	WWII
*#The Last Blitzkrieg	Col	WWII
*#Operation Petticoat	Univ	WWII
*Paratroop Command	AI	WWII
Submarine Seahawk	AI	WWII
#Surrender Hell	AA	WWII
*Tank Commandos	AI	WWII
*#Up Periscope	WB	WWII
Verboten	UA	WWII
North by Northwest	MGM	Cold
*On the Beach	UA	Cold
We Shall Return	N.A	Cold
The World, the Flesh, and the Devil	MGM	Cold
Battle Flame	AA	Korea
*Operation Dames	AI	Korea
Pork Chop Hill	UA	Korea

1960

The Enemy General	Col	WWII
*Five Branded Women	Par	WWII
#The Gallant Hours	UA	WWII
*#Hell to Eternity	AA	WWII
*#The Mountain Road	Col	WWII
Never So Few	MGM	WWII
The Rookie	20th	WWII
Ski Troop Attack	FG	WWII
Under Ten Flags	Par	WWII
*Man on a String	Col	Cold
#All the Young Men	Col	Korea
*#Wake Me When It's Over	20th	Korea

1961

#Armored Command	AA	WWII
#Battle at Bloody Beach	20th	WWII
Bridge to the Sun	MGM	WWII
*#Cry for Happy	Col	WWII

FILM TITLE	RELEASING COMPANY	WAR
*The Guns of Navaronne	Col	WWII
Heroes Die Young	AA	WWII
#Judgment at Nuremburg	UA	WWII
#On the Double	Par	WWII
Operation Bottleneck	UA	WWII
Operation Eichmann	AA	WWII
Seven Women from Hell	20th	WWII
The Steel Claw	WB	WWII
Then There Were Three	Parade	WWII
*#The Wackiest Ship in the Army	Col	WWII
*#All Hands on Deck	20th	Cold
Capture that Capsule	Riveriera	Cold
Rocket Attack USA	Exploit	Cold
*The Secret Ways	Univ	Cold
*The Sergeant Was a Lady	Univ	Cold
#Marines Let's Go	20th	Korea
Sniper's Ridge	20th	Korea

1962

The Counterfeit Traitor	Par	WWII
Four Horsemen of Apocalypse	MGM	WWII
*#Hell Is For Heroes	Par	WWII
*Hitler	AA	WWII
*The Horizontal Lieutenant	MGM	WWII
*#The Longest Day	20th	WWII
*#Merrill's Marauders	WB	WWII
*#No Man Is An Island	Univ	WWII
#The Pidgeon that Took Rome	Par	WWII
*#The War Lover	Col	WWII
#Airborne	Art D.	Cold
*Brushfire	Par	Cold
Escape from East Berlin	MGM	Cold
*Satan Never Sleeps	20th	Cold
#The Manchurian Candidate	UA	Korea
*The Nun and the Sergeant	UA	Korea
*War Hunt	UA	Korea

1963

*#Captain Newman, M.D.	Univ	WWII
Cry of Battle	AA	WWII
#The Great Escape	UA	WWII
Operation Bikini	AI	WWII
*#PT 109	WB	WWII
The Quick and the Dead	N.A.	WWII
The Raiders of Leyte Gulf	Hemi	WWII
*The Victors	Col	WWII

FILM TITLE	RELEASING COMPANY	WAR
*#A Gathering of Eagles	Univ	Cold
The Prize	MGM	Cold
*#Soldier in the Rain	AA	Cold
*#The Ugly American	Univ	Cold
*The Hook	MGM	Korea
The Young and the Brave	MGM	Korea

1964

*The Americanization of Emily	MGM	WWII
Back Door to Hell	20th	WWII
Ensign Pulver	WB	WWII
*#Father Goose	Univ	WWII
*McHale's Navy	Univ	WWII
The Secret Door	AA	WWII
The Secret Invasion	UA	WWII
633 Squadron	UA	WWII
The Thin Red Line	AA	WWII
*#36 Hours	MGM	WWII
The Walls of Hell	Hemi	WWII
*Dr. Strangelove	Col	Cold
*Fail Safe	Col	Cold
*Seven Days in May	Par	Cold
*The Seventh Dawn	UA	Cold
War is Hell	AA	Korea
A Yank in Vietnam	AA	Vietnam

1965

*Battle of the Bulge	WB	WWII
*#In Harm's Way	Par	WWII
McHale's Navy Joins the Air Force	Univ	WWII
*King Rat	Col	WWII
Morituri	20th	WWII
*The Naked Brigade	Univ	WWII
*#None But the Brave	WB	WWII
The Ravagers	Hemi	WWII
*The Train	UA	WWII
*Up from the Beach	20th	WWII
Von Ryan's Express	20th	WWII
*#The Bedford Incident	Col	Cold
*Operation C.I.A.	AA	Cold

1966

*#Ambush Bay	UA	WWII
I Deal in Danger	20th	WWII
*Is Paris Burning	Par	WWII

FILM TITLE	RELEASING COMPANY	WAR
Once Before I Die	Goldstone	WWII
What Did You Do in the War, Daddy?	UA	WWII
Wounded in Action	Myriad	WWII
Agent for H.A.R.M.	Univ	Cold
*#The Russians Are Coming, The Russians Are Coming	UA	Cold
*The Silencers	Col	Cold
*Torn Curtain	Univ	Cold

1967

#Beach Red	UA	WWII
*Counterpoint	Univ	WWII
*The Dirty Dozen	MGM	WWII
#First to Fight	WB	WWII
A Man Called Dagger	MGM	WWII
*#Tobruk	Univ	WWII
*The Young Warriors	Univ	WWII
Come Spy with Me	20th	Cold
*The Venetian Affair	MGM	Cold

1968

#The Devil's Brigade	UA	WWII
Hell in the Pacific	Cinerama	WWII
*#In Enemy Country	Univ	WWII
*The Longest Hundred Miles	N.A.	WWII
*Mission Batangas	N.A.	WWII
#The Private Navy of Sergeant O'Farrell	UA	WWII
The Secret War of Harry Frigg	Univ	WWII
Snow Treasure	AA	WWII
#The 1,000 Plane Raid	N.A.	WWII
*Warkill	Univ	WWII
#The Bamboo Saucer	World	Cold
*#Ice Station Zebra	MGM	Cold
Panic in the City	Commonwealth	Cold
The Wicked Dreams of Paula Schultz	UA	Cold
Sergeant Ryker	Univ	Korea
*#The Green Berets	WB	Vietnam

1969

*Bridge at Remagen	UA	WWII
Castle Keep	Col	WWII
Secret of Santa Victoria	UA	WWII
*The Chairman	20th	Cold
*#Topaz	Univ	Cold

FILM TITLE	RELEASING COMPANY	WAR
1970		
*Catch-22	Par	WWII
Hornet's Nest	UA	WWII
*Kelly's Heroes	MGM	WWII
The McKenzie Break	UA	WWII
#Too Late the Hero	N.A.	WWII
*#Patton	20th	WWII
*#Tora Tora Tora	20th	WWII
Which Way to the Front	WB	WWII
Kremlin Letter	N.A.	Cold
M*A*S*H*	20th	Korea

---

*Content analysis based on screening.

#Received assistance from Department of Defense.

[a]Abbreviations: AA--Allied Artists; AI--American International; Art D.--Art Diamond; Col--Columbia; EL--Eagle Lion; FC--Film Classics; Hemi--Hemisphere; Lip--Lippert; MGM-Metro-Goldwyn-Mayer; Mono--Monogram; Par--Paramount; PRC--Producers Releasing Company; Rep--Republic; SG--Screen Gems; SR--States Rights; 20th--20th Century Fox; UA--United Artists; Univ--Universal; WB--Warner Brothers; N.A.--Not Available.

APPENDIX III

OTHER CONTENT ANALYSIS RESULTS

TABLE 72

THE AMERICAN HERO, 1939-1947

	1939-1941	1942	1943	1944	1945	1946-1947	Total
Minority Membership							
Ethnic	- %	1.2%	2.8%	- %	- %	- %	1.1%
Not native	-	1.2	1.4	-	-	-	0.7
Not minority	100.0	97.8	95.8	100.0	100.0	100.0	98.2
Total	100.0	100.0	100.0	100.0	100.0	100.0	100.0
Support of War Policy							
Support	89.5	91.8	92.2	95.7	95.8	92.3	92.4
Neutral	5.3	8.2	8.3	2.2	4.2	7.8	6.5
Legal opposition	-	-	-	2.2	-	-	0.4
No answer	5.3	-	-	-	-	-	0.7
Total	100.0	100.0	100.0	100.0	100.0	100.0	100.0
How Officer's Rank Obtained							
Direct commission	2.7	3.5	5.6	2.2	-	-	3.2
OCS	-	-	1.4	4.4	8.3	7.8	2.2
Promotion	-	1.2	-	-	-	7.8	0.7
Battlefield	-	-	1.4	-	-	-	0.4
No answer	97.4	95.1	91.6	93.6	91.7	84.6	93.6
Total	100.0	100.0	100.0	100.0	100.0	100.0	100.0
Reason for Not Being in Military							
Occ. deferment	7.9	11.8	5.6	6.5	4.2	15.4	8.3
Not required	-	4.7	6.9	4.4	4.2	7.8	4.7
Physically unfit	-	3.5	4.2	4.4	-	-	2.9
Age, family	-	1.2	4.2	2.2	4.2	-	2.2
Completed service	-	-	-	-	4.2	15.4	1.1
Other	-	3.5	4.2	-	-	7.8	2.5
No answer	92.1	75.3	75.0	82.6	83.3	54.0	78.4
Total	100.0	100.0	100.0	100.0	100.0	100.0	100.0

TABLE 72--Continued

	1939-1941	1942	1943	1944	1945	1946-1947	Total
Health							
Healthy	100.0%	92.9%	94.5%	93.5%	75.0%	92.3%	92.8%
War injury	-	1.2	2.8	8.7	16.7	-	4.0
Non-war injury	-	1.2	1.4	-	4.2	-	1.1
Mental problem due to war	-	-	1.4	-	8.3	-	1.1
War handicap	-	-	-	-	-	7.8	0.4
No answer	-	4.7	-	-	-	-	1.4
Total	100.0	100.0	100.0	102.2	104.2	100.0	101.8
Life and Death							
Lives	97.4	87.1	86.1	93.5	91.7	84.6	89.6
War death	2.7	8.2	13.9	6.5	8.3	7.8	8.6
No answer	-	4.7	-	-	-	7.8	1.8
Total	100.0	100.0	100.0	100.0	100.0	100.0	100.0
Change as Result of War							
No change	73.7	91.2	79.2	86.5	75.0	84.6	80.2
Behavior	23.7	8.2	17.6	10.8	16.7	-	13.7
Knowledge	5.3	8.2	5.6	2.2	4.2	15.4	6.1
Attitude	15.8	9.4	11.1	4.4	16.7	-	10.1
Total	118.5	117.0	114.5	103.9	112.6	100.0	110.1
Secondary Goal							
Love	13.2	16.5	30.6	34.8	25.0	15.4	23.7
Patriotism	10.5	15.3	12.6	17.4	16.7	7.8	14.0
War task	10.5	5.9	9.7	2.2	8.3	30.8	8.2
Honesty	13.2	4.7	4.2	2.2	-	-	4.7
Family	-	4.7	4.2	6.5	8.3	-	4.3
Justice	2.7	4.7	4.2	-	8.3	7.8	4.3
Safety	2.7	2.3	2.8	2.2	4.2	-	2.5
Revenge	-	2.3	5.6	-	-	-	2.2
Money	-	2.3	-	4.4	-	7.8	1.8
Adventure	2.7	1.2	1.4	2.2	-	-	1.4
Comfort	-	2.3	-	2.2	-	7.8	1.4
Escape Law	2.7	2.3	1.4	-	-	-	1.4
Individualism	5.3	2.3	-	-	-	-	1.4
Fame	2.7	-	-	2.2	-	7.8	1.1

TABLE 72--Continued

	1939-1941	1942	1943	1944	1945	1946-1947	Total
Truth	- %	2.3%	1.4%	- %	- %	- %	1.1%
Sex	2.7	1.2	-	-	-	-	o.7
Health	-	1.2	-	-	-	7.8	0.7
Power	2.7	-	-	-	-	-	0.4
No answer	26.3	27.1	22.2	23.9	29.2	7.8	24.5
Total	100.0	100.0	100.0	100.0	100.0	100.0	100.0

Primary Obstacle to Achieving Goals

	1939-1941	1942	1943	1944	1945	1946-1947	Total
Other people	44.7	48.2	31.8	26.1	12.5	46.2	36.7
Legal convention	34.2	16.5	33.3	34.8	33.3	23.1	28.1
Self	10.5	12.9	16.6	21.7	16.7	-	14.7
Social conven.	5.3	5.9	9.7	6.5	12.5	7.8	7.6
Circumstance	-	4.7	4.2	2.2	4.2	23.1	4.3
Illness	-	1.2	1.4	-	4.2	-	1.1
No answer	5.3	10.6	2.8	8.7	16.7	-	7.6
Total	100.0	100.0	100.0	100.0	100.0	100.0	100.0

Secondary Obstacle to Achieving Goals

	1939-1941	1942	1943	1944	1945	1946-1947	Total
Other people	5.3	10.6	11.1	17.4	8.3	15.4	10.8
Legal convention	2.7	7.1	6.9	2.2	4.2	7.8	5.4
Circumstance	7.9	-	9.7	-	8.3	7.8	4.7
Social conven.	5.3	1.2	5.6	-	4.2	15.4	3.6
Self	2.7	2.3	-	-	4.2	-	1.4
Illness	2.7	-	1.4	-	4.2	-	1.1
No answer	73.9	78.8	65.3	80.4	66.7	61.5	73.0
Total	100.0	100.0	100.0	100.0	100.0	100.0	100.0

Secondary Method of Achieving Goals

	1939-1941	1942	1943	1944	1945	1946-1947	Total
Force	5.3	10.6	12.6	8.7	29.2	-	11.2
Charm	18.4	4.7	12.6	2.2	-	-	7.9
Hard work	2.7	9.4	5.6	2.2	12.5	7.8	6.5
Trickery	10.5	2.3	5.6	2.2	16.7	15.4	6.1
Knowledge	-	4.7	6.9	6.5	4.2	15.4	5.8
Persuasion	2.7	4.7	5.6	8.7	-	-	4.7
Luck	-	1.2	4.2	4.4	4.2	7.8	2.9
No answer	60.5	74.1	45.8	63.0	33.3	47.8	58.6
Total	100.0	100.0	100.0	100.0	100.0	100.0	100.0

TABLE 72--Continued

	1939-1941	1942	1943	1944	1945	1946-1947	Total
War Status of Romantic Partner							
Ally spy	- %	5.9%	- %	2.2%	- %	- %	2.2%
Ally soldier	-	1.2	1.4	2.2	4.2	-	1.4
Ally civilian	7.9	5.9	6.9	8.7	8.3	-	6.8
American spy	5.3	3.5	1.4	8.7	8.3	-	3.2
Am. soldier	2.7	3.5	2.8	10.9	4.2	7.8	4.7
Am. civilian	28.8	36.5	48.7	47.8	16.7	38.4	38.8
Enemy spy	5.3	-	-	-	-	-	0.7
Enemy soldier	-	-	1.4	-	-	-	0.4
Enemy civilian	-	1.2	1.4	-	-	7.8	1.1
Neutral civilian	2.7	1.2	1.4	-	-	-	1.1
No answer	47.4	41.2	34.7	29.3	61.5	30.8	39.6
Total	100.0	100.0	100.0	100.0	100.0	100.0	100.0
Partner's Social Status							
Same as hero	23.7	24.7	29.2	47.8	20.8	38.5	29.9
Lower	7.9	3.5	4.2	6.5	4.2	-	4.7
Higher	13.2	16.5	23.6	13.0	4.2	23.1	16.5
Unclear	21.1	14.1	2.8	4.4	8.3	7.8	9.7
No answer	34.2	41.2	40.3	28.3	61.5	30.8	39.2
Total	100.0	100.0	100.0	100.0	100.0	100.0	100.0
Primary Concern							
War	76.3	76.5	73.6	71.7	50.0	38.5	70.9
Romance	10.5	5.9	16.6	17.4	12.5	23.1	12.6
Other	13.2	11.6	8.5	10.9	20.8	15.4	11.9
No answer	-	5.9	1.4	-	16.7	23.1	4.7
Total	100.0	100.0	100.0	100.0	100.0	100.0	100.0
Secondary Concern							
Romance	52.6	48.2	41.7	52.2	20.8	38.5	45.0
War	15.8	15.3	23.6	23.9	29.2	15.4	20.1
Other	5.3	12.9	12.6	2.2	4.2	7.8	9.0
No answer	26.3	23.5	22.2	21.7	45.8	38.5	25.9
Total	100.0	100.0	100.0	100.0	100.0	100.0	100.0

TABLE 72--Continued

	1939-1941	1942	1943	1944	1945	1946-1947	Total
			Third Concern				
Romance	5.3%	12.9%	9.7%	8.7%	8.3%	15.4%	10.1%
War	2.7	3.5	2.8	4.4	4.2	7.8	3.6
Other	2.7	4.7	6.9	-	-	-	3.6
No answer	89.5	78.8	80.6	87.4	87.5	77.8	83.7
Total	100.0	100.0	100.0	100.0	100.0	100.0	100.0
Number	38	85	72	46	24	13	278

[a]Data derived from questions 12, 14, 19, 21, 22, 23, 24, 26, 27, 28, 30, 32, 33, and 38 Form B in Appendix I. Questions 9, 10, 11, 13, 34, 35, and 37 of Form B were not included because their results were too scattered. All other results are included in the body of the thesis.

[b]Categories for which there were no responses were omitted.

TABLE 73

ALLIES AND ENEMIES, 1939-1947

	Ally	Enemy
Support of War Policy		
Support	75.9%	87.5%
Neutral	5.4	12.5
Illegal opposition	9.5	-
Neutral	5.4	-
Legal opposition	1.3	-
Other	1.3	-
No answer	1.3	-
Total	100.0	100.0
Reason for Not Being in Military		
Not required	8.1	-
Occupational deferment	5.4	-
Completed service	4.1	6.3
Age, family	2.7	12.5
Other	5.4	-
No answer	74.3	81.3
Total	100.0	100.0
Health		
Healthy	77.0	93.7
War injury	17.6	-
Mental problem due to war	5.8	6.3
Non-war mental problem	1.3	-
Total	102.7	100.0
Life and Death		
Lives	79.2	62.5
War death	18.9	37.5
Non-war death	1.3	-
Total	100.0	100.0

TABLE 73--Continued

	Ally	Enemy
Change as Result of War		
No change	76.5%	62.5%
Behavior	21.6	37.5
Attitude	17.6	6.3
Knowledge	6.8	-
Total	121.6	106.3
Secondary Goal		
Love	16.2	-
Patriotism	16.2	6.3
Justice	9.5	-
Individualism	6.8	-
War task	6.8	-
Safety	5.4	6.3
Family	4.1	-
Escape law	2.7	-
Honesty	2.7	-
Money	2.7	-
Comfort	1.3	6.3
Fame	1.3	-
Revenge	1.3	-
Sex	1.3	-
Truth	1.3	-
Power	-	12.5
No answer	20.3	68.8
Total	100.0	100.0
Primary Obstacle to Achieving Goals		
Legal convention	52.7	18.8
Other people	27.1	56.3
Self	9.5	6.3
Social convention	8.1	18.8
Circumstance	1.3	-
No answer	1.3	-
Total	100.0	100.0

TABLE 73--Continued

	Ally	Enemy
Secondary Obstacle to Achieving Goals		
Legal convention	8.1%	6.3%
Other people	8.1	12.5
Circumstance	5.4	-
Self	4.1	6.3
Social convention	2.7	-
Illness	1.3	-
No answer	70.3	75.0
Total	100.0	100.0
Secondary Method of Achieving Goals		
Force	14.9	6.3
Knowledge	13.5	6.3
Trickery	13.5	6.3
Charm	6.8	-
Hard work	5.4	6.3
Persuasion	5.4	6.3
Luck	2.7	-
No answer	40.5	68.8
Total	100.0	100.0
War Status of Romantic Partner		
Ally spy	1.3	-
Ally soldier	5.4	-
Ally civilian	31.1	-
American soldier	2.7	-
American civilian	2.7	-
Enemy spy	1.3	-
Enemy civilian	2.7	12.5
Neutral civilian	1.3	-
No answer	51.4	87.5
Total	100.0	100.0
Partner's Social Status		
Same as hero	18.9	-
Higher	6.8	6.3
Lower	2.7	6.3
Unclear	18.9	-
No answer	52.7	87.5
Total	100.0	100.0

TABLE 73--Continued

	Ally	Enemy
Romantic Outcome		
Unwilling breakup	17.6%	6.3%
Marriage	16.2	-
Romance continues	2.7	-
Willing breakup	-	6.3
Uncertain	4.1	-
No answer	59.5	87.5
Total	100.0	100.0
Primary Concern		
War	82.4	93.8
Other	14.9	-
Romance	1.3	6.3
No answer	1.3	-
Total	100.0	100.0
Secondary Concern		
Romance	40.5	6.3
War	12.2	6.3
Other	8.1	6.3
No answer	39.2	81.3
Total	100.0	100.0
Third Concern		
Romance	9.5	6.3
War	5.4	-
Other	-	-
No answer	85.1	93.8
Total	100.0	100.0
Number	74	16

[a]Data derived from questions 14, 21, 22, 23, 24, 26, 27, 28, 30, 32, 33, 36, and 38 Form B in Appendix I. Questions 9, 10, 11, 12, 13, 19, 34, 35, and 37 of Form B were not included because their results were too scattered. All other results are included in the body of the thesis.

[b]Categories for which there were no responses were omitted.

TABLE 74

FILM RESULTS, 1939-1947

	1939-1941	1942	1943	1944	1945	1946-1947	Total
Action	40.0%	42.1%	45.2%	43.4%	35.7%	60.0%	43.2%
Comedy	24.0	19.0	14.8	18.4	10.7	6.7	17.3
Mystery	14.0	24.8	12.2	7.9	14.3	13.3	15.6
General drama	20.0	6.6	10.4	14.5	35.7	20.0	13.3
Western	-	3.3	3.5	1.3	-	-	2.2
Romance	-	1.7	0.9	1.3	-	-	1.0
Fantasy	-	0.8	-	1.3	-	-	0.5
Expose	-	-	-	1.3	-	-	0.2
Musical	-	1.7	11.3	10.5	-	-	5.7
No answer	2.0	-	1.7	-	3.6	-	1.0
Total	100.0	100.0	100.0	100.0	100.0	100.0	100.0

Historical Base

	1939-1941	1942	1943	1944	1945	1946-1947	Total
Fictitious	94.0	94.2	90.0	88.2	67.9	80.0	89.4
Some truth	4.0	5.8	8.7	6.6	17.9	13.3	7.7
True story	2.0	-	1.7	5.3	10.6	6.7	2.7
No answer	-	-	-	-	3.6	-	0.2
Total	100.0	100.0	100.0	100.0	100.0	100.0	100.0

Locale

	1939-1941	1942	1943	1944	1945	1946-1947	Total
United States	54.0	54.5	50.0	43.4	25.0	46.7	48.6
Britain	16.0	9.1	1.7	3.9	3.6	-	6.2
Germany	12.0	4.1	3.5	7.9	3.6	6.7	5.7
France	4.0	3.3	2.6	7.9	7.1	13.3	4.7
Pacific Islands	-	2.5	2.6	7.9	7.1	6.7	3.7
Atlantic Ocean	4.0	3.3	2.6	2.6	-	6.7	3.0
China	-	4.1	3.5	1.3	7.1	-	3.0
Pacific Ocean	-	0.8	5.2	3.9	3.6	-	2.7
Philippines	-	3.3	3.5	1.3	7.1	-	2.7
North Africa	-	1.7	5.2	2.6	-	-	2.5
Soviet Union	-	-	2.6	3.9	3.6	-	1.7
Japan	-	-	0.9	2.6	10.7	-	1.5
Burma	2.0	1.7	0.9	-	7.1	-	1.2
Norway	-	0.8	3.5	-	-	-	1.2
Central Africa	2.0	1.7	0.9	-	-	-	1.0
Czechoslovakia	-	-	2.6	1.3	-	-	1.0
Panama	2.0	2.5	-	-	-	-	1.0
Italy	-	-	-	-	7.1	6.7	0.7
Poland	-	0.8	-	2.6	-	-	0.7
Portugal	-	0.8	-	2.6	-	-	0.7

TABLE 74--Continued

	1939-1941	1942	1943	1944	1945	1946-1947	Total
Switzerland	2.0%	- %	- %	- %	3.6%	6.7%	0.7%
Austria	2.0	-	0.9	-	-	-	0.5
Iceland	-	0.8	0.9	-	-	-	0.5
Turkey	-	-	1.7	-	-	-	0.5
Belgium	-	-	-	1.3	-	-	0.2
Brazil	-	-	-	-	-	6.7	0.2
Central America	-	0.8	-	-	-	-	0.2
Yugoslavia	-	-	0.9	-	-	-	0.2
Other Asian	-	-	1.7	1.3	-	-	0.7
Other European	-	0.8	1.7	1.3	-	-	1.0
Other	-	1.7	0.9	1.3	3.6	-	1.2
Total	100.0	100.0	100.0	100.0	100.0	100.0	100.0

War Message

	1939-1941	1942	1943	1944	1945	1946-1947	Total
Anti-enemy	16.0	14.9	13.9	18.4	14.3	20.0	15.6
Pro-military	18.0	7.4	11.3	17.1	21.4	-	12.3
Pro-patriotism	8.0	9.9	12.2	2.6	-	13.3	8.4
Pro-ally	6.0	9.9	6.9	3.9	10.7	-	6.7
Anti-pacifism	-	2.5	-	3.9	-	6.7	1.7
Pro-labor	-	-	3.5	2.6	-	-	1.5
Pro-Hollywood	-	-	0.9	3.9	-	-	1.0
Pro-farmers	-	-	1.7	-	-	-	0.5
Anti-status quo	-	-	-	-	-	6.7	0.2
Pro-democracy	-	-	0.9	-	3.6	-	0.5
Pro-FBI	-	-	0.9	-	-	-	0.2
Pro-youth	-	-	-	1.3	-	-	0.2
Anti-military	-	-	-	-	3.6	-	0.2
No answer	52.0	57.3	46.9	46.1	46.4	53.3	53.6
Total	100.0	100.0	100.0	100.0	100.0	100.0	100.0

Secondary Reasons for Victories[a]

	1939-1941	1942	1943	1944	1945	1946-1947	Total
Individuals	10.0	9.1	20.9	5.3	14.3	-	11.9
Methods	6.0	11.6	17.4	2.6	3.6	-	9.6
Resources	2.0	5.8	12.2	10.5	3.6	-	7.7
Goals	4.0	7.4	8.7	3.9	3.6	6.7	6.4
Circumstance	-	-	2.6	1.3	-	-	1.0
Supreme being	-	0.8	-	1.3	-	-	0.5
Total	22.0	26.5	61.7	25.0	25.0	6.7	37.0

TABLE 74--Continued

	1939-1941	1942	1943	1944	1945	1946-1947	Total

Immediate and Ultimate Results of Fighting

	1939-1941	1942	1943	1944	1945	1946-1947	Total
Imm. victory	42.0%	68.6%	53.0%	38.2%	50.0%	73.3%	54.1%
Ult. victory	-	-	0.9	5.3	7.1	60.0	3.9
Imm. defeat	4.0	5.8	7.8	5.3	3.6	-	5.7
Ult. defeat	-	-	-	-	3.6	-	0.2
Imm. deadlock	-	1.7	3.5	-	-	-	1.5
Ult. deadlock	-	-	-	-	-	-	-
Imm. undetermin.	8.0	5.8	3.4	7.9	7.1	-	5.7
Ult. undetermin.	12.0	13.2	13.0	6.6	7.1	-	10.9
Imm. not applic.	46.0	18.2	31.3	50.0	39.3	26.7	33.1
Ult. not applic.	88.0	86.8	87.0	86.8	82.1	40.0	84.9
Total	200.0	200.0	200.0	200.0	200.0	200.0	200.0

Consequence of Film Events to War Effort

	1939-1941	1942	1943	1944	1945	1946-1947	Total
Limited-major	6.0	19.8	11.3	11.8	10.7	26.7	13.8
Overall-major	-	-	3.5	3.9	-	40.0	3.2
Limited-minor	6.0	21.5	20.0	7.6	28.6	-	16.3
Overall-minor	-	9.1	9.6	7.9	21.4	-	8.4
Limited-unrelated	20.0	18.2	21.7	55.3	35.7	6.7	27.2
Overall-unrelated	12.0	10.7	16.5	60.5	42.9	6.7	24.0
Limited-undeter.	33.0	23.1	15.7	15.8	7.1	26.7	20.5
Overall-undeter.	8.0	12.4	19.1	19.7	14.3	26.7	15.8
Limited-not app.	30.0	19.0	32.2	5.3	17.9	40.0	22.2
Overall-not app.	80.0	66.1	50.4	11.8	21.4	26.7	48.6
Total	200.0	200.0	200.0	200.0	200.0	200.0	200.0

Second Major Film Themes

	1939-1941	1942	1943	1944	1945	1946-1947	Total
War	8.0	15.7	12.2	9.2	25.0	40.0	14.1
Love	12.0	5.8	13.9	17.1	3.6	6.7	10.9
Patriotism	10.0	9.9	12.2	14.5	3.6	-	10.9
Violence	4.0	14.9	7.0	6.6	17.9	6.7	9.6
Foreigners	6.0	3.3	7.0	9.2	14.3	-	6.2
Law enforcement	16.0	5.0	6.1	1.3	7.1	6.7	6.2
Comradship	4.0	3.3	9.9	9.2	7.1	-	4.4
Armed forces	6.0	0.8	3.5	5.3	-	-	3.0
Science	4.0	2.5	1.7	5.3	-	6.7	3.0
Entertainment	-	1.7	3.5	5.3	-	6.7	2.7
Public affairs	-	-	6.1	1.3	7.1	-	2.5
Inner conflict	2.0	2.5	0.9	1.3	3.6	-	1.7

TABLE 74--Continued

	1939-1941	1942	1943	1944	1945	1946-1947	Total
Medical	2.0%	0.8%	1.7%	1.3%	7.1%	- %	1.7%
Business	-	-	3.5	2.6	-	-	1.5
Family	2.0	0.8	0.9	-	-	6.7	1.0
Minorities	-	0.8	-	1.3	3.6	-	0.7
Nature	2.0	-	1.7	-	-	-	0.7
Press	2.0	-	1.7	-	-	-	0.7
Materialism	-	-	-	-	3.6	-	0.2
Mental health	-	-	-	1.3	-	6.7	0.5
No answer	18.0	32.2	15.7	7.9	-	13.3	18.2
Total	100.0	100.0	100.0	100.0	100.0	100.0	100.0

Other Major Film Themes

	1939-1941	1942	1943	1944	1945	1946-1947	Total
War	20.0	31.4	34.8	68.4	57.1	40.0	40.0
Love	54.0	33.1	40.0	26.3	42.9	40.0	35.1
Patriotism	18.0	19.0	38.3	38.2	10.7	33.3	27.9
Violence	12.0	13.2	17.4	10.5	-	13.3	12.8
Family	4.0	25.6	5.2	7.9	3.6	-	11.4
Foreigners	14.0	13.2	8.7	9.2	14.3	6.7	11.1
Comradship	6.0	5.0	13.0	10.5	14.3	6.7	10.1
Armed forces	6.0	5.8	11.3	5.3	21.4	13.3	8.6
Accidents	10.0	14.0	5.2	3.9	-	-	7.7
Science	12.0	9.9	2.5	5.3	10.7	13.3	7.4
Public affairs	6.0	-	4.3	1.3	7.1	13.3	3.2
Medical	4.0	2.5	1.7	5.3	3.6	-	3.0
Nature	4.0	3.3	1.7	3.9	3.6	-	3.0
Materialism	6.0	3.3	0.9	2.6	3.6	-	2.7
Religion	2.0	2.5	1.7	5.3	3.6	-	2.7
Minorities	4.0	4.1	1.7	1.3	-	-	2.5
Mental health	-	3.3	0.9	-	-	6.7	1.5
Education	-	0.8	1.7	1.3	-	6.7	1.2
Alcoholism	-	0.8	0.9	-	-	-	0.5
Fine arts	-	-	-	2.6	-	-	0.5
Superstition	-	-	-	1.3	-	-	0.2
Total	194.0	225.6	208.7	197.4	217.9	240.0	218.0
Number	50	121	115	76	28	15	405

[a]Secondary reasons for victories include second and third most important reasons according to the films.

[b]Data derived from questions 11, 14, 16, 30, the second part of 34, 40, 41, and the second and third parts of 43 Form A in Appendix I. Questions 1-8 were not quantified and questions 15, 19, 35, 36, 37, and the second parts of 26, 27, 28, 29, and 31 received sparse responses; thus, those answers were not included in the tables. Data from all other questions are included in the body of the thesis.

[c]Categories for which there were no responses were omitted.

TABLE 75

THE AMERICAN HERO, 1948-1962

	WWII	Cold	Korea	Total
Minority Membership				
Non-white	2.6%	1.2%	- %	1.6%
Ethnic	1.8	1.2	-	1.2
Religious	0.9	1.2	-	0.8
Not native	-	1.2	-	0.4
Not minority	94.7	95.1	100.0	95.9
Total	100.0	100.0	100.0	100.0
Support of War Policy				
Support	90.4	90.1	98.0	91.8
Neutral	8.8	6.2	2.0	6.6
Illegal opposition	0.9	2.5	-	1.2
Other	-	1.2	-	0.4
Total	100.0	100.0	100.0	100.0
How Officer's Rank Obtained				
OCS	7.9	1.2	2.0	4.5
Promotion	5.3	-	4.1	3.3
Direct commission	4.4	-	4.1	2.9
ROTC	0.9	1.2	2.0	1.2
Service academy	2.6	-	-	1.2
Battlefield	1.8	-	-	0.8
No answer	77.2	97.5	87.8	86.1
Total	100.0	100.0	100.0	100.0
Reason for Not Being in Military				
Completed service	1.8	3.7	-	2.0
Occ. deferment	-	6.2	-	2.0
Age, family	-	1.2	-	0.4
Not required	0.9	-	-	0.4
Other	0.9	-	-	0.4
No answer	96.5	8.9	100.0	94.7
Total	100.0	100.0	100.0	100.0

TABLE 75--Continued

	WWII	Cold	Korea	Total
Healthy	81.6%	92.6%	79.6%	84.8%
War injury	11.4	6.2	14.3	10.3
Mental problem due to war	2.6	1.2	6.1	2.9
War handicap	2.6	-	-	1.2
Non-war injury	1.8	-	-	0.8
Non-war handicap	0.9	-	-	0.4
Non-war mental prob.	0.9	-	-	0.4
Total	101.8	100.0	100.0	100.8

Life and Death

	WWII	Cold	Korea	Total
Lives	91.2	95.1	89.8	92.2
Non-war death	7.9	-	2.0	4.1
War death	0.9	4.9	8.2	3.7
Total	100.0	100.0	100.0	100.0

Change as Result of War

	WWII	Cold	Korea	Total
No change	78.1	92.7	77.6	79.5
Attitude	13.2	13.6	12.2	13.2
Behavior	14.6	7.4	10.2	11.7
Knowledge	5.3	8.6	-	5.3
Total	110.5	112.3	100.0	108.2

Secondary Goal

	WWII	Cold	Korea	Total
Love	15.8	25.9	28.6	21.7
Patriotism	12.3	18.5	12.2	14.3
War task	6.1	7.4	8.2	7.0
Safety	7.0	4.9	6.1	6.1
Family	5.3	4.9	4.1	4.9
Comfort	5.3	3.7	2.0	3.7
Justice	1.8	4.9	4.1	3.3
Money	2.6	4.9	2.0	3.3
Honesty	4.4	1.2	-	2.4
Health	3.5	-	-	1.6
Truth	1.8	2.5	-	1.6
Adventure	0.9	-	2.0	0.8
Individualism	0.9	-	2.0	0.8
Power	0.9	-	2.0	0.8
Revenge	1.8	-	-	0.8
Sex	-	1.2	2.0	0.8
No answer	30.7	19.8	24.5	25.8
Total	100.0	100.0	100.0	100.0

TABLE 75--Continued

	WWII	Cold	Korea	Total
Primary Obstacle to Achieving Goals				
Legal convention	36.0%	38.3%	36.7%	36.9%
Other people	22.8	34.6	20.4	26.2
Self	15.8	14.8	18.4	16.0
Social convention	7.9	6.2	12.2	8.2
Circumstance	6.1	2.5	8.2	5.3
Illness	5.3	-	4.1	2.9
No answer	7.0	3.7	-	4.5
Total	100.0	100.0	100.0	100.0
Secondary Obstacle to Achieving Goals				
Legal convention	18.4	18.5	34.7	21.7
Other people	18.4	7.4	22.4	15.6
Circumstance	12.3	6.2	8.2	9.4
Self	7.9	6.2	4.1	6.6
Social convention	5.3	7.4	2.0	4.9
Illness	5.3	1.2	6.1	3.7
No answer	34.2	53.1	22.4	38.1
Total	100.0	100.0	100.0	100.0
Secondary Method of Achieving Goals				
Force	9.6	12.3	24.5	13.5
Persuasion	8.8	13.6	2.0	9.0
Hard work	6.1	8.6	10.2	7.8
Knowledge	9.6	4.9	6.1	7.3
Trickery	6.1	6.2	6.1	6.1
Charm	4.4	4.9	8.2	5.4
Luck	3.5	4.9	4.1	4.1
No answer	51.8	44.4	38.8	46.7
Total	100.0	100.0	100.0	100.0
War Status of Romantic Partner				
Ally spy	-	1.2	-	0.4
Ally civilian	13.2	6.2	10.2	12.3
American spy	0.9	2.5	-	1.2
American soldier	8.8	4.9	10.2	7.8
American civilian	14.0	32.1	26.5	22.5
Enemy spy	-	4.9	-	1.6
Enemy civilian	6.1	4.9	2.0	4.9

TABLE 75--Continued

	WWII	Cold	Korea	Total
Neutral civilian	2.6%	2.5%	6.1%	3.3%
No answer	54.4	40.7	44.9	48.0
Total	100.0	100.0	100.0	100.0

Partner's Social Status

	WWII	Cold	Korea	Total
Same as hero	18.4	32.1	34.7	26.2
Lower	6.1	7.4	4.1	6.1
Higher	6.1	4.9	2.0	4.9
Unclear	5.3	8.6	6.1	6.6
No answer	54.4	40.7	44.9	48.0
Total	100.0	100.0	100.0	100.0

Primary Concern

	WWII	Cold	Korea	Total
War	70.2	77.8	71.4	73.0
Other	16.7	16.0	22.4	17.6
Romance	13.2	6.2	6.1	9.4
Total	100.0	100.0	100.0	100.0

Secondary Concern

	WWII	Cold	Korea	Total
Romance	42.1	44.4	40.8	42.6
War	21.1	13.6	18.4	18.0
Other	21.9	12.3	16.3	13.5
No answer	14.9	29.6	24.5	25.8
Total	100.0	100.0	100.0	100.0

Third Concern

	WWII	Cold	Korea	Total
Romance	11.4	14.8	10.2	12.3
War	6.1	2.5	6.1	4.9
Other	1.8	6.2	4.1	3.7
No answer	80.7	76.5	79.6	79.1
Total	100.0	100.0	100.0	100.0

[a]Data derived from questions 12, 14, 19, 21, 22, 23, 24, 26, 27, 28, 30, 32, 33, and 38 Form B in Appendix I. Questions 9, 10, 11, 13, 34, 35, and 37 of Form B were not included because their results were too scattered. All other results were included in the body of the thesis.

[b]Categories for which there were no responses were omitted.

TABLE 76

ALLIES AND ENEMIES, 1948-1962

	World War II		Cold War	
	Ally	Enemy	Ally	Enemy
Support of War Policy				
Support	70.6%	50.0%	66.7%	14.3%
Neutral	23.5	25.0	-	-
Illegal opposition	-	12.5	16.7	28.6
Legal opposition	-	-	-	28.6
Other	5.9	12.5	-	28.6
No answer	-	-	16.7	-
Total	100.0	100.0	100.0	100.0
Reason for Not Being in Military				
Age, family	11.8	6.3	-	-
Not required	11.8	-	-	-
Occupational defer.	5.9	12.5	-	-
Completed service	-	-	-	-
Other	5.9	-	33.3	-
No answer	64.7	81.3	66.7	100.0
Total	100.0	100.0	100.0	100.0
Health				
Healthy	100.0	100.0	100.0	71.4
War injury	-	-	-	28.6
Total	100.0	100.0	100.0	100.0
Life and Death				
Lives	76.5	50.0	100.0	85.7
War death	11.8	50.0	-	14.3
Non-war death	5.9	-	-	-
Total	100.0	100.0	100.0	100.0
Change as Result of War				
No change	76.5	62.5	83.3	57.1
Behavior	11.8	6.3	16.7	42.9
Attitude	5.9	6.3	16.7	14.3
Knowledge	5.9	25.0	-	14.3
Total	100.0	100.0	116.7	128.6

TABLE 76--Continued

	World War II		Cold War	
	Ally	Enemy	Ally	Enemy

Secondary Goal

	Ally	Enemy	Ally	Enemy
Love	35.3%	6.3%	-	28.6%
Honesty	11.8	25.0	16.7	-
Patriotism	11.8	6.3	-	-
Safety	11.8	12.5	33.3	14.3
Family	5.9	6.3	-	28.6
Individualism	5.9	6.3	-	-
Money	5.9	-	-	-
Revenge	5.9	6.3	-	-
Justice	-	6.3	16.7	-
Sex	-	6.3	-	14.3
War task	-	-	16.7	-
Truth	-	-	-	14.3
No answer	5.9	18.8	16.7	-
Total	100.0	100.0	100.0	100.0

Primary Obstacle to Achieving Goals

	Ally	Enemy	Ally	Enemy
Legal convention	47.1	43.8	50.0	85.7
Other people	23.5	37.5	33.3	-
Circumstance	11.8	-	-	-
Social convention	11.8	6.3	-	14.3
Self	5.9	12.5	-	-
No answer	-	-	16.7	-
Total	100.0	100.0	100.0	100.0

Secondary Obstacle to Achieving Goals

	Ally	Enemy	Ally	Enemy
Legal convention	29.4	25.0	16.7	-
Self	11.8	-	16.7	-
Circumstance	5.9	6.3	-	-
Illness	5.9	12.5	16.7	-
Other people	5.9	12.5	-	71.4
No answer	41.2	40.0	50.0	28.6
Total	100.0	100.0	100.0	100.0

TABLE 76--Continued

	World War II		Cold War	
	Ally	Enemy	Ally	Enemy

Secondary Method of Achieving Goals

Force	17.6%	12.5%	-	14.3%
Trickery	17.6	18.8	16.7	-
Charm	11.8	-	-	-
Knowledge	5.9	31.3	-	-
Persuasion	-	12.5	-	-
Hard work	-	-	16.7	42.9
Luck	-	-	16.7	-
No answer	47.1	25.0	50.0	28.6
Total	100.0	100.0	100.0	100.0

War Status of Romantic Partner

Ally spy	5.9	-	-	-
Ally civilian	23.5	-	33.3	14.3
American spy	5.9	-	16.7	-
American soldier	11.8	6.3	-	-
Enemy spy	-	-	-	14.3
Enemy civilian	-	31.3	-	71.4
Neutral civilian	-	6.3	-	-
No answer	52.9	56.7	50.0	-
Total	100.0	100.0	100.0	100.0

Partner's Social Status

Same as hero	11.8	25.0	-	14.3
Higher	11.8	6.3	33.3	42.9
Lower	-	6.3	-	14.3
Unclear	23.5	6.3	16.7	14.3
No answer	52.9	56.7	50.0	14.3
Total	100.0	100.0	100.0	100.0

Romantic Outcome

Unwilling breakup	29.4	25.0	-	14.3
Marriage	5.9	12.5	16.7	42.9
Romance continues	5.9	-	33.3	28.6
Willing breakup	-	6.3	-	-

TABLE 76--Continued

	World War II		Cold War	
	Ally	Enemy	Ally	Enemy
Uncertain	5.9%	- %	- %	- %
No answer	52.9	56.7	50.0	14.3
Total	100.0	100.0	100.0	100.0
	Primary Concern			
War	82.4	50.3	83.3	85.7
Romance	11.8	6.3	-	14.3
Other	5.9	31.3	-	-
No answer	-	6.3	16.7	-
Total	100.0	100.0	100.0	100.0
	Secondary Concern			
Romance	29.4	25.0	16.7	85.7
Other	23.5	6.3	-	-
War	17.6	25.0	-	-
No answer	29.4	43.8	83.3	14.3
Total	100.0	100.0	100.0	100.0
	Third Concern			
Other	5.9	-	-	-
Romance	5.9	12.5	-	-
War	-	12.5	-	-
No answer	88.3	75.0	100.0	100.0
Total	100.0	100.0	100.0	100.0
Number	17	16	6	7

[a]Data derived from questions 14, 21, 22, 23, 24, 26, 27, 28, 30, 32, 33, 36, and 38 Form B in Appendix I. Questions 9, 10, 11, 12, 13, 19, 34, 35, and 27 of Form B were not included because their results were too scattered. All other results are included in the body of the thesis.

[b]Categories for which there were no responses were omitted.

TABLE 77

FILM RESULTS, 1948-1962

	WWII	Cold	Korea	Total
Format				
Action	50.9%	36.5%	74.5%	50.0%
General drama	26.1	21.2	918	21.8
Comedy	13.7	22.1	9.8	15.8
Mystery	3.1	17.3	-	7.3
Romance	5.0	1.0	5.9	3.8
Musical	0.6	1.0	-	0.6
Expose	0.6	-	-	0.3
Fantasy	-	1.0	-	0.3
Total	100.0	100.0	100.0	100.0
Historical Base				
Fictitious	73.9	88.5	82.4	79.6
Some truth	16.8	7.7	9.8	13.1
True story	9.3	4.8	7.8	7.6
Total	100.0	100.0	100.0	100.0
Locale				
United States	14.3	51.9	13.7	26.6
Korea	-	-	80.4	13.0
Pacific Islands	17.2	-	2.0	9.1
Germany	13.7	3.8	-	8.2[a]
France	9.3	2.9	-	5.7
Italy	7.5	1.0	-	4.1
Japan	5.0	1.9	3.9	3.8
Pacific Ocean	6.8	1.0	-	3.8
China	3.1	5.8	-	3.5
Britain	5.0	1.0	-	2.8
Philippines	5.0	-	-	2.5
Indo-China	0.6	4.8	-	1.9
Hungary	-	3.8	-	1.3
Czechoslovakia	-	2.9	-	0.9
Greece	0.6	1.9	-	0.9
Soviet Union	-	2.9	-	0.9
Austria	-	1.9	-	0.6
Belgium	1.2	-	-	0.6
Holland	0.6	1.0	-	0.6
North Africa	1.2	-	-	0.6
Tangiers	-	1.9	-	0.6

TABLE 77--Continued

	WWII	Cold	Korea	Total
Turkey	0.6%	1.0%	- %	0.6%
Arctic	-	1.0	-	0.3
Australia	-	1.0	-	0.3
Borneo	0.6	-	-	0.3
Burma	0.6	-	-	0.3
Canada	-	1.0	-	0.3
Israel	0.6	-	-	0.3
Malaya	0.6	-	-	0.3
Mediterranean	0.6	-	-	0.3
Mongolia	0.6	-	-	0.3
Morocco	-	1.0	-	0.3
New Guinea	0.6	-	-	0.3
Okinawa	0.6	-	-	0.3
Roumania	0.6	-	-	0.3
Other European	1.2	2.9	-	1.6
Other Asia	-	1.0	-	0.3
No answer	-	1.0	-	0.3
Total	100.0	100.0	100.0	100.0

War Message

	WWII	Cold	Korea	Total
Anti-enemy	6.8	51.9	11.8	22.2
Pro-military	16.2	17.3	13.7	16.2
Anti-military	3.2	1.9	-	2.2
Pro-enemy	2.5	-	-	1.3
Anti-war	-	1.9	-	0.6
Pro-U.N.	1.3	-	-	0.6
Pro-patriotism	-	1.9	2.0	1.0
Anti-pacifism	-	1.0	-	0.3
Anti-status quo	-	-	2.0	0.3
No answer	70.2	24.0	70.6	55.1
Total	100.0	100.0	100.0	100.0

Secondary Reasons for Victories[b]

	WWII	Cold	Korea	Total
Methods	9.9	14.4	15.7	12.3
Individuals	8.7	12.7	9.8	10.1
Resources	7.6	6.7	9.8	7.6
Goals	3.7	2.9	-	2.8
Circumstance	1.9	1.9	-	1.6
Other	-	1.9	-	0.6
Total	31.7	40.4	35.3	25.6

TABLE 77--Continued

	WWII	Cold	Korea	Total
Immediate and Ultimate Results of Fighting				
Imm. victory	54.6%	56.7%	45.1%	53.8%
Ult. victory	31.1	1.0	3.9	16.8
Imm. defeat	3.7	4.8	3.9	4.1
Ult. defeat	-	2.9	-	0.9
Imm. deadlock	1.9	-	3.9	1.6
Ult. deadlock	-	1.9	2.0	0.6
Imm. undeterminable	3.7	6.7	3.9	4.7
Ult. undeterminable	2.5	7.7	11.8	5.7
Imm. not applicable	36.0	31.7	43.1	35.8
Ult. not applicable	66.5	87.5	82.4	75.9
Total	200.0	200.0	200.0	200.0
Consequence of Film Events to War Effort				
Limited-major	66.4	23.1	15.7	22.2
Overall-major	7.5	4.8	2.0	5.7
Limited-minor	6.2	1.9	7.8	5.1
Overall-minor	6.2	1.0	2.0	3.8
Limited-unrelated	35.4	26.0	29.4	31.3
Overall-unrelated	36.6	26.0	29.4	32.0
Limited-undetermin.	29.2	37.4	31.4	32.3
Overall-undetermin.	29.2	32.7	31.4	32.3
Limited-not applic.	5.6	11.5	15.7	9.2
Overall-not applic.	20.5	35.6	35.3	27.8
Total	200.0	200.0	200.0	200.0
Outcome				
Happy-success	71.5	81.4	72.5	74.9
Unhappy-success	9.5	3.9	7.8	7.4
Mixed-success	3.8	3.9	-	3.2
Unhappy-failure	5.1	3.9	2.0	4.2
Happy-mixed	-	1.0	-	0.3
Unhappy-mixed	0.6	1.0	3.9	1.3
Mixed-mixed	,9.5	4.8	13.7	8.0
Total	100.0	100.0	100.0	100.0
Second Major Film Themes				
War	16.8	12.5	17.6	15.5
Love	15.5	8.7	11.8	12.7
Armed forces	8.1	13.5	17.6	11.4

TABLE 77--Continued

	WWII	Cold	Korea	Total
Violence	10.6%	8.7%	9.8%	9.8%
Foreigners	8.1	14.4	-	8.9
Inner conflict	9.3	1.9	5.9	6.3
Comradship	4.3	3.8	9.8	5.1
Nature	5.0	2.9	2.0	3.8
Public Affairs	2.5	6.7	2.0	3.8
Science	1.2	3.8	7.8	3.2
Patriotism	2.5	1.9	3.9	2.5
Minorities	1.9	1.9	-	1.6
Law enforcement	-	3.8	-	1.3
Family	0.6	1.0	2.0	0.9
Fine arts	1.2	-	2.0	0.9
Medical	1.2	1.0	-	0.9
Religion	-	1.9	2.0	0.9
Entertainment	-	1.9	-	0.6
Mental health	0.6	-	2.0	0.6
Press	0.6	1.0	-	0.6
Alcoholism	-	-	2.0	0.3
Education	0.6	-	-	0.3
No answer	9.3	8.7	2.0	7.9
Total	100.0	100.0	100.0	100.0

Other Major Film Themes

	WWII	Cold	Korea	Total
War	37.3	42.3	37.3	38.9
Love	29.2	40.4	33.3	33.5
Patriotism	19.9	32.7	15.7	23.4
Armed forces	28.6	7.7	25.4	21.2
Foreigners	21.1	20.2	9.8	19.0
Violence	13.7	9.6	25.5	14.2
Inner conflict	16.1	6.7	21.6	14.0
Science	8.7	20.2	17.6	14.0
Comradship	16.1	4.8	11.8	11.7
Family	5.6	12.5	5.9	7.9
Nature	10.6	5.8	-	7.3
Public affairs	1.9	10.6	3.9	5.1
Materialism	3.7	1.9	2.0	2.8
Accidents	1.2	3.8	3.9	2.5
Law enforcement	1.9	3.8	2.0	2.5
Religion	1.2	1.9	5.9	2.2
Entertainment	1.2	2.9	1.0	1.9
Medical	-	-	11.8	1.9
Minorities	3.1	-	-	1.6
Press	1.9	1.0	2.0	1.6
Mental health	-	1.0	3.9	0.9

TABLE 77--Continued

	WWII	Cold	Korea	Total
Alcoholism	0.6%	- %	- %	0.3%
Business	0.6	-	-	0.3
Education	-	1.0	-	0.3
Total	224.2	230.7	241.2	229.1
Number	161	104	51	316

[a]Germany's total includes 1.0 percent for East Germany and 0.3 percent for West Germany.

[b]Secondary reasons for victories include second and third most important reasons according to the films.

[c]Data derived from questions 11, 14, 16, 30, the second part of 34, 40, 41, 42, and the second and third parts of 43 Form A in Appendix I. Questions 1-8 were not quantified and questions 15, 19, 35, 36, 37, and the second parts of 26, 27, 28, 29, and 31 received sparse responses; thus, those answers were not included in the tables. Data from all other questions are included in the body of the thesis.

[d]Categories for which there were no responses were omitted.

TABLE 78

THE AMERICAN HERO, 1963-1970

	WWII	Cold	Korea	Vietnam	Total
Support of War Policy					
Support	74.0%	76.2%	20.0%	100.0%	70.5%
Neutral	20.0	23.9	20.0	-	20.5
Illegal opposition	4.0	-	-	-	2.6
Other	2.0	-	-	-	1.3
No answer	-	-	60.0	-	3.8
Total	100.0	100.0	100.0	100.0	100.0
How Officer's Rank Obtained					
OCS	4.0	-	-	-	2.6
Direct commission	-	-	20.0	-	1.3
Promotion	2.0	-	-	-	1.3
Service academy	2.0	-	-	-	1.3
No answer	92.0	100.0	80.0	100.0	92.3
Total	100.0	100.0	100.0	100.0	100.0
Reason for Not Being in Military					
Mentally unfit	-	4.8	-	-	1.3
Completed service	-	4.8	-	-	1.3
Other	2.0	4.8	-	-	2.6
No answer	98.0	85.7	100.0	100.0	93.6
Total	100.0	100.0	100.0	100.0	100.0
Health					
Healthy	80.0	95.2	100.0	100.0	85.9
War injury	18.0	4.8	-	-	12.8
Non-war injury	2.0	-	-	-	1.3
Total	100.0	100.0	100.0	100.0	100.0
Life and Death					
Lives	86.0	90.5	80.0	100.0	86.7
War death	14.0	4.8	20.0	-	11.5
Non-war death	-	4.8	-	-	1.3
Total	100.0	100.0	100.0	100.0	100.0

TABLE 78--Continued

	WWII	Cold	Korea	Vietnam	Total
Change as Result of War					
No change	70.0%	81.0%	100.0%	100.0%	75.3%
Attitude	12.0	4.8	-	-	8.9
Behavior	10.0	4.8	-	-	7.7
Knowledge	4.0	4.8	-	-	3.8
No answer	4.0	4.8	-	-	3.8
Total	100.0	100.0	100.0	100.0	100.0
Secondary Goal					
Love	18.0	4.8	20.0	50.0	15.4
Safety	14.0	-	20.0	-	10.3
Comfort	10.0	-	20.0	-	7.7
Patriotism	2.0	23.9	-	-	7.7
War task	8.0	4.8	-	50.0	7.7
Sex	4.0	9.5	-	-	5.1
Individualism	4.0	4.8	-	-	3.8
Money	2.0	9.5	-	-	3.8
Power	2.0	9.5	-	-	3.8
Family	2.0	-	20.0	-	2.6
Justice	2.0	4.8	-	-	2.6
Escape law	2.0	-	-	-	1.3
Honesty	2.0	-	-	-	1.3
No answer	28.0	28.6	20.0	-	26.9
Total	100.0	100.0	100.0	100.0	100.0
Primary Obstacle to Achieving Goals					
Legal convention	46.0	23.9	40.0	-	38.2
Other people	24.0	42.9	-	100.0	29.4
Self	12.0	9.5	20.0	-	11.5
Circumstance	4.0	9.5	20.0	-	5.1
Social convention	4.0	-	20.0	-	3.8
Illness	4.0	-	-	-	2.6
No answer	6.0	14.3	-	-	7.7
Total	100.0	100.0	100.0	100.0	100.0
Secondary Obstacle to Achieving Goals					
Legal convention	30.0	19.0	-	-	24.4
Illness	10.0	4.8	-	-	10.3
Other people	14.0	-	40.0	-	10.0

TABLE 78--Continued

	WWII	Cold	Korea	Vietnam	Total
Social convention	8.0%	4.8%	- %	50.0%	7.7%
Circumstance	6.0	9.5	-	-	6.4
Self	-	-	20.0	-	1.3
No answer	32.0	61.9	40.0	50.0	41.0
Total	100.0	100.0	100.0	100.0	100.0

Secondary Method of Achieving Goals

	WWII	Cold	Korea	Vietnam	Total
Force	18.0	9.5	20.0	-	15.6
Trickery	8.0	28.6	-	-	12.9
Knowledge	12.0	9.5	-	50.0	11.5
Persuasion	4.0	9.5	-	50.0	6.4
Charm	2.0	4.8	-	-	2.6
Hard work	2.0	4.8	-	-	2.6
No answer	54.0	33.3	80.0	-	48.4
Total	100.0	100.0	100.0	100.0	100.0

War Status of Romantic Partner

	WWII	Cold	Korea	Vietnam	Total
Ally civilian	10.0	4.8	-	50.0	8.7
American spy	2.0	9.5	-	-	3.8
American soldier	6.0	-	20.0	-	5.1
American civilian	8.0	28.6	20.0	-	14.1
Enemy spy	-	4.8	-	-	1.3
Enemy soldier	2.0	-	-	-	1.3
Enemy civilian	4.0	4.8	-	-	3.8
Neutral civilian	2.0	9.5	-	-	3.8
No answer	66.0	38.6	60.0	50.0	57.7
Total	100.0	100.0	100.0	100.0	100.0

Partner's Social Status

	WWII	Cold	Korea	Vietnam	Total
Same as hero	16.0	38.6	40.0	50.0	24.4
Higher	4.0	-	-	-	2.6
Lower	2.0	4.8	-	-	2.6
Unclear	6.0	4.8	-	-	5.1
No answer	72.0	52.4	60.0	50.0	58.9
Total	100.0	100.0	100.0	100.0	100.0

TABLE 78--Continued

	WWII	Cold	Korea	Vietnam	Total
Primary Concern					
War	86.0%	95.2%	40.0%	100.0%	87.2%
Other	10.0	4.8	60.0	-	11.5
Romance	4.0	-	-	-	2.6
Total	100.0	100.0	100.0	100.0	100.0
Secondary Concern					
Romance	28.0	52.4	40.0	50.0	35.9
War	18.0	-	20.0	-	12.8
Other	16.0	4.8	-	50.0	12.8
No answer	38.0	42.3	-	-	38.6
Total	100.0	100.0	20.0	-	100.0
			100.0	100.0	
Third Concern					
Romance	8.0	4.8	-	-	6.4
Other	4.0	4.8	-	-	2.6
War	-	-	40.0	-	2.6
No answer	88.0	90.5	60.0	100.0	88.5
Total	100.0	100.0	100.0	100.0	100.0
Number	50	21	5	2	78

[a]Data derived from questions 14, 21, 22, 23, 24, 26, 27, 28, 30, 32, 33, and 38 Form B in Appendix I. Questions 9, 10, 11, 12, 13, 19, 34, 35, and 37 Form B were not included because their results were too scattered. All other results are included in the body of the thesis.

[b]Categories for which there were no responses were omitted.

TABLE 79

ALLIES AND ENEMIES, 1963-1970

	World War II		Cold War	
	Ally	Enemy	Ally	Enemy
Support of War Policy				
Support	80.0%	75.0%	100.0%	100.0%
Neutral	10.0	25.0	-	-
Illegal opposition	10.0	-	-	-
Total	100.0	100.0	100.0	100.0
Reason for Not Being in Military				
Age, family	-	-	100.0	-
Not required	10.0	-	-	-
Other	10.0	-	-	-
No answer	80.0	100.0	-	100.0
Total	100.0	100.0	100.0	100.0
Health				
Healthy	90.0	100.0	100.0	100.0
War injury	10.0	-	-	-
Total	100.0	100.0	100.0	100.0
Life and Death				
Lives	90.0	75.0	100.0	100.0
War death	10.0	25.0	-	-
Total	100.0	100.0	100.0	100.0
Change as Result of War				
No change	70.0	75.0	100.0	100.0
Attitude	30.0	25.0	-	-
Behavior	20.0	-	-	-
Total	120.0	100.0	100.0	100.0

TABLE 79--Continued

	World War II		Cold War	
	Ally	Enemy	Ally	Enemy
Secondary Goal				
Patriotism	20.0%	25.0%	- %	- %
Safety	20.0	25.0	-	-
Individualism	10.0	-	-	-
Sex	10.0	-	100.0	-
War task	10.0	25.0	-	-
Truth	-	25.0	-	-
Love	-	-	-	100.0
No answer	30.0	-	-	-
Total	100.0	100.0	100.0	100.0
Primary Obstacle to Achieving Goals				
Legal convention	60.0	100.0	-	-
Other people	20.0	-	100.0	100.0
Self	20.0	-	-	-
Total	100.0	100.0	100.0	100.0
Secondary Obstacle to Achieving Goals				
Other people	20.0	-	-	-
Legal convention	10.0	-	100.0	100.0
Self	10.0	-	-	-
No answer	60.0	100.0	-	-
Total	100.0	100.0	100.0	100.0
Secondary Method of Achieving Goals				
Hard work	40.0	25.0	-	-
Force	20.0	-	-	-
Knowledge	20.0	-	-	-
Luck	-	25.0	-	-
Persuasion	-	25.0	-	-
Trickery	-	-	100.0	-
No answer	20.0	25.0	-	100.0
Total	100.0	100.0	100.0	100.0

TABLE 79--Continued

	World War II		Cold War	
	Ally	Enemy	Ally	Enemy

War Status of Romantic Partner

Ally spy	- %	- %	100.0%	- %
Ally civilian	10.0	-	-	-
American soldier	10.0	-	-	-
American civilian	-	-	-	100.0
No answer	80.0	100.0	-	-
Total	100.0	100.0	100.0	100.0

Partner's Social Status

Lower	10.0	-	-	-
Same as hero	-	-	100.0	-
Unclear	10.0	-	-	-
No answer	80.0	100.0	-	100.0
Total	100.0	100.0	100.0	100.0

Romantic Outcome

Marriage	10.0	-	-	-
Unwilling breakup	-	-	100.0	-
Romance continues	-	-	-	100.0
No answer	90.0	100.0	-	-
Total	100.0	100.0	100.0	100.0

Primary Concern

War	90.0	75.0	100.0	-
Romance	10.0	-	-	100.0
Other	-	25.0	-	-
Total	100.0	100.0	100.0	100.0

Secondary Concern

Other	10.0	25.0	-	-
Romance	10.0	-	100.0	-
War	10.0	-	-	100.0
No answer	70.0	75.0	-	-
Total	100.0	100.0	100.0	100.0

TABLE 79--Continued

	World War II		Cold War	
	Ally	Enemy	Ally	Enemy
	Third Concern			
Other	- %	- %	100.0%	- %
No answer	100.0	100.0	-	100.0
Total	100.0	100.0	100.0	100.0
Number	10	4	1	1

[a]Data derived from questions 14, 21, 22, 24, 25, 26, 27, 28, 30, 32, 33, 36, and 28 Form B in Appendix I. Questions 9, 10, 11, 12, 13, 19, 34, 35, and 37 of Form B were not included because their results were too scattered. All other results are included in the body of the thesis.

[b]Categories for which there were no responses were omitted.

TABLE 80

FILM RESULTS, 1963-1970

	WWII	Cold	Korea	Vietnam	Total
Format					
Action	68.8%	56.5%	20.0%	100.0%	63.8%
Comedy	15.6	4.3	20.0	-	12.8
General drama	15.6	26.1	60.0	-	20.2
Mystery	-	13.6	-	-	3.2
Total	100.0	100.0	100.0	100.0	100.0
Historical Base					
Fictitious	78.1	100.0	100.0	100.0	85.1
Some truth	14.1	-	-	-	9.6
True story	7.8	-	-	-	5.3
Total	100.0	100.0	100.0	100.0	100.0
Locale					
Phillippines	20.3	-	-	-	13.8
Germany	9.4	8.7	-	-	11.7[a]
United States	3.1	34.8	20.0	-	11.7
Italy	9.4	4.3	-	-	7.4
Pacific Ocean	10.9	-	-	-	7.4
Pacific Islands	7.8	-	-	-	5.3
Britain	7.8	-	-	-	4.3
France	6.3	-	-	-	4.3
Korea	-	-	80.0	-	4.3
Vietnam	-	4.3	-	100.0	4.3
Belgium	3.1	-	-	-	2.1
China	-	8.7	-	-	2.1
Japan	3.1	-	-	-	2.1
Yugoslavia	3.1	-	-	-	2.1
Arctic	-	4.3	-	-	1.1
Atlantic Ocean	-	4.3	-	-	1.1
Carribean	-	4.3	-	-	1.1
Cuba	-	4.3	-	-	1.1
Greece	1.6	-	-	-	1.1
Guadalcanal	1.6	-	-	.	1.1
Mexico	-	4.3	-	-	1.1
North Africa	1.6	-	-	-	1.1
Norway	1.6	-	-	-	1.1

TABLE 80--Continued

	WWII	Cold	Korea	Vietnam	Total
Pearl Harbor	1.6%	- %	- %	- %	1.1%
Scotland	1.6	-	-	-	1.1
Sweden	-	4.3	-	-	1.1
Other European	4.7	4.3	-	-	4.3
Other Asian	-	8.7	-	-	2.1
Total	100.0	100.0	100.0	100.0	100.0

War Message

	WWII	Cold	Korea	Vietnam	Total
Anti-enemy	3.1	60.9	20.0	-	17.0
Anti-military	3.1	13.6	40.0	-	7.4
Anti-war	9.4	-	-	-	6.4
Pro-military	6.3	-	-	50.0	5.3
Pro-ally	1.6	-	-	50.0	3.2
Pro-internation.	-	8.7	-	-	2.1
Pro-patriotism	1.6	-	-	-	1.1
No answer	75.0	13.6	40.0	-	56.4
Total	100.0	100.0	100.0	100.0	100.0

Secondary Reasons for Victories[b]

	WWII	Cold	Korea	Vietnam	Total
Resources	14.1	21.7	40.0	-	17.0
Methods	14.1	13.0	-	-	12.8
Individuals	7.8	17.4	-	-	9.6
Circumstance	1.6	-	-	-	1.1
Other	1.6	4.3	-	-	2.1
Total	39.1	56.9	40.0	-	42.6

Immediate and Ultimate Results of Fighting

	WWII	Cold	Korea	Vietnam	Total
Imm. victory	62.5	56.5	-	100.0	58.5
Ult. victory	23.4	-	-	-	16.0
Imm. defeat	4.7	-	-	-	3.2
Ult. defeat	-	-	-	-	-
Imm. deadlock	1.6	17.4	20.0	-	6.4
Ult. deadlock	1.6	4.3	20.0	-	3.2
Imm. undetermin.	7.8	8.7	-	-	7.4
Ult. undetermin.	9.4	13.6	-	-	9.6
Imm. not applic.	23.4	17.4	80.0	-	24.5
Ult. not applic.	65.6	82.6	80.0	100.0	71.3
Total	200.0	200.0	200.0	200.0	200.0

TABLE 80--Continued

	WWII	Cold	Korea	Vietnam	Total
Consequence of Film Events to War Effort					
Limited-major	25.0%	60.9%	- %	- %	31.9%
Overall-major	6.3	8.7	-	-	6.4
Limited-minor	6.3	4.3	-	-	5.3
Overall-minor	-	-	-	-	-
Limited-unrelated	28.1	8.7	80.0	-	37.5
Overall-unrelated	28.1	30.4	80.0	-	30.9
Limited-undetermin.	31.3	26.1	20.0	100.0	30.9
Overall-undetermin.	28.1	26.1	20.0	-	26.6
Limited-not applic.	3.1	-	-	-	2.1
Overall-not applic.	25.0	21.7	-	100.0	24.5
Total	200.0	200.0	200.0	200.0	200.0
Outcome					
Happy-success	56.3	60.9	40.0	100.0	57.4
Unhappy-success	7.8	4.3	-	-	6.4
Mixed-success	9.4	13.6	-	-	9.6
Happy-failure	6.3	8.7	20.0	-	7.4
Mixed-failure	1.6	4.3	-	-	2.1
Mixed-mixed	10.9	8.7	40.0	-	11.7
No answer	6.3	-	-	-	4.3
Total	100.0	100.0	100.0	100.0	100.0
Second Major Film Themes					
War	37.5	-	20.0	-	26.6
Love	14.1	26.1	-	-	16.0
Violence	14.1	8.7	20.0	-	12.8
Armed forces	9.4	13.6	20.0	50.0	11.7
Science	-	21.7	-	-	6.4
Foreigners	3.1	8.7	-	50.0	5.3
Patriotism	3.1	8.7	20.0	-	5.3
Comradship	6.3	-	-	-	4.3
Family	1.6	4.3	20.0	-	3.2
Accidents	3.1	-	-	-	2.1
Public affairs	1.6	4.3	-	-	2.1
Law enforcement	-	4.3	-	-	1.1
Mental health	1.6	-	-	-	1.1
Religion	1.6	-	-	-	1.1
No answer	3.1	-	-	-	2.1
Total	100.0	100.0	100.0	100.0	100.0

TABLE 80--Continued

	WWII	Cold	Korea	Vietnam	Total
	Other Major Film Themes				
Love	28.1%	39.1%	40.0%	50.0%	31.9%
Foreigners	29.7	21.7	40.0	50.0	28.7
Patriotism	26.6	34.8	-	40.0	28.7
War	18.8	34.8	40.0	-	23.4
Armed forces	25.0	4.3	60.0	-	21.3
Violence	15.6	13.6	20.0	-	14.9
Comradship	4.7	8.7	60.0	20.0	9.6
Science	7.8	17.4	-	-	9.6
Inner conflict	10.9	4.3	-	-	8.5
Public affairs	7.8	8.7	-	-	7.4
Accidents	4.7	13.6	-	-	6.4
Nature	7.8	-	-	-	5.3
Law enforcement	4.7	4.3	-	-	4.3
Family	3.1	4.3	-	-	3.2
Fine arts	4.7	-	-	-	3.2
Materialism	1.6	8.7	-	-	3.2
Medical	3.1	-	-	-	2.1
Mantal health	3.1	-	-	-	2.1
Religion	-	-	20.0	-	1.1
Total	209.4	217.4	260.0	250.0	214.9
Number	64	23	5	2	94

[a]Germany's total includes 2.1 percent for East Germany.

[b]Secondary reasons for victories include second and third important reasons according to the films.

[c]Data derived from questions 11, 14, 16, 30, the second part of 34, 40, 41, 42, and the second and third parts of 43 Form A in Appendix I. Questions 1-8 were not quantified and questions 15, 19, 35, 36, 37, and the second parts of 26, 27, 28, 29, and 31 received sparse responses; thus, those answers were not included in the tables. Data from all other questions are included in the body of the thesis.

[d]Categories for which there were no responses were omitted.

APPENDIX IV

CONTENT ANALYSES BASED ON SCREENINGS AND REVIEWS

TABLE 81

COMPARISON OF CONTENT ANALYSES BASED
ON SCREENINGS AND REVIEWS

Question	A%	B%	C%	D%	Chi S.	P
			Form A			
11	89.7	10.3	-	-	-	-
12	75.9	10.3	13.8	-	3.4	.05-.10
13	97.8	1.3	-	0.9	-	-
14	98.7	0.9	-	-	-	-
15	99.1	0.9	-	-	-	-
16	29.3	3.9	3.9	62.9	15.4	.001
17	97.4	1.3	-	1.3	60.6	.001
18	87.5	2.2	-	10.3	217.8	.001
19	45.7	6.0	35.8	12.5	10.3	.001-.005
20A	92.7	7.3	-	-	-	-
20B	69.0	17.7	8.2	5.2	4.1	.025-.05
20C	28.9	9.9	18.5	42.7	41.9	.001
21	95.3	4.7	-	-	-	-
22	58.2	1.3	3.0	37.5	217.9	.001
23	52.2	1.7	4.7	41.4	172.6	.001
24	51.3	6.5	5.6	32.3	103.2	.001
25A	61.6	8.2	3.0	27.2	112.5	.001
25B	34.5	7.3	9.5	48.7	20.6	.001
26A	15.9	3.0	8.2	72.8	111.6	.001
26B	4.7	2.6	3.0	89.7	76.0	.001
26C	1.3	-	2.2	96.6	60.3	.001
27A	8.6	1.7	5.2	84.5	114.2	.001
27B	1.3	-	1.7	97.0	10.2	.001-.005
27C	0.9	-	0.9	98.3	9.8	.001-.005
28A	29.7	9.5	11.2	49.6	72.6	.001
28B	8.6	6.0	10.3	75.0	37.8	.001
28C	1.7	1.7	4.7	91.8	7.9	.005
29AA	10.3	4.7	3.4	81.5	99.4	.001
29AB	2.6	2.2	0.9	94.4	1.5	.20-.25
29AC	3.0	-	-	97.0	210.3	.001
29EA	9.9	3.4	2.6	84.0	99.3	.001
29EB	1.7	1.7	3.0	93.5	36.5	.001
29EC	0.4	0.4	0.9	98.3	0.5	.30-.50
30	47.0	11.2	9.5	32.3	75.2	.001
31A	15.5	8.6	22.0	53.9	21.1	.001
31B	3.4	1.7	3.0	91.8	73.6	.001
31C	11.4	3.4	13.6	71.6	112.3	.001
32	37.9	19.0	19.0	25.9	10.7	.001-.005
33	27.6	7.3	26.3	38.7	30.2	.001
34A	49.6	22.4	10.3	17.7	18.9	.001

TABLE 81--Continued

Question	A%	B%	C%	D%	Chi S.	P
34B	24.1	20.3	15.1	40.5	16.9	.001
34C	6.9	5.3	5.6	86.6	53.4	.001
35	29.7	5.3	4.7	60.3	141.9	.001
36	20.2	5.6	11.3	62.9	80.1	.001
37	28.9	13.4	6.9	50.9	763.1	.001
38	27.6	14.2	7.8	50.4	64.7	.001
39	33.6	12.9	13.8	39.6	17.9	.001
40A	50.4	9.1	9.5	25.0	69.4	.001
40B	26.7	9.1	11.6	52.6	67.2	.001
41A	62.9	29.3	4.7	3.0	0.9	.30-.50
41B	51.7	24.6	12.1	11.6	4.3	0.25-.50
42	83.6	15.9	-	0.4	0.4	.50-.70
43A	69.0	31.0	-	-	-	-
43B	53.4	44.0	1.7	0.9	0.1	.80-.90
43C	59.7	25.1	5.9	9.3	33.8	.001

Form B

1	96.9	3.1	-	-	-	-
2	100.0	-	-	-	-	-
3	92.4	2.7	4.9	-	-	-
4	78.0	14.3	7.6	-	15.4	.001
5	70.9	9.0	15.7	4.5	17.0	.001
6	48.0	13.0	13.5	25.1	46.7	.001
7	72.2	5.4	10.3	11.7	52.8	.001
8	99.6	-	-	0.4	2.0	.10-.20
9	99.6	-	-	0.4	2.0	.10-.20
10	100.0	-	-	-	-	-
11	5.0	-	0.4	94.2	10.4	.001-.005
12	98.2	1.8	-	-	-	-
13	99.6	0.4	-	-	-	-
14	96.0	4.0	-	-	-	-
15	84.3	5.4	2.2	8.1	17.1	.001
16	68.6	4.9	-	26.5	171.3	.001
17	65.0	5.4	0.4	29.1	165.5	.001
18	61.0	9.4	-	29.6	148.8	.001
19	17.0	4.9	6.3	71.7	99.8	.001
20	39.0	17.9	10.8	32.3	39.7	.001
21	10.3	3.6	4.9	80.3	92.2	.001
22	16.1	2.2	6.3	75.3	118.8	.001
23	97.8	2.2	-	-	-	-
24	16.6	6.7	9.4	67.3	67.2	.001
25	71.3	28.3	0.4	-	-	-
26	54.3	27.4	12.6	5.8	-	-
27	75.3	24.2	0.4	-	-	-

TABLE 81--Continued

Question	A%	B%	C%	D%	Chi S.	P
28	37.7	29.1	13.0	26.9	5.0	.025-.05
29	68.6	30.5	0.4	0.4	-	-
30	30.0	26.0	21.9	21.9	0.2	.90
31	87.9	10.3	0.9	0.9	3.5	.05-.10
32	49.8	6.3	5.8	29.1	156.9	.001
33	41.7	15.7	7.6	35.0	63.4	.001
34	49.3	4.9	8.5	37.2	115.6	.001
35	8.1	0.4	45.7	45.7	12.4	.001
36	46.2	7.2	7.2	39.5	110.1	.001
37	44.4	3.6	16.1	35.9	83.7	.001
38	78.9	16.6	4.5	-	0.9	.30-.50

[a]The Yates Correction was used in calculating Chi Square. Chi square could not be calculated for some squares because of too few frequencies.

[b]Letters following question numbers indicate parts of the question.

The Arno Press Cinema Program

THE LITERATURE OF CINEMA

Series I & II

Agate, James. **Around Cinemas.** 1946.

Agate, James. **Around Cinemas.** (Second Series). 1948.

American Academy of Political and Social Science. **The Motion Picture in Its Economic and Social Aspects,** edited by Clyde L. King. **The Motion Picture Industry,** edited by Gordon S. Watkins. *The Annals,* November, 1926/1927.

L'Art Cinematographique, Nos. 1-8. 1926-1931.

Balcon, Michael, Ernest Lindgren, Forsyth Hardy and Roger Manvell. **Twenty Years of British Film, 1925-1945.** 1947.

Bardèche, Maurice and Robert Brasillach. **The History of Motion Pictures,** edited by Iris Barry. 1938.

Benoit-Levy, Jean. **The Art of the Motion Picture.** 1946.

Blumer, Herbert. **Movies and Conduct.** 1933.

Blumer, Herbert and Philip M. Hauser. **Movies, Delinquency, and Crime.** 1933.

Buckle, Gerard Fort. **The Mind and the Film.** 1926.

Carter, Huntly. **The New Spirit in the Cinema.** 1930.

Carter, Huntly. **The New Spirit in the Russian Theatre, 1917-1928.** 1929.

Carter, Huntly. **The New Theatre and Cinema of Soviet Russia.** 1924.

Charters, W. W. **Motion Pictures and Youth.** 1933.

Cinema Commission of Inquiry. **The Cinema: Its Present Position and Future Possibilities.** 1917.

Dale, Edgar. **Children's Attendance at Motion Pictures.** Dysinger, Wendell S. and Christian A. Ruckmick. **The Emotional Responses of Children to the Motion Picture Situation.** 1935.

Dale, Edgar. **The Content of Motion Pictures.** 1935.

Dale, Edgar. **How to Appreciate Motion Pictures.** 1937.

Dale, Edgar, Fannie W. Dunn, Charles F. Hoban, Jr., and Etta Schneider. **Motion Pictures in Education: A Summary of the Literature.** 1938.

Davy, Charles. **Footnotes to the Film.** 1938.

Dickinson, Thorold and Catherine De la Roche. **Soviet Cinema.** 1948.

Dickson, W. K. L., and Antonia Dickson. **History of the Kinetograph, Kinetoscope and Kinetophonograph.** 1895.

Forman, Henry James. **Our Movie Made Children.** 1935.

Freeburg, Victor Oscar. **The Art of Photoplay Making.** 1918.

Freeburg, Victor Oscar. **Pictorial Beauty on the Screen.** 1923.

Hall, Hal, editor. Cinematographic Annual, 2 vols. 1930/1931.

Hampton, Benjamin B. A History of the Movies. 1931.

Hardy, Forsyth. Scandinavian Film. 1952.

Hepworth, Cecil M. **Animated Photography: The A B C of the Cinematograph.** 1900.

Hoban, Charles F., Jr., and Edward B. Van Ormer. **Instructional Film Research 1918-1950.** 1950.

Holaday, Perry W. and George D. Stoddard. **Getting Ideas from the Movies.** 1933.

Hopwood, Henry V. **Living Pictures.** 1899.

Hulfish, David S. **Motion-Picture Work.** 1915.

Hunter, William. **Scrutiny of Cinema.** 1932.

Huntley, John. **British Film Music.** 1948.

Irwin, Will. **The House That Shadows Built.** 1928.

Jarratt, Vernon. **The Italian Cinema.** 1951.

Jenkins, C. Francis. **Animated Pictures.** 1898.

Lang, Edith and George West. **Musical Accompaniment of Moving Pictures.** 1920.

London, Kurt. **Film Music.** 1936.

Lutz, E ⌐dwin⌐ G ⌐eorge⌐. **The Motion-Picture Cameraman.** 1927.

Manvell, Roger. **Experiment in the Film.** 1949.

Marey, Etienne Jules. **Movement.** 1895.

Martin, Olga J. **Hollywood's Movie Commandments.** 1937.

Mayer, J. P. **Sociology of Film: Studies and Documents.** 1946. New Introduction by J. P. Mayer.

Münsterberg, Hugo. **The Photoplay: A Psychological Study.** 1916.
Nicoll, Allardyce. **Film and Theatre.** 1936.

Noble, Peter. **The Negro in Films.** 1949.

Peters, Charles C. **Motion Pictures and Standards of Morality.** 1933.

Peterson, Ruth C. and L. L. Thurstone. **Motion Pictures and the Social Attitudes of Children.** Shuttleworth, Frank K. and Mark A. May. **The Social Conduct and Attitudes of Movie Fans.** 1933.

Phillips, Henry Albert. **The Photodrama.** 1914.

Photoplay Research Society. **Opportunities in the Motion Picture Industry.** 1922.

Rapée, Erno. **Encyclopaedia of Music for Pictures.** 1925.

Rapée, Erno. **Motion Picture Moods for Pianists and Organists.** 1924.

Renshaw, Samuel, Vernon L. Miller and Dorothy P. Marquis. **Children's Sleep.** 1933.

Rosten, Leo C. **Hollywood: The Movie Colony, The Movie Makers.** 1941.

Sadoul, Georges. **French Film.** 1953.

Screen Monographs I, 1923-1937. 1970.

Screen Monographs II, 1915-1930. 1970.

Sinclair, Upton. **Upton Sinclair Presents William Fox.** 1933.

Talbot, Frederick A. **Moving Pictures.** 1912.

Thorp, Margaret Farrand. **America at the Movies.** 1939.

Wollenberg, H. H. **Fifty Years of German Film.** 1948.

RELATED BOOKS AND PERIODICALS

Allister, Ray. **Friese-Greene: Close-Up of an Inventor.** 1948.

Art in Cinema: A Symposium of the Avant-Garde Film, edited by Frank Stauffacher. 1947.

The Art of Cinema: Selected Essays. New Foreword by George Amberg. 1971.

Balázs, Béla. **Theory of the Film.** 1952.

Barry, Iris. **Let's Go to the Movies.** 1926.

de Beauvoir, Simone. **Brigitte Bardot and the Lolita Syndrome.** 1960.

Carrick, Edward. **Art and Design in the British Film.** 1948.

Close Up. Vols. 1-10, 1927-1933 (all published).

Cogley, John. **Report on Blacklisting. Part I: The Movies.** 1956.

Eisenstein, S. M. **Que Viva Mexico!** 1951.

Experimental Cinema. 1930-1934 (all published).

Feldman, Joseph and Harry. **Dynamics of the Film.** 1952.

Film Daily Yearbook of Motion Pictures. Microfilm, 18 reels, 35 mm. 1918-1969.

Film Daily Yearbook of Motion Pictures. 1970.

Film Daily Yearbook of Motion Pictures. (Wid's Year Book). 3 vols., 1918-1922.

The Film Index: A Bibliography. Vol. I: The Film as Art. 1941.

Film Society Programmes. 1925-1939 (all published).

Films: A Quarterly of Discussion and Analysis. Nos. 1-4, 1939-1940. (all published).

Flaherty, Frances Hubbard. **The Odyssey of a Film-Maker: Robert Flaherty's Story.** 1960.

General Bibliography of Motion Pictures, edited by Carl Vincent, Riccardo Redi, and Franco Venturini. 1953.

Hendricks, Gordon. **Origins of the American Film.** 1961-1966. New Introduction by Gordon Hendricks.

Hound and Horn: Essays on Cinema, 1928-1934. 1971.

Huff, Theodore. **Charlie Chaplin.** 1951.

Kahn, Gordon. **Hollywood on Trial.** 1948.

New York Times Film Reviews, 1913-1968. 1970.

Noble, Peter. **Hollywood Scapegoat: The Biography of Erich von Stroheim.** 1950.

Robson, E. W. and M. M. **The Film Answers Back.** 1939.

Seldes, Gilbert. **An Hour with the Movies and the Talkies.** 1929.

Weinberg, Herman G., editor. **Greed.** 1971.

Wollenberg, H. H. **Anatomy of the Film.** 1947.

Wright, Basil. **The Use of the Film.** 1948.

DISSERTATIONS ON FILM

Beaver, Frank Eugene. **Bosley Crowther:** Social Critic of the Film, **1940-1967.** First publication, 1974.

Benderson, Albert Edward. **Critical Approaches to Federico Fellini's "8½".** First publication, 1974

Berg, Charles Merrell. **An Investigation of the Motives For and Realization of Music to Accompany the American Silent Film, 1896-1927.** First publication, 1976

Blades, Joseph Dalton, Jr. **A Comparative Study of Selected American Film Critics, 1958-1974.** First publication, 1976

Cohen, Louis Harris. **The Cultural-Political Traditions and Developments of the Soviet Cinema: 1917-1972.** First publication, 1974

Dart, Peter. **Pudovkin's Films and Film Theory.** First publication, 1974

Davis, Robert Edward. **Response to Innovation:** A Study of Popular Argument About New Mass Media. First publication, 1976

Facey, Paul W. **The Legion of Decency:** A Sociological Analysis of the Emergence and Development of a Social Pressure Group. First publication, 1974

Karimi, A. M. **Toward a Definition of the American Film Noir (1941-1949).** First publication, 1976

Karpf, Stephen L. **The Gangster Film:** Emergence, Variation and Decay of a Genre, 1930-1940. First publication, 1973

Lounsbury, Myron O. **The Origins of American Film Criticism, 1909-1939.** First publication, 1974.

Lyons, Robert J[oseph]. **Michelangelo Antonioni's Neo-Realism:** A World View. First publication, 1976

Lyons, Timothy James. **The Silent Partner:** The History of the American Film Manufacturing Company, 1910-1921. First publication, 1974

McLaughlin, Robert. **Broadway and Hollywood:** A History of Economic Interaction. First publication, 1974

North, Joseph H. **The Early Development of the Motion Picture, 1887-1909.** First publication, 1973

Pryluck, Calvin. **Sources of Meaning in Motion Pictures and Television.** First publication, 1976

Rimberg, John. **The Motion Picture in the Soviet Union, 1918-1952.** First publication, 1973

Sands, Pierre N. **A Historical Study of the Academy of the Motion Picture Arts and Sciences (1927-1947).** First publication, 1973

Shain, Russell Earl. **An Analysis of Motion Pictures About War Released by the American Film Industry, 1939-1970.** First publication, 1976

Stuart, Fredric. **The Effects of Television on the Motion Picture and Radio Industries.** First publication, 1976

Wead, George. **Buster Keaton and the Dynamics of Visual Wit.** First publication, 1976

Wolfe, Glenn J. **Vachel Lindsay:** The Poet as Film Theorist. First publication, 1973